Advance Praise for Give Nonkilling a Chance

We live in auspicious times. Humankind stands at a crossroads where our thinking awaits to manifest deep strategic shifts. Prof Anoop Swarup is an extraordinary thinker and far-sighted scholar and this book is compiled in memoriam and as a sequel to the work of visionary thinker late Glenn D. Paige. This book brings a message to the world that is of crucial importance: Killing is not an inherent part of human nature! Violence is 'a preventable disease'! The task of the day for each of us is to help build killing-free societies, and ultimately, to form a peaceful global society. Peace can no longer be a word that describes silence achieved through oppression and killing. True peace only flows from mutually enriching dialogue among citizens who respect each other as equal in dignity, who practice loving unity in enriching diversity, and who jointly care for all life on our home planet. Prof Anoop Swarup has gathered a group of extraordinary authors from across the globe for this book. It will be an indispensable guiding light for everyone embarking on this path.

—**Evelin Lindner**, *MD, PhD, (Dr. med. and Dr. psychol.); Founding President, Human Dignity and Humiliation Studies; nominated three times for the Nobel Peace Prize in 2015, 2016, and 2017*

This book, *Give Nonkilling a Chance*, is a very laudable contribution by Prof Anoop Swarup, a distinguished academician, thinker, poet, former diplomat and above all, an innovative leader of several peace initiatives in different parts of the world with whom I have had the privilege to having a lasting association of over three decades. I hope this book will turn out to be a reliable 'Handbook' on Nonkilling Society and a companion volume to several thought-provoking books, studies and anthologies left behind by Prof Glenn D. Paige.

Let me again congratulate Prof Swarup on his leadership for a Nonkilling Society across the globe as the Chairperson of Center for Global Nonkilling at Hawaii in the footsteps of Late Prof Glenn D. Paige.

—**Prof Dr Neelakanta Radhakrishnan**, *Chairman, Indian Council of Gandhian Studies and Gandhi Peace Mission, India*

Everyone knows of the moral integrity of Gandhi and Mandela. Would you have had them on your wish list as dinner guests? At the dinner, how would you and your friends have responded if either of them looked directly into your eyes and asked, 'Would you be prepared to make a personal sacrifice to protect the sanctity of life?' Imagine pausing... staring back into the depth of their eyes before answering. I believe that you and every person would unequivocally say 'yes'. The elevated question then is, what action would you offer to Gandhi or Mandela to contribute to stop killing?

I invite you to read this enlightening and expansive compilation of educative and informative articles by the highly respected Dr Anoop Swarup to enhance your understanding. Expanding your knowledge of what global thought leaders are articulating will inspire you. Killing is not theoretical. It is the definitive ending of a Divine creation. It is the breaking of a Universal covenant.

This powerful publication is an invitation for you to personally take just one action or say one word as a Transformational Leader for Nonkilling to be part of a collective energy of change that will reverberate around our world.

—**Garry Prigg,** *Founder & CEO of International Consultants to Business and Who I Am Dynamics; acclaimed Speaker and Author of Living My Life with Purpose... Now and 'The Power of Giving'*

Revered political scientist and cosmodignifier Glenn D. Paige has given humanity an extraordinary, multidimensional, life-supporting approach which is creatively known as NONKILLING. The evergrowing and everlasting influence of his idea(l)s is now cogently shown by this multi-authored volume eloquently edited by Anoop Swarup, who has eminently succeeded Glenn D. Paige as president of the pioneering Center for Global Nonkilling. This publication will contribute significantly to the globalising of the Paigean legacy and should become a top-priority reading for all scholars/students committed to probing the dignifying *Peace-Nonviolence-Nonkilling* continuum. The Glenn Paige legacy inspiringly lives on. Nonkillingly, his disciples and practitioners have a sublime mission to carry on!

—**Francisco Gomes de Matos**, *peace linguist; Professor Emeritus of Linguistics, Federal University of Pernambuco, and president of the Board, ABA Global Education, Recife, Brazil*

A culture of killing and hatred is closing in on humanity today. My heart bleeds when I see that thousands of innocent men, women and children are killed in the name of caste, colour and creed across the world. Lord Mahavira, the twenty-fourth Tirthankara of the nonviolent Jain tradition, said, 'All *jivas*, small or big, want to live. No one wants to die, so killing any of them is a sin.' The essence of his message is that killing of not only humans and animals but any form of life is a heinous crime. *Ahimsa* (nonviolence) is the highest religion. Prof Glenn D. Paige was a practical man. He steered clear of the doctrinaire definition of nonviolence and instead coined the new word 'Nonkilling'. It is much simpler and gives a clear message to ordinary humans. That's why his movement of Nonkilling inspired thousands of people across the world, including the young and the old. His selfless dedication, determination and simplicity left an indelible impression on my mind. My friendship with him dates back more than 30 years and we remained in constant touch sharing our visions till he breathed his last. The book *Give Nonkilling a Chance* is a befitting tribute to the memory of this great soul and I commend the efforts made by Prof Anoop Swarup to continue his legacy of Nonkilling.

—**Dr Sohan Lal Gandhi** *is the International President of Anuvrat Global Organization (ANUVIBHA), a transnational centre for peace and nonviolent action. He has been in the forefront of national and international campaigns of nonviolence and has travelled extensively delivering lectures and organizing nonviolence leadership training camps in various parts of the world. He has edited and authored several books.*

I thoroughly enjoyed reading the chapters and the introduction. This is one of the best books for the global readers to understand the importance of peace and nonviolence.

The book provides the world with a chance to stop killing. I believe that if the chance is taken, people will see Nonkilling prevailing across the globe and they would be able to live together in harmony, 100 per cent, as Nonkilling paves the way for eternal, immortal and everlasting peace. On the giant shoulders of all peace lovers, the contribution of this book to the humanity resonates the birth of light from the first second of the universe where human life is born to live. Killing is the death of life and the end of the light. Giving Nonkilling a chance is the last plea to all.

—**Maorong Jiang** *serves as the Director of the Asian World Center at Creighton University. He founded the Asian World Nonkilling Consortium in 2014. He is a member of the Governing Council for the Center for Global Nonkilling. Since 2003, Jiang has been with Creighton University teaching both graduate and undergraduate courses in Political Science, International Relations, East-West Studies, Asian Studies and modern Eastern/Western history. Jiang has an MA in Asian Religions and a PhD in Political Science from the University of Hawaii at Manoa.*

http://www.creighton.edu/ccas/politicalscience/faculty/maorongjiang/

Give Nonkilling a Chance

Are Nonkilling Societies Possible?

Edited by

ANOOP SWARUP

KONARK

Konark Publishers Pvt Ltd
New Delhi • Seattle

Konark Publishers Pvt. Ltd
206, First Floor,
Peacock Lane, Shahpur Jat,
New Delhi 110 049
Tel : +91-11-4105 5065
Mob : +91-93552 93900, +91-93552 94900
e-mail: india@konarkpublishers.com
website: www.konarkpublishers.com

Konark Publishers International
8615, 13th Ave SW,
Seattle, WA 98106
Phone: (415) 409-9988
e-mail: us@konarkpublishers.com

ISBN 978-93-220-0894-9

Edited by Jaishree Balasubramanian

Jacket Design by Dushyant Parasher

Typeset by Saanvi Graphics, Noida

Printed and bound at Thomson Press (India) Ltd.

IN MEMORIAM

Late Prof Glenn Durland Paige

Dedication

Nonkilling and Peace, not only in our times but also for our future generations, is going to be one of the defining paradigms of the Anthropocene age. It was indeed the wizard in Glenn Durland Paige, a political scientist and humanist extraordinaire, much ahead of his times who understood this better than anyone else in our times. He raised the level of human consciousness to evolve the very idea based on a strong scientific thesis to reinforce and redefine the core purpose of nonkilling, going beyond the traditional precept of nonviolence as the best means for universal peace.

I had the privilege to speak to Professor Paige just a week back before his demise to follow up on our earlier interactions, when prophetically enough; he spoke of his own end and the future of the Nonkilling movement and the Center for Global Nonkilling. I could perceive his own vision of the looming shadow of his own struggle and the end in sight but more importantly what struck me most was his conviction, the dream and the desire for me and the Nonkilling fraternity to strive and reach beyond for a 'Nonkilling world'. The intensity and the enlightened approach of a visionary genius and his wit and wisdom even in death was awe inspiring. It is this appeal from his last few words to me that brings me to the profound nature of his own contribution that I will briefly dwell upon.

Well the apparent question to our mind that remained post Second World War was whether nonkilling societies and a killing-free world was possible? The prevailing pessimism left an emphatic answer, 'No!' It was presumed that killing is inevitable because of human nature, competition, scarce resources, and other factors. However, in 2002 that was to change with a resounding 'Yes' as asserted in the Nonkilling Global Political Science, a monumental work and fact finding by Professor Paige that promised to revolutionize our pessimist world view on two principal grounds. Firstly, nonkilling predominates over killing in human nature and secondly, most humans have not killed and do not kill contrary to the perpetuated myth. Furthermore, nonkilling knowledge and practice already exist in global human experience that if creatively combined and advanced in any society, promise progress toward making Nonkilling societies universally possible for a peaceful world, which can focus on the Sustainable Development Goals enshrined by the United Nations. Responses to the Nonkilling thesis have been remarkable; the book is being translated into 41 languages accessible to over 4 billion speakers. Over 600 scholars in 300 academic institutions in 73 countries have joined in 19 disciplinary research committees that are contributing to a scientific paradigm shift from acceptance of killing to discover and apply nonkilling knowledge as a common heritage for all mankind.

Glenn Durland Paige was born on June 28, 1929 in Brockton, Massachusetts, in the north eastern part of the United States known as New England. He grew up in Rochester, New Hampshire, with summers in Provincetown, Cape Cod, Massachusetts. He served in the US Army (1948-52). He was a graduate of Phillips Exeter Academy (1947), Princeton University (A.B., politics, 1955), Harvard University (A.M., East Asian regional studies, 1957) and Northwestern University (Ph.D. political science, 1959). After teaching at Seoul National University (1959-61), and Princeton University (1961-67), he taught at the University of Hawai'i (1967-92). He lived in Honolulu since 1967 and travelled widely as the Founder and past Chair of the Center for Global Nonkilling. His own experiential times as a Korean War veteran indeed molded his thinking and work in his celebrated books on Nonkilling Global Political Science (2002), and The Scientific Study of Political Leadership (1977).

Professor Paige will be remembered for this unique vision, mission and enterprise to promote change toward the measurable goal of a killing-free world in reverence to life that aims for infinite creativity and discovery to advance the spiritual, scientific, skills and arts capabilities of humankind, for nonkilling change for tomorrow's global society.

To a humanist and a pioneer who evoked interdisciplinary creativity to empower humanity with confidence that killing-free societies are possible, I pen a few lines in memoriam as we bid him goodbye:

'In times of mindless terror, killings and fight,
Let us rebuild the bonds, and bridges that are right,
With Gandhi, King, Mandela and Paige in sight,
In infinite creativity, and reverence to life so bright,
Let each of us be a center of nonkilling, and a knight,
Sure, enough billions of us can advance, live and light,
Forever in our goal of nonkilling, peace to delight,
Eternal be Glenn's vision and mission, a triumph of god's might.'

I end my tribute to a great soul in gratitude and in eternal reverence to life in Glenn's own words:

'No More killing!

Nonkilling Culture in infinite reverence to human ingenuity crosses all lines'

'Everyone can be a Center for Global Nonkilling and usher in the next stage of Human Evolution.'

Anoop Swarup

Contents

Foreword

Prof Dr Neelakanta Radhakrishnan

While describing what exactly is true leadership and how does it differ from management or dictatorship, James MacGregor Burns, the author of the landmark book *Leadership,* states:

> Leadership is leaders acting—as well as caring, inspiring and persuading others to act—for certain shared goals that represent the values—the wants and needs, the aspirations and expectations—of themselves and the people they represent. And the genius of leadership lies in the manner in which leaders care about, visualize, and act on their own and their followers' values and motivations. (P23).

The unique leadership provided by five leaders from five different parts of the globe offers significant parallels in their campaigns and efforts to employ nonviolent methods in the realization of a Nonkilling Society. They are Mahatma Gandhi, Martin Luther King Jr., Nelson Mandela, Glenn D. Paige and Daisaku Ikeda.

The global nonviolent awakening which began with Gandhi is now a powerful alternative vision and creative option before humanity justifying King's assertion that 'the word "nonviolence"' is no longer an option for intellectual analysis; it is an imperative of action'.

Let me reproduce the following summation of Mark Kurlansky from his book ***Nonviolence: The History of a Dangerous Idea***:

1. *There is no proactive word for nonviolence.*
2. *Nations that build military forces as deterrents will eventually use them.*
3. *Practitioners of nonviolence are seen as enemies of the state.*
4. *Once a state takes over a religion,the state loses its nonviolent teachings.*
5. *A rebel can be defanged and co-opted by making him a saint after he is dead.*
6. *Somewhere behind every war there are always a few founding lies.*
7. *A propaganda machine promoting hatred always has a war waiting in the wings.*
8. *People who go to war start to reassemble their enemy.*
9. *A conflict between a violent and nonviolent force is a moral argument. If the violent side can provoke the nonviolent side into violence, the violent side has won.*
10. *The problem lies not in the nature of man but in the nature of power.*
11. *The longer a war lasts, the less popular it becomes.*
12. *The state imagines it is impotent without a military because it cannot conceive power without force.*
13. *It is not the largest but the best organized and most articulate group that prevails.*
14. *All debate momentarily ends with an 'enforced silence' once the first shots are fired.*
15. *A shooting war is not necessarily to overthrow an established power but is used to consolidate the revolution itself.*
16. *Violence does not resolve. It always leads to more violence.*
17. *Warfare produces peace activists. A group of veterans is a likely place to find peace activists.*
18. *People motivated by fear do not act well.*

19. *While it is perfectly feasible to convince a people faced with brutal repression to rise up in a suicidal attack on their oppressor, it is almost impossible to convince them to meet deadly violence with nonviolent resistance.*
20. *Wars do not have to be sold to the general public if they can be carried out by an all-volunteer professional military.*
21. *Once you start the business of killing, you just get 'deeper and deeper' without limits.*
22. *Violence always comes with a supposedly rational explanation which is only dismissed as irrational if the violence fails.*
23. *Violence is virus that infests and takes over.*
24. *The miracle is that despite all of society's promotion of warfare, most soldiers find warfare to be a wrenching departure from their own moral values.*
25. *The hard work of beginning a movement to end war has already been done.*

What King said about Gandhian methods offers very valuable insights into his understanding of Gandhi. He wrote:

> 'Gandhi was probably the first person in history to lift the love ethic of Jesus above mere interaction between individuals to a powerful and effective social force on a large scale; Love for Gandhi was a potent instrument for social and collective transformation. It was in this Gandhian emphasis on love and nonviolence that I discovered the method for social reform that I had been seeking for so many months...The intellectual and moral satisfaction that I failed to gain from the utilitarianism of Bentham and Mill, the revolutionary methods of Marx and Lenin, the social contract theory of Hobbes, the 'back to nature' optimism of Rousseau, and the superman philosophy of Nietzsche, I found in the nonviolent resistance philosophy of Gandhi. I came to feel that this was the only morally and practically sound method open to oppressed people in their struggle for freedom.'

The leadership provided by Gandhi and King received extensive analysis by Homer A. Jack who tells us 'both (Gandhi and King) led large political movements, using the method of Satyagraha. Both held no public office, yet both exerted more power and gained more adulation than most elected statesmen of their time. Both were charismatic. Votaries of nonviolence, both ironically, died by the bullet. Both were acknowledged in death, and even in life, as the greatest humanitarians of their time. The world truly grieved at the passing of both. Both died in the very midst of their work for harmony and amity, both feeling a sense of disappointment and not of victory.'

If Gandhi demonstrated the infinite frontiers of 'freedom from fear' and stressed the importance of religion in everyday life, King amplified the power of human will to rise in revolt against unjust man-made barriers which denied fellow human beings their inalienable right to live in peace, with dignity and honour.

Gandhi and King are complementary in several respects; both have influenced a large number of eminent men and women in different parts of the world. Buddhist philosopher and peacebuilder Ikeda says about Gandhi and King: 'Armed only with an unyielding faith in the power of dialogue, Gandhi and King awakened people to the sublime dignity of their own lives, as well as the lives of others. In this way they worked to construct a spreading solidarity of peace and nonviolence, one person at a time. The struggle waged by these two prophets of peace clearly demonstrates the path forward as we seek to create a world free from war and violence in the 21st century.' Great men radiate greatness just as iridium emits light. Their creative minds absorb hidden or latent aspects of society and adapt them for the welfare of all people. This has been happening all the time. While Gandhi successfully grafted traditional wisdom to create new non-violent techniques, King adapted the Gandhian techniques of social and political mobilization in a new idiom and phrase to suit the temperament and aspirations of Black Americans. Gandhi provided the frame and King expanded it. King's philosophy and methods were so effective that he convinced both the white and the black population that violence was not a valid means of solving social problems. In this process, he emerged as the fountain-head of resolute determination as revealed in the marching song, 'we shall overcome... The translation of the song into most of the world's languages and the adoption of King's methods for conflict resolution are proof of the growing influences of King on humanity.

What King said about Gandhi offers very valuable insights in to his understanding of Gandhi. He wrote Gandhi was probably the first person in history to lift the love ethic of Jesus above mere interaction between individuals to a powerful and effective social force on a large scale; Love for Gandhi was a potent instrument for social and collective transformation. It was in this Gandhian emphasis on love and nonviolence that I discovered the method for social reform that I had been seeking for so many months.

The intellectual and moral satisfaction that I failed to gain from the utilitarianism of Bentham and Mill, the revolutionary methods of Marx and Lenin, the social contract theory of Hobbes, the 'back to nature' optimism of Rousseau, and the superman philosophy of Nietzsche, I found in the nonviolent resistance philosophy of Gandhi. I came to feel that this was the only morally and practically sound method open to oppressed people in their struggle for freedom.

If Gandhi demonstrated the infinite frontiers of 'freedom from fear' and stressed the importance of religion in everyday life, King amplified the power of human will to rise in revolt against unjust man-made barriers which denied fellow human beings their inalienable right to live in peace, with dignity and honour.

Ikeda, like Gandhi and King, is a master in establishing instant communication with the masses. Ikeda's strategies are not copied from any textbook. Communication is a great art. Effortless communication with the masses is a gift. Ikeda revealed exceptional qualities as a communicator. In an age of cell phones, e-mail, internet and fax, when impersonal and mechanical devices dominate and control the entire gamut of the communication process, the social reformer, moral activist, religious and political activist find ways to create bonds with people and establish credible lines of communication of his message reach their hearts.

Ikeda gradually expanded his activities and campaigns from Japan. The launch of world-wide *kosen-rufu* witnessed a new style and a new leadership. What Ikeda said about Gandhi and King truly applies to his own self:

'They (Gandhi and King) believed ceaselessly in the capacities for good that reside in the human spirit. They uncovered and discovered

the capacity for good in all people, equally and without exception. Committed first and foremost to the inner transformation of the individual, they worked with vibrant energy to inspire people to bring forth their very highest, their most noble potential.'

Mandela's transformation into a nonviolent votary and the manner in which he pioneered the Truth and Reconciliation Commission under the leadership of Archbishop Desmond Tutu offered new ideas and leadership.

While all these epoch making initiatives were taking place a restless champion of nonviolence in the person of Prof Glenn D. Paige in Hawaii who conceived the seminal idea of Nonkilling Political Science and Nonkilling Society ignited a considerable segment of thinkers, political strategists, scientists and peace activists and today all over the world are convinced thanks to the ceaseless efforts of this pioneering thinker that a nonkilling society is possible.

The network of thinkers and peace activists who subscribed to the idea of a nonkilling society, Prof Glenn D. Paige has created and the institutional frame he has offered besides spreading the vision of a nonkilling future he has amplified, are bound to influence humanity in the coming days.

Prof Anoop Swarup, a distinguished academician, thinker, poet, former diplomat and above all an innovative leader of several peace initiatives in different parts of the world with whom I have the privilege to a lasting association of over three decades, is currently leading the Center for Global Nonkilling, established and nourished by Prof Paige.

I hope this book, GIVE NONKILLING A CHANCE, a very laudable contribution by Prof Anoop Swarup, will turn out to be a reliable 'Handbook' on Nonkilling Society and a companion volume to several thought-provoking books, studies and anthologies left behind by Prof Glenn Paige. I also hope this book will ultimately rise to the level of a tribute to Glenn Paige whose revolutionary ideas and efforts will be understood, appreciated and followed by generations to come, since they are both vital reminders and guidance to us all.

Let me again congratulate Prof Swarup on his leadership for Nonkilling Society in the footsteps of Prof Paige.

Preface

Anoop Swarup

> *A breadth of will blows eternally through the universe of souls in the direction of the Right and Necessary.*
>
> —Ralph Waldo Emerson

In one of his last few messages to me, Glenn Durland Paige, the Founding Chair of the Center for Global Nonkilling (CGNK – in Consultative Status to the UN), at Hawaii while handing over the reins of the Chair wrote to me inter alia, on this ambitious book project, *'your creative idea of pairing Nonviolence and Nonkilling is very constructive in bridging them ....'*. This exchange as I recall was in the aftermath of the launch of the book *Give Nonviolence a Chance* and my address at the India International Centre in New Delhi on 19 August 2016 commemorating the works of Dr N. Radhakrishnan, in the presence of former Prime Minister Dr Manmohan Singh, the intelligentsia and some very prominent Parliamentarians. I did mention it then about Glenn, and the extraordinary work at CGNK and argued our view, that *'Nonkilling is the natural corollary to Nonviolence and Peace, as the latter cannot be achieved unless we commit ourselves to the measurable goal of universal Nonkilling by means of infinite creativity in reverence to life'*.

It was in this context that Glenn felt that the proposed book, even if repetitive, will be a follow-up companion to commemorate a decade of his historic *Nonkilling Global Political Science* thesis and the title suggested was, *Give Nonkilling a Chance: Beyond Glenn D. Paige and Nonkilling Global Political Science*. However, I had to rename it in keeping with Glenn's own desire. Though I have removed his name from the title, this book is a commemoration of a decade of work from across the globe since then and essentially a reflection of Glenn's eternal quest, '*Are* Nonkilling societies possible?' This book also echoes the Sustainable Development Goal 16.1, introduced at our behest, to significantly reduce all forms of violence and related deaths everywhere and the UNESCO Charter which states, '*since wars begin in the minds of men, it is in the minds of men that the defences of peace must be constructed,*' the book is a humble approach to a concept that I had earlier introduced, *Affirmative Nonkilling,* in contrast to 'Illusive Nonkilling', since killing begins in the minds of men and women, it is here that the change toward a Nonkilling society must begin. Thanks to the Director of the Center for Global Nonkilling scholar Joam Evans Pim, the book is a modest attempt to bring together scholarly works, even though published earlier, of very eminent experts who have been committed over the last decade to promote change towards the measurable goal of a killing-free world in reverence to life. These articles are a veritable reflection of the researches and discoveries by advancing the Spiritual and Scientific, Skills and Arts, Anthropology, Geography and History, Linguistics and Teaching, Media and Music, Leadership, Values and Ethos and other creative pursuits from across the globe.

I will fail to explain the spirit behind the book unless I reflect on the genesis and the idea of nonkilling in its entirety. The very philosophy and spirit of 'existentialism' is 'in being' as it revolves around the central question of our own existence in reverence to life where the individual has freedom and choice to choose his own destiny over a life time. In killing and death, this is not possible or even conceivable as the individual not only loses his own dignity but also life as such. Even the 'utilitarian' view of life would recommend a course of human civilizational ascent that achieves greatest happiness and best opportunities for the greatest number of people but obviously not at the cost of human life even if it is purported to be for the overall good of all. My rationale for such an assumption being the fact that as scientifically and empirically proved, no human can ever be happy with '*killing*' an individual let alone, genocide and wars, as it is not innate to human nature.

Incidentally, we tend to anthropomorphize the limits when it comes to our ability to understand even animal behavior. In *Wild Justice,* Marc Bekoff and Jessica Pierce have married years of behavioral and cognitive research on animals to reveal moral traits that include fairness, empathy, trust and reciprocity and are explicit in their moving repertoire, '*Yet what are we to make of a female gorilla in a German zoo who spent days mourning the death of her baby? Or a wild female elephant who cared for a younger one after she was injured by a rambunctious teenage male? Or a rat who refused to push a lever for food when he saw that doing so caused another rat to be shocked?*'

The contributions and researches over the past few years and particularly the last few decades do conclusively establish that humans do not rejoice, even if the individual or a race or a clan or a country, be it for religious or even for political differences was found to be enemy or labelled to be evil. Such an argument does preclude unavoidable deaths in self-defence as these are not killings, which in all cases have to be the last resort only. There being no denying of the fact that political and religious conflicts during the course of human history have led to innumerable brutalities and loss of countless lives, and the trend shows no signs of abatement. Thus, this book attempts to make a humble plea to the world at large to 'give Nonkilling a chance'.

It is the timelessness of the precept, practice and pursuit of spirituality, nonkilling and nonviolent peace during our own Darwinian evolutionary process gives hope to human civilizational ascent. Let me briefly explain this taking recourse to the past 200,000 years since *Homo sapiens* evolved, which indeed has been an extraordinary journey. Amazingly enough, from our own primate roots with stone tools, we became insanely brilliant masterminds with complex language, control and computers to run the planet with agriculture and technology. How and why of this intelligence explosion will remain an enduring mystery, but the pre-eminence of the scientific study of human origins and the evolution of rational thought and spirituality is that it nails the myth that '*no human revolution can ever happen*' that may change human nature. The sudden and revolutionary emergence of language, consciousness, and culture but more importantly *to perceive ourselves as others, our morality, ethics and spirituality* will foster *universal nonkilling peace* and it is my belief, may well turn out to be our ultimate saviour from a doomsday.

It is a matter of record and I must recall that in post-industrial age, atrocities such as genocides have been neither rare nor infrequent but rather enormous in their number, scale and scope. It reveals from datasets that just in over 200 episodes of mass atrocities over the last hundred odd years there have been two such events per year, where governments alone have each time killed at least 1,000 innocent civilians. The estimated fatalities are over a billion and the total does not consider victims suffering collateral physical and psychological trauma perpetrated by state and nonstate actors, the military casualties, not to speak of causalities below the threshold and their economic consequences for the rest. In stark contrast, and on an individual human scale when we consider the past many centuries, it is estimated that less than 0.5 per cent of all humans that ever existed actually killed others. Indeed, this finding of Glenn Durland Paige, founding Chair of the Center for Global Nonkilling, in his seminal work, *Nonkilling Global Political Science* was an eye-opener. Also, anthropological, and other scientific evidence points out that in certain societies and cultures 'killing' is down to statistically insignificant levels. In these circumstances, let us ask whether a reconciliation amongst humans and faiths and of science and spirituality for universal nonkilling peace is possible? Can a nonkilling society evolve and exist. A resounding 'yes!' is being asserted at the Center for Global Nonkilling at Hawaii that I now Chair in the footsteps of Glenn D. Paige. In my own talks and many exchanges with late Professor Paige, it was apparent that he was influenced by the work of A. Richard Konrad who did challenge way back in 1974, the conventional assumption, that *readiness to kill from rape to holocaust was the only effective way* to cope with the challenge before humanity. We as humans have evolved the so called 'violent problem-solving alternatives' resting on three assumptions: that all nonviolent alternatives have been identified; that all have been tried; and that all have failed.

From a spiritual perspective, a nonkilling society is a human community, smallest to largest, local to global, characterized by no killing of humans, and no threats to kill; no weapons designed to kill humans and no justifications for using them; and no conditions of society dependent upon threat or use of killing force for maintenance or change. Here it may not be out of context to mention that it was Johan Galtung who introduced the term 'positive peace' to imply the simultaneous presence of many desirable states of mind and society, such as harmony, justice, equity, etc. and 'negative peace' as historically denoting the 'absence of war' and other forms of wide scale violent human conflict. It is my case in point, that as a parallel analogy nonkilling peace should also be recognized as an 'affirmative nonkilling' that is positive and structural such as promoting education, learning and advocacy against killing in contrast to 'illusive nonkilling' that is negative and non-structural such as fostering the concept of 'a war to end all wars' and capital punishment or coercive practices to achieve the ultimate goal against killings. Implicitly, a society with negative peace should not be witnessing crimes though living under oppression while societies characterized by positive peace could be witnessing human prosperity in terms of social and economic development. That indeed is not the case as we see, and it is in this perspective, in today's world of violence, killings and terror that the question remains as to how we promote the objective of nonkilling peace by ensuring such conditions through '*affirmative nonkilling*'. Hence this book!

Perhaps, the institutionalization and promotion of a 'Global Nonkilling Index' on scientific lines for sociological and societal introspection may best foster the paradigm of nonkilling peace and nonviolence amongst societies and the political leadership of countries. Yes, for a revolution to take place from our erstwhile Darwinian evolutionary roots, we do need a utopian vision and mission. In this context it will not be out of context for me to delve briefly into the Kardashev scale to adjudge, even if vaguely, humanity's own civilizational ascent over the last millennia! It was physicist and futurist, Carl Sagan, followed by Michio Kaku, who suggested that humans may attain Type I status in 100–200 years, Type II status in a few thousand years, and Type III status in 100,000 to a million years. Unfortunately, the predictive interpolation and extrapolation perhaps did consider the energy requirement, technological prowess and scientific achievements but overlooked humanity's own nonkilling creative potential and its spiritual attainments for universal peace. No doubt, developing a holistic approach and model in order to promote universal nonkilling peace through *affirmative nonkilling* goes much beyond, using nonviolence the earlier narrative and the tactic by the wholesome rejection of *illusive nonkilling* world view of the past is the way forward. To develop a new principled and strategic paradigm of the nonkilling future for holistic civilizational change is a small and humble, yet a bold step through this book.

'Are Nonkilling Societies Possible?' Joám Evans Pim, the Director of the 'Center for Global Nonkilling', in his Prologue raises the eternal question and that is the theme of the book. He highlights the researches and the developments during the past decade and half since 2002, citing the publication of the World Report on Violence and Health that clearly identified violence as 'a preventable disease'. He mentions that in the same year, Glenn Paige, published his seminal work *Nonkilling Global Political Science* that from different disciplinary perspectives, reached the same conclusion: 'Killing is preventable and, thus, societies that are free from killing are indeed possible'. I recall having exchanged similar notes with Glenn during my planned presentation of the 'United Nations Development Programme' (UNDP), draft road map for the institution of the Sustainable Development Goals (SDGs) in replacement to the Millennium Development Goals (MDGs), post 2015 during an invited talk to the Confederation of Indian Industry (CII), on 23 January 2013. Indeed, the 'Center for Global Nonkilling' had played a catalyst role in the introduction of SDG 16.1 that I believe, will significantly shape international development policies until 2030 as the set targets have to be met, if not fully, at least substantially. Joám explains that besides the overarching SDG 16.1, other goals specifically address different types and contexts of violence (4a, 4.7, 5.2, 5.3, 16.2) and a number of risk factors closely connected to lethality. There is no doubt from my own discourse with Glenn and other researchers, so well brought out now by Joám, that envisioning of a critical mass of scientific community is not at all far-fetched but perhaps already happening now. Emerging from scientific facts into a mass movement would eventually be reflected best in Joám's words, 'replace the assumption of lethal inescapability with the premise of nonkilling potentiality or, in other words, if it would shift from the predominant killing—accepting perspective to a nonkilling perspective'. Joám I must mention made the task of bringing out the book exceptionally simple as many of the essays offered in this book are his own collections over the past decade, as he aptly reflects 'these are, however, brief and exploratory, do provide grounds for confidence in possibilities for a major paradigm shift'.

Leslie Sponsel makes remarkable reflections on the possibilities of a *Nonkilling Society through Nonkilling Anthropology* highlighting the inherent nonviolent nature of human beings by citing the existence of nonkilling societies. Analyzing nonkilling from the point of view of an anthropologist, it is the Yanomami tribes who are stigmatized as fierce and aggressive but after careful study and analysis of their ethnography it can be safely concluded that the Yanomami's as a society do not kill. It is also well surmised in closing that, 'Nonkilling and peace are scientific facts' as a nonviolent society is the precursor to the full realization of human potential and creativity.

James Tyner and Joshua F. J. Inwood, in their introduction to *Nonkilling Geographies,* highlight the role of geography in achieving a nonkilling society. Their superb analysis leads us to the perennial question: why do people adapt violence as the only means to solve a problem when it is not the inherent trait of humans? Their argument begins with an eloquent quote by Martin Luther King Jr. 'A time comes when silence is betrayal'. Indeed, as they elaborate, it is the significance of time and space that determines militarism, materialism and racism, so well emphasized by King. The dictum that 'the growth and prosperity of an empire is achieved at the expense of others' has been exemplified in reference to Glenn D Paige's views that a 'nonkilling society is a possibility, but they insist that the creation of such a society would require efforts globally' and go on to emphasize geography's pivotal role in its promotion. The concept of 'spaces of socialization', is well expounded where people act as per their understanding of race and gender. This becomes the central theme in our understanding: why people kill either directly or by observing others and the spaces in turn give birth to a militarized society—a society that not only promotes but also justifies violence as the best means to tackle violence.

Antony Adolf, in his Chapter on *Preconditional, Didactic and Predictive Histories* brilliantly makes his case that history can be best employed to ensure the importance of nonkilling in a society. He states in his article that 'History, as a rule, is about the 'when' and 'where' of 'what was done' by 'whom' and sometimes, about the 'why'. He further questions, 'what does history mean? And what does it do?' He raises the moot point that, 'history is concerned only with what happened but ignores what did not happen'. He is the author of the book, *Peace: A World History.* He asserts that history is focussed on violence, which disturbs the long-standing peace repeatedly whereas History of Nonkilling focusses on the efforts made time and again to restore order and peace. Indeed, as stressed by Mahatma Gandhi and Leo Tolstoy, nonviolence should be followed for both moral and political reasons. Martin Luther King Jr. and Petra Kelley also adopted it and the initiative was taken to incorporate its principles to create harmony and equality in our society. Thus 'History' can be understood as a study when people have invariably tried to resolve disputes and conflicts and have leaned towards a non-violent approach. Throughout history, as we understand, long standing peace gets interrupted by episodes of conflict and violence, which time and again ended by mutual cooperation and peace treaties. Therefore, when we study the history of mankind we do understand and appreciate the importance of world peace. The conclusions arrived by Antony Adolf are monumental, *if didactic approach is employed in the study and understanding of history many lives across the globe can be saved.*

David Haws, on *Nonkilling Professional Ethics and Engineering: the Public Good* makes a strong case by stating that death remains the unchanged reality of human life but it does not mean that the value of human life is reduced or denied. Rather, to my mind it is the other way around. This value of human life is undermined or denied by the acts of violence and killing. From the point of view of an engineer, it is stated that nonkilling is an important goal and 'Engineers without Borders', is best asserted as public good is one of the goals for engineers. If this goal is realized then nonkilling society becomes an eminent possibility. The need of the hour is to have a moral dialogue between professional engineers so as to realize the importance of ethics along with science.

Antonio Draggo, on *The Scientific Nature of Nonkilling,* brilliantly adopts the scientific approach to achieving the goal of a nonkilling society. Though scientists may have questioned the scientific basis of Gandhi's nonviolence, science does not recognize any rationale or logic in ethics, Draggo adopts theoretical science to provide grounds for his nonkilling perspectives and reiterates that the nonkilling principle is both ethical and scientific. The connection between science and nonkilling being subtle can be proved in many ways. Draggo concludes by his proposed conditioning of human mind to an ethical attitude, emphasizing the obligation of science in achieving a nonkilling society.

In his effusive paper on *Nonkilling Media*, Philip Lee sheds light on the importance of means of communication in realizing the nonkilling goal. He highlights how significant communicative actions are in resolving or even creating conflicts and it is the Nonkilling media which comes into play with the aim to acknowledge the truth and denounce falsehood. The central theme of NonKilling media is that by making people aware of the '*multiple realities*', they can create their own opinions about various issues. It is the media that may save people from all kinds of deceptive propaganda and develop an empathetic attitude towards people of different race and religion. Philip Lee makes a powerful case for Media as a very powerful instrument in engraining positive attitude in the hearts and minds of people, and in enabling them to look beyond their self-interests for humanity. It is this surmise that has led me to coin the term 'Affirmative Nonkilling' for positive approach to building the foundation for nonkilling peace.

Patricia Friedrich and our revered Nonkilling poet laureate, Francisco Gomes de Matos, explore the wonderful approach through *Nonkilling Linguistics* as they believe it plays a vital role in creating a Nonkilling society. Patricia and Francisco believe that it is Nonkilling linguistics and a Nonkilling society which are complementary to each other. Their paper highlights the role of linguistics in the peaceful use of languages at the individual, group, community, national and international levels. They make a strong case that it is the nonkilling society that presupposes the importance of linguistics in attaining peace. To fulfil the goal of a nonkilling society, collaboration of nonkilling linguistics with other disciplines is critical for an 'interdisciplinary approach' towards a nonkilling paradigm. Therefore, immediate need is to denounce all forms of killing, particularly those labelled as *'justifiable'* by means of nonkilling linguistics and actions. Needless to emphasize that the importance of linguistics in health and life is not only underscored but also understood by all.

In their article on *An Educational Model for Teaching Nonkilling Ethics,* authors Todd Junkins and Dracia Narvaez lay emphasis on ethics, and its importance in a harmonious society. They state that, 'ethics requires care about and awareness of how one's actions affect others and how to take appropriate actions.' The importance of moral development and psychological roots of ethical judgment are discussed by the authors in their thesis that education becomes the key to developing a response and conditioning which builds the psycho social framework for morality and ethics. *Integrative Ethical Education (IEE)* plays a pivotal role in developing nonkilling skills on four pillars—expertise development, well-structured and caring environment, active communal involvement and encouragement of self-regulation. Here two primary methods of moral education are also described such as traditional character education and rational moral education. Therefore right to education becomes the building block of a nonkilling society.

Culture of violence began as the course of civilizations had gradually transferred and transformed from generation to generation is the revealing assertion by Piero P Giorgi in his path-breaking paper on *Spirituality and Nonkilling*. History tells numerous tales about violent wars and killings. He notes that this violence can be countered through a different spiritual approach that enables a person to realize the importance of nonkilling peace. Piero calls this transformation of the society as an 'ambitious aim', therefore, emphasizing its pre-eminence. This revolution is also 'slow, legal and local' as it takes at least two to three generations to occur. To explain it further, he states that it is legal because it employs legal methods and is local as it occurs locally and is adapted to local resources.

One of the most steadfast proponents of a *Nonkilling Society,* the Vice Chair of the Center for Global Nonkilling, is Chaiwat Satha-Anand who makes a fervent plea in his article titled *Teaching Nonkilling to the States* that the States who kill, be taught the principles of nonkilling. I do acknowledge that though the article is forwarded to me, courtesy Joám, it is essentially Chaiwat's earlier contribution *per se* on *Nonkilling Security and the State,* edited by Joám Evans Pim and co-published by the Center for Global Nonkilling and Creighton University, Honolulu and Omaha (May 2013), is again reproduced in its entirety, due to Chaiwat's remarkable findings and deductions on the role of the State so relevant even now in the turbulence, wars and violence that we face. The Thai State example observed closely is an excellent illustration about a State's response to violence. In order to explain the concepts of nonkilling and the utmost importance of nonviolence, he extensively relies on Thomas Hobbes, 'Leviathan', rationale that, 'states exist in order to prevent killing of one-person by another', and Emmanuel Kant's 'Perpetual Peace' derived from a 'non-war categorical imperative.' Though the thesis by Hobbes does run in contrast and in reference to the 'Gandhian' thought, that *'the State does not have a soul',* to explore the possibility of a Nonkilling State, Chaiwat does brings us face to face with a dilemma whether, 'Is it right to Teach Nonkilling to the States'. In retrospect I believe that these excellent arguments may well be used as a challenge to convince the States to adopt a nonkilling policy so well concluded by Chaiwat himself, 'to secure national security by nonkilling' in order to achieve the universal nonkilling goal.

Vivek Patkar, in his well-argued article on *Mathematics for Building a Nonkilling Ethos* brings out the scientific rationale by stating how mathematics, as a human activity, can be used for both constructive and destructive purposes. To illustrate, the laws of mathematics that Johannes Kepler conceptualized for his three laws of planetary motion proved helpful in the designing of guns and cannons. The author compares mathematics with fire, the two of them being pure and neutral in their nature, but do make a difference in how we humans use them. Therefore, he makes a strong case of a necessity to educate our youth about the use of mathematics in creating a nonkilling society. He also cites the example of Non-Euclidean Geometry and its role in realizing the goal. Vivek concludes that the future of mankind depends on the development and use of mathematics, as it is interconnected with the development of peaceful societies. So well argued and so close to my own prescription, from human evolution to human revolution, '*if there is peace in the world, these concepts of mathematics can be used for realizing greater goals such as inter-galactic travel*'.

Anis Hamadeh, a versatile writer, musician, painter, journalist, an expert on Islamic Studies, editor of Anis Online, author of *Understanding Islam* (2013, in German) and translator of 'Nonkilling Global Political Science' into German (2009) explores the role of arts such as: literature, television shows, cartoon series, music pieces and even paintings in cultivating nonkilling ideas. She is affirmative and unequivocal in her conviction that 'arts manifested in these forms has a profound influence on the audience and can play a great role in organizing the masses'. By creative measures in art, the author suggests that sensitivity towards nonkilling can be created.

In his brilliant contributing article on *Music in Peacebuilding, the Nonkilling Dimension: A new prelude to 'Nonkilling Arts*, Olivier Urbain, who had on my request very graciously and despite his extremely busy engagements revised his original piece published earlier, passionately elaborates music and activities that impact such as ambivalence, musicking, booster, non-universality, power balance, repetition and industry amplification. He eloquently raises the matter, 'What is the role of the arts in making a nonkilling society possible?' and further states that 'once people start producing nonkilling arts all over the world, how do we find out which society creates more nonkilling arts (of the explicit type)? Would those be the less violent societies (showing that people express the overall culture of their societies), or the more violent ones (showing that people need the arts to express their most urgent needs)? Olivier to my mind is spot on when he mentions that this concept is at least a few tens of thousands of years old, perhaps as old as humanity. It was Glenn Paige who provided us a way to think about the issue in a systematic manner as the set of questions are indeed a pure stroke of genius: 'Is a nonkilling society possible? If no, why not? If yes, why?'

Expressed, as numerous works of art across centuries best expressed by Romain Rolland who quotes Tolstoy, 'Art must suppress violence, and only art can do so' (...) Art Young observes, 'Nonviolence is more than a system of political thought; it is the stuff of poetry and of life.'

Dennis Morgan in his article on *Image of a Nonkilling Future* addresses the challenges, which various civilizations had to face in order to ensure their existence. In the words of Arnold Toynbee (Toynbee), 'when a civilization collapses, it is due to the inefficiency of the "creative minority".' Thus, the creative minority has to adapt to a 'new wiser conceptual framework' in order to protect modern civilization and save the society in times of crisis. Dennis concludes by saying, 'The image of a nonkilling future has a social image to make based upon anthropological and historical precedents, as well as current sociological research'. The responsibility of the creative minority is to fill this nonkilling image for civilizational course correction and survival with the right colours. The question that may remain to be answered is how much influence will this creative minority have, in reshaping the future?

During the course of her doctoral research it was Katyayani Singh who came up with the thought that a nonkilling societal paradigm can be best achieved with great leadership and perhaps this work may not be complete if we do not address this paradigm space. Based on my earlier work on leadership and followership, I was of the opinion that leadership and followership for a nonkilling society do go hand in hand for achieving our ultimate vision, *'Is a Nonkilling Society Possible'*? Hence the article at the end to capture not only the wisdom of all the earlier authors but also to make it possible, *Leadership, Followership and the Nonkilling Paradigm*. The importance of socio-political leaders in establishing peace is highlighted, as it is indeed not only their own leadership impact on the followers that helps their followers to determine the future course of action for posterity. It is true, that 'all great leaders have been great followers' and in their lives they have emulated others as well. Leaders and their followers as much as their philosophy do determine the shape and the course of human civilizational ascent, where principles of a 'nonkilling world community' ultimately would rest. When people begin to kill in the name of political thought or philosophy, or religion or even so-called dogmas it is the leaders who have to provide the wisdom and the conscientious path to the society as a whole for the future forward. In this penultimate article we have tried to chart the success of certain charismatic leaders of the twentieth century and have evaluated them as a test case, in our attempt to predict the possibilities that exist for a nonkilling society in reference, as to how far these *leaders and followers* were able to establish an '*affirmative nonkilling society*'.

In his Epilogue, our mentor at the Center for Global Nonkilling, the nonkilling veteran and the venerable peace activist, Balwant Bhaneja aptly explains that the idea of nonkilling paradigm is not at all an abstract model but has scientific basis. He highlights and concludes that the scientific ideas of Paige in his seminal work *Nonkilling Global Political Science* do reflect the creative pursuits and ways that the idea of nonkilling can be developed and promoted. Bill (Bhaneja) also shares his personal emails, a treasure trove, that he had exchanged with Paige on subjects such as Nonviolence limits of Jains of India, abortion, death of self, cures for killing and policy and even the politics and connections that may one day make it eminent for human civilization to have a nonkilling society.

I dedicate this work and acknowledge with profound gratitude, my source of inspiration, my predecessor, founder Chair of the 'Center for Global Nonkilling', Glenn Durland Paige who not only wanted me to initiate this project but had wished that I carry forward his work, for our nonkilling shared destiny.

My grateful thanks to Joám Evans Pim for his liberally sharing his own collection of edited works on nonkilling and for timely and prompt advice from time to time. I owe my immense gratitude to distinguished Prof Dr N. Radhakrishnan, Advisor, for his gracious Foreword and Bhaneja, our Governing Board Member, for his concluding Epilogue as also his inspirational interventions, to Glenda Paige for her sure and steady motivation in all our endeavours, and finally all our reviewers for their generous recommendations and our very eminent contributors for the excellent articles that made this book possible, for a better tomorrow, for a nonkilling world.

Perhaps this project may have not seen the light of the day but for Shri K.P.R. Nair of Konark Publishers for his constant encouragement and his very able editorial and cover design team, especially Coordinating Editor Jiza Joy. Not in the least, I do acknowledge with thanks, the efforts of Ms Katyayani Singh, who is pursuing her doctorate on the subject and all those who have directly or indirectly been a part of this endeavour in the imminent hope that this work will one day prove to be a turning point in our human civilizational ascent.

'To reach a port we must set sail –
Sail not tie at anchor
Sail not drift...'
—Franklin D. Roosevelt

References

Bekoff, Marc and Jessica Pierce. (2009). *Wild Justice: The Moral Lives of Animals*. Chicago: University of Chicago Press.

Paige, G. D. (2009). *Nonkilling Global Political Science*. Honolulu: Center for Global Nonkilling.

Swarup, A. (2018). *Shifting the Way We Think About Nonkilling, Vision of Humanity*. Accessed 12 July 2018, <http://visionofhumanity.org/economists-on-peace/shifting-way-think-nonkilling/>

Acknowledgements

Since 2009, the Center for Global Nonkilling published a multidisciplinary series of scientific explorations of the possibilities for a nonkilling paradigm shift. These series included the collective volumes: *Toward a Nonkilling Paradigm, Nonkilling Societies, Nonkilling History: Shaping Policy with Lessons from the Past, Engineering Nonkilling: Scientific Responsibility and the Advancement of Killing-Free Societies, Nonkilling Geography, Nonkilling Futures: Visions, Nonkilling Linguistics: Practical Applications, Nonkilling Psychology, Nonkilling Korea: Six Culture Exploration, Nonkilling Media, Nonkilling Security and the State, Nonkilling Balkans,* and *Nonkilling Spiritual Traditions*.

Although the series is ongoing and various additional volumes are under preparation, to commemorate the life of Prof Glenn D. Paige and the decade-long explorations, a selection of texts from the published books has been compiled and prepared for greater dissemination. It must be noted that some of the texts have been written a decade ago, without any revision or updated references. Fortunately, the seeds of these and other contributions have grown to fertilize the fields of nonkilling scientific discovery, also contributing to applied science and policy making, as evidenced by the recent Sustainable Development Goals target 16.1, which in essence captures the nonkilling spirit formulated by Glenn D. Paige in his seminal work, *Nonkilling Global Political Science* (2002).

As the title suggests, the purpose of the compilation is to arouse, awaken and amplify intellectual discussion and discourse on the philosophy of nonkilling and to look beyond the 'Nonkilling Global Political Science' of Glenn D. Paige and to seek answers to the eternal question: Is a Nonkilling Society Possible? The book attempts to bring to light new ideas, researches and discoveries, particularly the practicability of the principles and precepts, in today's contemporary world.

I acknowledge with gratitude all contributors and it is my fervent hope that the book will not only provide intellectual recourse and the next level of thought on the very foundation of the philosophy of nonkilling originally propounded but also to encourage thought leaders and readers to move beyond and to dwell upon the principles and practice of its values internationally.

Anoop Swarup

Prologue

Joám Evans Pim

In September 2015, the United Nations adopted the newly drafted Sustainable Development Goals (SDGs) as the post-2015 development agenda. The SDGs replaced the Millennium Development Goals that expired at the end of 2015 and, for the first time, include an item explicitly addressing the need for 'peaceful and inclusive societies', setting the goal to 'significantly reduce all forms of violence and related death rates everywhere' (16.1). Just 6 years before, in 2009, the Center for Global Nonkilling published the book *Toward a Nonkilling Paradigm*, arguing for such a strategic shift in our global thinking and agenda.

The SDGs will significantly shape international development policies until 2030 and set targets to be met by major national and international agencies. Besides the overarching SDG 16.1, other goals specifically address different types and contexts of violence (4a, 4.7, 5.2, 5.3, 16.2) and a number of risk factors closely connected to lethality. However, the possibility of significantly reducing death rates and building killing-free societies is still strongly questioned by social constructions that assume killing as an inherent part of human nature.

The field of violence prevention has grown significantly over the past decade, signalled in 2002 with the publication of the *World Report on Violence and Health* that clearly identified violence as 'a preventable disease'. In the same year, Prof. Glenn D. Paige, a political scientist and founder of the Center for Global Nonkilling, published his seminal work *Nonkilling Global Political Science*, which from a different disciplinary perspective, reached the same conclusion: killing is preventable and, thus, societies that are free from killing are indeed possible. The book explored some of the accumulative supportive evidence for nonkilling policies that provide a solid base for taking SDG 16.1 seriously and making the case for the necessary build up to escalate their application.

Over a decade after the publication of both *Nonkilling Global Political Science* and the *World Report on Violence and Health*, we have much of the needed knowledge to drastically reduce death rates everywhere and to start building killing-free societies, as sought by SDG 16.1. This book, which republishes a collection of materials that the Center for Global Nonkilling has disseminated over the past decade, provides some elements of that common knowledge of humanity that can assist us in putting an end to the global disease of lethality.

Failure to seize the opportunity presented by the SDGs and the accumulation of a knowledge base that sustains the possibility of ending killing in this crucial point in history, may not only prove a strategic failure in the efforts to prevent and reduce violence, but may also jeopardize other global goals and the future of humanity. SDGs are indeed interdependent, and failure to address certain targets will obstruct advances in others. By continuing to ignore killing as a preventable problem, on the basis of our social bias toward the inevitability of violence, and disregarding violence prevention as an integral part of the solution,we are undermining the possibilities for real social change in the 21st century and beyond.

About the Selection

Since 2009, the Center for Global Nonkilling under the guidance of Prof. Glenn D. Paige, published a multidisciplinary series of scientific explorations of the possibilities for a nonkilling paradigm shift. The series included the collective volumes: *Toward a Nonkilling Paradigm, Nonkilling Societies, Nonkilling History: Shaping Policy with Lessons from the Past, Engineering Nonkilling: Scientific Responsibility and the Advancement of Killing-Free Societies, Nonkilling Geography, Nonkilling Futures: Visions, Nonkilling Linguistics: Practical Applications, Nonkilling Psychology, Nonkilling Korea: Six Culture Exploration, Nonkilling Media, Nonkilling Security and the State, Nonkilling Balkans, Nonkilling Spiritual Traditions* and *Nonkilling Education*.

Although the series is ongoing and various additional volumes are under preparation, to commemorate the life of Prof. Glenn D. Paige and the decade-long explorations, a selection of texts from the published books has been compiled and prepared for greater dissemination, particularly in India. It must be noted that some of the texts have been written a decade ago, without any revision or updated references. Fortunately, the seeds of these and other contributions have grown to fertilize the fields of nonkilling scientific discovery, also contributing to applied science and policy making, as evidenced by the recent Sustainable Development Goals target 16.1, which in essence captures the nonkilling spirit formulated by Glenn D. Paige in his seminal *Nonkilling Global Political Science*.

The series of publications exploring different disciplinary approaches to nonkilling arose from a crucial question formulated by Prof Glenn D. Paige:

> 'Is a Nonkilling Society Possible?' Paige defines this form of society as 'a human community, smallest to largest, local to global, characterized by no killing of humans and no threats to kill; no weapons designed to kill humans and no justifications for using them; and no conditions of society dependent upon threat or use of killing force for maintenance or change.'

Even if the term itself is not new, Paige provided a new way to think about the problem of lethality in an alternative and systematic way, through this simple but far reaching question.

Paige's approach, characterized by the measurability of its goals (killing and nonkilling can be quantified and related to specific causes) and the open-ended generative systems nature of its realization (appealing to infinite human creativity and variability), trespasses the limits of an ideology for social change entailing a new scientific model based on the refutation of killing-accepting science and the societal premises rooted in the widespread acceptance of lethality (in all of its forms) and lethal intent. As Charles Collyer reminds us, the 'familiar word, nonviolence, is almost comforting in its generality' while nonkilling 'confronts and startles us with its specificity' (2003: 371), urging us to take concrete action.

Even if written from the stand point of political science, an explicit request is directed to other fields to bring about a 'disciplinary shift to nonkilling creativity,' through a four-part logic of analysis focused on the causes of killing; the causes of nonkilling; the causes of transition between killing and nonkilling; and the characteristics of killing-free societies (2009 [2002]: 73). The fourth item in this framework implies the need to understand existing killing-free societies, setting an appeal to anthropologists, sociologists and others. Recalling Kenneth Boulding's so-called 'First Law' ('Anything that exists is possible'), Paige (and much of the evidence brought forward in this book) reminds us that nonkilling societies do exist in spite of having passed largely unnoticed to most in the scientific community.

To counter the 'historic and current systemic bias of the disproportionate amount of attention given to violence and war' (Sponsel, 1996a: 113-114) peace, nonviolence and nonkilling need not only be held as legitimate subjects of research, but must be considered seriously, systematically and intensively. As Leslie Sponsel points out: 'You cannot understand or achieve something by ignoring it' (1996: 14). Readers have probably realized that what is being said here is not in any way a revelation. Some of the authors who are contributing to this volume have been repeating the same crucial fact for decades: nonkilling societies, as those imagined by Paige in his book, are not a utopian dream; they are a genuine real actuality that is currently in existence and has been so for millennia. It can probably be said louder but not more clearly. This volume provides firm evidence that the only feasible answer to Paige's question ('Is a Nonkilling Society Possible?') is undoubtedly affirmative.

Shifting our Worldview

An average person in the US watches approximately 30 hours of television every week. That equates to nearly 4 and half hours a day, an estimate common to most industrialized countries. During those 4 and half hours, viewers have a choice of programming which usually ranges from several thousand individual or serial killings in crime fiction serials to multiple complete annihilations of the whole human species and all planetary life available on film. Counting individual murders alone, an average child in the US will have viewed 16,000 killings by the age of 18 according to a study by the American Academy of Child and Adolescent Psychiatry. Television series exclusively focussed on killings break audience figures leading all rankings ('Criminal Minds' in CBS has a DVR of 13.5 million viewers), spearheading a multibillion dollar industry for the socialization of lethality and its institutions.

News channels also broadcast in multiple and repetitive occasions every single intentional killing or public act of violence that takes place in the 'civilized' world, together with escalating threats, military deployments and security hazards that constantly siege the average viewer. While the World Health Organization (2002) calculated that an average of 4,000 people are killed from self-inflicted, interpersonal or collective violence every day—of which the most part is attributed to suicide—every television spectator is presented with several billion human killings every day, including nuclear holocaust, planetary extinction and every single form of random or organized interpersonal or collective form of lethality. In a society increasingly shaped by what is conveyed by the screen, this statistical anomaly has more far reaching consequences that can be imagined, especially in the increasing number of youths that have in the media one of their main sources of socialization and worldview formation.

In the same year Paige published *Nonkilling Global Political Science*, John Kavanaugh also pointed out how '[t]he principle of nonkilling is not a recommendation of passivity,' as the 'primary commitment to the inherent dignity of personal life requires us to intervene on behalf of the defenceless or the victim' with the only moral limit of 'the direct intended killing of the aggressor' (2002: 123). Moving beyond, Paige argues that nonkilling is not only about the rejection of killing, but also implies constructive engagement in societal transformation:

> This means unequivocal engagement in abolition of war and its weapons, abolition of poverty, nonkilling expression of human rights and responsibilities, proactive promotion of environmental sustainability, and contribution to problem-solving processes that respond to human needs and evoke infinite creative potential in individuals and in humankind as a whole. (2009: 102)

Certainly, all theories that were the catalysts for significant paradigm shifts were previously dismissed as 'utopian,' 'idealistic,' and 'unrealistic' (Kuhn, 1962), in this case by the institutionalized lethality-accepting scholarly communities that challenge nonkilling's scientific status, credibility and viability. As Jesús Ibáñez explains, 'majority science' always operates as a selective filter of reality, in such a way that only the portion that dominant ideology provides goes through' (1985: 33). Alternative approaches such as nonkilling tend to be considered deviant, if not simply unnoticed. Following this logic, Ibáñez distinguishes between dogmatic, sedentary or majority science and critical, nomadic or minority science.

While the first assumes the mainstream position of power and unity; the latter adopts the multiple views of those who resist from the base of the hierarchical system; While the first approach does not challenge the existing reality; the latter seeks its transformation; While the first is responsible for reproducing and maintaining the knowledge that has been previously generated; the latter constantly creates alternatives on the fringes of sedentary science; While the first considers the latter 'prescientific,' 'subscientific' or 'parascientific,' the latter considers the first as 'meta-scientific' and hylomorphic, as 'all passivity is on the side of matter' and 'no production exists beyond reproduction' (1985: 38-39).

Following society's general orientation toward the belief that affirms the inevitability and legitimacy of killing in human relations, most scientists could be accordingly labelled as 'killing' or 'lethality-accepting.' Using the gradual taxonomy suggested by Paige, the following perspective would describe a possible spectrum of orientations:

> prokilling—consider killing positively beneficial for self or civilization; killing-prone—inclined to kill or to support killing when advantageous; ambikilling—equally inclined to kill or not to kill, and to support or oppose it; killing-avoiding—predisposed not to kill or to support it but prepared to do so; nonkilling—committed not to kill and to change conditions conducive to lethality. (2009: 77)

On Paradigm Shifts

The concept of paradigm shift was introduced by Thomas Kuhn in *The Scientific Structure of Scientific Revolutions* (1962) as a theory to explain epistemological change through history. In spite of its flaws and setbacks, successive debates and modifications have led to a widely accepted model on the mechanisms that shape scientific revolution (see Lakatos and Musgrave, 1970; Kordig, 1973; Fuller, 2000), which, in Kuhn's terms, is 'a noncumulative developmental episode in which an older paradigm is replaced in whole or in part by an incompatible new one' (1962: 91).

According to this approach, normal science is based on the unprecedented and open-ended scientific achievements that are acknowledged by a scientific community, constituting a paradigm (1962: 10). Paradigms serve as instruments for endo-culturalization and doctrinal training within the scientific community. Acceptance of defined doctrine by students is required as part of their initiation thus creating consensus on the basic rules and standards. These standards are consecrated through a series of institutional instruments as professional societies or academic journals, and—eventually—the general understanding that the bases of the paradigm no longer need to be discussed (as they are already enshrined in textbooks).

As a paradigm reaches its position as normal science it will focus its efforts on the reinforcement of its theoretical and experimental foundations, leaving no space for the analysis of anomalies or the development of new theories, as it is 'directed to the articulation of those phenomena and theories that the paradigm already supplies' (1962:24). But anomalies that cannot be understood within an existing scientific framework still appear, creating discrepancies between theory and facts. Kuhn assumes that anomalies exist in all paradigms, even though they tend to be considered as acceptable margins of error or, more often, simply ignored and excluded from the focus of debate (1962: 64). In the history of science there have always been points in which the excess of significant anomalies have jeopardized the prevailing scientific paradigms, bringing them into a state of crisis (see Kuhn, ch. 7).

These inexorable anomalies, together with changes in socially constructed knowledge and belief systems and growing academic criticism, seed the ground for scientific revolutions or paradigm shifts (transition from normal to extraordinary science). A paradigm is not limited to dominant theories but encompasses the worldview of the scientific community at a certain point in time. Understandably, the change of the scientists' worldview is not a simple consequence of the accumulation of adverse anomalies within a discipline, but, moreover, a result of deep alterations of social, historic and cultural conditions and possibilities.

A paradigm shift is thus a long social process that implies significant changes in how disciplines function, slowly modifying views on what is thinkable or unthinkable, altering intellectual strategies for problem-solving and modifying terminology usage and conceptual frameworks in a changing universe of discourse. When anomalies become more generally acknowledged, explicit discontent, new articulations of the paradigm and new discoveries proliferate. As Kuhn expresses it, 'a scientist's world is qualitatively transformed as well as quantitatively enriched by fundamental novelties of either fact or theory' (1962: 7). At this stage new ideas or those who had previously been consigned to the margins of academic thought are brought forward and engage the previously accepted theoretical framework in an epistemological challenge.

Followers of the institutionalized paradigm that has started to be questioned will close ranks until a new alternative emerges and gains acceptance. Conversion from one paradigm to another is not necessarily immediate or spontaneous and, according to Max Planck, can be more the result of a generational turnover: 'A new scientific truth does not triumph by convincing its opponents and making them see the light, but rather because its opponents eventually die, and a new generation grows up that is familiar with it' (in Kuhn, 1962: 151). On the contrary, Kuhn does believe in conversions, that 'occur not despite the fact that scientists are human but because they are' (1962: 152). When a paradigm reaches its crisis and consensus within the established framework of 'normal science' ceases to exist, a period of 'revolutionary science' arises, as the bolder members of the scientific community start to point out weaknesses and explore alternatives for the previously unchallenged assumptions. Challenging a paradigm certainly requires audacity, as desertion will initially be framed as the exclusion from scientific practice, as defined by the dominant paradigm (1962: 34).

Any scientific community will encompass both conservative and more 'daring' individuals. The first will harshly resist any theoretical change brought forward by the latter elements, and a period in which both paradigms co-exist—in a troubled relation—will occur. During this initial period the emerging paradigm (still precarious and incomplete) will be highly criticized for being unable to solve apparent anomalies, only replacing the previous one (and thus completing the shift) when it has overcome its inconsistencies and gained unity. The result of this process is not simply a different or improved theoretical model or, in other words, 'handling the same bundle of data as before, but placing them in a new system of relations with one another by giving them a different framework' (1962: 85), but a completely altered worldview (thus the incommensurability of old and new paradigms presented in the Kuhnian approach). Allegiance to a new paradigm is not based exclusively on its past achievements (usually still immature) but rather on 'which paradigm should in the future guide research on problems many of which neither competitor can yet claim to resolve completely' (1962: 157).

As Kuhn believed problem-solving is the basis of science, the success of a new paradigm ultimately depends on its ability to 'resolve some outstanding and generally recognized problem that can be met in no other way' (1962: 168). Or, summarizing, being able to resolve more problems and resolve them better than its predecessor. A new paradigm implies a redefinition of science itself as problems that were previously considered trivial or nonexistent become focal points of scientific development (1962:103). The emerging paradigm will initially have a small number of supporters (disqualified and considered suspect by the mainstream scientific community) who are ultimately responsible for improving their proposal, exploring its possibilities and persuading others to join. As the number of aligned scientists increases so will the quantity of books, articles, instruments and experiments. If successful and appealing, a spiral process will be unleashed through which the emerging paradigm will enter its phase of normal science. In this sense, paradigm shifts share parallels with the diffusion of innovation theories where new inventions and discoveries are described on an innovation curve ranging from initial resistance, innovators, then early adapters, late majority, and finally laggards (Rogers, 1995).

A Nonkilling Paradigm Shift

In *Nonkilling Global Political Science*, Prof Glenn D. Paige envisioned what kind of science would emerge if the scientific community would replace the assumption of lethal inescapability with the premise of nonkilling potentiality or, in other words, if it would shift from the predominant killing—accepting perspective to a nonkilling perspective (2009: 73):

> What values would inspire and guide our work? What facts would we seek? What explanatory and predictive theories would we explore? What uses of knowledge would we facilitate? How would we educate and train ourselves and others? What institutions would we build? And how would we engage with others in processes of discovery, creation, sharing, and use of knowledge to realize nonkilling societies for a nonkilling world?

In a 'disciplinary shift to nonkilling creativity,' Paige argued, the acceptance of killing as a social, cultural, political, economic, biological, technological, etc. imperative becomes unthinkable or, at the very least problematical, as both approaches are, using Kuhnian terms, incompatible and incommensurable. Certainly, if killing is considered inevitable or acceptable within the scientific community little effort will be devoted to deepening our understanding of killing and possible alternatives that will remove the conditions behind lethality. As the criteria for determining legitimate problems and solutions also change, Paige called for a greater emphasis on the understanding of killing within the framework of a four-part logic of analysis. This focus is on the causes of killing; causes of nonkilling; causes of transition between killing and nonkilling; and the characteristics of killing-free societies (2009: 73).

This causational approach is crucial, as each case of killing and nonkilling must be analyzed seeking to understand the underlying 'processes of cause and effect, however, complex and interdependent' (2009: 74). Not only is it necessary to know 'who kills whom, how, where, when, why and with what antecedents, contextual conditions, individual and social meanings, and consequences,' but also why and how so many in human history have chosen life over lethality when confronted with the most adverse circumstances, and why and how collective or individual transitions and oscillations from killing to nonkilling and vice-versa have occurred (an irreversible linear progression is not assumed), taking into account every variable from individual decision making to structural killing and nonkilling determinant factors (idem).

In his proposal, Paige also identifies five zones (portrayed as a 'funnel of killing' and a 'unfolding fan of nonkilling alternatives') in which practical transformative alternatives must be developed in the process of applying the theoretical knowledge derived from nonkilling analysis: the killing zone (the place of bloodshed); the socialization zone (where people learn to kill); the cultural conditioning zone (where acceptance of killing as unavoidable and legitimate is predisposed); the structural reinforcement zone (providing socio economic relations, institutions, and material means predisposing and supporting killing);and the neuro biochemical capability zone (comprising physical and neurological factors that contribute to both killing and nonkilling behaviors). The focal point of nonkilling scientific research resides on the need for effective transformative applications in the scope of this 'funnel of killing.'

For the emergence of these alternatives a normative and empirical shift from the killing imperative to the imperative not to kill must occur through a cumulative process of interacting ethical and empirical discoveries. As Kuhn stated, a scientific revolution does not come about simply through accumulation, but rather through transformation, altering the foundational theoretical generalizations (1962: 85). Paige points out that this inevitably requires normative, factual, theoretical, applied, educational, institutional and methodological nonkilling revolutions. Normative ethical progression would have to move from 'killing is imperative,' to 'killing is questionable,' to 'killing is unacceptable,' to 'nonkilling is imperative.' In parallel, an empirical progression should shift from 'nonkilling is impossible,' to 'nonkilling is problematic,' to 'nonkilling is explorable,' to 'nonkilling is possible' (2009: 75-79).

As a factual shift, nonkilling deepens into the gathering of evidence for nonkilling human propensities and capabilities, usually discarded or ignored by killing-accepting 'normal science' that sees them as trivial or non-existent anomalies, but that are extremely significant in the context of nonkilling fact-gathering. As a theoretical shift, nonkilling faces the challenge of articulating normative and empirical theories that can effectively tackle the problems from the range of phenomena it confronts. As an applied shift, nonkilling must assist global transformation toward killing-free societies, designing ways where theoretical knowledge can relate to the problem-solving needs of the 'unfolding fan of nonkilling alternatives.' As an educational shift, nonkilling has to challenge the authority of killing-accepting academic traditions; unless the horizon of rules and standards within the scientific community is widened to include nonkilling alternatives and competencies for research, teaching, consultancy, leadership, civic action and critical reflection, disagreement over lethality is not likely to occur. As a methodological shift, nonkilling must overcome not only the conceptual and theoretical framework that limit the understanding of nonkilling capabilities but also instrumental and methodological impediments that condition selection, evaluation, criticism and analysis of necessary data on killing and nonkilling. Finally, an institutional shift foresees the establishment of nonkilling as normal science, designing new organizational outlines for disciplines, sub disciplines and interdisciplinary relations, not only focussing on the academic arena but moreover on the field of social practice (Paige, 2009: 79-85).

Kuhn presented an analogy between the framework of scientific revolutions leading to paradigm shifts and political revolutions that bring about social transformation (see Kuhn, ch. 9). Considering both imply an alteration of the worldview held by communities, it is not odd to see how political and scientific revolutions are sometimes closely linked in human history. Nonkilling is not an exception, as its implications clearly go beyond the sphere of politics or academic research, questioning and potentially transforming (or perhaps rehabilitating) human relations. A movement toward nonkilling (either expressed using this term or simply embracing the idea behind it) is already happening in the fields of civil action, education, politics and science.

We believe that the essays offered in this book, however, brief and exploratory, provide grounds for confidence in possibilities for a major shift from lethality-accepting science to an ethically-orientated nonkilling paradigm empowering social and cultural transitions toward killing-free societies. This process is currently underway. But it will require much greater commitment not only by the scientific community but by society as a whole. Paradigm shifts are inevitable, open-ended, and impermanent. Nonkilling will certainly not be the final phase in scientific development. But it will surely be a crucial contribution to the advancement of knowledge and action for continuation of human and planetary life.

References

Collyer, Charles E. (2003). 'A Nonkilling Paradigm for Political Scientists, Psychologists, and Others,' *Peace and Conflict*, 9(4):371-372.

Fuller, Steve. (2000). *Thomas Kuhn: A Philosophical History for Our Times*. Chicago: University of Chicago Press.

Ibáñez, Jesús. (1985). *Del algoritmo al sujeto*. Madrid: Siglo XXI.

Kavanaugh, John F. (2002). *Who Count as Persons? Human Identity and the Ethics of Killing*. Washington: Georgetown University Press

Kordig, C. R. (1973). 'Discussion: Observational Invariance,' *Philosophy of Science*, 40:558-569.

Kuhn, Thomas. (1962). *The Scientific Structure of Scientific Revolutions*. Chicago: University of Chicago Press.

Lakatos, Imre; Musgrave, Alan, eds. (1970). *Criticism and the Growth of Knowledge*, Vol. 4. Cambridge: Cambridge University Press.

Paige, Glenn D. (2009 [2002]). *Nonkilling Global Political Science*. Honolulu: Center for Global Nonkilling. Available at: <http://www.nonkilling.org>.

Sponsel, Leslie E. (1996a). 'The Natural History of Peace: A Positive View of Human Nature and Its Potential,' in Gregor, Thomas A., ed., *The Natural History of Peace*. Nashville: Vanderbilt University Press, ch. 4, pp. 95-125.

1

Reflections on the Possibilities of a Nonkilling Society and a Nonkilling Anthropology

Leslie E. Sponsel
University of Hawaii

That since wars begin in the minds of men, it is in the minds of men that the defences of peace must be constructed.

—UNESCO Constitution, November 16, 1945

Everyone has the right to life, liberty and security of person.

—UN, Universal Declaration of Human Rights, December 10, 1948, Art. 3

The time has come to set forth human killing as a problem to be solved rather than to accept enslavement by it as a condition to be endured forever.

—Paige, 2002: 145

Is a nonkilling society possible? What are the possibilities of a nonkilling political science? These are the two elemental, central, and pivotal questions that Glenn D. Paige (2002) raises and explores in his ground breaking book which is generating a quiet but accelerating and far-reaching revolution in theory and praxis throughout the world (Bhaneja, 2008). This essay addresses these two questions and related matters from the perspective of one anthropologist and cites some of the extensive literature for documentation and as sources for further information, although no attempt has been made at a thorough literature review, especially for periodicals.

The particular approach to anthropology used here needs to be clearly specified at the outset. American anthropology may be defined as the holistic scientific and scholarly study of human unity and diversity in all of its aspects throughout time and space. It encompasses the five subfields of archaeology, biological (or physical) anthropology, cultural anthropology, linguistic anthropology, and applied anthropology. In varying ways and degrees, American anthropologists share a concern for human evolution, human diversity (biological, cultural, and linguistic), culture and cultures, fieldwork, and comparison (especially cross-cultural). Anthropology is also unique in its scope which ranges from in-depth studies of local communities to surveys of the human species as a whole (Birx, 2006; Perry, 2003; Salzman and Rice, 2004).

Nonkilling Society

Is a nonkilling society possible? Without any hesitation, my answer is affirmative. As a political scientist, Paige pursues the framework of nation states or countries noting that today there are 195 such entities. In contrast, an anthropologist would more likely pursue the framework of cultures. Estimates of the number of extant cultures in the world today are around 7,000 (Summer Institute of Linguistics, 2008). Furthermore, whereas countries typically range in age from a few decades to a few centuries, cultures are centuries to millennia old. Accordingly, examples of nonkilling and peaceful cultures can also be important evidence in answering Paige's first question in the affirmative. Such socio-cultural systems generally accord with Paige's (2002: 1) definition of a nonkilling society as '... characterized by no killing of humans and no threats to kill; no weapons designed to kill humans and no justification for using them; and no conditions of society dependent upon threat or use of killing for maintenance or change.'

At the same time, the logic that Paige pursues regarding the frequency of killing by humans is affirmed as well by anthropology. He argues that women seldom kill other humans, and that only a minority of men kill other humans (cf. Levinson, 1994; WHO, 2002). To phrase it another way, the overwhelming majority of humans have not been involved directly in any kind of killing. The Yanomami are an anthropological case in point. They were stereotyped and stigmatized in a derogatory way as 'the fierce people' by Napoleon Chagnon (1968, 1992). However, if one actually scrutinizes his own ethnography (description of a culture), then it is apparent that most individuals within the Yanomami society do not kill others. There is no mention of a woman killing a man or another woman. Raids and other forms of intergroup aggression are not ubiquitous in space and time by any means. Not all men from a village participate in a raid on another village. Also, Chagnon mentions that often many members of a raiding party find excuses to retreat rather than participate in the entire process (Sponsel, 1998).

Other anthropologists who have conducted research with the Yanomami, some living with them for many more years than Chagnon, such as Bruce Albert, Gale Goodwin Gomez, Kenneth Good, Jacques Lizot, and Alcida Ramos, have all called into serious question Chagnon's characterization of the Yanomami as the 'fierce people.' Apparently as a result of such authoritative criticism, Chagnon dropped that subtitle from later editions of his book, yet his characterization in the text persists anyway (Sponsel, 1998). The ethnography by Chagnon together with the wealth of dozens of other books on the Yanomami could be examined to identify a multitude of examples of nonkilling and peaceful behaviors that prevail in the daily life of most individuals and communities (see especially Dawson, 2006; Ferguson, 1992, 1995; Good, 1991; Lizot, 1985; Peters, 1998; Ramos, 1987, 1995; Smole, 1976; Sponsel, 1998, 2006c).

A nonkilling society is not only just a possibility as Paige theorizes, rather in reality many such societies actually exist today. The most famous one is the Semai of the Malaysian forest. They fit Paige's criteria for a nonkilling society and were first described through field research by Robert Knox Dentan (1968). Years later Clayton Robarcheck (1992, 1996, 1998a,b) independently confirmed Dentan's characterization of the Semai. Much later Clayton and Carole Robarcheck worked among the Waorani who were supposedly one of the most violent societies known, as will be discussed here later. In an ingenious comparison between the Semai and Waorani, the Robarchecks (1992, 1998a) concluded that the worldview of each of these two cultures was the single most important influence on whether they were peaceful or warlike. Otherwise, they were very similar in many respects such as their subsistence economy.

Beyond the Semai, dozens of other nonkilling societies have been extensively documented in the anthropological record. David Fabbro (1978) published the earliest modern cross-cultural study identifying the basic attributes of existing peaceful societies which accord with Paige's criteria. The most systematic and extensive documentation of such societies is by Bruce D. Bonta (1993, 1996, 1997). He compiled an annotated bibliography of 47 cultures that are generally nonviolent and peaceful (Bonta, 1993). A wealth of information on these and other aspects of this subject are archived on his encyclopaedic website called 'Peaceful Societies' (http://www.peacefulsocieties.org). By now there are several other surveys and inventories of nonviolent and peaceful societies including those by Baszarkiewicz and Fry (2008), Bonta and Fry (2006), Melko (1973, 1984), and van der Dennen (1995). Three edited books of ethnographic case studies of nonviolent and peaceful cultures also have been published (Howell and Willis, 1989; Montagu, 1978; Sponsel and Gregor, 1994). Most recently, Fry (2006, 2007) has systematically and vigorously argued, with ample evidence, for the human potential and actuality of nonviolence and peace.

Given this extensive documentation of nonkilling and peaceful socio-cultural systems, the only way that any author, scholar, or scientist can possibly assert that human nature is inherently murderous and warlike is by ignoring the ample evidence to the contrary from a multitude of diverse sources. Nevertheless, that fact has not prevented many from doing so as apologists for warfare (Barber, 1996; Cannel and Macklin, 1974; Ehrenreich, 1998; Feibleman, 1987; Ghiglieri, 1987, 1999; Guilaine and Zammit, 2001; Kaplan, 1994, 2000; Keeley, 1996; LeBlanc and Register, 2003; Otterbein, 1993, 1999, 2004; Smith, 2007; Wrangham and Peterson, 1996). Either they have not adequately covered the documentation that is readily available in the published literature, or they just purposefully ignore other arguments and evidence that do not fit their own ideology, theory, arguments, advocacy, and so on. In either of these two instances, their science, scholarship, and writing is seriously deficient and suspect, to say the very least (Frankfurt, 2005). Yet, the unproven assumption that human nature is inherently murderous and warlike still dominates publications by a vocal minority of anthropologists and others to the nearly total exclusion of any serious and systematic attention to nonkilling and peace. For a most recent example, see Holmes (2008).

Most simple hunter-gatherer bands epitomize Paige's attributes of a nonkilling society (Kelly, 2000). They are grounded in an ethos of routine cooperation, reciprocity, and nonviolent conflict resolution as documented for the San and Mbuti of Africa, Semai of Malaysia, and many others (Bonta, 1993, 1996, 2008; Dentan, 1968; Fry, 2006, 2007; Kelly, 2000). Furthermore, for 99 per cent of human existence, from more than two million to roughly 10,000 years ago, humans lived almost exclusively as simple hunter-gatherers (Hart and Sussman, 2009; Kelly, 2000; Lee and DeVore, 1968; Shepard, 1973). Accordingly, although captivating, William Golding's (1999) novel *Lord of the Flies* which was originally published in 1954, and the ensuing two movies are by no means accurate anthropologically as a reflection on human nature. A more recent variant on the Hobbesian theme is the film called *Apocalypto* which appears to have been made to insult the Mayan people.

With regard to nonlethal weapons and weapon-free societies (Paige, 2002: 109, 113), it is important to note that weapons specifically designed for warfare do not appear archaeologically until very late in human prehistory, although tools employed in hunting, such as a spear or a bow and arrow could easily be used to kill or injure another human being. The archaeological record does not evidence any regular warfare until relatively late in human prehistory (Ferguson, 2002, 2006; Fry, 2006, 2007; Grossman, 2008; Guilaine and Zammit, 2001; Keegan, 1993; Keeley, 1996; Kelly, 2000; LeBlanc and Register, 2003).

Paige (2002: 101) refers to the twentieth century as 'the era of lethality.' Anthropology, with its unique combination of temporal depth and spatial breadth offers great hope in this regard, because such widespread lethality is an extremely recent aberration in human nature, judging by evidence from evolution and prehistory accumulated by archaeologists and evidence from the record of some 7,000 cultures in the world (ethnographies) and from cross-cultural comparisons (ethnology). Torture, terrorism, genocide, weapons of mass destruction, and the like are all relatively rare in the vast range of human experience (cf. Levinson, 1994). The 'era of lethality' endures for decades or so, not millennia or millions of years. However, structural violence in various forms and degrees is coincident with the origin of inequality (social stratification) which emerges most of all with civilization at the state level of socio-political organization and complexity (Bodley, 2008a).

Actually warfare and the institution of the military are relatively recent inventions, as noted long ago by Margaret Mead (1940). There is relatively little evidence of warfare until the Neolithic some 10,000 years ago, depending on the region. The military as a social institution is mostly coincident with the evolution of the state around 5,000 years ago, depending on the region (Bodley, 2008a; Fry, 2006, 2007; Keegan, 1993; Kelly, 2000). Moreover, anyone who is a genuine evolutionist realizes that change is inevitable; thus, there is no reason to think that warfare and the institution of the military, not to mention other lethal aspects of humankind or a culture, are inevitable and eternal. Humanity as a whole cannot return to a hunter-gatherer lifestyle, at least at the current level of world population and given economic dependence and preference (Shepard, 1973). However, hunter-gatherers can provide heuristic models of the socio-cultural possibilities of a nonkilling society (Fry, 2006, 2007; Kelly, 2000).

Resource scarcity and the resulting competition may well lead to conflict, violence, and even warfare as many have asserted (Hastings, 2000; Homer-Dixon et al., 1993; Kaplan, 1994, 2000; Klare, 2001, 2002; Lanier-Graham, 1993; Myers, 1996; Renner, 1996). But as Fredrik Barth (1956) demonstrated for three different ethnic groups in the Swat Valley of Pakistan, niche differentiation may be an alternative. They effectively reduced most direct competition by developing different foci for land and resource use as well as complementary trading relationships. However, this interethnic system was probably, seriously disrupted by refugees from the successive Soviet and American invasions of Afghanistan.

The above are indisputable scientific facts, this in spite of the biased approaches, pseudoscience, and disinformation campaigns of a few anthropologists and others who have gained notoriety. Without meaning to denigrate the substantial contribution of anthropologists who have focused on studying warfare and other forms of aggression, such as Eller (1999, 2006), Ferguson (1995, 2007) and Nordstrom (1997, 1998), clearly a vocal minority are in effect apologists for war (cf. Paige, 2002: 136). (For additional case studies, see compilations such as those by Fried et al., 1968; Ferguson and Farragher, 1988; Ferguson and Whitehead, 1992; Ferguson, 2003; Nordstrom and Robben, 1995.) Since at least the 1960s the apologists for war pursue and even champion the pivotal assumption that humans are innately, instinctively, genetically, or biologically programmed to be aggressive, and, therefore, that war is an inevitable manifestation of human nature (Ardrey, 1961; 1966, 1976; Chagnon, 1992; Ghiglieri, 1987, 1999; Keeley, 1996; Lorenz, 1966; Morris, 1967, 1969; Otterbein, 1993, 1999, 2004, 2008; Wrangham and Peterson, 1996). Their absolutist, universalist, and essentialist posture conveniently ignores the contrary examples within our own species of *Homo sapiens* and, as will be discussed later, from our closest relatives in the animal kingdom, the chimpanzees (see Bonta, 1993, 1996; Dennen, 1995; Fry, 2006, 2007; Howell and Willis, 1989; Melko, 1973, 1984; Montagu, 1978; Sponsel, 1996a; Sponsel and Gregor, 1994).

Some of these apologists for warfare claim to have discovered extraordinarily violent and warlike societies, such as the Yanomami in the Brazilian and Venezuelan Amazon. However, the Yanomami, although not free from low levels and frequencies of some types of aggression do not pursue warfare by any meaningful definition of the term and are relatively nonviolent in their daily lives (Barash and Webel, 2002; Gelvin, 1994; Keegan, 1993; Jeong, 2000; Sanders, 2008; Sponsel, 1998; Stoessinger, 2008). Chagnon (1968, 1992) stereotyped and stigmatized the Yanomami as the 'fierce people,' and even after he dropped that designation as the subtitle of his famous (now infamous) book, his fixation on aggression still exaggerated it to the point of being misleading (Good, 1991; Sponsel, 1998, 2006c). Chagnon exemplifies some anthropologists who have been so focused on the violent aspects of a society, often to the point of obsession, that they have provided a grossly distorted and problematic perspective, neglecting the far greater frequency of nonviolence and peace in the daily life of most people in the society.

It should also be noted that, even within relatively violent societies, most people are nonkilling in their own behavior (cf. Nordstrom, 1997, 1998). Furthermore, there are individuals, groups, and subcultures that explicitly pursue nonkilling and pacifism such as the Amish. In addition, even in the midst of wars, such as the recent ones in Afghanistan and Iraq, there are medical doctors and other persons who have saved lives and reduced suffering instead of the opposite. Nevertheless, the prevalence of many forms of violence in American society and culture to the point of obsession in the media and elsewhere should be obvious, especially with inventories like that by Paige (2002). Transcending this phenomenon is as much a problem for science as for society as Paige discusses.

History provides examples of nation states such as Germany and Japan that have been transformed from a society frequently engaged in war to one pursuing peace. Costa Rica is an instructive example as well. This country abolished the military and instead invested its resources in life-enhancing activities. Cases like Costa Rica merit much greater recognition, documentation, and analysis by anthropologists and others (Biesanz et al., 1982).

Among ethnographic cases, perhaps the most remarkable example of a rapid transformation from a killing to a nonkilling society is the Waorani of the Ecuadorian Amazon, as amply documented by the Robarcheks (1992, 1996, 1998a,b). Traditionally the Waorani were frequently involved in inter-group feuding. Through contact with American missionaries the Waorani imagined the possibilities of a nonkilling and peaceful society; they considered this to be far more attractive, and within a few decades the majority of the Waorani communities voluntarily changed. The Waorani demonstrate the plasticity and adaptability of human nature. Accordingly, they hold the promise for the possibility of other societies undergoing such a transformation, another case of an affirmative answer to Paige's first question. It is also noteworthy that many societies in Oceania and elsewhere, which had traditionally engaged in some kind of warfare to some degree, were rapidly pacified by Western colonial forces, albeit often through violent means (Bodley, 2008b; Ferguson and Whitehead, 1992; Rodman and Cooper, 1979).

There are also societies which have courageously persisted in their pacifist commitment in the face of terrible violence. The Amish are pacifists, like the Hutterites, Mennonites, and Quakers. Americans and many in the rest of the world were shocked when a psychotic gunman shot to death five girls and wounded five others in an Amish one-room school in Lancaster County, Pennsylvania, on 2 October 2006. Many people were impressed as well, when representatives from the same Amish community attended the funeral of the gunman, whom police had killed, in order to forgive and comfort his widow and children. The Amish did not respond to this horrific crime by initiating a cycle of blood revenge (Kraybill, 2008; Kraybill, et al., 2006). This should have been a lesson to the larger world, and especially American society in general and its government. It has direct relevance to the aftermath of the terrible unjust tragedy of the 9/11 attacks. What if a similar Christian response had been pursued then? What if the US federal government had responded to 9/11, not by military attack on Afghanistan, but instead capitalized on world sympathy and advocated concerted action by its leaders through the United Nations, Interpol (International Criminal Police Organization), and other nonkilling means? Whether or not this would have brought to justice the surviving perpetrators of the September 11 attacks (also referred to as 9/11) is uncertain. However, it is certain that US militarism has not achieved that goal in the many years since 2001. Moreover, it is certain that in the interim hundreds of thousands of innocent civilians, including women, children, and elderly, have been killed and injured, so-called collateral damage. Millions have been displaced as refugees internally and beyond their homeland in Afghanistan and Iraq. Billions of dollars have been sacrificed from constructive life-enhancing initiatives to promote nutrition, health, education, economy, and other things in the USA and elsewhere. As Mahatma Gandhi observed, an eye for an eye leads to blindness. All of the vast resources—personnel, financial, institutional, technological, and so on—of the Pentagon, State Department, CIA, and other US federal government agencies failed to prevent 9/11. The time is long overdue to open the minds of government leaders and the populace regarding the nonkilling alternatives available for dispute resolution and conflict prevention (Barnes, 2007; Bonta, 1996; Fry and Bjorkqvist, 1997; Kemp and Fry, 2004; Ury, 1999, 2002).

Tibet also provides a particular case to illustrate several crucial points previously identified. During its long history, in spite of some episodes of violence, Tibet was transformed into a mostly nonviolent society. The spread of Buddhism was the seminal influence in this transformation. Today the power and wealth of Tibetans are not military, political, and/or economic, but religious and cultural. That Tibetans have suffered terribly since the 1950 invasion and occupation by the Chinese, with more than a million killed and thousands imprisoned and tortured to this day, and that more than 100,000 Tibetans have risked their lives in the Himalayan winter to flee to exile as political refugees in adjacent countries and beyond, does not diminish this power. Although initially there was militant resistance to the Chinese invasion by some Tibetans, subsequently under the leadership of His Holiness the 14th Dalai Lama of Tibet, Tibetans appear to present the most outstanding case of a nonviolent response to violent invasion, occupation, and suppression. While this nonkilling approach has not liberated Tibet from Chinese imperialism, it has avoided far worse conflict and suffering by the Tibetans who are greatly outnumbered and outgunned by the Chinese. It may be only a matter of time before the situation improves significantly, although it could be decades or more before the central government of the People's Republic of China promotes a more democratic society and moral civilization in the entire country. However, there is reason for optimism, given the religiosity, courage, and resilience of Tibetans. There is also some hope, given historical precedents such as the expulsion of the British colonial empire from India, the dissolution of the apartheid system in South Africa, and the overthrow of the Ferdinand Marcos regime in the Philippines, all generated by the nonviolent actions of courageous and persistent leaders and commoners in the face of overwhelming lethal force. (For more on Tibet see Blondeau; Buffetrille, 2008; Dalai Lama, 1987; Kapstein, 2006; Shakya, 1999; Sperling, 2004;

Thurman, 2008, and the official website of the Tibetan Government in Exile at <http://www.tibet.com>.)

To go even deeper, into human nature, that is, while many biologists and psychologists might favour nature over nurture as the primary determinant and shaper of aggression, some have revealed strong evidence to the contrary. Of all of the species in the animal kingdom, the closest to humans are the common and pygmy chimpanzees, *Pan troglodytes* and *P. paniscus*, respectively. Only after many years of observations on a few social groups of the common chimpanzee at Gombe Stream Reserve in Tanzania did Jane Goodall and her research associates discover what they described as the rudiments of war (Goodall, 1986; Wrangham and Peterson, 1996; Ghiglieri, 1987, 1999). However, Margaret Power (1991) and others have argued that this aggression may be influenced by external factors, at least in part, and especially by the primatologists provisioning the chimpanzees with bananas in order to bring them closer for more detailed observation.

In sharp contrast to some groups of the common chimpanzees, independent studies of the pygmy chimpanzees, also called bonobos, have not revealed comparable aggression either in the wild or in captive colonies. In fact, they are just the opposite. They seem to pursue behavior according to the motto make love and not war! Bonobos use a wide variety of sexual behaviors to avoid or reduce tensions within the group on a daily basis (Kano, 1990, 1992; Waal, 1989, 1996, 2006; Waal and Lating, 1997). However, the 'scientists' who favour the Hobbesian view of human nature, apparently have ideological blinders that channel them to emphasize violence to the near exclusion of nonviolence, stressing the common chimpanzees at Gombe and largely ignoring other common chimpanzee groups elsewhere where such behavior has not been observed. They also downplay the evidence of the peaceful bonobos. (See Aureli and de Waal; 2000; Harcourt and de Waal, 1992; Kohn, 1990.)

As a heuristic exercise, Leslie E. Sponsel (1996a) marshalled the arguments and evidence for the natural history of peace, pursuing just the opposite position from that of the apologists for war. The fields of biology, primate ethology, human ethology, human palaeontology, prehistoric archaeology, ethnography, and ethnology were surveyed. The basic conclusions were that: (1) although conflict is inevitable and common, violence is not; (2) human nature has the psychobiological potential to be either nonviolent/peaceful or violent/warlike; (3) nonviolence and peace appear to have prevailed in many prehistoric and pre-state societies; (4) war is not a cultural universal; and (5) the potential for the development of a more nonviolent and peaceful world is latent in human nature as revealed by the natural history of peace (Sponsel, 1996a: 114-115).

Douglas P. Fry (2006, 2007) elaborated this approach further in much greater detail. He observes that the 'Man the Warrior' model asserts that war is ubiquitous in time and space, natural, normal, and inevitable. Fry asserts that this reflects a Western cultural bias that selectively focuses on certain kinds of evidence to the exclusion of contrary evidence. He observes that this Hobbesian model also stems from muddled thinking that confuses almost any kind of aggression such as homicide or blood feuding with warfare. Fry concludes that the 'Man the Warrior' model is fantasy instead of fact. Moreover, he warns that this model is dangerous because it may contribute to policies of belligerent militarism as well as to inaction by peace advocates, if war is considered to be an inevitable manifestation of human nature. Fry argues that evolutionary pressures would select for restraint and for the ritualization of aggression to reduce harm, as well as for alternatives in nonviolent conflict resolution because the costs of aggression can far exceed any possible benefits. He affirms that war can be eliminated in the twenty-first century by transcending the narrow, unrealistic, and culturally biased mentality of 'Man the Warrior' and the associated belligerent militarism, and replacing it with an emphasis on extending nonviolent conflict management alternatives practiced within democratic nation states to an international system of world and regional cooperative governance and justice such as in the United Nations and the European Union.

Such studies are an independent and objective confirmation of the assertions in the UNESCO 'Seville Statement on Violence' of 16 May 1986, cited by Paige (2002: 39-40). (See Adams, 1989.) They affirm as well the statement in the charter of UNESCO; namely, that just as war begins in the minds of men, then so can peace (Barnaby, 1988). They sustain Mead's (1940) contention that war is only an invention, and that, as such, it can be transcended.

What is needed more than ever is a collaborative project to research nonviolence and peace in both theory and practice with a commitment, expert personnel, and adequate resources on a scale equivalent to the Manhattan Project of WWII. If that war effort was so important to the world, then why isn't a peace effort even far more so? Modern warfare is simply much too expensive in terms of human deaths, injuries, and suffering as well as money, resources, and the environment (Andreas, 2004; Cranna and Bhinda, 1995; Hastings, 2000; Lanier-Graham, 1993; US Army, 2008). Indeed, war is rapidly becoming an unaffordable anachronism in the twenty-first century (cf. Younger, 2007). Just consider the fact that a significant percentage of the American troops returning from Afghanistan and Iraq are bringing the war home in the form of not only physical injuries, but also post-traumatic stress syndrome, substance abuse, domestic violence, homelessness, and even suicide. The expense of all of this—medical, psychological, and social as well as economic—will be long-term and immense (Grossman, 1995; Hedges and Al-Arian, 2007; McNair, 2002). (Also see 'Iraq Body Count' at <http://www.iraqbodycount.org>.) Incidentally, the facts that soldiers have to be trained to injure and kill other human beings, and that many of those who do so often suffer serious emotional problems that may endure over many years, are yet another line of evidence invalidating the Hobbesian myth of dismal human nature. (Also see <http://www.refusingtokill.net>.)

As in political science (Paige, 2002: 74), likewise in anthropology, authors who have dared to consider the possibilities of nonviolence and peace have been variously accused, stigmatized, and dismissed as unrealistic, idealistic, romantic, or utopian dreamers (Otterbein, 1999; Sponsel, 1990, 1992, 2000b, 2005). But such feeble attempts at a counter-argument are not sustainable in the face of the wealth of scientific evidence that has been rapidly accumulating since the 1970s.

In summary, although anthropology certainly has its limitations, it offers a far broader temporal and spatial perspective than that of political science which tends to be constrained by its focus on the governments and politics of historic and contemporary nation states

(Barash and Webel, 2002; Jeong, 2000). Anthropology offers not only an affirmative answer to Paige's first question, but also amplification and substantiation based on numerous and diverse well-documented cases in the real world. Paige discusses how individuals in different contexts from different professions or disciplines and countries answer his elemental question. No doubt he would also find a variety of responses to this question if he were to ask individuals in societies such as the Amish, Semai, Tibetans, Waorani, and Yanomami. Hopefully, future anthropological researchers may do just that.

Nonkilling Anthropology

What are the possibilities for a nonkilling anthropology? At first glance, probably most anthropologists would be puzzled to consider the idea of either a killing anthropology or a nonkilling anthropology. However, consider this logic: either you are part of the solution or a part of the problem; there is no space for neutrality. For example, if you witness a person who is apparently being beaten to death and do nothing to intervene, such as call for anyone nearby to help and telephone the police, then are you not complicit in murder to some degree? Similarly, if you are an anthropologist in a killing society and do nothing to intervene in any way, then are you not complicit in the killing to some degree? Moreover, even from an egocentric perspective, it might be argued that ignoring the human suffering caused directly and indirectly by a killing society diminishes one's own humanity and increases one's own suffering, because we are all interconnected and interdependent (cf. Dalai Lama, 1999). Such considerations may stimulate some to contemplate the possibilities of a killing anthropology and a nonkilling anthropology.

Answering Paige's second question is much more difficult than answering the first one because it requires thinking more 'outside of the box,' since much of anthropology supports, indirectly if not directly, and inadvertently if not intentionally, the military-industrial-media-academic complex. To be blunt, the modern war-making machine's main effect, if not primary purpose, is usually to generate death, destruction, and suffering, as for example in the March 2003 US 'shock and awe' bombing campaign over the city of Baghdad. At the same time, it should be mentioned that I respect those in the military who serve honourably and even place themselves in harm's way; however, I respect even more highly someone like the courageous First Lieutenant Ehren Watada who refuses to serve in an unjust Iraq War in spite of tremendous institutional, social, and legal pressures to conform (<http://www.thankyoult.org>). Another difficulty with the nonkilling aspects of anthropology is that they are so diffuse that a special effort is required to identify and explicate them. Furthermore, much of what would help generate a nonkilling anthropology is at the early stage of critical analysis and focused on the military as an institution, its origin, evolution, structure, functions, beliefs, values, symbols, rituals, customs, and practices, rather than on positive alternatives, such as the interrelated human rights and peace movements and organizations throughout the world.

In recent decades, an increasing number of publications have critically analyzed in historical perspective the relationships between anthropology and war since colonial times to the current wars in Afghanistan and Iraq. This endeavour is not to be confused with the anthropological study of war as such. (See Ben-Ari, 2004; de Wolf, 1992; Frese and Harrell, 2003; Goldschmidt, 1979; Gordon, 1988; Gough, 1968; Gusterson, 1996, 2003, 2007; Hickey, 2002; Hymes, 1999; Jell-Bahlsen, 1985; Mabee, 1987; Neel, 1994; Patterson, 2001; Penny and Bunzl, 2003; Price, 2008; Schaft, 2004; Simons, 1997, 1999; Starn, 1986; Stauder, 1974; Suzuki, 1981; Wakin, 1992; Williams, 1986.) Among other influences, pursuit of this subject reflects the correlated development since the 1960s of a code of professional ethics for anthropologists emphasizing the primary ethical principle of 'do no harm.' That code was largely stimulated by the reaction to covert counter-insurgency research by anthropologists in Thailand during the American war in Vietnam and adjacent countries, although its roots are deeper in time and broader in experience (Fluehr-Lobban, 2002, 2003; Hymes, 1999; Whiteford and Trotter, 2008; Wakin, 1992).

At the same time, some anthropologists have been pacifists, such as Edward B. Tylor and Franz Boas, although rarely does this surface in their research and publications. It was not until the 1960s, and in connection with the Vietnam War in particular, that a variant of what might be called nonkilling anthropology began to develop. Perhaps more than any other single anthropologist before or since, Ashley Montagu as a prominent public scientist pioneered the groundwork for a nonkilling anthropology through many of his publications, addressing nonviolence and peace as well as violence, including even structural violence (racism, sexism, ageism) (Lieberman et al., 1995; Montagu, 1968, 1972, 1989, 1998; Sponsel, 2006b; cf. Paige 2002: 97). He rigorously challenged the idea that there is any biological basis for racial superiority, distinguishing between biological and social ideas about race (Montagu, 1998). Montagu (1972) was one of the leaders in the development of the UNESCO Statement on Race. Likewise, he critically analyzed and dismissed the Hobbesian view of human nature (Montagu, 1976). He edited the first anthology documenting nonviolent and peaceful societies (Montagu, 1978). Montagu and Matson (1983) scrutinized dehumanization as a tactic facilitating violence toward 'the other' (Staub 1989). More recently, several other pioneers laying the groundwork for a nonkilling anthropology stand out in various ways, including Baszarkiewicz and Fry (2008), Bodley (2008a,b), Bonta (1993, 1996, 1997), Dentan (1968), Ferguson (1995, 2002, 2003, 2006, 2007, 2008), Fry (2006, 2007), González (2004), Graeber (2004), Gusterson (1996, 2003, 2007), Hymes (1999), Kyron and Rubenstein (2008), Lutz (2001, 2002), Nordstrom (1997, 1998), Nordstrom and Robben (1995), Price (2004, 2008), Sanders (2008), Sluka (2000), Sponsel (1994a,b,c, 1996a,b,c, 1997a,b, 2000b, 2006b), Sponsel and Good (2000), and Strathern and Stewart (2008).

Recently, the US military initiated the special program called the Human Terrain System (HTS) that embeds anthropologists and other social scientists with troops on the ground in conflict zones in Afghanistan, Iraq, and probably elsewhere as well. The main purpose appears to be to enhance the cultural information and understanding of the soldiers in order to help make their operations more effective (Kipp et al., 2007; McFate, 2005a,b; Renzi, 2006; Sewall et al., 2007). It is claimed that HTS reduces conflict, saves lives, and may shorten the wars; however, so far these assertions have not been proven. One HTS anthropologist, Marcus Griffin, even maintains a website from Iraq (<http://marcusgriffin.com>).

The American Anthropological Association (AAA) is the major professional organization of anthropologists in the USA, with a membership of well over 10,000. Its executive officers charged a special commission with investigating the role of anthropologists in the HTS (AAA ad hoc Committee on the Engagement of Anthropology with US Security and Intelligence Communities, or CEAUSSIC). The results of their inquiry were summarized in an Executive Board Statement on 31 October 2007. Their 62-page Final Report was posted on 4 November 2007. The main conclusion is that anthropologists involved in HTS may compromise or violate the principles in the 1998 AAA Code of Ethics in various ways. They may not be able to openly disclose their purpose or obtain voluntary consent from informants, and their information may be used by the military in ways that harm their informants and/or others in their community. Another concern was that anthropologists working anywhere in the world might be mistakenly identified as associated with the US military and/or HTS and thereby their personal safety might be placed at risk (<http://www.aaanet.org>). Several prominent anthropologists have been very critical of HTS, among them Roberto J. González (2007, 2008), Hugh Gusterson (2003, 2007), and David H. Price (2000, 2007). An organization was formed among such critics called the Network of Concerned Anthropologists (<http://concerned.anthropologists.googlepages.com>). (Ferguson, 1988; Fluehr-Lobban, 2002, 2003; Glazer, 1996; Whitehead and Trotter, 2008.)

There is no doubt that anthropology can be relevant in facilitating cross-cultural understanding and communication for example, in the pioneering research by Edward T. Hall (1990) on proxemics (spatial relationships). The main problem is the ends to which anthropology is a means—causing harm or promoting welfare, violence or nonviolence, war or peace, militarism or pacifism, and so on. As part of the creative challenge of a nonkilling anthropology, it is imperative to imagine the practical possibilities of a nonkilling alternative to HTS. For example, some anthropologists might have less concern if the field anthropologists were engaged with the US Department of State instead of the Department of Defence, but that would also depend on current government policies. For instance, by now it is widely recognized in the US and worldwide that many of the policies of President George

W. Bush's administration have been disastrous, to say the least (Carter, 2005; Chomsky, 2001; Gore, 2007; Govier, 2002; Singer, 2004; Wright and Dixon, 2008).

In thinking through Paige's chapter 3, one of the challenges is that anthropologists usually focus on culture and community, whereas political scientists tend to focus on power and polity, especially in the context of the nation state. However, anthropology also deals with many subjects basic to political science such as human nature, the origin of the state as civilization, and the emergence and maintenance of social inequality. In any case, thinking through the relevance of this chapter for anthropology has the potential to transform the discipline, if not even to revolutionize it. In the first paragraph of chapter 3, Paige poses several questions about political science that can be pursued through anthropology as well as other disciplines. For example, his third question asks what values would inspire and guide the work? His sixth question asks what uses of knowledge would we facilitate? These two questions were previously answered in another context by the present author who pointed to the various United Nations declarations and conventions on human rights as a framework for developing anthropological thinking and actions (Sponsel, 1994a; 1995: 277-278; 1996b, c; 1997a, b; 2001). Before and since then, many other anthropologists have conducted research on human rights theory and practice (Bell et al., 2001; Downing and Kushner, 1988; Messer, 1993; Nagengast and Turner, 1997; Nagengast and Vélez-Ibáñez, 2004). Anthropologists have also addressed the important issue of universal human rights versus cultural relativism mentioned by Paige (2002: 117). (See Bell et al., 2001; Herskovits, 1972; Nagengast and Turner, 1997.) Three tasks for applied science that Paige (2002: 104) identifies are prevention, intervention, and post-traumatic nonkilling transformations, and each of these can be pursued through various forms of applied anthropology (e.g., Rubenstein, 2008). Articulating teaching, research, and service with human rights, even in a general way as a conceptual framework, can generate more social meaning and significance in the anthropological endeavour.

For the professional training of nonkilling anthropologists, the curriculum and the pedagogy would need to be substantially changed, if not revolutionized (cf. Paige 2002: 127-129). The curriculum would need to be reoriented from a structure around standard courses on subfields, topics, areas, and methods to one more explicitly focused on the important problems and issues of contemporary society and the world. It would have to emphasize aspects of nonviolence and peace, although not to the exclusion of also considering violence and war. These are among some possibilities for a curriculum:

- Unity and Diversity of Humankind
- Professional Values and Ethics in Anthropology
- History of Anthropology from War to Peace
- History of Colonial and Development Anthropology
- Anthropology of Colonialism and Neocolonialism
- Cultural Evolution, Change, and Revolution
- Anthropology of Violence and War
- Anthropology of Nonviolence and Peace
- Science, Technology, and Economics as if People Mattered
- Quality of Life: Environment, Water, Food, and Health
- Anthropology of Environmentalism, Environment, and Gaia
- Comparative Religion: Worldviews, Values, and Spiritual Ecology
- Alternative Political and Legal Systems
- Culture in Conflict Management and Resolution
- Problems and Solutions in Applied Anthropology
- Human Rights and Advocacy Anthropology
- Collaborative Ethnographic Methods

Each of these courses would address as feasible Paige's (2002: 72-74) four principles of logical analysis (see below). (Also see McKenna, 2008; Smith, 1999.) Although some of these courses mirror traditional ones, the focus would be significantly changed. For example, the orientation of a course on Alternative Political and Legal Systems, formerly political and legal anthropology, would shift to themes such as the mechanisms of nonviolent dispute resolution traditionally practiced by hunter-gatherer cultures (Avruch, 1998; Bonta, 1996; Bonta and Fry, 2006; Fry and

Bjorkqvist, 1997; Greenhouse, 1985; Kemp and Fry, 2004; Rubinstein, 2008; Wolfe and Yang, 1996).

The faculty would be dedicated as much to teaching and service as to research, genuinely recognizing and rewarding the significance of all three. They would be engaged in cooperative rather than competitive activities aimed at applying their science to understanding and helping to resolve practical problems and issues, rather than advancing egocentric career trajectories by pursuing the latest academic fashions and theoretical fantasies. Accordingly, overall there would be a shift in emphasis, albeit not exclusively, from basic to applied aspects of anthropology (Barker, 2004; Fry and Bjorkqvist, 1997; Gwynne, 2003; Johnston, 2007; Johnston and Barker, 2008; Kemp and Fry, 2004; Paine, 1985; Sponsel, 2001; and Ury, 1999, 2004).

At the same time, there are economic obstacles to be overcome. For example, at the University of Hawaii, in spite of near unanimous opposition from faculty and students, some top administrators and a few researchers in the physical sciences recently embraced a 5-year contract for $50,000,000 from the US Navy for the development of a University Applied Research Center. At the same time, it is simply inconceivable that even a fraction of that amount would ever be invested in the annual budget of the Spark M. Matsunaga Institute for Peace at the University of Hawaii. Such are the priorities in a killing society and in the most militarized state in the union (Blanco, 2009; Kajihiro, 2007). Killing remains more profitable than nonkilling. As General Dwight Eisenhower also warned in his farewell presidential speech to the nation on 17 January 1961: 'The prospect of domination of the nation's scholars by Federal employment, project allocations, and the power of money is ever present—and is gravely to be regarded.' (See Feldman, 1989; Giroux, 2007; Simpson, 1998.)

Likewise, within the professional organization of the American Anthropological Association and others, the structures and priorities would have to radically change. For example, within the AAA the Committee on Ethics and the Committee for Human Rights would have to be given top priority with corresponding financial and other resources. The themes of the annual conventions would have to place far greater emphasis on the more applied aspects of anthropology.

Current priorities are crystal clear. For instance, the topical index of key words from sessions at the 2008 annual convention of the AAA lists 10 sessions on violence and eight on war, but only one on peace and none on nonviolence. On the other hand, it lists nine sessions on human rights and a dozen on ethics which is more positive, a much larger number than prior to the 1990s (AAA, 2008). Incidentally, the AAA is not atypical in this respect. As another example, the second edition of the multidisciplinary *Encyclopedia of Violence, Peace, and Conflict* (Kurtz, 2008) contains 289 entries, but only 10 (3.5 per cent) with nonviolence and 29 (10 per cent) with peace in their titles, although these topics may receive some attention in articles without these words in their titles.

Many of the phenomena that Paige (2002: 133) worries about were not problems until the evolution of the state, and especially modern nations, so they are very recent (Nagengast, 1994). Contemporary issues include abortion, capital punishment, conscription, war, armed revolution, terrorism, genocide, criminality, social violence, disarmament, and economic demilitarization (Paige, 2002: 133; cf. Levinson, 1994). According to Paige (2002: 111-112), five problems that are globally salient are: continued killing and the need for disarmament, poverty and the need for economic equality, violations of human rights and the need for greater respect for human dignity and human rights, destruction of nature, and other-denying divisiveness that impedes problem-solving cooperation. (See Donnelly, 2003; Mahoney, 2007.) In one way or another, anthropologists have been addressing these and related matters to varying degrees. Indeed, there are many books on each of these subjects, but if any one might be singled out, including as a possible textbook, then it would be *Anthropology and Contemporary Human Problems* by John H. Bodley (2008a).

Paige concludes chapter 3 by inviting '... thought about what political science would be like if it took seriously the possibility of realizing nonkilling societies in a nonkilling world.' He goes on to write that 'Acceptance of such a possibility implies active political science engagement in nonviolent global problem-solving' (Paige, 2002: 97). This is certainly a provocative question for anthropology as well. Applied, advocacy, action, public, and engagement are various qualifiers associated with anthropology that deals with practical problem solving in promoting human survival, welfare, justice, dignity, and rights in various ways and degrees (Barker, 2004; Besteman and Gusterson, 2005; Eriksen, 2006; González, 2004; Gwynne, 2003; Johnston, 1994, 1997, 2007; Johnston and Barker 2008). Already many anthropologists are contributing to the development of a nonkilling society and nonkilling world, although not exactly with those terms in mind. There is still enormous potential for further work in this regard. However, a major obstacle is that often such practical work is not considered to be as prestigious or valuable as basic research, as for example, in the assessment for tenure and promotion of academic faculty at universities and colleges, and especially among those who are still under the illusion that science is apolitical and amoral (cf. Giroux 2007).

The framework and questions for research and praxis that Paige develops so boldly and profoundly in his book and other work opens up an entire new world of exciting and promising possibilities for anthropological research, teaching, and service with potentially far reaching practical consequences. His pursuit of a medical model for the sciences, humanities, and other professions pivoting around a central concern for saving lives, reducing suffering, and promoting well-being calls for a paradigm shift, if not, even a revolution. While he emphasizes nonkilling, ultimately this transcends stopping the negative—lethality, to also advance the positive—protection and enhancement of the quality of life. In the present author's opinion, the subject of human rights provides the conceptual and practical framework for such a noble endeavour.

Discussion

Paige challenges the prevailing assumption that (1) killing is an inescapable or inevitable part of human nature or of the human condition, and the corollary that (2) it must be accepted in political theory and practice as well as elsewhere. He implies that this assumption stems from the long history of American warfare and militarism by citing numerous examples (Paige, 2002: 7-8). Even more revealing and disturbing are the detailed historical inventories of these aggressive activities in sources such as Andreas (2004) and Churchill (2003). Thus, a systemic bias toward violence including war appears to be a product of Western and especially American history and culture (Duclos, 1997;

Hofstadter and Wallace, 1971; Keegan, 1993; Lewis, 2006; Palmer, 1972; Sponsel, 1994a, 1996a). The US is grounded in the invasion and conquest of the continent by European colonial displacement or compulsory relocation, forced assimilation and acculturation, and downright ethnocide and genocide of a multitude of indigenous societies (Bodley, 2008b; Churchill, 1997; Diamond, 1999; Ferguson and Whitehead, 1992; Jaimes, 1992; Kroeber, 1961; Patterson, 2001; Starkey, 1998; Steele, 1994). Another factor is the militarism and warfare that permeates US history (Andreas, 2004; Churchill, 2003; Hedges, 2002; Hillman, 2004; Ury, 2002). Since at least WWII, the Hobbesian view of human nature has been increasingly reinforced by the development of the industrial-military complex that President Dwight Eisenhower warned about in his farewell speech to the nation.

Moreover, subsequent developments have resulted in an industrial-military-media-academic complex that infiltrates American society like a cancer, with the most rapid and penetrating growth during the administration of President George W. Bush as part of the post-9/11 paranoia it helped to create and maintain. Thus, for instance, for several years Americans were kept terrified with a system of periodic colour coded alerts and other tactics that helped generate the lucrative profits of the weapons, military, and security industries since 9/11. The interconnected weapons and oil industries are not only the most profitable ones in the world along with illegal drugs, but also the most powerful politically as well as economically (Andreas, 2004). It is sad to say that peace is likely to emerge and prevail globally only when it becomes more profitable than war.

American anthropologists who stress a Hobbesian view of human nature may be culturally as well as ideologically biased (Clark, 2002; Curti, 1980). On the one hand not all American anthropologists share the ideology that encompasses the Hobbesian view (Kegley and Raymond, 1999: 20-21, 245; Patterson, 2001). On the other hand, to some degree all American anthropologists share the same generic culture. In anthropology, the common assumption about dismal human nature and the inevitability of war and other forms of aggression still appears to prevail, even though most reject simplistic and reductionist biological determinism. This is reflected in the fact that there are many more books on violence and war than on nonviolence and peace, whether general surveys or particular case studies. Those on nonviolence and peace number about a dozen, whereas there are many times more on violence and war (Ferguson and Farragher, 1988; Sponsel, 1994a, b, 1996a, c; Wiberg, 1981). Members of the American Anthropological Association may list their specializations in a special online directory. The specializations available for listing in the AAA form include conflict, conflict resolution, ethnic conflict, violence, and warfare, but revealingly, neither nonviolence nor peace are listed.

The idea of human nature also needs to be problematized (Cannel and Macklin, 1974; Curti, 1980; Sponsel, 2007; Stevenson and Haberman, 1998). Logically, human nature may or may not exist, it may be uniform or multifarious, it may good or bad, and so on. For example, some anthropologists would argue that there is no single, uniform human nature; instead, there are numerous human natures as expressed in the diversity of some 7,000 different cultures extant in the world today. From such a perspective, human nature is manifest in cultural diversity and is generated by nurture (social environment) instead of nature (genetics). Human nature is tremendously plastic and adaptable as well as diverse, the latter the expression of the former two attributes (Sponsel, 2007). Thus, many anthropologists would see cultural relativism as their primary disciplinary value, while some extreme cultural relativists would even dispute the existence of any meaningful cross-cultural universals common to all of humanity (Brown, 1991; Herskovits, 1972). Furthermore, within science and academia, there are many different theories of human nature (Cannel and Macklin, 1974; Curti, 1980; Feibleman, 1987; Stevenson and Haberman, 1998). Likewise, each of the world's religions has a somewhat different concept of human nature distinctive to their own worldview (Matthews, 2004). This diversity itself undermines the assumptions of a single, uniform human nature, and of the inevitably of violence and war in spite of the reductionist and simplistic speculations of the apologists for war.

As a political scientist concerned with international relations, Paige tends to focus on the modern nation state. Anthropology also problematizes this focus because the state is actually a relatively recent invention and could well be a transitory stage of political organization in cultural evolution (cf. Ferguson, 2003; Nagengast, 1994). As conceived by anthropologists, the state is basically coincident with civilization and only about 5,000 years old, depending on the region. Actually 99 per cent of human existence from origins dating back to at least two million years ago was dominated exclusively by hunting-gathering lifestyles. If there is anything universal in human culture and/or such a thing as human nature, it then most likely is a result of this hunter-gatherer legacy (Lee and DeVore, 1968; Shepard, 1973). Moreover, the overwhelming majority of hunter-gatherer societies are mostly egalitarian, cooperative, nonkilling, and peaceful, as demonstrated by evidence from archaeology, ethnohistory, ethnography, and ethnology, this notwithstanding the contrary opinions of the apologists for warfare (Kelly, 2000).

As a political scientist, Paige considers power to be pivotal in society and in his discipline, and power is political with economics, religion, and other factors secondary. The parallel focus in anthropology is culture. Culture is pivotal in society and in the discipline. However, both of these are only partial considerations, albeit very important ones. Particular circumstances can be decisive. For instance, in the case of Tibet as previously discussed, Buddhism as a religion is pivotal, and the power of the Dalai Lama as a spiritual leader is primary even in exile. Given the relationship of Tibetans with China and other countries, these factors also become political, but that is secondary, even though it is often difficult to consider the religious and political as separate in this case, especially given Tibet's history since the Chinese invasion and occupation. Similarly, in the case of the Middle East, religion is a tremendous influence; it is not simply a matter of secular politics. In Islam, politics is subordinated to religion. It is impossible to understand the Middle East purely in secular terms (Eickelman, 2002; Eickelman and Piscatori, 1996; Esposito and Mogahed, 2007; Khan, 2006).

Paige is challenging not only the inevitability of killing, but also its efficacy and legitimacy. A nonkilling anthropology would reject these tenets as well. However, legitimacy invokes normative considerations, and some might reject this by claiming that science must be amoral as well as apolitical to maintain neutrality for the sake of objectivity. But that is an illusion. To take an extreme case, the Manhattan Project was grounded in hard science. Yet Paige (2002: 81) notes that 19 out of 150 scientists on the Manhattan Project voted against any military use of the atomic bombs. The present author does not see any difference in incinerating Jews in the Nazi concentration camps and in incinerating Japanese in the cities of Hiroshima and Nagasaki. Both are absolutely immoral. Furthermore, the scientists who made these atrocities possible cannot be considered amoral and apolitical. Indeed, they can be considered complicit in such crimes against humanity (cf. Christopher, 1999).

Postmodernists have called into question the assertion that science is neutral, objective, apolitical, amoral, and the like. As an example, in the controversy over the scandalous behavior of some researchers working with the Yanomami generated by the publication of the book *Darkness in El Dorado* by investigative journalist Patrick Tierney (2000), some of those who portrayed themselves as scientists clearly exhibited behavior that was the opposite of scientific, lacking in objectivity, rife in political ideology, and downright unethical and immoral (Borofsky, 2005; Fluehr-Lobban, 2003; Gregor and Gross, 2004; Gross, 2004; Robin, 2004; Sponsel, 2006a; Sponsel and Turner, 2002; Tierney, 2000). The larger hidden agenda of many of the negative responses to Tierney was to try to invalidate a penetrating critic of one example of Cold War anthropological research (also see Neel, 1994; Price, 2008; Wax, 2008).

The above are some of my reservations, qualifications, and elaborations regarding Paige's book and thesis. At the same time, what he has to say is extremely important, and increasingly so, given the so-called global war on terrorism, the dire problems of globalization, the developing consequences of global warming with all of its widespread and profound impacts on society and the environment, and the increasing militarization of the planet including its infiltration of scientific and academic institutions (Giroux, 2007). These are all interrelated and acting in synergy to the point of being not only alarming, but potentially catastrophic, to say the least.

Consequently, the time is not only propitious, but also urgent to consider the possibilities of a nonkilling society at every level—family, community, national, international, and global. Paige's four-component logical analysis is most valid and useful; namely, to consider the conditions, processes, and consequences of (1) a killing society, (2) a nonkilling society, (3) the transition from a nonkilling to a killing society, and (4) the transition from a killing to a nonkilling society. Tibet could be a very revealing case study for illuminating these four components. In various ways anthropology offers evidence and insights that are very relevant to all four of these components, ranging from the earlier work of Franz Boas, Margaret Mead, Ruth Benedict, and Ashley Montagu, and others to the most recent work of pioneers previously mentioned.

Finally, Paige (2002: 143) asserts that: 'Every political scientist and each person can be *a centre* for global nonviolence to facilitate transition to a nonkilling world.' More anthropologists need to become such a centre. In 1993, I was privileged to participate in a small multidisciplinary conference titled 'What We Know About Peace' in Charleston, South Carolina, sponsored by the Harry Frank Guggenheim Foundation (Gregor, 1996). However, I was disillusioned when it became clear that almost all of the participants were talking about war instead of peace. One participant asserted that peace is the presence of war (Tuzin, 1996: 3). Thank you, Glenn Paige, for opening some minds to the social and scientific possibilities of nonkilling and peace.

Conclusions

Glenn Paige (2002) has dared to ask the very profound and provocative primary question: Is a nonkilling society possible? From my perspective as an anthropologist who has paid some attention to anthropological aspects of peace and nonviolence, and not only war and violence unlike most colleagues, I find the answer to this question quite simple. It is possible to conceive of a nonkilling society as such societies exist in reality as revealed by the evidence presented by archaeology, ethnohistory, history, ethnography, and ethnology. Nonkilling is an actuality, not merely a possibility. Nonkilling and peace are scientific facts; the evidence is overwhelming and undeniable, as alluded to in this essay and sustained by documentation, such as Bonta's website. The time is long overdue to systematically make this explicit and pursue it in every constructive way possible to create a nonviolent and life-enhancing society for the realization of the human potential for freedom, justice, peace, harmony, and creativity. Anthropology has an important role to play in such a noble and vital endeavour, if only more anthropologists can be open to the revolutionary possibilities of a nonkilling society and a nonkilling anthropology.

References

Adams, David (1989). 'The Seville Statement on Violence: A Progress Report,' *Journal of Peace Research*, 26(2):113-121.

American Anthropological Association (2008). *Program American Anthropological Association 107TH Annual Meeting, November 19-23, 2008, San Francisco, California*. Arlington: American Anthropological Association.

Andreas, Joel (2004). *Addicted to War: Why Can't the U.S. Kick Militarism*. Oakland: AK Press. Also see: <http://www.addictedtowar.com>.

Ardrey, Robert (1961). *African Genesis: A Personal Investigation into the Animal Origins and Nature of Man*. New York: Atheneum.

Ardrey, Robert (1966). *The Territorial Imperative: A Personal Inquiry into the Animal Origins of Property and Nations*. New York: Atheneum.

Ardrey, Robert (1976). *The Hunting Hypothesis: A Personal Conclusion Concerning the Evolutionary Nature of Man*. New York: Atheneum.

Aureli, Filippo; Waal, Frans B.M. de, eds. (2000). *Natural Conflict Resolution*. Berkeley: University of California Press.

Avruch, Kevin (1998). *Culture and Conflict Resolution*, Washington: United States Institute of Peace Press.

Barash, David P.; Webel, Charles P. (2002). *Peace and Conflict Studies*. Thousand Oaks: Sage Publications.

Barber, Benjamin R. (1996). *Jihad vs. McWorld: How Globalism and Tribalism are Reshaping the World*. New York: Ballantine Books.

Barker, Holly M. (2004). *Bravo for the Marshallese: Regaining Control in a Post-Nuclear, Post-Colonial World*. Belmont: Wadsworth/Thomson Learning.

Barnaby, Frank, ed. (1988). *The Gaia Peace Atlas*. New York: Doubleday.

Barnes, Bruce E. (2007). *Culture, Conflict, and Mediation in the Asian Pacific*. Lanham: University Press of America.

Barth, Fredrik (1956). 'Ecological Relationships of Ethnic Groups in Swat, North Pakistan,' *American Anthropologist*, 58:1079-1089.

Baszarkiewicz, Karolina; Fry, Douglas P. 2008. 'Peaceful Societies,' in Kurtz, Lester, ed., *Encyclopedia of Violence, Peace, & Conflict*, San Diego: Elsevier 2:1557-1570.

Bell, Lynda S.; Nathan, Andrew J.; Peleg, Ilan, eds. (2001). *Negotiating Culture and Human Rights*. New York: Columbia University Press.

Ben-Ari, Eyal (2004). 'The Military and Militarization in the United States,' *American Ethnologist*, 31(3):340-348.

Besteman, Catherine; Gusterson, Hugh, eds. (2005). *Why America's Top Pundits are Wrong: Anthropologists Talk Back*. Berkeley: University of California Press.

Bestman, Catherine, et al. (2009). *Network of Concerned Anthropologists: The Counter-Counterinsurgency Manual or, Notes on Demilitarizing American Society*. Chicago: Prickly Paradigm Press.

Bhaneja, Balwant (2008). 'Nonkilling Political Science,' in Kurtz, Lester, ed., *Encyclopedia of Violence, Peace, & Conflict*, San Diego: Elsevier 2:1356-1363.

Biesanz, Richard; Biesanz, Karen Zubris; Biesanz, Mavis Hitunen (1982). *The Costa Ricans*. Prospect Heights: Waveland Press, Inc.

Birx, H. James, ed. (2006). *Encyclopedia of Anthropology*. Thousand Oaks: Sage.

Blanco, Sebastian (2009). *U.S. Militarism in Hawaii: A People's History*. Kihei: Koa.

Blondeau, Anne-Marie; Buffetrille, Katia, eds. (2008). *Authenticating Tibet: Answers to China's 100 Questions*. Berkeley: University of California Press.

Bodley, John H. (2008a). *Anthropology and Contemporary Human Problems*. Lanham: AltaMira Press.

Bodley, John H. (2008b). *Victims of Progress*. Lanham: AltaMira Press.

Bonta, Bruce D. (1993). *Peaceful Peoples: An Annotated Bibliography*. Metuchen: Scarecrow Press.

Bonta, Bruce D. (1996). 'Conflict Resolution among Peaceful Societies: The Culture of Peacefulness,' *Journal of Peace Research*, 33:403-420.

Bonta, Bruce D. (1997). 'Cooperation and Competition in Peaceful Societies,' *Psychological Bulletin*, 121:299-320.

Bonta, Bruce D. (2008). 'Peaceful Societies: Alternatives to Violence and War,' Available at: <http://www.peacefulsocieties.org>.

Bonta, Bruce D.; Fry, Douglas P. (2006). 'Lessons for the Rest of Us: Learning from Peaceful Societies,' in Fitzduff, M.; Stout, C. E., eds., *The Psychology of Resolving Global Conflicts: From War to Peace*. Westport: Praeger 1:175-210.

Borofsky, Robert, ed. (2005). *Yanomami: The Fierce Controversy and What We Can Learn from It*. Berkeley: University of California Press.

Brown, Donald E. (1991). *Human Universals*. New York: McGraw-Hill, Inc.

Cannel, Ward; Macklin, June (1974). *The Human Nature Industry: How Human*

Nature is Manufactured, Distributed, and Consumed in the United States and Parts of Canada. Garden City: Anchor Press/Doubleday.

Carter, Jimmy (2005). *Our Endangered Values: America's Moral Crisis*. New York: Simon and Schuster.

Chagnon, Napoleon A. (1968). *Yanomamo: The Fierce People*. New York: Holt, Rinehart and Winston.

Chagnon, Napoleon A. (1992). *Yanomamo*. Fort Worth: Harcourt Brace Jovanovich.

Chomsky, Noam (2001). *9-11*. New York: Seven Stories Press.

Christopher, Paul (1999). *The Ethics of War and Peace: An Introduction to Moral and Legal Issues*. Upper Saddle River: Prentice Hall.

Churchill, Ward (1997). *A Little Matter of Genocide: Holocaust and Denial in the Americas 1492 to the Present*. San Francisco: City Lights Books.

Churchill, Ward (2003). *On the Justice of Roosting Chickens: Reflections on the Consequences of U.S. Imperial Arrogance and Criminality*. Oakland: AK Press.

Clark, Mary E. (2002). *In Search of Human Nature*. New York: Routledge.

Cranna, Michael; Bhinda, Nils (1995). *The True Cost of Conflict: Seven Recent Wars and Their Effects on Society*. New York: New Press.

Curti, Merle (1980). *Human Nature in American Thought: A History*. Madison: University of Wisconsin Press.

Dalai Lama, His Holiness the XIVth (1987). *The Buddhism of Tibet*. Ithaca: Snow Lion Publications.

Dalai Lama, His Holiness the XIVth (1999). *Ethics for the New Millennium*. New York: Riverhead Books.

Dawson, Michael (2006). *Growing Up Yanomamo*. Enumclaw: WinePress.

Dennen, J.M.G. van der (1995). *The Origin of War*. Groningen: Origin Press.

Dentan, Robert K. (1968). *The Semai: A Nonviolent People of Malaya*. New York: Holt, Rinehart and Winston.

Diamond, Jared (1999). *Guns, Germs, and Steel: The Fates of Human Societies*. New York: W.W. Norton & Company.

Donnelly, Jack (2003). *Universal Human Rights in Theory and Practice*. Ithaca: Cornell University Press.

Downing, Theodore E.; Kushner, Gilbert, eds. 1988. *Human Rights and Anthropology*. Cambridge: Cultural Survival.

Duclos, Dennis (1997). *The Werewolf Complex: America's Fascination with Violence*. New York: Berg.

Ehlers, Tracy Bachrach (1980). 'Central America in the 1980's: Political Crisis and the Social Responsibility of Anthropologists,' *Latin American Research Review* XXV(3):141-155.

Ehrenreich, Barbara (1998). *Blood Rites: Origins and History of the Passions for War*. New York: Holt.

Eickelman, Dale F. (2002). *The Middle East and Central Asia: An Anthropological Approach*. Upper Saddle River: Prentice Hall.

Eickelman, Dale F.; Piscatori, James (1996). *Muslim Politics*. Princeton: Princeton University Press.

Eller, Jack David (1999). *From Culture to Ethnicity to Conflict: An Anthropological Perspective on International Ethnic Conflict*. Ann Arbor: University of Michigan Press.

Eller, Jack David (2006). *Violence and Culture: A Cross-Cultural and Interdisciplinary Approach*. Belmont: Thomson Higher Education.

Eriksen, Thomas Hylland (2006). *Engaging Anthropology: The Case for a Public Presence*. New York: Berg.

Esposito, John L.; Mogahed, Dalia (2007). *Who Speaks for Islam?: What A Billion Muslims Really Think*. New York: Gallup Press.

Fabbro, David (1978). 'Peaceful Societies: An Introduction,' *Journal of Peace Research*, XV(1):67-83.

Feibleman, James Kern (1987). *The Destroyers: The Underside of Human Nature*. New York: Peter Lang.

Feldman, Jonathan (1989). *Universities in the Business of Repression: The Academic-Military-Industrial Complex and Central America*. Boston: South End Press.

Ferguson, R. Brian (1988). 'Anthropology and War: Theory, Politics, Ethics,' in Turner, Paul R.; Pitt, David, eds.,*The Anthropology of War and Peace: Perspectives on the Nuclear Age*. Cambridge: Bergin and Garvey Publishers, pp. 141-159.

Ferguson, R. Brian (1992). 'Tribal Warfare,' *Scientific American*, 266(1):108-113.

Ferguson, R. Brian (1995). *Yanomami Warfare: A Political History*. Santa Fe: School of American Research Press.

Ferguson, R. Brian (2002). 'The "Violent" Human: Archaeological and Historical Evidence,' in Ury, William, ed., *Must We Fight? From the Battlefield to the Schoolyard: A New Perspective on Violent Conflict and Its Preservation*. San Francisco: Jossey-Bass, pp. 26-38.

Ferguson, R. Brian, ed. (2003). *The State Under Siege: Political Disintegration in the Post-Cold War World*. London: Routledge.

Ferguson, R. Brian (2006). 'Archaeology, Cultural Anthropology, and the Origins and Intensification of War,' in Arkush, Elizabeth N.; Allen, Mark W., eds., *The Archaeology of Warfare: Prehistories of Raiding and Conquest*. Gainesville: University Press of Florida.

Ferguson, R. Brian (2007). 'Eight Points on War,' *Anthropology News*, 48(2):5-6.

Ferguson, R. Brian (2008). 'Ten Points on War,' *Social Analysis*, 52(2):32-49.

Ferguson, R. Brian; Farragher, Leslie E. (1988). *The Anthropology of War: A Bibliography*. New York: Harry Frank Guggenheim Foundation Occasional Paper 1.

Ferguson, R. Brian; Whitehead, Neil L., eds. (1992). *War in the Tribal Zone: Expanding States and Indigenous Warfare*. Santa Fe: School of American Research.

Fluehr-Lobban, Carolyn (2002). 'A Century of Ethics and Professional Anthropology,' *Anthropology News*, 43(3):20.

Fluehr-Lobban, Carolyn, ed. (2003). *Ethics and the Profession of Anthropology: Dialogue for Ethically Conscious Practice*. Walnut Creek: AltaMira Press.

Fluehr-Lobban, Carolyn (2006). *On Truth*. New York: Alfred A. Knopf.

Frankfurt, Harry G. (2005). *On Bullshit*. Princeton: Princeton University Press.

Frese, Pamela R.; Harrell, Margaret C., eds. (2003). *Anthropology and the United States Military: Coming of Age in the Twenty-first Century*. New York: Palgrave Macmillan.

Fried, Morton; Harris, Marvin; Murphy, Robert, eds. (1968). *The Anthropology of Armed Conflict and Aggression*. Garden City: Doubleday & Company, Inc.

Fry, Douglas P. (2006). *The Human Potential for Peace: An Anthropological Challenge to Assumptions about War and Violence*. New York: Oxford University Press.

Fry, Douglas P. (2007). *Beyond War: The Human Potential for Peace*. New York: Oxford University Press.

Fry, Douglas P.; Bjorkqvist, Kaj, eds. (1997). *Cultural Variation in Conflict Resolution: Alternatives to Violence*. Mahwah: Lawrence Erlbaum Associates, Publishers.

Gelvin, Michael (1994). *War and Existence: A Philosophical Inquiry*. University Park: Pennsylvania State University Press.

Ghiglieri, Michael P. (1987). 'War among the Chimps,' *Discover*, 8(11):67-76.

Ghiglieri, Michael P. (1999). *The Dark Side of Man: Tracing the Origins of Male Violence*. Reading: Perseus Books.

Giroux, Henry A. (2007). *The University in Chains: Confronting the Military-Industrial-Academic Complex*. Boulder: Paradigm Publishers.

Glazer, Myron Peretz (1996). 'Ethics,' in Levinson, David; Ember, Melvin, eds., *Encyclopedia of Cultural Anthropology*, vol. 2. New York: Henry Holt, pp. 389-393.

Golding, William (1999 [1954]). *Lord of the Flies*. New York: Penguin Books.

Goldschmidt, Walter, ed. (1979). *The Uses of Anthropology*. Washington: American Anthropological Association Special Publication 11.

González, Roberto J., ed. (2004). *Anthropologists in the Public Sphere: Speaking Out on War, Peace, and American Power*. Austin: University of Texas Press.

González, Roberto J. (2007). 'Towards Mercenary Anthropology?,' *Anthropology Today*, 23(3):14-19.

González, Roberto J. (2008). 'Imperial Tactics: Bribing the Tribes,' *Z Magazine*, 21(2):37-40.

González, Roberto J. (2009). *American Counterinsurgency: Human Science and the Human Terrain*. Chicago: Prickly Paradigm Press.

Good, Kenneth; Charnoff, David (1991). *Into the Heart: One Man's Pursuit of Love and Knowledge among the Yanomami*. New York: Simon and Schuster.

Goodall, Jane (1986). *The Chimpanzees of Gombe: Patterns of Behavior*. Cambridge: Cambridge University Press.

Gordon, Robert (1988). 'Apartheid's Anthropologists: The Genealogy of Afrikaner Anthropology,' *American Ethnologist*,15(3):535-553.

Gore, Al (2007). *The Assault on Reason*. New York: Penguin Books.

Gough, Kathleen (1968). 'Anthropology and Imperialism,' *Monthly Review*,19(11):12-24.

Govier, Trudy (2002). *A Delicate Balance: What Philosophy Can Tell Us About Terrorism*. Boulder: Westview Press.

Graeber, David (2004). *Fragments of an Anarchist Anthropology*. Chicago: Prickly Paradigm Press.

Greenhouse, Carol (1985). 'Mediation: A Comparative Approach,' *Man*, 20(1):90-114.

Gregor, Thomas A., ed. (1996). *The Natural History of Peace*. Nashville: Vanderbilt University Press.

Gregor, Thomas A.; Gross, Daniel R. (2004). 'Guilt By Association: The Culture of Accusation and the AAA's Investigation of *Darkness in El Dorado*,' *American Anthropologist*,106(4):687-698.

Griffin, Marcus. *Human Terrain System Anthropologist* (<http://www.marcusgriffin.com>).

Gross, Paul R. (2004). 'Politics and Science,' in Salzano, Francisco M.; Hurtado,

A. Magdalena, eds., *Lost Paradises and the Ethics of Research and Publication*. New York: Oxford University Press, pp. 59-69.

Grossman, Dave (1995). *On Killing: The Psychological Costs of Learning to Kill in War and Society*. New York: Little, Brown.

Grossman, Dave (2008). 'Evolution of Weaponry,' in Kurtz, Lester, ed., *Encyclopedia of Violence, Peace, & Conflict*, San Diego: Elsevier 3:2442-2455.

Guilaine, Jean; Zammit, Jean (2001). *Origins of War: Violence in Prehistory*. Malden: Blackwell Publishing.

Gusterson, Hugh (1996). *Nuclear Rites: A Weapons Laboratory at the End of the Cold War*. Berkeley: University of California Press.

Gusterson, Hugh (2003). 'Anthropology and the Military: 1968, 2003, and Beyond?' *Anthropology Today*,19(3):25-26.

Gusterson, Hugh (2007). 'Anthropology and Militarism,' *Annual Review of Anthropology*, 36:155-175.

Gwynne, Margaret A. (2003). *Applied Anthropology: A Career-Oriented Approach*. Boston: Allyn and Bacon.

Hall, Edward T. (1990). *The Hidden Dimension*. New York: Anchor Books.

Harcourt, A.H.; Waal, Frans B. M. de (1992). *Coalitions and Alliances in Humans and Other Animals*. New York: Oxford University Press.

Hart, Donna; Sussman, Robert W. (2009). *Man the Hunted: Primates, Predators, and Human Evolution*. Boulder: Westview Press.

Hastings, Tom H. (2000). *Ecology of War & Peace: Counting Costs of Conflict*. Lanham: University Press of America.

Hedges, Chris (2002). *War Is a Force that Gives Us Meaning*. New York: Public Affairs.

Hedges, Chris; Al-Arian, Laila (2007), 'The Other War,' *The Nation*, 285(4): 11-31.

Herskovits, Melville J. (1972). *Cultural Relativism: Perspectives in Cultural Pluralism*. New York: Random House.

Hickey, Gerald C. (2002). *Window on a War: An Anthropologist in the Vietnam Conflict*. Lubbock: Texas Tech University Press.

Hillman, James (2004). *A Terrible Love of War*. New York: Penguin.

Hofstadter, Richard; Wallace, Michael, eds. (1971). *American Violence: A Documentary History*. New York: Random House.

Holmes, Bob (2008). 'How Warfare Shaped Human Evolution,' *New Scientist*, 2682.

Homer-Dixon, Thomas F.; Boutwell, Jeffrey H.; Rathjens, George W. (1993). 'Environmental Change and Violent Conflict,' *Scientific American*, 268(2):38-45.

Howell, Signe; Willis, Roy, eds. (1989). *Societies at Peace: Anthropological Perspectives*. New York: Routledge.

Hymes, Dell, ed. (1999). *Reinventing Anthropology*. Ann Arbor: University of Michigan Press.

Jaimes, M. Annette, ed. (1992). *The State of Native America: Genocide, Colonization, and Resistance*. Boston: South End Press.

Jell-Bahlsen, S. (1985). 'Ethnology and Fascism in Germany,' *Dialectical Anthropology*, 9: 337-347.

Jeong, Ho-Won (2000). *Peace and Conflict Studies: An Introduction*. Aldershot: Ashgate.

Johnston, Barbara Rose, ed. (1994). *Who Pays the Price? Examining the Sociocultural Context of the Environmental Crisis*. Washington: Island Press.

Johnston, Barbara Rose, ed. (1997). *Life and Death Matters: Human Rights and the Environment at the End of the Millennium*. Thousand Oaks: AltaMira Press.

Johnston, Barbara Rose, ed. (2007). *Half-Lives & Half-Truths: Confronting the Radioactive Legacies of the Cold War*. Santa Fe: School for Advanced Research Press.

Johnston, Barbara Rose; Barker, Holly M. (2008). *The Rongelap Report: Consequential Damages of Nuclear War*. Walnut Creek: Left Coast Press, Inc.

Kajihiro, Kyle (2007). 'A Brief Overview of Militarization and Resistance in Hawaii' Honolulu: DMZ-Hawaii/Aloha 'Aina, pp. 1-12 (<http://www.dmzhawaii.org>).

Kano, Takayoshi (1990). 'The Bonobo's Peaceful Kingdom,' *Natural History*, 11:62-71.

Kano, Takayoshi (1992). *The Last Ape: Pygmy Chimpanzee Behavior and Ecology*. Stanford: Stanford University Press.

Kaplan, Robert D. (1994). 'The Coming Anarchy,' *Atlantic Monthly*, 273(2):44-76.

Kaplan, Robert D. (2000). *The Coming Anarchy: Shattering the Dreams of the Post Cold War*. New York: Random House/Vintage.

Kapstein, Matthew T. (2006). *The Tibetans*. Malden: Blackwell Publishing.

Keegan, John (1993). *A History of Warfare*. New York: Random House/Vintage.

Keeley, Lawrence H. (1996). *War Before Civilization: The Myth of the Peaceful Savage*. New York: Oxford University Press.

Kegley, Jr., Charles W.; Raymond, Gregory A., eds. (1999). *How Nations Make Peace*. New York: St. Martin's Press.

Kelly, Raymond C. (2000). *Warless Societies and the Origin of War*. Ann Arbor: University of Michigan Press.

Kemp, Graham; Fry, Douglas P., eds. (2004). *Keeping the Peace: Conflict Resolution and Peaceful Societies Around the World*. New York: Routledge.

Khan, Arshad (2006). *Islam 101: Principles and Practice*. San Jose: Khan.

Kipp, J.; Grau, L.; Prinslow, K.; Smith, D. (2006). 'The Human Terrain System: ACORDS for the 21st Century', *U.S. Army Professional Writing Collection*, 4:1-9.

Klare, Michael T. (2001). 'The New Geography of Conflict,' *Foreign Affairs*, 80(3):22-49.

Klare, Michael T. (2002). *Resource Wars: The New Landscape of Global Conflict*. New York: Harry Holt.

Kohn, Alfie (1990). *The Brighter Side of Human Nature: Altruism and Empathy in Everyday Life*. New York: Basic Books.

Kraybill, Donald B. (2008). *The Amish of Lancaster County*. Mechanicsburg: Stackpole.

Kraybill, Donald B.; Nolt, Steven M.; Weaver-Zercher, David L. (2006). *Amish Grace: How Forgiveness Transcended Tragedy*. New York: Jossey-Bass.

Kroeber, Theodora (1961). *ISHI in Two Worlds: A Biography of the Last Wild Indian in North America*. Berkeley: University of California Press.

Krug, E. et al., eds. (2002). *World Report on Violence and Health*. Geneva: World Health Organization.

Kurtz, Lester, ed. (2008). *Encyclopedia of Violence, Peace, & Conflict*. San Diego: Elsevier.

Kyrou, Christos N.; Rubenstein, Robert A. (2008). 'Cultural Anthropology Studies of Conflict,' in Kurtz, Lester, ed., *Encyclopedia of Violence, Peace, & Conflict*. San Diego: Elsevier 1: 515-521.

Lanier-Graham, Susan D. (1993). *The Ecology of War: Environmental Impacts of Weaponry and Warfare*. New York: Waker and Company.

Lassiter, Luke Eric (2005). *The Chicago Guide to Collaborative Ethnography*. Chicago: University of Chicago Press.

LeBlanc, Steven A.; Register, Katherine E. (2003). *Constant Battles: The Myth of the Peaceful, Noble Savage*. New York: St. Martin's Press.

Lee, Richard B.; DeVore, Irven, eds. (1968). *Man the Hunter*. Chicago: Aldine.

Levinson, David (1994). *Aggression and Conflict: A Cross-Cultural Encyclopedia*. Santa Barbara: ABC-CLIO.

Lewis, Andrian R. (2006). *The American Culture of War: The History of U.S.*

Military Force from World War II to Operation Iraqi Freedom. New York: Routledge.

Lieberman, Leonard; Lyons, Andrew; Lyons, Harriet (1995). 'An Interview with Ashley Montagu,' *Current Anthropology*, 36(5):835-844.

Lizot, Jacques (1985). *Tales of the Yanomami: Daily Life in the Venezuelan Forest*. New York: Cambridge University Press.

Lorenz, Konrad (1966). *On Aggression*. New York: Harcourt, Brace and World.

Lutz, Catherine (2001). *Homefront: A Military City and the American 20th Century*. Boston: Beacon Press.

Lutz, Catherine (2002). 'Making War at Home in the United States: Militarization and the Current Crisis,' *American Anthropologist*,104(3):723-735.

Mabee, Carleton (1987). 'Margaret Mead and Behavioral Scientists in World War II: Problems in Responsibility, Truth, and Effectiveness,' *Journal of the History of the Behavioral Sciences*, 23:3-13.

MacNair, Rachel M. (2002). *Perpetration-Induced Traumatic Stress: The Psychological Consequences of Killing*. Westport: Praeger Publications.

Mahoney, Jack (2007). *The Challenge of Human Rights: Origin, Development, and Significance*. Malden: Blackwell Publishing.

Matthews, Warren (2004). *World Religions*. Belmont: Wadsworth/Thomson Learning.

McFate, Montgomery (2005a). 'Anthropology and Counterinsurgency: The Strange Story of their Curious Relationship,' *Military Review*, 24-38.

McFate, Montgomery (2005b). 'The Military Utility of Understanding Adversary Culture,' *Joint Force Quarterly*, 38:42-48.

McKenna, Brian (2008). 'A Good Military Education is Hard to Find,' *Society for Applied Anthropology Newsletter*, 19(2):13-18.

Mead, Margaret (1940). 'Warfare: It's Only an Invention—not a Biological Necessity,' *Asia*, 15:402-405.

Melko, Matthew (1973). *52 Peaceful Societies*. Oakville, Ontario: Canadian Peace Research Institute.

Melko, Matthew (1984). 'Peaceful Societies,' in Laszlo, Ervin; Youl Yoo, Jong, eds.,*World Encyclopedia of Peace*. New York: Pergamon Press, 2:268-270.

Messer, Ellen (1993). 'Anthropology and Human Rights,' *Annual Review of Anthropology*, 22:221-249.

Montagu, Ashley (1968). *The Natural Superiority of Women*. New York: Macmillan.

Montagu, Ashley (1972). *Statement on Race: An Annotated Elaboration and Exposition of the Four Statements on Race Issued by the United Nations*

Educational, Scientific, and Cultural Organization. New York: Oxford University Press.

Montagu, Ashley, ed. (1976). *The Nature of Human Aggression*. New York: Oxford University Press.

Montagu, Ashley (1978). *Learning Non-Aggression: The Experience of Non-Literate Societies*. New York: Oxford University Press.

Montagu, Ashley (1989). *Growing Young*. Granby: Bergin & Garvey Publishers.

Montagu, Ashley (1998). *Man's Most Dangerous Myth: The Fallacy of Race*. Walnut Creek: AltaMira Press.

Montagu, Ashley; Matson, Floyd (1983). *The Dehumanization of Man*. New York: McGraw-Hill.

Morris, Desmond (1967). *The Naked Ape: A Zoologist's Study of the Human Animal*. London: Cape.

Morris, Desmond (1969). *The Human Zoo*. New York: McGraw-Hill.

Myers, Norman (1996). *Ultimate Security: The Environmental Basis of Political Instability*. Washington: Island Press.

Nagengast, Carole (1994). 'Violence, Terror, and the Crisis of the State,' *Annual Review of Anthropology*, 23:109-136.

Nagengast, Carole; Turner, Terence, eds. (1997). 'Universal Human Rights versus Cultural Relativity,' *Journal of Anthropological Research*, 53(3):267-381.

Nagengast, Carole, Vélez-Ibáñez, Carlos G., eds. (2004). *Human Rights: The Scholar as Activist*. Oklahoma City: Society for Applied Anthropology.

Neel, James V. (1994). *Physician to the Gene Pool: Genetic Lessons and Other Stories*. New York: John Wiley.

Nordstrom, Carolyn (1997). *A Different Kind of War Story*. Philadelphia: University of Pennsylvania Press.

Nordstrom, Carolyn (1998). 'Deadly Myths of Aggression,' *Aggressive Behavior*, 24(2):147-159.

Nordstrom, Carolyn; Robben, Antonious, eds. (1995). *Fieldwork Under Fire: Contemporary Studies of Violence and Survival*. Berkeley: University of California Press.

Otterbein, Keith F. (1993). *Feuding and Warfare: Selected Works of Keith F. Otterbein*. New York: Gordon and Breach.

Otterbein, Keith F. (1999). 'A History of Research on Warfare in Anthropology,' *American Anthropologist*, 101(4):794-805.

Otterbein, Keith (2004). *How War Began*. College Station: Texas A&M University Press.

Otterbein, Keith F. (2008). 'Clan and Tribal Conflict,' in Kurtz, Lester, ed., *Encyclopedia of Violence, Peace, & Conflict*. San Diego: Elsevier, 1:268-275.

Paige, Glenn D. (2009 [2002]). *Nonkilling Global Political Science*. Honolulu: Center for Global Nonkilling. Available at: <http://www.nonkilling.org>.

Paine, Robert, ed. (1985). *Advocacy and Anthropology*. St. John's: Memorial University of Newfoundland Institute of Social and Economic Research.

Palmer, Stuart (1972). *The Violent Society*. New Haven: College and University Press Publishers.

Patterson, Thomas C. (2001). *A Social History of Anthropology in the United States*. New York: Berg.

Penny, H. Glenn; Bunzl, Matti, eds. (2003). *Worldly Provincialism: German Anthropology in the Age of Empire*. Ann Arbor: University of Michigan Press.

Perry, Richard J. (2003). *Five Key Concepts in Anthropological Thinking*. Upper Saddle River: Pearson Education, Inc./Prentice Hall.

Peters, John F. (1998). *Life Among the Yanomami: The Story of Change among the Xilixana on the Mucajai River in Brazil*. Orchard Park: Broadview Press.

Power, Margaret (1991). *The Egalitarians–Human and Chimpanzee: An Anthropological View of Social Organization*. New York: Cambridge University Press.

Price, David H. (2000). 'Anthropologists as Spies,' *The Nation*, 271(16):24-27.

Price, David H. (2004). *Threatening Anthropology: McCarthyism and the FBI's Surveillance of Activist Anthropologists*. Durham: Duke University Press.

Price, David H. (2007). 'Counterinsurgency Anthropologist Montgomery McFate's,' *Counterpunch*, 30 October. Available at: <http://www.counterpunch.org/price 10302007.html>.

Price, David H. (2008). *Anthropological Intelligence: The Development and Neglect of American Anthropology in the Second World War*. Durham: Duke University Press.

Price, David H. (2008). David H. Price Faculty Homepage. Available at: <http://www.homepages.stmartin.edu/fac_staff/dprice>.

Ramos, Alcida Rita (1987). 'Reflecting on the Yanomami: Ethnographic Images and the Pursuit of the Exotic,' *Cultural Anthropology*, 2(3):284-304.

Ramos, Alcida Rita (1995). *Sanuma Memories: Yanomami Ethnography in Times of Crisis*. Madison: University of Wisconsin Press.

Renner, Michael (1996). *Fighting for Survival: Environmental Decline, Social Conflict, and the New Age of Insecurity*. New York: W.W. Norton & Company.

Renzi, Fred (2006). 'Networks: Terra Incognita and the Case for Ethnographic Intelligence,' *Military Review*, 16-22.

Robarchek, Clayton A.; Robarchek, Carole J. (1992). 'Cultures of War and Peace: A Comparative Study of the Waorani and Semai,' in Silverberg, James; Gray, J. Patrick, eds., *Aggression and Peacefulness in Humans and Other Primates*. New York: Oxford University Press, pp. 189-213.

Robarchek, Clayton A.; Robarchek, Carole J. (1996). 'Waging Peace: The Psychological and Sociocultural Dynamics of Positive Peace,' in Wolfe, A. W.; Yang, H., eds. *Anthropological Contributions to Conflict Resolution*. Athens: University of Georgia Press, pp. 64-80.

Robarchek, Clayton A.; Robarchek, Carole J. (1998a). 'Reciprocities and Realities: World Views, Peacefulness, and Violence among Semai and Waorani,' *Aggressive Behavior*, 24:123-133.

Robarchek, Clayton A.; Robarchek, Carole J. (1998b). *Waorani: The Contexts of Violence and War*. Fort Worth: Harcourt Brace College Publishers.

Robin, Ron (2004). *Scandals & Scoundrels: Seven Cases that Shook the Academy*. Berkeley: University of California Press.

Rodman, Margaret; Cooper, Matthew, eds. (1979). *The Pacification of Melanesia*. Ann Arbor: University of Michigan Press.

Rubenstein, Robert A. (2008). *Peacekeeping Under Fire: Culture and Intervention*. Boulder: Paradigm Publishers.

Salzman, Philip Carl; Rice, Patricia C., eds. (2004). *Thinking Anthropologically. A Practical Guide for Students*. Upper Saddle River: Pearson Education/ Prentice Hall.

Sanders, Andrew (2008). 'Anthropology of Warriors,' in Kurtz, Lester, ed., *Encyclopedia of Violence, Peace, & Conflict*. San Diego: Elsevier, 3:2432-2442.

Schafft, Gretchen E. (2004). *From Racism to Genocide: Anthropology in the Third Reich*. Urbana: University of Illinois Press.

Sewall, Sarah et al. (2007). *The U.S. Army/Marine Corps Counterinsurgency Field Manual*. Chicago: University of Chicago Press.

Shakya, Tsering (1999). *The Dragon in the Land of Snows: A History of Modern Tibet Since 1947*. New York: Penguin Group (USA) Inc.

Shepard, Paul (1973). *The Tender Carnivore and the Sacred Game*. New York: Scribner.

Simmons, Anna (1997). *The Company They Keep: Life Inside the U.S. Army Special Forces*. New York: Free Press.

Simmons, Anna (1999). 'War: Back to the Future,' *Annual Review of Anthropology*, 28:73-108.

Simpson, Christopher, ed. (1998). *Universities and Empires: Money and Politics in the Social Science during the Cold War*. New York: New Press.

Singer, Peter (2004). *The President of Good and Evil: Questioning the Ethics of George W. Bush*. New York: Penguin Group.

Sluka, Jeffrey A., ed. (2000). *Death Squad: The Anthropological State of Terror*. Philadelphia: University of Pennsylvania Press.

Smith, David Livingstone (2007). *The Most Dangerous Animal: Human Nature and the Origins of War*. New York: St. Martin's Press.

Smith, Linda Tuhiwai (1999). *Decolonizing Methodologies: Research and Indigenous Peoples*. New York: Zed Books Ltd.

Smole, William J. (1976). *The Yanomama Indians: A Cultural Geography*. Austin: University of Texas Press.

Sperling, Elliot (2004). *The Tibet-China Conflict: History and Polemics*. Washington: East-West Center Washington.

Sponsel, Leslie E. (1990). 'Ultraprimitive Pacifists: The Tasaday as a Symbol of Peace,' *Anthropology Today*, 6(1):3-5.

Sponsel, Leslie E. (1992). 'Our Fascination with the Tasaday: Anthropological Images and Images of Anthropology,' in Headland, Thomas N., ed.,*The Tasaday Controversy: Assessing the Evidence*. Washington: American Anthropological Association Special Publication No. 28, ch. 18, pp. 200-212.

Sponsel, Leslie E. (1994a). 'The Mutual Relevance of Anthropology and Peace Studies,' in Sponsel, Leslie E.; Gregor, Thomas A., eds., *The Anthropology of Peace and Nonviolence*. Boulder: Lynne Rienner Publishers, ch. 1, pp. 1-36.

Sponsel, Leslie E. (1994b). 'Toward a Pedagogy of the Anthropology of Peace,' in Sponsel, Leslie E.; Gregor, Thomas A., eds., *The Anthropology of Peace and Nonviolence*. Boulder: Lynne Rienner Publishers, ch. 11, pp. 259-269.

Sponsel, Leslie E. (1994c). 'Book Review: *Societies at Peace: Anthropological Perspectives* co-edited by S. Howell and R. Willis,' *American Ethnologist*, 20(2):396-397.

Sponsel, Leslie E. (1995). 'Relationships among the World System, Indigenous Peoples, and Ecological Anthropology,' in Sponsel, Leslie E., ed., *Indigenous Peoples and the Future of Amazonia: An Ecological Anthropology of an Endangered World*. Tucson: University of Arizona Press, ch. 13, pp. 263-293.

Sponsel, Leslie E. (1996a). 'The Natural History of Peace: A Positive View of Human Nature and Its Potential,' in Gregor, Thomas A., ed., *The Natural History of Peace*. Nashville: Vanderbilt University Press, ch. 4, pp. 95-125.

Sponsel, Leslie E. (1996b). 'Human Rights and Advocacy Anthropology,' in Levinson, David; Ember, Melvin, eds. *The Encyclopedia of Cultural Anthropology*. New York: Henry Holt and Co., 2:602-607.

Sponsel, Leslie E. (1996c). 'Peace and Nonviolence,' in Levinson, David; Ember, Melvin, eds.,*The Encyclopedia of Cultural Anthropology*. New York: Henry Holt, 3:908-912.

Sponsel, Leslie E. (1997a). 'Human Rights,' *The Dictionary of Anthropology*, Barfield, Thomas, ed. Oxford: Blackwell Publishers, pp. 248-250.

Sponsel, Leslie E., (1997b). 'Peace and Nonviolence,' *The Dictionary of Anthropology*, Barfield, Thomas, ed. Oxford: Blackwell Publishers, pp. 350-352.

Sponsel, Leslie E. (1998). 'Yanomami: An Arena of Conflict and Aggression in the Amazon,' *Aggressive Behavior*, 24(2):97-122.

Sponsel, Leslie E. (2000b). 'Response to Otterbein,' *American Anthropologist*, 102(4):837-840.

Sponsel, Leslie E. (2001). 'Advocacy in Anthropology,' in Smelser, N.J.; Baltes, Paul B., eds., *International Encyclopedia of the Social and Behavioral Sciences*. Oxford: Pergamon Press, pp. 204-206.

Sponsel, Leslie E. (2005). 'Noble Savage and Ecologically Noble Savage,' in Taylor, Bron, ed., *Encyclopedia of Religion and Nature*. New York: Continuum, 2:1210-1212.

Sponsel, Leslie E. (2006a). 'Darkness in El Dorado Controversy,' in Birx, H. James, ed., *Encyclopedia of Anthropology*. Thousand Oaks: Sage Publications, 2:667-673.

Sponsel, Leslie E. (2006b). 'Ashley Montagu,' in Birx, H. James, ed., *Encyclopedia of Anthropology*. Thousand Oaks: Sage Publications, 4:1620-1622.

Sponsel, Leslie E. (2006c). 'Yanomamo,' in Birx, H. James, ed., *Encyclopedia of Anthropology*. Thousand Oaks: Sage Publications, 5:2347-2351.

Sponsel, Leslie E. (2007). 'Human Nature,' in Robbins, Paul, ed. *Encyclopedia of Environment and Society*. Thousand Oaks: Sage Publications, 3:886-889.

Sponsel, Leslie E.; Good, Kenneth R. (2000). 'Anthropologists Debate Future of War,' *Anthropology News*, 41(2):19-20.

Sponsel, Leslie E.; Gregor, Thomas A., eds. (1994). *The Anthropology of Peace and Nonviolence*. Boulder: Lynne Rienner Publishers.

Sponsel, Leslie E.; Turner, Terence (2002). 'Counterpoint: Charges of Wrongdoing by Anthropologists,' *The Chronicle of Higher Education*, 2 (Reviews), B13.

Starkey, Armstrong (1998). *European and Native American Warfare, 1675-1815*. Norman: University of Oklahoma Press.

Starn, Orin (1986). 'Engineering Internment: Anthropologists and War Relocation Authority,' *American Ethnologist*, 13:700-720.

Staub, Ervin (1989). *The Roots of Evil: The Origins of Genocide and Other Group Violence*. New York: Cambridge University Press.

Stauder, J. (1974). 'The "Relevance" of Anthropology to Colonialism and Imperialism,' *Radical Science Journal*, 1:38-61.

Steele, Frank (1994). *Warpaths: Invasions of North America*. New York: Oxford University Press.

Stevenson, Leslie; Haberman, David L. (1998). *Ten Theories of Human Nature*. New York: Oxford University Press.

Stoessinger, John G. (2008). *Why Nations Go to War*. Belmont: Thomson.

Strathern, Andrew J.; Stewart, Pamela J. (2008). 'Anthropology of Violence and Conflict, Overview,' in Kurtz, Lester, ed., *Encyclopedia of Violence, Peace, & Conflict*. San Diego: Elsevier, 1:75-86.

Summer Institute of Linguistics (2008). *Ethnologue*. <http://www.ethnologue.com>.

Suzuki, Peter T. (1981). 'Anthropologists in the Wartime Camps for Japanese Americans: A Documentary Study,' *Dialectical Anthropology*, 6:23-60.

Thurman, Robert (2008). *Why the Dalai Lama Matters: His Act of Truth as the Solution for China, Tibet, and the World*. New York: Simon & Schuster/Atria Books.

Tierney, Patrick (2000). *Darkness in El Dorado: How Scientists and Journalists Devastated the Amazon*. New York: W.W. Norton & Company.

Tuzin, Donald (1996). 'The Spectre of Peace in Unlikely Places: Concept and Paradox in the Anthropology of Peace,' in Gregor, Thomas, ed., *A Natural History of Peace*. Nashville: Vanderbilt University Press, pp. 3-33.

Ury, William L. (1999). *The Third Side: Why We Fight and How We Can Stop*. New York: Penguin Putnam, Inc.

Ury, William L., ed. (2002). *Must We Fight? From the Battlefield to the Schoolyard—A New Perspective on Violent Conflict and Its Preservation*. San Francisco: Jossey-Bass.

US Army (2008). *War Surgery in Afghanistan and Iraq: A Series of Cases, 2003-2007*. Washington: U.S. Department of Defense.

Waal, Frans de (1989). *Peacemaking Among Primates*. Cambridge: Harvard University Press.

Waal, Frans de (1996). *Good Natured: The Origins of Right and Wrong in Humans and Other Animals*. Cambridge: Harvard University Press.

Waal, Frans de (2006). *Primates and Philosophers: How Morality Evolved*. Princeton: Princeton University Press.

Waal, Frans de; Lating, Frans (1997). *Bonobo: The Forgotten Ape*. Berkeley: University of California Press.

Wakin, Eric (1992). *Anthropology Goes to War: Professional Ethics and Counterinsurgency in Thailand*. Madison: University of Wisconsin Center for Southeast Asian Studies, Monograph No. 7.

Wax, Dustin M., ed. (2008). *Anthropology at the Dawn of the Cold War*. Ann Arbor: Pluto Press.

Whiteford, Linda M.; Trotter II, Robert T. (2008). *Ethics for Anthropological Research and Practice*. Long Grove: Waveland Press, Inc.

World report on violence and health. (2002). Geneva: World Health Organization.

Wiberg, Hakan (1981). 'JPR 1964-1980—What Have We Learned About Peace?,' *Journal of Peace Research,* XVIII(2):111-148.

Williams, Emilio (1986). *A Way of Life and Death: Three Centuries of Prussian-German Militarism: An Anthropological Approach*. Nashville: Vanderbilt University Press.

de Wolf, Jan J. (1992). 'Ethnology in the Third Reich,' *Current Anthropology*, 33(4):473-475.

Wolfe, A.W.; Yang, H., eds. (1996). *Anthropological Contributions to Conflict Resolution.* Athens: University of Georgia Press.

Wrangham, Richard; Peterson, Dale (1996). *Demonic Males: Apes and the Origins of Human Violence*. Boston: Houghton Mifflin Company.

Wright, Ann; Dixon, Susan (2008). *Dissent: Voices of Conscience*. Kihei: Koa Books.

Younger, Stephen M. (2007). *Endangered Species: How We Can Avoid Mass Destruction and Build a Lasting Peace*. New York: HarperCollins Publishers.

2

An Introduction to Nonkilling Geographies: Opening New Spaces

James Tyner
Kent State University

Joshua F.J. Inwood
University of Tennessee

On 4 April 1967, one year to the day of his assassination, Dr Martin Luther King Jr. publicly denounced the war in Vietnam. It was imperative, morally and spiritually, to speak out. According to King (1986a; 231), 'A time comes when silence is betrayal.' King explained that throughout his public work within the Civil Rights movement, he began to view the on-going war in Vietnam as commensurate with the entrenched poverty and racism that permeated the United States. In other words, the massive killing of Vietnamese by American forces occupied the same moral plane as the discrimination, exploitation, and oppression of African-Americans in the US. Moreover, King realized that to remain silent on the war was to betray his core values. Specifically, it would be immoral to attempt to build his Beloved Community at home while ignoring the plight of Vietnamese abroad (Inwood, 2009).

During his sermon, King powerfully linked the growth of militarism, materialism, and racism through time and space. In so doing, he implicated wider social, religious, and academic institutions in American society as being complicit in the death and destruction that is meted out every day in the name of the American Empire. The promotion of empire, in other words, does carry a cost; most often measured in the lives of oppressed peoples of colour that have the misfortune of living in those spaces deemed of strategic economic or military value by American politicians. King's imploring of his audience to make the connection between Vietnam and the American Civil Rights movement was an attempt to connect the direct physical violence—the killing—with the institutional and structural violence that was foundational to the economic and political systems of the United States.

Nearly a half-century later, in the shadow of innumerable global interventions, in the shadow of genocides and famines, in the shadow of rampant gun violence in the United States, King's call to 'break the silence' looms over us in uncomfortable ways. It is again time to break the silence.

Stated differently, as educators—but more immediately as citizens of the world—we have a responsibility to act, to end the violence that permeates our culture and our institutions in ways that do not just end conflict, but also lay the foundations for a positive peace and a nonkilling society to take root. At this moment, within the United States, when a war culture so dominates geopolitical discourse, to *not* do something is an ultraconservative response that maintains a status quo which more often than not directly impacts the marginalized and the most vulnerable in our society. To know that poverty exists, and do nothing; to know that infants and children are starving, and do nothing; to know that women are being raped and killed through organized mass violence, and do nothing, is to participate in a culture of impunity (Tyner, 2009). As Susan Opotow (1990: 3) explains, 'Although harm that results from unconcern ... may not involve malevolent intent, [this] can nevertheless result in exploitation, disruption of crucial services, suffering, the destruction of communities, and death.'

As long as killing—and here we refer quite explicitly to the direct physical violence of taking life—remains an organizing principle of our modern society, we can neither deny nor ignore our responsibility to address the interrelationships of war, violence, and inequality and to help our students and colleagues understand the linkages between these seemingly intractable problems.

Glenn Paige, professor emeritus of political science at the University of Hawaii and the founder and Chair of the Governing Council of the Center for Global Nonkilling (formerly Center for Global Nonviolence), provides a working definition of a nonkilling society. According to Paige (2002: 1), such a society is 'a human community, smallest to largest, local to global, characterized by no killing of humans and no threats to kill; no weapons designed to kill humans and no justifications for using them; and no conditions of society dependent upon threat or use of killing force for maintenance or change.'

This is a tall order—but certainly a laudable goal. There are some, of course, who will decry this as utopian thinking; that violence, but especially killing, is a natural part of humanity; that geopolitics requires violence. How else, it is asked, are we to stop this century's Hitlers, Stalins, or Pol Pots? Of course, we could counter with the question of what type of society permits the emergence of these brutal rulers. Is there no space to promote a more just society—to eliminate the structural and institutional inequalities that lead to violence?

Glenn Paige (2002: 161) maintains that a nonkilling (and more broadly, nonviolent) society is possible, but any effort to promote such as society must be global. In other words, *geography* must figure prominently in such an effort. Indeed, as outlined by Paige (2002: 74-75), a beginning point in the promotion of a nonkilling society is to concentrate on the various zones—or spaces—of a nonkilling society; attention, both scholarly and politically, must be directed toward those spaces in which violence is (re)produced, maintained, justified, and legitimated. At a most immediate, proximate level, we must direct attention to the 'space of killing': the space where actual violence takes place—the space of the murderer, for example, or the rapist. These personal spaces are produced through social relations and interactions; these are the spaces where men and women *act*. However, these spaces are themselves coded by dominant and embodied conceptions of race, sex, gender, and so on—the 'spaces of socialization'. Here is where people learn to kill, directly by training or vicariously by observation. These are the spaces in which violence is learned—and learned to be accepted. More broadly, we are confronted with the 'spaces of cultural conditioning'. It is within these spaces that we observe how religion, for example, and other ideologies have provided reasons and justifications for violence more broadly and killing more specifically. We see here also the salience of media, education, and other institutions. Lastly, we need to direct attention to those 'spaces of structural reinforcement': the economic and political practices that permeate society, such as the promotion of capitalism and attendant colonial and neo-colonial practices. In total, we must direct attention as to how structural and institutional violence likewise provides the context for direct personal violence and, ultimately, killing.

These spaces are not exclusive, but instead operate in tandem, producing a militarized society that both condones and in fact promotes violence and killing as justifiable solutions. This is seen most clearly, but by no means solely, in the emergence of 'war culture'. Thus, as an initial testing of the waters, of a preliminary sketch of the spaces of violence, we provide a brief narrative of war culture and militarism.

War Culture, Militarism and Death

Many societies throughout history have exhibited some form of militarism (Vagts, 1959). However, a fundamental shift occurred between the late eighteenth and early twentieth centuries (Gat, 2008; Creveld, 2008). During this period there evolved an expanded role of civilian participation in military preparation. Indeed what is distinctive about the advent of militarism during this era is the changing character of military-industrial relations.

The rise of militarism of Western societies throughout the late nineteenth and early twentieth centuries dramatically altered the conduct of warfare in two significant ways. First, modern war has become directed primarily against civilians (Pilisuk, 2008; Slim, 2008; Tanaka and Young, 2009). Throughout the twentieth century, civilians in general (and children in particular) have comprised an ever increasing proportion of the direct and indirect causalities of war and other major armed conflicts (Carlton-Ford et al., 2000). During the First World War, civilian casualties comprised between five and 19 per cent of all war deaths; by the Second World War this figure jumped to approximately 50 per cent (Carlton-Ford et al., 2000; Bartrop, 2002). If one looks at all the armed conflicts that occurred during the late twentieth and early twenty-first century, at least 80 per cent of the approximately 20 million people killed and 60 million wounded in declared wars, civil war and other conflicts have been civilians (Slim, 2008). Of these casualties, three out of every five have been children (Carlton-Ford et al., 2000: 401). Hugo Slim (2008: 3) concludes that

> 'It is obvious from the massive violence against civilian populations around the world and throughout history, that most warring parties do not see civilians as humanitarian agencies might like them to. Either they do not find civilians particularly innocent or they decide that innocent or not, killing them is useful, necessary, or inevitable in their wars.'

Second, the advent of industrial capitalism as the dominant mode of production has altered the growth of the military-industrial complex. Quite simply, the industrial revolution radically affected the way wars are waged, as well as how wars are planned (Horne, 2002). Hossein-Zadeh (2006) explains that the arms industries of past empires were not subject to capitalist market imperatives. Those 'industries' that produced military weaponry up to the 18TH and 19TH centuries were, for the most part, owned and operated by imperial governments. Armaments and munitions were not produced by market-driven corporations but instead arms production was dictated by immediate war requirements. This all changed with the advent of the industrial revolution and the concept of total war. Under this newer form of capitalism—horrifically played out during the First World War—the nature of arms production, and perhaps most importantly war itself, underwent a profound transformation.

These new forms of accumulation and production introduced concepts that had previously not been part of the human consciousness: mass mobilization, mass political movements, mass media, mass education, and a far more chilling notion emerged: *mass death* (Bartrop, 2002: 519). The killing fields of Ypres, Verdun and Flanders turned war death into a grizzly and heretofore unparalleled horror. The combined death toll of the First World War amounted to nearly 10 million individuals and when coupled with other casualties (disease, malnutrition etc.) the figure surpasses 32 million—so if you calculated war death as a kind of macabre production quota, the 'Great War' was able to turn out 5,600 deaths for each day of the war's duration (Bartrop, 2002: 520).

Among the many factors that contributed to such a devastatingly high death toll was the growth of a military-industrial-academic complex (Vagts, 1959; Downing, 1992; Epkenhans, 2003; Barnes, 2008). As the war bogged down into trench warfare, new or recent innovations were utilized in vain and grotesque attempts to break the stalemate: machine guns, chemical/biological weapons, armored vehicles and aircraft. Governments on both sides of the war increasingly turned to civilian scientists and engineers to provide technical assistance to military action which subsequently reinforces and reproduces the conditions necessary for a killing society (Johnson, 1994). As Alfred Vagts (1959: 463) explains, the rise of the military-industrial-academic complex 'led to an intensification of the horrors of warfare.' Thus, by the 1940's civilians 'not only had anticipated war more eagerly than the professionals, but played a principle part in making combat, when it came, more absolute, more terrible than was the current military wont or habit' (Vagts, 1959: 463).

The most obvious consequence of this shift in conducting war is that civilian populations pay the price for the industrial design, production and use of modern weapons. The advent of more sophisticated landmines and aerial munitions, for example, has contributed to more devastating practices of indiscriminate warfare strategies. The widespread military practice of 'strategic bombing' is a case in point. Although originating with dropping bombs from hot-air balloons in the late eighteenth century, aerial bombing campaigns 'came of age' in the First World War. When the war ended, both Germany and the Allied powers were engaged in indiscriminate bombing, killing or injuring several thousand civilians (Tanaka, 2009: 2). From there the practice only intensified, marked by the horrific use of carpet bombing in both the Second World War and the Vietnam War.

Yet the increase and acceptance of civilian deaths is only a symptom of the larger consequences of the shift in the production and execution of war. One cannot separate the debilitating consequence of twentieth century warfare from a 'war culture' which legitimizes the death of innocents by discursively constructing them as 'collateral damage' and accepts violence, intolerance and inequality as a natural part of the human condition. As Chris Hedges (2002: 3) writes, 'war forms its own culture.' Indeed, a 'mythology' of war emerges, particular during times of conflict. Hedges (2002: 21) explains:

> In mythic war we imbue events with meanings they do not have. We see defeats as signposts on the road to ultimate victory. We demonize the enemy so that our opponent is no longer human. We view ourselves, our people, as the embodiment of absolute goodness. Our enemies invert our view of the world to justify their own cruelty. In most mythic wars this is the case. Each side reduces the other to objects—eventually in the form of corpses.

Militarism and the promotion of a war culture directly contributes to attitudes of moral exclusion which legitimates violence at multiple scales—from the death of civilians in war zones to domestic violence Boal et al., (Gilligan, 1996; 2005; Kellner, 2008; Tyner, 2009). Dr King realized this when he wrote an essay titled 'A Testament of Hope' that in fighting the War in Vietnam, the US society was 'perpetuating racism [and] tolerating almost 40 million poor during an overflowing material abundance [...] our moral values and our spiritual confidence sink, even as our material wealth ascends' (King, 1986b: 315). By legitimating violence we not only accept civilian deaths, we also accept geographic divisions which none-too-subtly reinforce an 'us or them' binary that has a deleterious effect at all scales of society.

Susan Opotow (2001: 156) explains that militarism and war culture relies on a framework of exclusionary justice. For example, she argues that *moral inclusion* 'in the scope of justice means applying considerations of fairness, allocating resources, and making sacrifices to foster another's well being', while *moral exclusion* 'rationalizes and excuses harm inflicted on those outside the scope of justice. Excluding "others" from the scope of justice means viewing them as unworthy of fairness, resources, or sacrifice, and seeing them as expendable, undeserving, exploitable, or irrelevant.' This logic was perhaps made most famous by President George W. Bush's pronouncement in the wake of 11 September 2001 terror attacks that you are 'either with us or against us' (President Bush November 6, 2001).[1] By discursively packaging the world into two camps, President Bush not only legitimated any subsequent military actions against those who 'oppose us', but also consigned to the sidelines those civilians and innocents who have been caught in the crossfire. War culture and militarism thus treat innocents as 'collateral damage,' their deaths an unfortunate consequence of war. This creates a situation in which the death and injury suffered by civilians caught in war zones is discursively and materially excluded from consideration. Ironically, this has led Barry Sanders (2009) to conclude that in the twentieth and twenty-first centuries, human beings no longer die. He explains (p. 3) that Nazis did not see humans when they looked at Jews, but rather vermin and cockroaches. They saw a multitude of pests in desperate need of wholesale extermination.... [and] in the more recent past, we read of entire villages of Vietnamese 'pacified'; Tutsis and Serbs 'ethnically cleansed'; men, women, and the youngest of children in Darfur and Chad 'lost to religious strife.' Sanders (p. 3) is left wondering how we arrived 'at a state of affairs so catastrophic that fathers, sons, husbands, wives, daughters, lovers, and friends ... could have collapsed so conclusively into images, pixels, ciphers, ghosts, gross numbers, into the palatable euphemisms of death?'

The binary division of the world, a hallmark of war culture and militarism, also promotes a broader acceptance of violence because it hides the gruesome realities of modern armed conflict. Chris Hedges (2002: 83) explains, 'We do not smell the rotting flesh, hear the cries

---

1 As quoted on CNN: <http://archives.cnn.com/2001/US/11/06/gen.attack.on.terror/>.

of agony, or see before us blood and entrails seeping out of bodies.' The designer of a landmine or a machine gun does not always (if ever) witness the effects of his or her labour, neither does the chemist who discovers a more lethal poisonous gas, or the engineer who designs a more effective delivery system. Most of the US population, *including the vast majority of our students,* are not adequately aware of the daily realities of US military interventions in Afghanistan, Iraq, Pakistan and myriad other war zones. Because of the discursive and physical distance war culture creates—the geographic separation of militarism from actual warfare—the deadly consequences are often ignored; as has been observed countless times, 'War is always more popular with those who don't experience it' (Kurlansky, 2006: 141).

The Path Ahead

In this introductory chapter, we provide neither conclusions nor directions. Rather, we provide a starting point. We maintain that a nonkilling *and* nonviolent society is possible. Such an endeavour, however, requires work and dedication. We also maintain that geography must be front and center in such a pursuit. Geography, in particular, can (and has) contributed significantly to our understanding of the various 'spaces' of killing. However, to date, there has been no overarching, singular focus promoted by geographers toward nonkilling. This present volume constitutes the first direct engagement by a panel of geographers to think through the idea of a 'nonkilling' society. Contributors were asked to think broadly, to expand our intellectual—and moral—horizon to question killing and nonkilling, violence and nonviolence. And in the pages that follow, readers will experience a vast array of ideas, an unfolding of a larger intellectual quest that has the singular goal of contributing toward a nonkilling and nonviolent world.

As Martin Luther King Jr. so eloquently remarked: *Now is the time to break the silence*. This book serves as a clarion call: to provoke discussion, to begin a dialogue, to speak out. Because there are too many in the world who cannot.

References

Bartrop, Paul (2002). 'The Relationship Between War and Genocide in the Twentieth Century: A Consideration,' *Journal of Genocide Research*, 4(4): 519-532.

Boal, Iain; Clark, T. J.; Matthews, Joseph and Watts, Michael (2005). *Afflicted Powers: Capital and Spectacle in a New Age of War*. London: Verso.

Carlton-Ford, Steve; Hamill, Ann and Houston, Paula (2000). 'War and Children's Mortality,' *Childhood*, 7: 401-419.

Creveld, Martin Van (2008). *The Changing Face of War: Combat from the Marne to Iraq*. New York: Ballantine Books.

Epkenhans, Michael (2003). 'Military-Industrial Relations in Imperial Germany, 1870-1914,' *War in History*, 10: 1-26.

Gat, Azar (2008). *War in Human Civilization*. Oxford: Oxford University Press.

Gilligan, James (1996). *Violence: Reflections on a National Epidemic*. New York: Vintage Books.

Hedges, Chris (2002). *War is a Force That Gives Us Meaning*. New York: Anchor Books.

Horne, John (2002). 'Civilian Populations and Wartime Violence: Towards an Historical Analysis.,' *International Social Science Journal*, 54: 483-484.

Hossein-Zadeh, Ismael (2006). *The Political Economy of U.S. Militarism*. New York: Palgrave Macmillan.

Inwood, Joshua (2009). 'Searching for the Promised Land: Examining Dr Martin Luther King's Concept of the Beloved Community,' *Antipode*, 41: 487-508.

Johnson, Hubert C. (1994). *Breakthrough! Tactics, Technology, and the Search for Victory on the Western Front in World War I* . Novato: Presidio.

Kellner, Douglas (2008). *Guys and Guns Amok: Domestic Terrorism and School Shootings from the Oklahoma City Bombing to the Virginia Tech Massacre*. Boulder: Paradigm Publishers.

King Jr., Martin Luther (1986a). 'A Time to Break the Silence,' in Washington, J., Ed., *A Testament of Hope: The Essential Writings and Speeches of Martin Luther King Jr*. San Francisco: Harpers Collins.

King Jr., Martin Luther (1986b). 'A Testament of Hope,' in Washington, J., Ed., *A Testament of Hope: The Essential Writings and Speeches of Martin Luther King Jr*. San Francisco: Harpers Collins.

Kurlansky, Mark (2006). *Nonviolence: Twenty-Five Lessons from the History of a Dangerous Idea*. New York: Modern Library.

Opotow, Susan (1990). 'Moral exclusion and injustice: an introduction,' *Journal of Social Issues*, 46(1): 1-20.

Opotow, Susan (2001). 'Reconciliation in Times of Impunity: Challenges for Social Justice,' *Social Justice Research*, 14: 149-170.

Paige, Glenn D. (2002). *Nonkilling Global Political Science*. Honolulu: Center for Global Nonviolence. Available online at: <http://www.nonkilling.org>.

Pilisuk, Marc, with Rountree, Jennifer Achord (2008). *Who Benefits from Global Violence and War: Uncovering a Destructive System*. Westport: Praeger Security International.

Slim, Hugo (2008). *Killing Civilians: Methods, Madness, and Morality in War*. New York: Columbia University Press.

Tanaka, Yuki (2009). 'Introduction,' in Tanaka, Yuki and Young, Marilyn B., Eds., *Bombing Civilians: A Twentieth-Century History*. New York: The New Press, pp. 1-7.

Tanaka, Yuki and Young, Marilyn B., eds. (2009). *Bombing Civilians: A Twentieth-Century History*. New York: The New Press.

Tyner, James A. (2009). *War, Violence, and Population: Making the Body Count*. New York: Guilford Press.

Tyner, James A. (2010). *Military Legacies: A World Made by War*. New York: Routledge.

Tyner, James A. (2011). *Space, Place, and Violence*. New York: Routledge.

Vagts, Alfred (1959). *A History of Militarism: Civilian and Military*. New York: Meridian.

3

Preconditional, Didactic and Predictive Histories: An Introduction to Nonkilling History

Antony Adolf
Author of *Peace: A World History*

Introduction: Rhinoceros for Breakfast and the Survival of Humanity

History is, as a rule, about the when and where of what was done by whom and even, sometimes, about the why. Overwhelmingly, focus is on the done. We know from material, documentary and firsthand evidence engrained by force of repetition, for example, that across Europe millions of Jews and others considered degenerate by Nazis were killed by them during World War II. As a result of this rule applied as the perennially predominant historical theory and practice, what was (and is) *not* done tends stalwartly to be considered at best historically uninteresting and at worst not history at all. To stress the point: no one cares why or how they did not eat rhinoceros for breakfast. But, we believe, they surely would if it explained why they are alive today and predict whether they may be tomorrow (sic). It is as usual the exception that proves the rule and, in the case of history, makes it possible both as a lived experience as well as a field of study, debate and always already impending influence on the present and future.

There is little if anything in history that more pertinently puts the practice of this valid rule—and especially its as-valid exception—into theory or vice versa than particular histories of nonkilling within ever-wider histories of nonviolence, peace and, ultimately, humanity and life on earth. Here, our concern with the particular is both informed by and informs the wider. In one sense, the historicization of nonkilling explains behavioral, psychological, social and other conventions or status quos that have *de facto* sustained our survival as a species literally from before time immemorial up to and including the moment you are reading this, despite constant blinding focus on their temporary lapses, such as violence, conflicts and wars. In a second sense, the histories of nonkilling are the interpreted records of attempts and successes at preventing or overcoming acts and systems of killing, which if they had failed completely you would not be reading this. Paradoxically, then, historicizing what did not happen (but makes the past, present and future possible) is at once radically revisionist in reversing the most elemental hierarchy of traditional historiography and dogmatically orthodox in reaffirming what was/not done, when, by whom, how and perhaps even why, as in traditional historiography.

We seek neither to reconcile nor to argue exclusively for one or the other of these two approaches by which arguably the most important events that never happened actually did not, can become intelligible and useful. Nor do we present a 'third way' of any kind because, strictly speaking, there cannot be: what is not part of the historical record is determined by the historical record rather than the other way around, in the same way that what is not known is determined by what is known. Instead, the case is made that only by taking these two approaches separately and together can any viable, pragmatic accounts of nonkilling specifically and nonviolence generally be given with the purpose of perpetuating the principles and learning from the practices thereby gained, debated and applied. The history, nonhistories to be precise, with which we are engaged are scientific in that they involve what is concurrently visible and invisible and equally legitimate, like the proverbial Newtonian apple, which in falling revealed the force of gravity. You can see apples falling, you cannot see gravity: it must be deduced or induced. Technically, gravity did not actually happen as the falling apple actually did, but the negative actuality of gravity explains why and how the apple positively fell on Newton's head in the late seventeenth century (or so his story goes), and can predict how other objects will fall in the present and future. The key difference between gravity and historicizing what did not happen are the vastly greater influence and concomitantly added complexity of continually evolving sets of conditions and participants involved in the latter, as in reflexive relativity not relativism (contrasted below).

A clear and unequivocal distinction must also be made between the facts of what actually did not happen and the fictions of what could, would or should have happened. It is feasible, if easier said than done, to account for rhinoceros not being eaten for breakfast; it is not for neon rhinoceros. This distinction, its methodological implications, its import to better understanding related (non)phenomena and (non) histories in ethical to socio-economic to political realms and beyond, their practical uses in policy formation, identity construction, conflict resolution, peacebuilding, the course of cultures and so on are at the heart of our project. *Deductive historicization* of what did not happen begins within the context of a theory, posits a hypothesis, collects data by observation and analyzes it, finally confirming or invalidating the hypothesis or theory. *Inductive historicization* of what did not happen is not the reverse. Beginning with observation, data and its analysis leads not to a hypothesis, but to the identification of patterns in the observed that then may form a hypothesis or theory that can inform inquiries into what did not happen in other ways. Deduction seeks specificity, induction generality, and so only the two together can provide a full view of what has not happened, the unification of which is a challenge unto itself. If you were to stack up all that has happened in one pile, and all that has not in another, the latter would immeasurably outproportion the former. Likewise, to account for every instance of nonkilling would be counterproductive if not nonsensical, and so foci of historical attention with the most contextually-relevant didactic and/or predictive potential must be determined. Thus it is our purpose here to show how to historicize what did not happen indicatively more than definitively.

Deductive Historicization

Positing nonkilling as a field of historiography is itself based in a theory and hypotheses that must be validated deductively before proceeding; doing so in tandem indicates how other related theories or hypotheses can similarly be validated. Namely, that the *concept of nonkilling* is: (a) sufficient to account for and/or explain at least a discrete set of historical phenomena, the theory; (b) of sufficient import to justify the allocation of resources and efforts to historicize it, hypothesis one, covered in the next section on inductive historicization; and (c) is didactical and/or has predictive powers, hypothesis two, covered in the conclusion below. Glenn D. Paige's foundational conceptualization of nonkilling is our starting point: the absence of killing, threats to kill, and conditions conducive to killing in human society (2009 [2002]). Our end-point must be how, if valid, the historiographical theory of nonkilling, and the hypotheses and observations upon which it rests, fits within those of nonviolence, peace and humanity more widely. However, to get to the deductive historicization of nonkilling, the spectacular extent to which historiographical theory and practice is currently and always has been paramountly preoccupied with killing, violence, conflict and war must be acknowledged, confronted and overcome, which can only be done cursorily here (see Adolf, 2009).

To witness the predominance of violence, conflict and war over nonkilling, nonviolence and peace in historiography first-hand, simply walk into any bookstore or library and ask for their military history section, or sections. Upon receiving your directions and following them, you will encounter stack upon stack and row upon row of erudite studies and their popularizations with focuses on aspects of war you did not even know existed, and you wish never had, even if the military is your chosen profession. Problematically, under the Dewey classification system used by many libraries, many of the various 'War' sections fall under 'Public Administration.' All the periods in warfare, all the types of warfare, all the strategies of warfare, all the instruments of warfare, all the causes and consequences of warfare, all the changes in warfare, all the conditions of and participants in warfare, all the approaches to studying warfare historically may stun you no matter what your predispositions toward warfare are and, by seeing all this at once, become. Then, you try to look for sections on nonkilling, nonviolence and peace history, only to realize that there is comparatively little to be stunned by, even if you know peace studies as a discipline is well-established (see Katz and López, 1989; Wallerstein, 1988). You may wonder who is to blame: scholars or writers, publishers or book-buyers, readers or funders. Does this situation say more about historians, their vehicles and audiences or about human history itself?

The answer to this question is decidedly that historians, their vehicles and audiences must be held accountable for not accounting for the better part of human history, qualitatively and quantitatively. This answer forms the deductive bedrock of the theory of nonkilling upon which its historicization is to be based for now. The widely held contention that the principal collective actors in history (groups of people, nation-states, etc.) have conceived of war as an end in itself is predicated on the fact that in being able to carry out wars against their enemies they were not busy killing themselves, each other or their allies (see Bobbitt, 2002). That they did not do so on bases of kin, clan, country or culture is of prime import. They all had to be alive in order to kill so many people, but historians are consistently more concerned with the latter acts than former states, and so put their carriage before their horse. Violence, conflicts and wars are for historians and readers generally like shiny things are for children: easy to focus upon and so attention-grabbing. As a historical fact nonkilling is, paradoxically, what makes them possible (though as an ethical principle against them) and what limits them in success or failure insofar as being and remaining alive is a precondition for each. Even the glorification of war is a testament to its abnormality. In this light, the intimate relationship between historians and war from ancient times up to the present is, from a factual point of view, fetishistic and perverse. Historians, by centring violence, conflict and war have also, if counter to their very intentions, contributed to their enduring legitimization, popularization and perpetuation by marginalizing nonkilling, nonviolence and peace. Here, in a troublesome way, we begin to see how the concept of nonkilling is not only sufficient to account for discrete sets of historical phenomena, but to a certain degree *a priori* in order to account for any.

Productive encounters with the explanatory powers of the concept of nonkilling requires moving into the realms of observation, data accumulation and analysis to be firmly grasped, links illustrated in the graph that follows. Two 'zones' Paige identifies as key to transformation in the present and future also, in retrospect, provide foci for finding, documenting and analysing nonkilling as a negative actuality in the past, with present and future import (the other three are discussed in different context below). The diverse and specific spatiotemporal locations in which predispositions toward killing are or are not instilled in individuals and/or groups Paige calls *cultural conditioning zones*. Within these zones, distinctions between and convergences of the two senses of the historicization of nonkilling put forth above become immediately evident. For example, nonkilling as a convention or status quo among the Semai and Tasaday tribes is well-documented, and begins with implicit enculturation mechanisms as children's games. In a more explicit but still within the same sense, nonkilling in Euro-American culture is enshrined in Hippocratic Oaths doctors take to do no harm, even as help (among other codes of conduct). The concept of nonkilling transcends these two very different cultural conditioning zones, but its manifestations and modes, participants and conditions are immanently within them.

Likewise in the second sense, nonkilling as attempts at preventing or overcoming acts and systems of killing have come down to us and exist in several domains, notably though not exclusively as religious injunctions and legal systems. Paige's *structural reinforcement zone* of institutions and material means brings out this sense. The degrees to which, for example, the Judaic and Christian divine Commandment not to kill has or has not been followed by adherents; the justifications put forth to break it (the 'just war' tradition) or uphold it (Church proscriptions on killing under the Pax and Truga Dei of the Middle Ages); the Buddhist Eightfold Path, at the centre of which is nonviolence toward all living creatures; the actual laws of different national traditions which prohibit and punish killing of different (but usually not all) kinds; the human and other resources allocated to enforce or uphold these laws, from police to peacekeepers; all these are insightful and practical foci of observation, data accumulation and analysis that can confirm or validate more specific historical hypothesis about nonkilling. Remember, however, that religions and laws do not (not) kill people, people do not (not) kill people. As mentioned here, they and the examples of the first sense above, taken together, double as the observational basis confirming the validity of the concept of nonkilling as a field of historiography. As the graph below shows, historiography—and particularly the deductive historicization of what did not happen—is a rude awakening to those who still hold that theory is of no consequence.

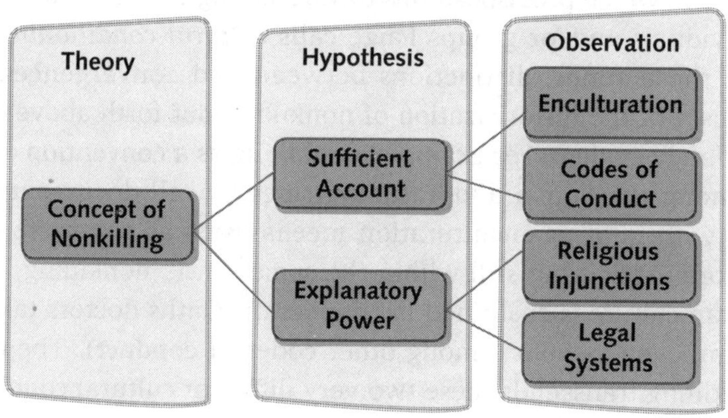

Figure 1. Deductive Historicization Visualized

Inductive Historicization

I did not kill anyone yesterday or today, did you?... No, did he?... No, did she?... No, did we?... No, did they? Why? Do you think I, you, he, she, we or they will tomorrow? Why?

The preceding elementary questions are but partially apt for nonkilling history fieldwork and more so for opening up discussions about how to conduct inductive historicization. From a historical standpoint, if we understand nonkilling as a 'not done' that is 'not done on purpose', what we lose of it as a normative status quo we gain as an individuated intention, as something special but not abnormal. When we do this, historicizing nonkilling turns into the psychology of nonviolence because the orientation of individual intent tends toward an obscurity from the point of view of an observer equipped with lenses and analytical tools meant for other tasks. The elusive historical question, *why*, proposed as an area of inquiry above can, should and must be asked, but its answers insofar as historicizing nonkilling is concerned are to be limited to the extra-individual: social, collective, material, systemic, structural, etc. It makes no sense to ask someone why they did not eat rhinoceros for breakfast when the asker knows the answer would be a product of imagination rather than memory, closely related as they are. However, knowing that rhinoceros was not eaten for breakfast opens up questions which the individual who did not, cannot answer but the historian can, a heuristic scenario that opens up to inductive historicization as a second, separate and equally insightful and practical as deductive historicization.

Just as deductive historicization requires acknowledging, confronting and overcoming historiographers' preoccupation with killing, violence, conflict and war, so the inductive requires overcoming among the most charged epithets that can be hurled at it, as at other humanistic disciplines, today: *relativism*. The basic tenet of cultural relativism is that social and collective norms (behavioral, truth regimes, power legitimization, beauty constitution, group formation) are determined exclusively within a given culture, heterogeneous as all are to some degree; are only valid within that culture; and so the norms of other cultures are irrelevant in ascribing value to them from the outside even if that is the only vantage point observers have. Universalism holds there are absolute norms valid in all times and places. The point here is not to debate relativism vs. universalism, but to distinguish them from the domain of historicizing what did not happen, particularly nonkilling. As we have seen, nonkilling, like nonviolence and peace, belong to a distinct category of norms that simultaneously transcend cultures and are imminently within them. The concept of *reflexive relativity*, in stark contrast with relativism and universalism, is in our particular case: nonkilling is culturally-specific (relative), inter-subjectively understood and enacted (reflexive), and historically constant (norm). Gravity on Earth and on the Moon has a different value because of astronomical factors; nonkilling in the Southern U.S. and Northern Nigeria in the 1970s likewise has different values because of historical factors. However, agency exists vis-à-vis norms like nonkilling that does not vis-à-vis gravity, no matter where you are. That is, no matter how well-established, nonkilling norms are always violable; technically, you cannot defy the law of gravity anywhere, no matter who you are. Reflexivity lies in this agency, omnipresent and circumscribed; relativity in this historicization, psychological as intent and historiographical as a wider actuality, positive or negative.

Some may counter that Paige's *neuro-biochemical capability zone*, comprising physical and neurological factors that contribute to both killing and nonkilling behaviors, reduces the psychological to a biological determinism that in the end invalidates the historiographical. It may be more precise to say, also as a first inductive step addressing the hypothetical line of questions above, that when neurology joins psychology and historiography to become biography, the lines are productively blurred. The life stories of individuals are a prime starting point for inductively historicizing nonkilling. Comparative biographical or autobiographical studies, within or across cultures and timeframes, can point both to how nonkilling as a status quo allowed agents to do or not do what they did, and can indicate how they were able to prevent killing or overcome acts and systems of killing in their own ways as defined participants in definite conditions. We know, for example, that the practitioners of certain philosophical (Stoic and Epicurean, among others) and religious schools (Zen, cenobite and eremite monks) retreated from highly violent societies or proscribed modes of intervention for their members inside in order to transform individuals and societies at once. We also know that they contingently succeeded, but the causes, consequences and means of the efforts have barely been scrutinized in relation to the import they may have as duplicable common denominator patterns of thought, behavior and otherwise.

Yet another ground for historical observation can be located through what Paige calls the *killing zone* (where people kill) and its correlates, killing-free zones (where people do not kill). In prehistoric societies the most common social structure was 'home bases,' where people lived and ate, and from where the animal killing site was always at a distance. With the introduction and sustenance of geo-semantic distinctions between 'military' and 'civilian' in Mesopotamia continuing to Roman, Medieval and modern times to today, war zones were often separated from militarily killing-free zones, civil wars and invasions here being the exception. Aerial bombing of towns and cities, atomic bombs and terrorist acts were shocking developments in warfare because they erased these long-held lines of demarcation between killing and killing-free zones. Gang warfare, police brutality and lone wolves in cities are historical forces, among many others, threatening killing-free zones considered militarily. Within twenty years of the first deployment of nuclear weapons, regional and world bodies created nuclear-free zones, and places for asylum and sanctuary exist in most cultures in some form. Nation-state neutrality, neutral-zones enforced by peacekeepers, buffer zones created to avoid war-triggering skirmishes between conflicting states, the list of nonkilling zones with distinct but comparable histories goes on. Considering the tremendous number of participants and conditions required for any item on this very topically limited list to be an actuality, historians of nonkilling, nonviolence and peace have their work cut out for them, and the beneficial roles they can play in world affairs also cut out for them.

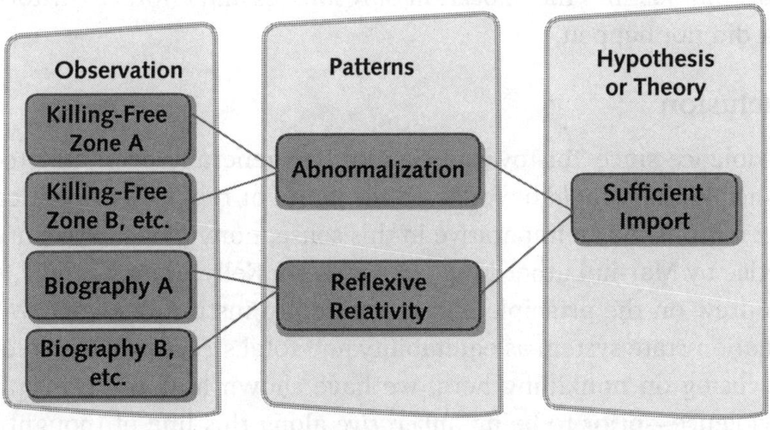

Figure 2. Inductive Historicization Visualized

Even within peace studies broadly, professional and activist documentation, critique and transformation of what is often called 'structural violence' significantly preponderates what may called 'structural nonviolence,' with nonkilling at its core. The Global Peace Index and Global Corruption Index are in this sense writing the history of the future. The point here is that there is significant tension between the two ways in which we have taken nonkilling. As a historical constant status quo, nonkilling is so obvious it has for the most part remained unseen. Deductive and inductive historicizations are ways to 'see' the history of nonkilling for their didactic and predictive enablement. The abnormalization of killing—making killing abnormality effective—can be reactive or proactive in preventing or overcoming acts and systems of killing. The tension is not represented in Figure 2, depicting the inductive historicization process we have just enacted as an example. If one becomes ubiquitous, universal status quo or universal abnormalization, the other would lose much of its import; but if history is any indication, then this tension is unlikely to be resolved any time soon, probably for the better. This is where inductive and deductive historicization combined can have their greatest impact: by providing the best possible theoretical or hypothetical lenses through which patterns based on observation can be identified. Patterns most closely or best relating to now or the future can be accurately determined, modified and applied, a process we turn to in closing, wherein lies the import that justifies the allocation of resources and efforts to historicize what did not happen.

Conclusion

Nonviolence since Tolstoy and Gandhi has generally been asserted as a principle that *should* be followed for moral or religious or political or other reasons. As an imperative in this sense, nonviolence was put into practice by Martin Luther King, Jr. and Petra Kelly, among others, who both drew on the principle and attempted to institutionalize it within the nation-state system as equitability and total structural nonviolence. In focusing on nonkilling here, we have shown how the principle of nonviolence—prior to being *imperative* along this line of thought and practice—has always been, is and is likely always to be a *precondition* of history; in other words a *necessity* for human and all life as we know it, the source of the perennial import of nonkilling to all branches of knowledge and action. Deductive and inductive historicization, then, are essential tools in experiential progressions that debunk the notion that nonkilling is impossible by accounting for participants and conditions in order to explain them and, in the end, to assert that not only is nonkilling possible, its indispensability is extendable as far and as deep as we can muster the wherewithal. Breaking with the playful rhinoceros-for-breakfast analogy, little is more serious than historicizing nonkilling, nonviolence and peace.

The purposes of proposing historical didacticism and predictive history as next steps after deductive and inductive processes are precisely to ensure that extending the indispensability (not to mention self-evident, to-be-discovered benefits) of nonkilling in particular as a synchronized stride within wider nonviolence and peace studies is expedient and effective through ongoing investigation, critical dialogue, innovation, adaptation and perpetuation. So before proceeding to the didactic and predictive, it is important to sketch where the historiography of nonkilling, and the hypotheses and observations upon which it rests, fit within those of nonviolence, peace and humanity more widely. Put simply and succinctly, nonkilling is at the core of nonviolence studies in that, by providing a fixed physiological basis (life/death), it also can provide practical, theoretical and empirical breakthroughs difficult to come by and even more difficult to apply in more ambiguous areas. The two fields of study are linked and run parallel to each other by the dichotomy supporting them, in each case the 'non' tied to the inferences of its absence, methodological, conceptual and otherwise. Continuing this linkage and parallel with peace studies requires reverting to notions of 'negative peace' as the absence of war, etc. and 'positive peace' as the presence of justice, etc., which have proven to be more limiting than enabling as historiographical concepts. The infrastructure of how peace is made, maintained and broken on the levels of individuals (within and between persons), societies (within groups) and collectives (between groups) may be more propitious for shared advances in peace, nonviolence and nonkilling historiography and studies generally, leading to a more complete, diverse, accurate, etc. overall understanding of human history and life on earth. Breaking with the heuristic gravity analogy, historicizing nonkilling, nonviolence and peace is not just an empirical science, or relativistic or universalistic, but a human and life science strictly bound by reflexive relativity.

To be effective, historical didacticism first and foremost must fend off the connotation of its term as being boring, preaching to the choir or belabouring. Here is where the historian's skill at defining profiles of their intended audiences and targeting them is vital. Students at different levels, policymakers in different areas, scholars or activists with different interests, people of different identities (age, class, ethnicity, gender, religion, etc.), professions, nationalities all stand to learn something from the history of nonkilling, nonviolence and peace. What that something is, however, and how to present it is the crux of shedding these connotations of didacticism so that its proper business through choices of subjects and methods of instruction can be carried out. With this in mind, two crucial modes of historical didacticism can be put forth. First by *analogy*, the drawing of which is always easier than the drawing of lessons from: for instance, no shortage of comparisons has been made between the US war in Iraq today and its war in Vietnam in 1960s. Futile for us to point out that had historians used the powers of historical didacticism through analogy to effectively inform a concerted effort within the US and abroad, lives may have been saved. It is in this spirit that H.G. Wells gave up fiction in order to write his *Outline of History* after the Versailles Treaty of 1919, and that history itself can be considered, in Paige's term, as a *socialization zone* where people learn (not) to kill. Of course, this is not to criticize historians for not being activist enough, but for not doing their jobs well enough. Drawing out relevant assumptions is a second crucial mode of historical didacticism, as say determining what underlay the Pax Romana, Pax Islamica, Pax Britanica and whether this can determine if or how a Pax Americana takes shape now. Historical didacticism makes possible a direly needed shift from a disingenuously amoral science aimed at professional or popular success to a self-aware and ethically responsible one, and no they are not mutually exclusive (Küng, 1991).

History can be predictive without being deterministic (say in an apocalyptic, Marxist or other teleogical sense) or hallucinogenic (say in any flavour of utopia or dystopia) if it is based on probabilities rather than creeds. All that teleological and hallucinogenic constructs achieve is privileging particular histories. This is another way historicizing nonkilling in particular, and nonviolence and peace more widely, can directly contribute to the peaceful coexistence of our planet's billions of inhabitants. As analogy and assumptions are two turnkeys for historical didacticism, *patterns* and *implications* are for predictive history. For example, advocates for global liberalism (nation-state sovereignty, free markets, individual liberties, etc.) today tend to present liberalism as a set of social and collective patterns based on the 'best' in Western traditions, universally applicable to local conditions and participants. Commonalities and innovations that inductively make up such historical patterns are of great import because they justify the reproduction of liberalism everywhere (see Thompson, 1992). Among the major shortcomings of alter-globalization movements is that their efforts to 'resist' this liberalism and implement albeit disconcerted alternatives are primarily deductive—except when they point out actual implications of liberalism (poverty, inequality). And so alter-globalization movements by and large neglect the primacy of the inductive in recognisng and implementing positive patterns, which liberalists have seized in their universalism and alter-globalists seem unable to in their relativism, even while their inductive critique of liberalism is compelling (see Houtart and Polet, 2001). The promising notion of progress on several paths at once, devoid of determinism, with individualized options and participations is itself devoid of patterns (if purposefully) because it scarcely builds on any, and so fails to offer the predictive powers the patterns of liberalism do despite their implications. The point here is to stress how patterns and implications can serve as aids to probabilistically predict the future based on interpretations of historical facts; in turn, such predictions become active, living arguments that do in the end influence the shape the future takes by influencing participants and conditions. Reflexive relativity and historical didacticism can serve as arbiters in these debates, which are worthy of never ending because the past, present and future depend on them.

What remains to be worked out, but is far beyond our mandate here, is how existing resources within what is still a zero-sum academic-economic game can be reallocated on a global scale to pragmatically address the tyrannical asymmetry of information available on nonkilling and killing respectively. For indeed they must or we risk being judged by posterity as those who missed the calling to set records straight, and so save humanity from itself for the last time. If we imagine that peace and the environmental movements started in the 1960s (which, of course, they did not even if they surely received a boost), and think of them today as competing for media attention, government and corporate support, private donations, social entrepreneur initiatives and technological developments, few if anyone would say that peace is 'winning.' Although it reinscribes the very structure it seeks to overturn, this last metaphor presents itself as a significant opportunity to figure out why environmentalism is doing so well, and peace from most points of view (though not the one held herein) could do so much better. Apparently the '60s peace symbol is, in North America, 'in' this summer as a fashion accessory or imprint on any piece of clothing you can imagine, including underwear. If the point of this essay can be summed up in one sentence, it's that while fashions change, wearing clothes does not.

References

Adolf, Antony (2009). *Peace: A World History*. Cambridge: Polity Press.

Bobbitt, Philip (2002). *The Shield of Achilles. War, Peace and the Course of History*. New York: Alfred A. Knopf.

Houtart, François and Polet, François, Eds. (2001). *The Other Davos: The Globalization of Resistance to the World Economic System*. London: Zed Books.

Katz, Neil H.; López, George A. (1989). 'Peace studies: past and future,' *The Annals of the American Academy of Political and Social Science*, 504(4): 14-22.

Küng, Hans (1991). *Global Responsibility: In Search of a New World Ethic*. London: Continuum.

Paige, Glenn D. (2009 [2002]). *Nonkilling Global Political Science*. Honolulu: Center for Global Nonkilling. Available at: <http://www.nonkilling.org>.

Thompson, Kenneth W. (1992). *Traditions and Values in Politics and Diplomacy*. Baton Rouge: Louisiana State University Press.

Wallerstein, Peter. (1988). *Peace Research: Achievements and Challenges*. Boulder: Westview Press.

4

Toward a Nonkilling Linguistics

Patricia Friedrich
Arizona State University
Francisco Gomes de Matos
Federal University of Pernambuco

More than a universally avoided violence
It's the constructing of peaceful permanence
More than preventing the evils of violence
Let's universally sustain Nonkilling sense.
(from *Nonkilling Sense*, a poem by Francisco Gomes de Matos, dedicated by the author to Glenn D. Paige)

It is the age-old question: are human beings naturally predisposed to violence and therefore bound to a perpetual and elusive quest for peace, or are we a peaceful group falling prey to the traps of aggression and hostility?

In *Nonkilling Global Political Science*, Paige (2009 [2002]) raises the question of whether or not a nonkilling society is possible and what would it take to build such a society. He explains that a nonkilling society is,

> a human community, smallest to largest, local to global, characterized by no killing of humans and no threats to kill; no weapons designed to kill humans and no justifications for using them; and no conditions of society depend upon threat or use of killing force for maintenance or change. (p. 21)

Paige acknowledges that the answer to the first part of his question is a product of one's 'personal experience, professional training, culture, and context' (p. 22). The answer to the second, in case one agrees that such a society is possible, would in our view, depend upon a collective effort in which each member of the society employs their expertise and special skills to contribute to the nonkilling paradigm. Our contribution to a nonkilling society would involve the use of languages and the social power derived from such use.

In our nonkilling linguistics we can express our desire for languages to be employed in all of their peace-making potential. It is easy enough to observe that languages can be employed as instruments of harm; one can, for example, hurt with the words he or she chooses or yet segregate and exclude those who share a different linguistic background. Thus, it seems intuitive to us that we need to tip the scale in the opposite direction by reinforcing instead those humanising uses of language which help boost respect for human dignity and social inclusion. By doing so we may in some direct and indirect ways be advancing a nonkilling mentality.

The linguistic power conveyed by the juxtaposition of the negative prefix *non* and the noun *killing* recalls another felicitous combination, namely, *nonviolence*, a Gandhian concept-term which according to Random House (1995: 891) originated in 1915, meaning 'the policy or practice of refraining from the use of violence, as in protesting oppressive authority.' That same source tells us that *violence* made its debut in written English at the beginning of the fourteenth century. How about *killing*, the reader might be wondering? The verb *kill* first appears in written form in 1175. According to the *American Heritage Dictionary* (2001: 469), *kill* can mean: To put to death; To deprive of life; To cause to cease operating. When, however, we add the prefix *non*, we positivize what would otherwise be destructive terms. Another history-making concept-term in that respect is, for example, that of *non-proliferation* as in the Nuclear Non-proliferation Treaty, signed in 1968 by the U.S.A., the then USSR, the UK and over 80 nonnuclear weapon states.

What these examples show is that language plays a significant role in the way we see and build the world because it has the power to transcend and transform. In the current state of affairs, Paige argues, 'Language reflects and reinforces lethality, contributing a sense of naturalness and inescapability' (p. 30). His examples are many; for instance, the way in which metaphors which make reference to violence, war and conflict abound in the English language. He reminds us of expressions such as 'making a killing in the stock market,' or being 'stab[bed] in the back,' or movie stars being dubbed 'bombshells.' We can add our own: Lou Dobbs's constant reference (2006, for example) to the 'war on the middle class,' the disagreements between men and women as 'the battle of the sexes,' or taking part in a discussion as engaging in a 'war of words.' There are also two ecolinguistically inappropriate—unfair!—nouns in English referring to animals: 'killer bee' (for African honeybee capable of stinging repeatedly) and 'killer whale' (large carnivore which is intelligent and relatively docile). Such labelling is biased against those species and again emblematic of our desensitizing toward the use of linguistically violent terms. English is not the only language through which we display violence-inspired metaphors. In Portuguese, for example, the combination of either 'morrer' or 'matar de vergonha' (to die or kill of embarrassment) fits this description as well (see also Arabic and Chinese for languages which extensively use linguistically violent terms). The existence, in several languages, of reference works on insulting words and expressions attests to the near-universal omnipresence of violent or *killing* communication across languages-cultures.

Because we live in a world which has, to a certain extent, been the backdrop for a rather indifferent attitude toward killing, allowing us to become also somewhat unmoved by it, linguists might be interested in mapping the lexicon of violence, an area which is in need of cross-cultural data collection. For a useful section on violence in a reference work, a starting point could be Glazier (1997: 634-38). That work features subsections on violent events, fights, attacks, violent actions, and violent persons. The listing of over 300 types of violent actions provides evidence to support the hypothesis that human beings are the most destructive creatures on Earth. However, we must also ask what listing would be made to exemplify the opposite, that is, the fact that human beings can/could be constructive creatures as well.

Other contexts of use also evidence this indifference and actually give away a certain acclamation of violence. A quick search through a movie guide (Maltin, 2008) for example revealed the popularity of such titles as *Kill Bill* (2003), *The Matador* (2005) and *A Time to Kill* (1996). An interesting challenge could be to try to find an equivalent number of titles displaying peace-fostering terms. This challenge could be a desirable practice among conscientization (to use a Freirean term) activities aimed at communicatively enhancing constructive vocabulary, humanizing uses of languages and linguistic activism.

Of course the role of language in both the maintenance of peace and unfortunately the pursuit of violence is not restricted to its more metaphorical or purely linguistic uses. Effective diplomacy through peace talks, for example, can mark the divide between practicing peace through constructive dialogue or engaging in war through armed conflict. Further pacific pursuit of agreement and understanding can be exemplified by the growingly researched phenomenon of public peace dialogue (Saunders, 1999).

At the micro-level, the use of language can signal our desire to respect and honour human dignity on the one hand, or to offend and attack one's self-esteem on the other. Recently, a friend of a senior author received a phone call from a stranger telling her that her daughter had been kidnapped. What ensued was a near-killing communicative exchange. The would-be kidnapping turned out to be a horrible prank, that is, an instance of *killing* use of Portuguese, for the mother, in this case, had to receive medical treatment to overcome the shock. Whereas this is an extreme example of both physical and psychological harm through language, human beings do indeed have the capacity to use linguistic boundaries to segregate, to deny membership, to belittle or conversely to educate, to empower, to establish contact and to elevate.

Surprisingly enough, given the ubiquitous nature of language, it took linguistics quite a long time to be more formally recognized as an important element of peace and the establishment of fairer social institutions. Luckily for us and our contemporaries, Peace Linguistics (Gomes de Matos, 1996; Crystal, 1999, 2004; Friedrich, 2007a and 2007b) now figures alongside Peace Psychology, Peace Education and other disciplines, among the contributing subjects helping in the development of interdisciplinary Peace Studies which in turn can inform those interested in the building of a nonkilling society.

However, the task ahead for linguistics scholars, teachers, language policy makers, government officials and language users themselves is not a small one. Language is so intricately connected to human experience that it can be said to permeate all aspects of our lives, from school to work, from entertainment to family relations, from conflict to diplomacy and governmental action. Yet, we often take language for granted and fail to recognize its power and reach, and we often trivialize its use. We neglect to engage in peace-fostering dialogue or we become cocooned in our own silence. We often find it hard to say 'I am sorry,' to yield to the other speaker, and to choose our words according to their potential for peace. We at times fall short of recognizing situations in which language, if used constructively, could avoid serious conflict both at the personal micro-level and at the global macro-level.

In a nonkilling society, language must play a pivotal role as a tool for peace, as it needs to be widely engaged. Language users need to be empowered, and constructive dialogue needs to replace violence. This chapter is organized around the idea that several elements related to language are central to the establishment of a nonkilling society. We will visit but a few. While these elements relate to linguistics in its more abstract form, which means that they do not refer to any one particular language and at the same time include all languages, examples of their applicability are given vis-à-vis existing languages and the dynamics of power that unite and unfortunately also divide them. While many of our examples come from English, we do not in any way mean to imply that the use of English is more 'harmful' than the use of any other language. We truly believe that the power to change a language as a vehicle of peace and nonkilling power lies within the realm of the users (i.e., language as an abstract entity cannot be to blame). Therefore, the list which includes many instances of uses of English is simply an acknowledgement that we share English with the readers and thus can rely on an understanding of our examples. Whereas the list is not exhaustive, it is guided by two encompassing, fundamental principles and two general pleas as follows:

- **First fundamental principle**: 'Language is a system for communicating in nonkilling ways.'
- **Second fundamental principle**: 'Language users should have the right to learn to communicate nonkillingly for the good of humankind.'
- **First plea**: 'Let us be communicative Humanizers, treating all language users with compassion and dignity.'
- **Second plea**: 'Let us opt for communicatively nonkilling uses of language.'

Respect for Language Users and the Uses they Make of Language

Languages are not autonomous entities. They exist to serve the perceived needs of the societies who build them. They are made into tools or weapons depending upon their users. They are not intrinsically good or bad; however, they are used as vehicles of good or evil by the people who utilize them. Each user of language impacts the language in many ways by modifying, creatively applying, denying, or embracing it. Each language user is also unique because no one's experience with language and with the world is the same as anyone else's. Even considering identical twins, obviously born to the same parents in the same place and roughly at the same time, we will come to realize that the twins' experiences with language are unique; each will speak to different users, read different books, and develop unique interests which in turn will help shape language use differently. Recognition of the multiplicity of users, realms of use, cline[1] of proficiency, and educational environments of different languages and language varieties is paramount to building a nonkilling society.

1 The continuum that extends itself from not proficient at all to fully competent.

Multiple users will present different linguistic features. Pronunciation will vary, and choice of vocabulary and type of variety will also oscillate according to the situation of communication, educational background, geographical location, gender and age of participants. While we must recognize and seize such diversity, we must also learn to refrain from using it against language users. How many times has violence resulted from denied membership due to linguistic separatism? How often do negative attitudes toward users or groups of users of specific dialects end up impacting people in nonlinguistic realms of life? Fought (2002: 127) provides an example of such attitudes. In a study conducted with college students from California about attitudes toward the various regional dialects of the United States, she found out that 'the South was labelled as a separate geographic area more frequently than any other region.' In addition, 'a majority of terms associated with the South are negative.' The same stigmatization of regional dialects is true for Japanese (Gottlieb, 2008).

Scientifically speaking, no evidence exists that using a certain linguistic variety correlates with accomplishment, intelligence or skill. Yet, people are often stereotyped and pigeonholed with dialectal variation and language proficiency as criteria, and these criteria are then later wrongly reapplied to include or to exclude users. In a nonkilling society, multiple linguistic expressions exist in harmony, and people have a chance to develop their full potential regardless of the native status of their language use (i.e., whether they are native speakers or not), the regional origin of their dialect, or the functional range of their language use.

Additionally, notions about cline of proficiency and frequency of use are not employed judgmentally. Some people will use a certain language for a variety of functions (e.g., the speaker of English who uses the language in his medical practice, to talk to his kids, to write in academic journals and to chat with friends) while others will use it for only one (e.g., the airport controller in a primarily Spanish speaking country who uses English for a specialized function at his workplace). In a nonkilling society, all kinds of users have a right to use such languages, and for those languages to be recognized and revered. They feel they are valuable members of their linguistic communities, and other members of such societies are grateful that because of those people's linguistic skills others have access to, for example, a medical diagnosis or the safe landing of their plane.

Thus, in a nonkilling society, beside the respect for dialectal variation, the questionable deficit approach to language use (i.e., the view which focuses of language users' shortcomings) is replaced with support for the further development of their skills and appreciation for the skills they already possess.

Respect for a Healthy Ecosystem of Languages

Recently, *The Economist* (October 23, 2008) published an article on endangered languages. The renowned publication reflected on the fate of thousands of languages which may disappear by the end of the twenty-first century, languages such as Hua, spoken in Botswana, and Manchu, from China. The most optimistic estimates foreshadow that about 50 per cent of the almost 7,000 languages of the world are endangered (Wurm, 2001; Gordon, 2005; Austin and Simpson, 2008); the most pessimistic bring the number of those endangered up to 90 per cent (Krauss, 1992).

Disagreements aside, most specialists concur that the rate at which languages are disappearing is unprecedented, and part of our inability to know what to do is intimately connected to its uniqueness—no historical antecedent tells us what needs to be done. Austin and Simpson (2008: 5) point out that besides being unparalleled, '[l]oss of linguistic diversity on this scale ... represents a massive social and cultural loss, not only to the speakers of particular languages but to humanity and science in general.' Scanlon and Singh (2006), referring to Maffi's scholarship (2001), cite colonization, the rise of the nation state, globalization, and environmental degradation as the most important phenomena contributing to the disruption of linguistic diversity and a healthy ecosystem of languages (see also Mühlhäusler, 2003).

The fact that many languages are currently endangered has to be juxtaposed with the fact that languages also do fade away more 'naturally' too and that some of the sociolinguistic phenomena accounting for such disappearance is beyond our scope of action.

Nevertheless, despite the fact that we might not be able to save all endangered languages, we do not need unnaturally to push for their demise. In a nonkilling society, the danger of languages displacing other languages is diminished because respect for language diversity also signifies that multilingualism is revered and encouraged (Phillipson, 1992). In that case, the need for languages of wider communication (which fulfil a pragmatic purpose) does not need to clash with the desire to build community and preserve local language and culture.

Notice, however, that the term 'preserve' is a tricky one; some preservation efforts are an attempt to catalogue and document the language as it was last conceived. Such efforts are to a large degree undertaken by language preservationists when there is no hope of a language surviving (e.g., when the last few speakers are of an advanced age and no young users can be found). The other complementary effort is to preserve a language's ability to continue changing, that is, to continue to be used functionally by a community. In this case, policy making, which includes sound educational policies, can be an important step to maintaining a language. Smith (2000: 174) argues '... mutual recognition of all linguistic heritage should be the goal. Without such mutual respect and tolerance, internal and international tension and hostilities may result.' While Smith is referring more specifically to languages indigenous to Europe, the researcher's reflection bears relevance to all relations among languages with regional and international status and those used only within smaller communities. It also establishes the connection between disrespect for linguistic diversity and social unrest (see also Fishman, ed., 2001).

Therefore, as individuals interested in upholding the ideals of a nonkilling society, ideals which can be extended to the nonkilling of languages, we should take measures to preserve dying languages, counteract unnatural homogenizing forces when necessary, and recognize the necessity of lingua francas (but strive to establish them alongside local languages). In a nonkilling society, languages and speakers of languages are not purposefully exterminated. There is no effort of an educational, political or armed forces nature to decimate linguistic groups and extinguish their language and culture.

Focus on Diplomacy: Negative Peace

Galtung's (1964) widely known concept of 'negative peace' refers to the absence of war, thus the word 'negative.' Attempts to uphold peace in situations where conflict has already erupted fall within the realm of negative peace. Thus, a great deal of the effort to re-establish and restore peace is undertaken by diplomacy. In a nonkilling society diplomacy also is the primary vehicle used to resolve differences because armed conflict is not an option. The use of language in diplomatic talks is paramount to sustaining a nonkilling paradigm. Gomes de Matos (2001) has created a very thorough list of principles for diplomatic communication to be carried out 'constructively.' Some highlights include:

- Avoidance of dehumanizing language
- Investment in handling differences constructively
- Emphasis on language with a potential for peace rather that language employed with a strategic agenda
- Focus on agreement rather than on polemics
- Avoidance of pompous language used to separate and hide

Gomes de Matos (2001) also speaks of the importance of upholding the ideals of diplomacy to the utmost degree and believing in the ability of diplomats and other representatives to pursue their ideals through pacific and honourable means. We would add that in a nonkilling society, efforts need to be undertaken and investments made in research and education so that we can increasingly understand which features of languages make them more apt to generating peace in diplomatic talks. As Gomes de Matos (2001) similarly points out, our efforts should not be to take advantage of language to 'win' peace talks but rather to arrive at the kind of understanding which will lead to longer lasting peace.

Focus on Building Strong Social Institutions: Positive Peace

Galtung's (1964) other form of peace, 'positive peace,' can also be framed in terms of language use. Positive peace refers to the building of strong social institutions which would help prevent war in the first place. As pointed out elsewhere (Friedrich, 2007b), language, as a uniquely human institution, can largely contribute to this effort because, if individuals see their linguistic rights respected, they will be less likely to engage in violent conflict. Amongst the necessary steps to building a strong language institution, we can highlight efforts to offer sound, peace-promoting education with a curriculum which emphasizes rights and duties, moral values and ethic, and sound linguistic skills. Complementary, a solid linguistic structure also relies on access to resources, information and opportunities by speakers of different languages and by users of various dialects. In a nonkilling society, individuals are encouraged to use their language-related skills for the development of society as a whole and for the upholding of human dignity.

Peace educators, peace psychologists, peace linguists and all those concerned with the nonkilling education of language users are urged to exercise their right to be communicatively creative for peaceful purposes and, in such spirit, to add, adapt, expand, refine, and probe the practices found most relevant to specific socio-cultural contexts. The overall goal should be to make learners aware of the open-ended practical activities aimed at enhancing one's nonkilling communicative potentialities. Group discussion of results achieved is desirable since communicating is above all an act of sharing. Examples of educational activities which could help fulfil this goal are:

Practice 1. Answering the question 'When do we kill a person linguistically?' by adding verbs or verb phrases to the list in the suggested answers.

Answer: When we antagonize, coerce, desecrate, frighten with threats of harm, intimidate violently, oppress, provoke in a violent way, exclude from our network.

Practice 2. Answering the question 'How can we humanize a person linguistically?' by adding verbs, phrases or sentences to the list of suggested answers.

Answer: When we refer to him or her in a respectful and admiring way. For instance, calling the person a peacebuilder, an expert, a connoisseur, a creative genius, a luminary, a mentor, a patriot, a prodigy, a role model, a trendsetter, a virtuoso, a visionary, a prophet.

Practice 3. By creating nonkilling sayings (adding to the challenge and the fun by using alliterations. rhymes,etc.). Examples: Wicked words wound the world/ Nonkilling words nourish nonviolence.

Practice 4. Creating constructive alliterations.

Example: Challenge yourself to add other letters:

AAA = Activate life-affirming assertions

MMM=Monitor manipulative messages (in the media)

TTT = Transform tension into tranquillity

VVV =Value a vital vocabulary

Practice 5. Creating a poem celebrating the power of nonkilling communication or celebrating the vision of a nonkilling 'planetary patriot,' such as Mahatma Gandhi or Johan Galtung.

Practice 6. Creating some entries for a dictionary of encouragement and praise, so conspicuously absent in the literature (there are Dictionaries of Insults in Portuguese) or a dictionary of (name of language) for nonkilling purposes.

Practice 7. By paraphrasing inspiring statements by Glenn Paige in his seminal book.

Practice 8. By adapting famous quotations to a nonkilling perspective. For example: Confucius' statement 'Without knowing the force of words, it is impossible to know men' could become 'Only by knowing the nonkilling power of words it is possible to humanize human beings communicatively.' Another example: 'Beauty is eternally gazing at itself in a mirror' (Kahlil Gilbron, *The Prophet*, 'On Beauty' [1923]) could become 'A nonkilling society is Humankind swimming in a Sea of Serenity.'

Practice 9. By listing more reasons for not killing, besides those mentioned by Glenn Paige.

Practice 10. By creating practical, transforming communicative alternatives. Examples: Turning an intended threat into a thought-provoking text; turning an intended intimidation into an invitation. In these two examples, the belief in loving one's linguistic neighbour is challengingly applied.

Practice 11. By composing a poem on 'Why more nonviolent people are needed.'

Practice 12. By completing a nonkilling paradigmatic set with nouns ending in –ation. Example: nonkilling is (a) moral obligation, spiritual elevation, humanizing conscientization, global salvation, life-affirming education, planetary cooperation, vital preservation, etc.

Practice 13. By engaging your students in this creatively humanizing activity of building a repertoire of actions to avoid, with the use of non+noun words in an alphabetically arranged paradigm (for a complete list, see appendix): nonaggression, nonanimosity, nonantagonism, nonattack(ing), nonbelligerance, nonbrutality, nonbombing, nonbombarding, nonconspiracy, nonconcealment.

When will educational systems include the systematic learning of nonkilling language in their language programmes? How can *peace* educators, psychologists, linguists and other peacebuilding humanizers get together and help design *nonkilling language* programmes for use in schools at all levels? Herein lies a formidable universal educational challenge. Besides learning to systematize one's nonkilling vocabulary, every planetary citizen could be educated in a Critical Nonkilling Linguistics framework, or in other words, learning to question *killing* uses of language(s). In such spirit, human beings would learn not to *kill* their 'linguistic neighbours' communicatively, by avoiding linguistically violent actions.

If we take the above considerations about education seriously, it becomes clear that a curriculum of nonviolence and peace should be the next step to fostering a nonkilling mentality. Such a curriculum should include teachings about communicative aspects of peace, linguistic ecology, peace linguistic terms and language appropriate for peace-fostering action. Crystal (2004) writes about the importance of fostering a curriculum of peace from the early grades. Alongside teachings about ecology, he explains, young students can receive education on linguistic ecology, linguistic rights and other language-related topics.

Other scholars have addressed the importance of the classroom as a site for all facets of peace education. Gomes de Matos (2002), reviewed by Rector (2003), explains aspects of his 'humanizing pedagogy' which integrates Dell Hymes's concept of *communicative competence* (1966) expanded to include *communicative peace*. He urges the reader to promote language uses which reflect a preoccupation with the linguistic rights of others as well as respect for the participants in communicative acts regardless of their status or of the communication site.

In Friedrich (2007a and 2007b), an argument is found for the importance of linguistic peace education in promoting encompassing peace and for the appreciation of the classroom as a prime environment for education about peace (Peace Education), education about linguistic forms which enhance peaceful communication (Peace Linguistics) and education about all things sociolinguistic which impact the ways in which we communicate (Peace Sociolinguistics).

In a nonkilling society, classroom education, as well as life-long education in all of these language-related aspects of peace, is taken very seriously and given a position of relevance and influence alongside other disciplines.

Respect for Individual Linguistic Choices

The matter of linguistic choices has largely become a political one. Whether one chooses to remain monolingual, embrace bilingualism or multilingualism, or primarily use a language other than one's native tongue has social implications. Furthermore, these choices are usually framed by critics in terms of group membership rather than individual decisions. The widely debated phenomenon of linguistic imperialism (Phillipson, 1992) is an example of how choices are made into political entities. Phillipson argues that the global use of English is a result of linguistic imperialism and that people in the 'periphery' (countries where English is acquired as second or foreign language) are victims of the imperialistic moves by countries such as the US. However, what theories of imperialism fail to recognize (among the many other elements brought forth by nonsupporters of this view) is that whether or not to use English or another language, is ultimately a matter of personal choice and that individuals in the so-called periphery make these choices consciously based on weighing the benefits and drawbacks of using a given language[2] (regardless of the original intentions of leaders in the alleged imperialistic countries).

In a nonkilling society, these choices are easier to make because language use is not seen as part of an 'either/or' paradigm in which languages are disseminated (rather than spread) for purposes of domination. Since human beings have an infinite capacity for language acquisition, if we could remove the fear that language could be used as a weapon of domination and subjugation, then individuals would be free to make these choices based on functional needs and personal interests. In that kind of society, we would also be able to abandon all metaphorical references to killing vis-à-vis languages of wider communication, e.g., 'killer languages,' as used by Skutnabb-Kangas (2000) to refer to English and other dominant languages, and we would focus on a language's capacity to bring people together instead while maintaining diversity and a healthy ecosystem of languages.

Respect for Language Change

Languages go through a natural process of birth, change and death. Many times the 'death' of a language actually means that it changed so much that it gave birth to new varieties which in time became so independent (and ultimately partially or totally unintelligible) that these varieties originate new languages.

Geopolitical phenomena also contribute to such a development because these new languages, by virtue of being embedded in different societies with different state-ruling and outside influences, continue the process of differentiation and modification. That was the case, for example, of Latin and such languages as Portuguese, Spanish, French, Italian and Romanian. Because of its spread and then concentration in different regions, different outside influences, and even different climates, what was once one (Latin) became many (Romance languages). So languages also die because their functional uses have

2 It is our belief that in former colonial contexts, the languages first introduced through imperial power have come to change so as to express the culture, values and linguistic choices of their users and have therefore defied the colonial structures that first brought them there. (See also Mufwene, 2001).

ceased, no new native speakers exist and, as a consequence, linguistic change within that language becomes stagnated.

Language change will occur whether we like it or not. In a nonkilling society, however, the process of language death is not accelerated unnaturally because linguistic decisions are forced upon language users; nor is language change arbitrarily stopped in the name of language purism. In a nonkilling society, there is no policy impeding users to employ a given language and no violent and unnatural attempts to impact the ecosystem of languages. Legislation exists to protect individual linguistic choice but not to forbid it (see also the section on North Korea in Kaplan and R. B. Baldauf, eds., 2003 and the work of Baldauf Jr. and Kaplan, 2003).

On the other hand, in a nonkilling society individuals are not punished for engaging in linguistic change processes. Change is not seen as corruption, impurity, or error. It is seen as a natural process of linguistic evolution, one which is brought about by social transformation and/or one which aims at transforming society as well.

Respect for Language Teachers, Language Learners, and Users with Special Language Needs

Language learning environments are not immune to some of the problems which plague other spheres of our society. In fact, in many cultures, learning settings suffer from a lack of resources and conditions because education has yet to be recognized in real and concrete terms as an important part of the foundation of any society which values human development. As a result, too often we see teachers working from a position of scarcity, with fewer resources than minimally necessary to perform their duties adequately. In other places, while the infrastructure is adequate, educational decisions are made capriciously or in the name of political interests.

In a nonkilling society educators are given a prominent social role because members of such a society recognize that violence is to a great degree a result of ignorance. Once we empower (the term is used in the *Freirean* sense) individuals to the point that they feel the safety of being in control of their own future (and education can do just that), they can feel less inclined to resort to violence.

In a nonkilling society, we empower language teachers, and in fact all teachers by offering them a safe, clean and appropriate environment in which to work. We compensate them with fair wages for the important service they provide, and we encourage them to make pedagogical decisions based on sound knowledge and experience, not on their political impact.

By supporting the work of teachers, we directly affect the lives of students and consequently the whole social structure in which they are embedded. The classroom has been shown to be a perfect site for peace education, peace linguistics education, and for discussing ecological concerns vis-à-vis languages with the students (Crystal, 2004). Any society which places education anywhere but in a prominent position is bound to be faced with ignorance which in turn breeds violence, disrespect for human dignity and a relentless sense of underdevelopment. On the other hand, any society which values education and places it amongst the strategic elements greatly contributing to social justice and dialogue (also as understood by Freire), is on its way to greater social inclusion and ultimately nonkilling potential.

People with language-related disabilities (e.g., hearing and speech impairment and impediment, paralysis impacting speech production, aphasia) also have a right to education and communication in a dignified manner. We have the opportunity to provide them with tools, adaptive technology and other forms of support to allow them to express themselves, to claim their rights, and to contribute to their communities. In a nonkilling society the rights of all language users, including those with language-related disabilities are not only acknowledged but also, and more importantly, observed.

Upholding of a Vocabulary of Peace rather than One of War

Because language changes both to *reflect* social transformation and to *affect* such transformation (e.g., we created the word 'computer' because society had changed and needed it, but we employ politically correct terms because we want to change society), revising our metaphors to express a preoccupation with peace is a necessary step to becoming nonkilling. In that paradigm, as mentioned elsewhere in this chapter, terms such as 'killer languages' (Skutnabb-Kangas, 2000: 46), which is attributed to Singaporean linguist Anne Pakir, are replaced with peace fostering ones. We stop the 'fight' for human rights and start the educational process toward upholding such rights. We do not scare social groups into action by denouncing the 'war on the middle class' but instead establish a dialogue in which different constituencies in society can pursue social justice.

Within that paradigm we also avoid resorting to 'scare tactics' or appeals to fear to sell products or change one's mind. Everywhere, from political campaigns to television commercials, we emphasize the positive rather than the negative. Fear tactics only make us perceive reality as one of danger rather than harmony, and fear only fuels violence. On the other hand, wise linguistic choices can help change our perception and act more sensibly toward one another.

Forging of New 'Humanizers'

Although linguists kept refining their enumeration of aspects of language, one trait was conspicuously absent: the humanizing nature of language use. Thus, in Gomes de Matos (1994) a plea was made for such a conceptual gap to be filled, since by merely stating that language is human we do not do justice to its humanizing power. Humanizing has to do with both acknowledging language as a system shared by human beings as well as investing in making language humane. Realistically, such characterization of language would be worded so as to cover both its humanizing and dehumanizing power, after all, linguists such as Bolinger (1980) and Crystal and Crystal (2000) have already expressed that language unfortunately can be employed as a weapon (Gomes de Matos, 2006: 159).

Humanizers are persons imbued with the ideals of human rights, justice, and peace and who apply such values in everyday interaction. In such a spirit, language users, depending on their humanizing or dehumanizing uses of languages, can be described as Humanizers or Dehumanizers, and of course we need many of the former. While language is a mental marvel for meaning-making used by members of one or more communities in varied sociocultural contexts for humanizing or dehumanizing purposes, the latter dimension seems to have received the most interest by linguists, especially when dealing with detrimental effects of language use. Jay (1999), for example, adopts a neuro-psycho-social approach for developing a theory of speech that can be explanatory of cursing. Of interest to researchers in Nonkilling Linguistics is his section on 'Do words wound?' in which he summarizes research on harmful, psychological effects of words on listeners. It seems appropriate for us as humanizers to ask that linguists take further interest in investigating the neurological, psychological and social makings of a theory of language which explains positive uses of language such as praising, comforting, and reassuring. Additionally, we need linguists, psychologists, sociologists and language users in general to employ their time, energy and knowledge in becoming humanizers themselves.

Implications for an Applied Peace Linguistics

An awareness of or conscientization about the need for a Nonkilling Society not only helps shed light on an equally needed Nonkilling Linguistics but also provides insights on actions to be implemented which can contribute to the rise and development of an Applied Peace Linguistics. Among the implications which could be drawn, derived from an initial study of Nonkilling Linguistics as presented here, five stand out:

a) Nonkilling Linguistics prioritizes nonkilling, peaceful, humanizing uses of languages at the individual, group, community, national, and international levels.
b) Nonkilling Linguistics needs to interact with many other fields so as to help build an interdisciplinary approach to Nonkilling communication, in varied types of societies.
c) The preparation of Nonkilling linguists calls for a keen perception and thorough analysis of both constructive and destructive ways of interacting intra- and internationally, in face-to-face or online situations.
d) Nonkilling Linguistics can also be thought of as a humanizing realization of an Applied Peace Linguistics. As such, it should be able to join other interdisciplinary areas within the ever-growing macro-field of Applied Linguistics. For an overview of the latter, see Kaplan (2002).

e) A steady, universal increase in the number of killings and homicides—sometimes deplorably labelled 'justifiable'—calls for immediate nonkilling action by all individuals and organizations committed to protecting and preserving human linguistic health and life.

May we close this section with a plea for the systematic application of principles and practices of Nonkilling Linguistics all over the world. May Glenn Paige's prophetic, transformative wisdom of a Nonkilling Society also influence the work of linguists committed to helping improve the living conditions of human beings as language users at the service of universal, communicative peace.

Conclusion

Our list of elements connecting language and peace or language and nonkilling ideas could go on for a long time. It would come to include the importance of empathy and sensitivity to different rhetorical patterns in cross-cultural communication (e.g., Kaplan, 1966; Hofstede, 1980; Friedrich et al., 2006). It would also describe the need to respect and preserve linguistic artifacts, from books to original manuscripts, so often destroyed for political reasons. What all of the elements above and the many still missing from the list have in common is their central role in making human beings, in their uniqueness as producers of complex linguistic expression, feel included, valued, and reverenced (see also Lee, Mikesell, Joaquin, Mates, and Schumann, 2009). Respect for human communication and human dignity is paramount to building a nonkilling society and as such should be pursued in all aspects of our lives.

Languages per se are not dehumanizing, lethal, or killing
It is the linguistic choices made by the users that may be
The new, universal challenge school systems could be facing
Has to do with why and how nonkilling language uses should be
May all education systems their citizens prepare
As communicative beings of an unprecedented kind
By assuring them of a human right beyond compare
Learning to use languages for the good of humankind.

References

American Heritage Dictionary of the English Language (2001). Boston: Houghton Mifflin.

Austin, P. K.; Simpson, A. (2008). 'Introduction,' in Austin, Peter K.; Simpson, Andrew, eds. *Endangered Languages*. Hamburg: Helmut Buske Velarg.

Baldauf Jr., R. B.; Kaplan, R. B. (2003). 'Language Policy Decisions and Power: Who are the Actors?' Ryan, P. M.; Terborg, R., Eds. *Language: Issues of Inequality*. México, D.F.: Universidad National Autónoma de México, pp. 19-40.

Bender, L., producer; Tarantino, Q., director (2003). *Kill Bill* (vol. I) [Motion picture]. United States: Miramax Films.

Bolinger, D. (1980). *Language, the Loaded Weapon: The Use and Abuse of Language Today*. London: Longman.

Brosnan, P.; Del Rio, R.; Furst, B.; Furst, S.; St. Clair, B., producers; Shepard, R., director (2005). *The Matador* [Motion picture]. United States: Stratus Film Co.

Crystal, D. (1999). *The Penguin Dictionary of Language*. London: Penguin.

Crystal, D.; Crystal, H. (2000). *Words on Words: Quotations about Language and languages*. London: Penguin.

Crystal, D. (2004). 'Creating a World of Languages,' Introductory Speech presented at the 10TH Linguapax Congress, Barcelona, FIPLV (International Federation of Language Teacher Associations), *World News*, 61:22-35.

Dobbs, L. (2006). *War on the Middle Class: How the Government, Big Business, and Special Interest Groups are Waging War on the American Dream and How to Fight Back*. New York: Viking Adult.

Elvin, W.; Grisham, J.; Lowry, H.; Milchan, A.; Nathanson, M. G., producers; Shumacher, J., director. (1996). *A Time to Kill* [Motion picture]. United States: Regency Enterprises.

Fishman, J., ed. (2001). *Can Threatened Languages be Saved?* Clevedon: Multilingual.

Fought, C. (2002). 'California students Perceptions of, You Know, Regions and Dialelects?' in Long, Daniel; Preston, Dennis, eds. *Handbook of Perceptual Dialectology*, Volume II. Philadelphia: John Benjamins.

Freire, P. (1970). *Pedagogy of the Oppressed*. New York: Continuum.

Friedrich, P.; Mesquita, L.; Hatum, A. (2006). 'The Meaning of Difference: Cultural and Managerial Homogeneity Stereotypes of Latin America,' *Management Research*, 4(1):53-71.

Friedrich, P. (2007a). 'English for Peace: Toward a Framework of Peace Sociolinguistics,' *World Englishes*, 26(1):72-83.

Friedrich, Patricia (2007b). *Language, Negotiation and Peace: The Use of English in Conflict Resolution*. London: Continuum Books.

Galtung, J. (1964). 'A Structural Theory of Aggression,' *Journal of Peace Research*, 1(2):95-119.

Glazier, S. (1997). *Word Menu*. New York: Random House.

Gomes de Matos, F. (1976). *Linguistica aplicada ao ensino de inglês*. São Paulo: McGraw-Hill do Brasil.

Gomes de Matos, F. (1994). 'A Thesis 20 Years On: The Theory-Praxis of the Rights of Language Learners,' in Barbara, Leila; Scott, Mike, eds., *Reflections on Language Learning: In honour of Antonieta Celani*. Clevedon: Multilingual Matters.

Gomes de Matos, F. (1996). *Pedagogia da Positividade: comunicação construtiva em Português*. Recife: Editora da Universidade Federal de Pernambuco.

Gomes de Matos, F. (2001). 'Applying the Pedagogy of Positiveness to Diplomatic Communication,' in Kurbalija, Jovan; Slavik, Hannah, eds. *Language and Diplomacy*. Msida: DiploProjects.

Gomes de Matos, F. (2002). *Comunicar para o bem: rumo à paz comunicativa*. São Paulo: Editora Ave-Maria, 2002.

Gomes de Matos, F. (2005). 'Using peaceful language,' in *Encyclopedia of Life-Support Systems*. Oxford: EOLOSS Publishers.

Gomes de Matos, F. (2006). 'Language, Peace, and Conflict Resolution,' in Deutsch, Morton; Coleman, Peter T.; Marcus, Eric C., eds., *The Handbook of Conflict Resolution*. San Francisco: Jossey-Bass.

Gomes de Matos, F. (2008). 'Learning to Communicate Peacefully,' in Bajaj, Monisha, ed., *Online Encyclopedia of Peace Education*. See: <http://www.tc.edu/ centers/epe/>.

Gordon, Raymond G., Jr., ed. (2005). *Ethnologue: Languages of the World*, Fifteenth edition. Dallas: SIL International. See: <http://www.ethnologue.com/>.

Gottlieb, N. (2008). 'Japan: Language Planning and Policy in Transition,' in Kaplan, R. K.; Baldauf, Jr., R. B., eds., *Asia, Vol. 1: Japan, Nepal and Taiwan and Chinese Characters*. Bristol: Multilingual Matters, pp. 102-169.

Hofstede, G. (1980). *Culture's Consequences: International Differences in Work-Related Values*. Newbury Park: Sage.

Hymes, D. (1966). 'Two Types of Linguistic Relativity (with Examples from Amerindian Ethnography,' in Bright, William, ed., *Sociolinguistics*: The Hague: Mouton, pp. 131-156.

Jay, T. (1999). *Why We Curse: A Neuro-Psycho-Social Theory of Speech.* Philadelphia; Amsterdam: John Benjamins.

Kaplan, R. (1966). 'Cultural Thought Patterns in Intercultural Education,' *Language Learning*, 16(1):1-20.

Kaplan, R.B., ed. (2002). *The Oxford Handbook of Applied Linguistics.* New York: Oxford University Press.

Kaplan, R.R.; Baldauf, R. B., eds. (2003). *Language and Language-in-Education Planning in the Pacific Basin*. Dordrecht: Kluwer.

Krauss, M. (1992). 'The World's Languages in Crisis,' *Language*, 68(1):6-10.

Lee, N.; Mikesell, L.; Joaquin, A.D.L.; Mates, A. W.; Schumann, J. H. (2009). *The Interactional Instinct: The Evolution and Acquisition of Language.* Oxford: Oxford University Press.

Maffi, L. (2001). *On Biocultural Diversity: Linking Language, Knowledge, and the Environment.* Washington: Smithsonian Institution Press.

Maltin, L. (2008). *2009 Movie Guide*. New York: Signet.

Mufwene, S. S. (2001). *The Ecology of Language Evolution*. Cambridge: Cambridge University Press.

Mühlhäusler, P. (2003). *Language of Environment, Environment of Language: A Course in Ecolinguistics.* London: Battlebridge.

Paige, G. (2009). Nonkilling *Global Political Science*. Honolulu: Center for Global Nonkilling.

Phillipson, R. (1992). *Linguistic Imperialism*. Oxford: Oxford University Press.

Random House Webster's College Dictionary of the English Language (1995). New York: Random House.

Rector, M. (2003). 'Review of Francisco Gomes de Matos, *Comunicar para o Bem: rumo à paz comunicativa,' Hispania, Journal of the American Association of Teachers of Spanish and Portuguese*, 86(3):529-531.

Saunders, H. H. (1999). *A Public Peace Process: Sustained Dialogue to Transform Racial and Ethnic Conflicts*. New York: St. Martin's Press.

Scanlon, C.; Singh, M. (2006). 'Theorizing the Decline of Linguistic Diversity,' *International Journal of the Sociology of Language*, 182:1-24.

Skutnabb-Kangas, T. (2008 [2000]). *Linguistic Genocide in Education-or Worldwide Diversity and Human Rights?* London: Longman Orient.

Smith, Rhona K. M. (2000). 'Preserving Linguistic Heritage. A Study of Scots Gaelic,' *International Journal of Minority and Group Rights*, 7(3):173-187.

Wurm, S. (2001). *Atlas of the World's Languages in Danger of Disappearing.* Paris: UNESCO.

Appendix

Here is the full list of terms positivized by the prefix Non. We invite you to add your own contribution to the list.

Nonaggression, nonanimosity, nonantagonism, nonattack(ing), nonatrocity
Nonbelligerance, nonbrutality, nonbombing, nonbombarding
Nonconspiracy, nonconcealment
Nondestruction, nondevastation, nondiscrimination, nondomination
Nonexploitation, nonexplosion, nonextermination, nonescalation
Nonfrightening, nonfear
Nongore
Nonharassment, nonhatred, nonhumiliation
Nonintimidation, noninvasion, nonintervention
Nonjeopardy, nonjeer
Nonkilling
Nonlethality
Nonmurdering
Nonnegativity, nonnegativism
Nonoffending, nonoppression
Nonpersecution
Nonquarrelling
Nonretaliation
Nonslandering, nonslaughter
Nonterror(ism), nontorture, nonthreat(ing)
Nonusurpation
Nonviolence, nonvillainy, nonvillification, nonvengeance
Nonwar, nonwarmaking, nonwickedness
Nonxenophobia
Nonzealotry

5

An Educational Model for Teaching a Nonkilling Ethic

Todd Junkins
University of Chicago

Darcia Narvaez
University of Notre Dame

Any deed that any human has ever committed... is possible for any of us.

—Zimbardo, 2007: 211

Every day people buy products whose origin is unknown to them, such as diamonds, chocolates, or roses, products linked to murder, slavery and environmental degradation—all are types of killing. Yet few people are aware of how their choices support such horrors. Ethics requires care about and an awareness of how one's actions affect others and taking appropriate action. However, today most people behave in ways that perpetuate harmful systems. How do we make people care, be aware and prepared for moral action? Systems, situations and selves each contribute to the complexity of ethics. This chapter will address the psychological roots of ethical judgments and moral development and the role of education in forming a psychology of nonkilling in human persons and human systems.

To understand the role of education in confronting killing, it is important to first understand the psychological and ethical roots of killing and nonkilling. To any given situation, whether momentary or sustaining, individuals bring a history that includes their conditioned selves (epigenetic dispositions shaped by others during sensitive periods) and cultivated selves (habits, beliefs, values, practices). This conditioned, cultivated, and biological person responds to and engages with the world, including the larger human community, in the form of systems and the situations those systems create. Every person is psycho-ethically influenced by systems, situations, and the conditioning and capacities of the self. We analyze ethical pressures from evolutionary, neurobiological and developmental perspectives using triune ethics theory (Narvaez, 2008). Second, we turn to the role of education in developing ethical systems, situations, and the self. In particular, we focus on the Integrative Ethical Education (IEE) model, which provides a framework for promoting individual and group change through the teaching of ethical skills (Narvaez, 2008). Educators can specifically target ethical sensitivities, motivations, judgments and behaviors related to killing and nonkilling.

Psycho-Ethical Roots of Killing and Nonkilling

Research has shown there are multiple sources of human behavior. We simplify these forces into three categories into systems, situations, and selves. The self, for the purposes of this paper, is defined as our conditioned, cultivated, and biological internal systems as well as our social and effective capabilities.

Systems and Situations

Zimbardo (2007) suggests that the 'higher-order factors,' such as the organization of power, are central in determining a person's action. Generally, people function in several systems at once. For example, in the United States, people exist simultaneously in a democratic system and a capitalist system. Democracy organizes political power and the capitalist system organizes economic power. Watching the behavior of the government,, it is easy to see how they operate in overlapping ways. Systems create situations through rules and roles. For instance, people in a democracy are required to follow certain agreed-upon rules, including those laid out in the Constitution. They are also expected to play certain roles, including as citizens, voters, organizers, and monitors of the balance of power.

However, while systems are necessary for organizing and maintaining sources of power, they are not morally neutral. In fact, according to Zimbardo (2007), all systems have moral requirements of their participants. Moreover, systems often become independent of their creators, evolving in unpredicted and uncontrolled directions. When these directions turn morally questionable, systems can become corrupt, forming 'hierarchies of dominance' (Zimbardo, 2007). These corrupt systems can then create situations that overwhelm an individual's normal order of desires, thereby creating internal conflict, especially in unfamiliar circumstances. As the system breaks down the individual's moral compass, demanding a new set of desires, the individual becomes increasingly confused and conflicted about his or her morals and choices. Over time, even in a brief amount of time, the system and situation together can form a 'crucible' of effects resulting in learned helplessness or violent revolt. A system of dominance can become so singularly powerful that it creates situations where people are led to act in fearful or raging behaviors.

This is especially true of a corrupt 'total system'—an all-encompassing situation in which a person does not have access to social support systems and information networks. When people are immersed in a 'total system,' human nature is altered in ways that challenge the individual's stability, personal consistency, character and morality. A total system can bring about what looks like a 'disengaged morality,' in which situational forces overwhelm and direct a participant's choices rather than being directed by the person's skill, deliberations, or intuitions. An apparent 'disengaged morality' results from the system's ability to corrupt and manipulate human needs and desires through dehumanization, anonymity, deindividuation, participant's cynical view of the system (fair and trustworthy?), internalized oppression or self-suppression, identification with the aggressor, habituated and uninterrupted deception, rationalization, fear of rejection, and so on (Zimbardo, 2007). However, moral disengagement is only seemingly so, as people always act based on a set of ethics; it is simply the ethical frame that changes.

'Total systems' can overwhelm a person's sense of self and ethics, leading to an act of killing. This is true in abusive relationships, war and oppressive situations like Zimbardo's prison experiment. The power of a total system is evident in combat zones, which produce 'atrocity-producing situations'. (Hedges, 2011: 223). Soldiers report the high intensity of war, constantly being on alert for their own mortal safety, resulting in the instinctual action of removing sudden threats so quickly and fully that civilians can be killed in the process. For instance, the intensity of war for soldiers riding in armoured patrol trucks on constant alert for improvised explosive devices and hidden combatants is so strong that the first indication of an enemy presence can result in a wide range and indiscriminate use of firepower. Situation-specific instincts indicate to the soldiers that this is necessary, but later reflection can leave feelings of guilt, as outside the moment of intensity, the actions are harder to justify.

The Self and Multiple Moral Selves

Individual selves react to system and situational forces. Triune Ethics Theory, TET (Narvaez, 2008) addresses the moral self-in-situation. Integrating findings from neurobiology, cognitive science, and affective neuroscience, TET does not emphasize deliberative reasoning, but what underlies human reason, 'motivational orientations that are rooted in evolved unconscious emotional systems shaped by experience that predisposes one to react to and act on events in particular ways' (Narvaez, 2008). These 'emotional command systems' assist animals in adapting to ever changing and new situations. Further, TET emphasizes how early social experience shape these emotional systems.

TET details three affectively-rooted moral orientations which have emerged from human evolution. The first and oldest of the three moral orientations is the Ethic of Safety (also called the Ethic of Security), focussed on self-preservation through self-protection, personal status, and ingroup dominance. The Ethic of Engagement represents relational attunement found in face-to-face affective relationships with others, particularly through caring and social bonds. The Ethic of Imagination, coordinates the older parts of the human brain, using reasoning for the purpose of adaptation to ongoing and future complex human social relationships. Each orientation is a mindset that can shift ethical norms. This is explained in more detail below. Systems, in the form of situational forces, interact with the individual's capacities and conditioning, eliciting or 'priming' specific moral orientations in conjunction with the individual self.

The Safety Ethic is found in the R-complex or extrapyramidal action nervous system, the basal ganglia and lower limbic system. These systems, related to survival and thriving in context, therefore contain the basic emotions of fear, anger, and basic sexuality. They relate to territorialism, imitation, deception, power struggles, and following routines. Present at birth, these systems are conditioned by early experience and shared with most animals. The separation distress system is also a vital part of mammalian survival, as infants cannot live without parental protection and care. In humans, these systems may be related to conformity and submission to authority out of fear of separation. The Safety Ethic becomes the 'default' ethical system when other systems fail.

When the Safety Ethic is stimulated it generally focuses on activating what has worked in the past, so habitual routines can be initiated automatically from conditioned experience. These brain systems generate a self-focus but remain 'calm' when the environment is perceived as safe and routines can be followed. Self-protective behaviors and values of these brain systems guard both the individual and the ingroup. In individuals, when physical survival is threatened, the parasympathetic system can trigger the fight-or-flight (rage) system, leading to a 'bunker' ethic, or the sympathetic system can trigger the freeze (fear) system, leading to a 'wallflower' ethic. This ethic prioritizes strengthening ingroup boundaries and succumbing to authority, as noted in studies of terror management (Rosenblatt, Greenberg, Solomon, Pyszczynski and Lyon, 1989; Nisbett and Cohen, 1996), therefore creating an attraction to 'strongmen' and tough policies on out-group persons (Jost, Glaser, Kruglanski, and Sulloway, 2003). For instance, when group self-preservation is threatened, tribalism, rivalry, or revenge can be triggered. These phenomena, based on instinctual fear of strangers in all animals, are also known as a 'superorganism' or mob mentality. In fact, when the rage system is active, revenge actually generates a chemical reward in the subcortical regions of the brain deepening the conditioning (de Quervain, et al., 2004), suggesting that revenge can become a conditioned habitual response.

The Safety Ethic has as its virtues allegiant ingroup loyalty (not the loyalty of love), self-control (especially of soft emotion), and obedience. However, they are so powerful, that they can override the rest of the brain when activated for self-preservation (MacLean, 1990). Once activated, the Safety Ethic can dominate the process of ethical action, overlooking critical information, relationships, and feelings in the sole pursuit of reestablishing a known position of security. The safety mindset is often maintained in groups through shaming, threat, and deception techniques (Shaver and Mikulincer, 2007; Staub, 1992). When the Safety Ethic is acting as the primary or highly dominant ethic, it is prone to ruthlessness and attaining a security goal at any cost. Such single-mindedness can lead not only to decreased sensitivity towards those who perceivably interfere with security goals, but also an inability to change goals and action plans. More so than the other ethics, the Safety Ethic decreases sensitivity to others and higher moral goals (e.g., Darley and Batson, 1973). For example, the individual becomes less responsive to helping others (e.g., Mikulincer, Shaver, Gillath and Nitzberg, 2005).

The Safety Ethic, stemming from older parts of the brain, is part of lower evolution and therefore represents the most basic goals of evolution, goodness of fit and self-interest (Loye, 2002). However, the driving force of human evolution is in the 'moral sense' (Darwin, 1871/1981), whose primary roots are in the parental instincts, which underlie the Ethic of Engagement.

The Ethic of Engagement is rooted in the upper limbic system and related structures, also labelled the visceral-emotional nervous system on the hypothalamic-limbic axis. It is this part of the brain that drives mammals, emotionally speaking, toward play and care/love. Play is a drive among mammals that is dominant among youngsters as it facilitates social relations and wellbeing for life. When children don't play enough, they are susceptible to disorders like ADHD (Panksepp, 1998).

Early care shapes the integrity, function and integration of multiple systems (Narvaez and Gleason, in press). These systems are 'co-constructed' with mammalian caregivers and formed over an extended period of childhood development. Mutually-responsive care (Kochanska, 2002), creates a strong social bond and well-functioning emotion systems that guide adaptation (Schore, 1994). However, the development of the moral sense, which may be humanity's greatest achievement, may be under threat from an abandonment of evolved principles of childrearing (Narvaez, Panksepp, Schore and Gleason, in press) and perhaps social living (Narvaez, Panksepp, Schore and Gleason, in press). Ancestral parenting practices, evolved over millions of years, included natural childbirth, years of nursing on demand, nearly constant touch, prompt responses to infant needs, and multi-age play groups, all of which have significant effects on brain and body development but which have been diminishing in the USA for some time (Narvaez, Panksepp, Schore and Gleason, in press). The significance of supportive infant care to properly generate a mammalian brain's emotional circuitry has been evident since Harlow's experiments on monkeys (for a review, see Harlow, 1986). The infant's nervous system is dependent on experience guided by the caregiver as an 'external psychobiological regulator,' fostering the child's sociality and ability to communicate, relate, and connect with another mammal's inner state (Lewis, Amini and Lannon, 2000). Moreover, care affects cardiac vagal tone and neuroendocrine systems, which are critical for managing stressful situations. This includes lowering peptidergic systems responsible for defensive behaviors associated with anxiety, fear and stress, thus allowing for greater social interaction and development of bonds in times of distress.

Inadequate or poor early care can set a low threshold for activating stress response systems in social situations undermining social bonding, effects that can persist throughout the lifespan (Ochsner and Gross, 2007: 103). Again, human nervous systems require caregiver co-construction, as human babies are born with only 25 per cent of their brains complete, unlike any other animal. Thus, caregiver 'training up' of a baby's self-regulation is vital in managing stress response (which underlies the Safety Ethic) and facilitating the growth of prosocial systems (underlying the Engagement Ethic). Without limbic regulation, mammals develop fickle systems that daily activities easily overwhelm. Abused and neglected children develop disorganized systems similar to those of isolated monkeys.

> 'Because the primate brain's intricate, interlocking neural barriers to violence do not self-assemble, a limbically damaged human is deadly. If the neglect is sufficiently profound, the result is a functionally reptilian organism armed with the cunning of the neocortical brain.' (Lewis, Amini and Lannon, 2000: 218)

Care-deprived infants develop aberrant brain structures and brain-behavioral disorders which lead to greater hostility and aggression towards others (Kruesi, et al., 1992). Finally, there can be a generational degradation as low-nurturing families or groups form individuals with higher risk of providing lowered nurturing care to their offspring compounding the possibility of deteriorating bonding and brain integrity over generations (Weaver, Szyf and Meaney, 2002).

Proper care then is required for normal formation of the brain circuitry responsible for sociality and accompanying moral functioning. Evolution prepares the brain for social engagement and moral agency, similar to the way evolution prepares the brain for learning language. But in both cases particular early experience appears to be required to foster capabilities (Narvaez and Gleason, in press).

The Imagination ethic, residing primarily in the prefrontal cortex and related structures represents the third strata of human brain evolution (MacLean, 1990). The prefrontal cortex (PFC) is vital to creativity, flexible thinking, and perspective taking. The PFC is the only part of the brain capable of interpreting or integrating internal stimuli or information with external stimuli or information (Goldberg, 2002). This area of the brain reaches its greatest size in humans. Key areas in the PFC that relate to moral behavior include the orbitofrontal cortex (OFC) and the anterior cingulate cortex (ACC). Found only in apes and humans and formed after birth, converging evidence suggests that the ACC is also critical to life-long emotion regulation, empathy and problem solving, and is equally reliant on caregiving for optimal development (Allman, Hakeem, Erwin, Ninchinsky and Hof, 2001).

Like the brain areas related to the Engagement Ethic, the development of brain areas related to the Ethic of Imagination requires a nurturing environment or else they may never be wired properly or established very strongly. The prefrontal cortex and its specialized units take decades to fully mature and are subject to damage from environmental factors both early (Anderson, Bechara, Damasio, Tranel and Damasio, 1999; Kodituwakku, Kalberg and May, 1999) and late in development (Newman, Holden and Delville, 2005). Schore (2003a; 2003b) marshals a great deal of evidence to show how the development of the orbitofrontal cortex (OFC) not only is vital to lifelong emotion regulation but is highly dependent on early co-regulation by the caregiver in the first months of life. For most people, an active Engagement Ethic may require a stable, caring, and safe context where the individual experiences a sense of belonging. This is exemplified in research showing children in caring classrooms tend to be more prosocial (Solomon, Watson and Battistich, 2002).

Early life stressful experiences may permanently damage the OFC, predisposing the person to psychiatric diseases such as depression or anxiety and suboptimal social and emotional functioning throughout life (Schore, 2003a, 2003b). Even with nurturing care early in life, the prefrontal cortex is susceptible to damage in adolescence and early adulthood, as it is not fully developed until the third decade (Giedd, Blumenthal, Jeffries, et al., 1999; Luna, Thulborn, Munoz, Merriam, Garver and Minshew, 2001). For example, the prefrontal cortex may be damaged by behavior choices, such as binge drinking (Bechara, 2005), or extensive violent videogame play which suppress activation of the prefrontal cortex even during normal problem solving, turning normal brains into ones that look like those of aggressive delinquents (Mathews, Kronenberger, Wang, Lurito, Lowe and Dunn, 2005). Orbitofrontal cortex damage leads to poor impulse control, dysregulation of emotion, and an inability to foresee consequences. Patients with OFC damage behave like immature adolescents, and, in severe cases, are plainly antisocial. They are unable to control impulses because their volitional control is damaged (Goldberg, 2002). As the association cortex for social behavior, the PFC generally appears to contain 'the taxonomy of all the sanctioned moral actions and behaviors' and its damage may lead to 'moral agnosia' (Goldberg, 2002).

TET suggests that ideal moral functioning resides in the coordination of both the conscious and unconscious mind. The Ethic of Imagination coordinates, then, the intuitions and instincts of the Engagement Ethic and Safety Ethic which operate on conditioned and implicitly extracted moral principles. The Imagination Ethic assesses the 'multiple elements' that are involved in moral decision-making in a particular situation, elements such as situational pressures, contextual cues, social influence, goals and preferences, mood, energy, environmental affordances, logical coherence, self-image, and prior history (Narvaez, 2008). Best keeping the self-preservation systems calm, the Imagination Ethic utilizes perspective taking, foresight, and reasoned argument to reflect abstractly and deliberately about moral options. The capacity to deliberative develops slowly over time with maturation (the PFC is not completely developed until the third decade) but also with experience and training. Some aspects of deliberation that are well rehearsed become automatic and unconscious, as with any expertise. With intellectual knowledge and deliberative skills, a person can reflect on the virtuousness of an action (Arpaly, 2003) and even deliberate about which environments to select to form their instincts (Hogarth, 2001).

Immature brain development, damage to systems from physical or drug abuse, or a habituated self-protection focus affects moral behavior. Keeping intact and nurturing the executive functions vital for the Imagination Ethic and the emotional regulation systems vital for the Engagement Ethic are critical for keeping under control the source of impulsive killing, the Safety Ethic. But cultural narratives and conditioned cultural response can also foster killing, which is the way that the Imagination Ethic can become vicious and foster planful killing, as in Nazi Germany.

The Relationship between Systems and the Self

The relationship between systems and the self is mutually influential. That is, systems and the situations they create act as ethical 'primes' for personal action. A situation's forces can activate one of the three ethical orientations, which are dependent on the interface between the person and the situation (Lapsley and Narvaez, 2004). When a situation activates an ethic, the person-by-context interaction influences perceived affordances (social, physical and action possibilities), perceptual sensitivities (Neisser, 1976), behavioral outcome expectancies and preferred goals (Mischel, 1973: 270), affective expectancies (Wilson, Lisle, Kraft and Wetzel, 1989), and rhetorical susceptibilities (attractive fallacies). For example, when the Safety Ethic is operating one notices the aspects of an environment that enhances self and in-group. Terror management studies that prime for the safety or Engagement Ethic manipulate whether the participant shows compassion or not (e.g., Mikulincer, Shaver, Gillath and Nitzberg, 2005). However, it is important to remember the 'person by context' interaction (Cervone, 1999). Not all individuals are affected by primes for self-concern. For example, although a situation may provide aggression cues which can encourage hostile thoughts, a person with a disposition high in agreeableness may respond instead with prosocial thoughts and actions (Meier, Robinson and Wilkowski, 2006). That is, a person with a strong Engagement Ethic can guide calm the Safety Ethic's concerns and move toward more prosocial and caring action (Narvaez, 2008). Moral exemplars are able to keep the Safety Ethic calm when in a distressing situation affording the possibility of considering a wider array of possible actions (e.g., Frankl, 1963). Again, systems create these charged situations.

However, the self can also privilege one of the three ethical systems based on conditioning (for example, 'be afraid of black people') or self-cultivation (for example, reading right-wing diatribes). In this case, one of the three ethics may become a dispositional orientation, a primary or base position in the self. This is evident among subjects in Milgram's experiment of obedience to authority. Those with more sophisticated moral reasoning often quit the experiment (Milgram, 1977). Cultivated, conditioned, and biological/genetic factors all affect the self's disposition. Some of these factors can be under the person's control (habits), and others are not (genes and early epigenetics). These tendencies are formed from childhood environmental support in formative years and later in significant life experience. For example, if a child has secure attachment or support system, they generally exhibit compassionate behavior (Mikulincer, Shaver, Gillath and Nitzberg, 2005). Further, if a person has poor attachment in early childhood which develops into an attachment disorder, they can be less empathetic and receptive to others (Eisler and Levine, 2002; Mikulincer and Shaver, 2005). This lack of attachment and bonding is associated with a 'stressed brain' resulting in poor social abilities. 'Stress during infancy that is severe enough to create insecure attachment has a dissociative effect, disrupting right hemispheric emotional functioning and species preservative behavior, and a permanent bias towards self-preservation can become an adult trait' (Henry and Wang, 1998). This 'bias' or tendency manifests the accompanying Ethic of Safety. When one's environment, or network of systems, is perceived as perpetually threatening, self-protection may become the dominant orientation of the self (Eisler and Levine, 2002). Another example is found in the research of Caldji, Diorio and Meaney (2003). Their work with rats found that 'the brains of infant rats subjected to stress from parental care are permanently altered in GABA-ergic function in the ventral medial prefrontal cortex and the amygdala. Chronic stress increases the ability of the amygdala to learn and express fear associations, while at the same time reducing the ability of the prefrontal cortex to control fear,' leading to a vicious cycle of greater fear and reactivity (Quirk, 2007 and Narvaez, 2008). However, an inner self oriented toward the Ethic of Imagination can see more than immediate self-interest and imagine alternative systems, reflect with detached judgment on moral problems, and resist unhelpful instincts and intuitions (Bandura, 1999). Further, with both Imagination and Engagement Ethics, an individual can act altruistically, contra-situation, in security charged situations (Frankl, 1963).

Role of Education: Shaping the Self for Moral Optimization

From this research, we have learned that both the self and systems are involved when killing occurs. We have also learned that a strong self requires early formation, co-construction by caregivers and systems which promote proper moral development and action. Finally, systems require proper oversight, keeping them morally in check lest a system turns oppressive, leading to inefficiency, ineffectiveness, and destruction of persons and the greater environment. How about formal education? We discuss how education can provide optimal situations for the development of nonkilling selves. We suggest a framework, the Integrative Ethical Education (IEE) (Narvaez, 2006), answering the question of what and how to teach.

How do we teach? Education as a System

IEE highlights those specific aspects of a humane system that provide optimal situations for the development of nonkilling selves. The four aspects suggested here are expertise development, well-structured and caring environments, active communal involvement, and the encouragement of self-regulation. Together, they create an optimal environment for training the self for the coordination of the Safety, Engagement, and Imagination Ethics.

Expertise Development. Humans have a mostly subconscious 'bounded rationality,' which applies 'good enough' heuristics for solving life's challenges (Gigerenzer and Selten, 2001; Kahneman, 2003). Built from recurring experiences, some initially conscious, heuristics are intuitions that are coded in implicit memory systems (e.g., 'don't rock the boat'). Sometimes these intuitions are not verbally expressible (Hasher and Zacks, 1984; Keil and Wilson, 1999). Many actions are chosen without formal reasoning, but through pattern recognition, as exemplified in experts when their skills are habituated and unmediated (Bargh and Ferguson, 2000). In fact, physiological perception and behavior are closely intertwined (Hurley, 2002). For example, biochemical-physiological states or 'somatic markers' built from frequent experience often drive decisions and resulting action (Damasio, 1999). Most learning occurs effortlessly from the patterns implicit in the environment including cultural practices, and manifests itself without awareness. If most human behaviors are not consciously controlled but automatic (Bargh and Chartrand, 1999; Bargh and Ferguson, 2000), there are implications for moral education (Lapsley and Narvaez, 2004; Narvaez and Lapsley, 2009). The conscious system and systems outside of conscious awareness all benefit from intentional environments that foster good intuitions and understanding, a characteristic of expert training.

In recent years it has been apparent to researchers that all learning is expertise development (Bransford, Brown and Cocking, 1999). In expert training individuals begin as novices and develop skills and capacities towards expertise. Thus in every domain one can structure instruction for expertise development based on what is known about how expertise is best generated (Hogarth, 2001). Narvaez has brought this approach into the realm of moral or ethical development with the Integrative Ethical Education model, (Narvaez, 2006, 2007, 2008). Traditionally, expertise is obtained through apprenticeship (Rogoff, 1990; Rogoff and Lave, 1984; Bransford, Brown and Cocking, 1999). In an apprenticeship model, the mentor demonstrates, guides, and directs learning and performance. The novice is immersed in real-life situations, extensively practicing and focussing on skill development under expert mentoring, which facilitates the development of appropriate intuitions (Ericsson and Smith, 1991). As Narvaez (Narvaez et al., 2004) points out, expertise instruction best follows a pattern of immersion that starts with exposure to multiple examples and opportunities, attention to facts and skills, practicing procedures, and integrating skills across multiple contexts. We discuss specific ethical skills below.

This immersed-situational approach coincides with Zimbardo's recommendations for *good* systems. However, it is important to remember that expertise can run in both directions. That is, humans can perfect dysfunction and antisocial behavior. 'The potential for perversion is inherent in the very processes that make human beings do all the wonderful things we do' (Zimbardo, 2007: 229). Just as communities can promote hate and dysfunction, students can perfect vices using the same methods described above. Humans can use the Imagination Ethic in a negative direction, creating what Zimbardo calls a 'hostile imagination.' Moreover, if the Engagement Ethic is never developed properly, a person can be left with an overactive Safety Ethic. The Imagination Ethic can continue to function, however, and *imagine* insensitive and antisocial solutions to the 'problems' the Safety Ethic proposes (vicious imagination). In order to optimize ethical expertise, an intentional environment is required that includes a set of caring relationships, a supportive climate, and a community that encourages prosocial self-development.

Caring Relationships. Second, perhaps most vital within an educational setting is the establishment of a well-structured and caring relationship between educator and student, in a way that forms a secure attachment—a factor that leads to a greater sense of belonging and promotes greater motivation and achievements (Klem and Connell, 2004; McNeely, Nonnemaker and Blum, 2002; Roeser, Midgley and Urdan, 1996). For students who have a history of poor parental bonding or come from abusive or neglectful environments, a secure bond may be more difficult to establish, requiring more patience and support, but a secure relationship is still possible (Watson and Eckert, 2003). The details of this relationship may vary by ethnicity and culture, so attention must be given to appropriate ways in which care and respect are shown. Nevertheless, the first foundation for nonkilling is a respectful, loving relationship with a mentor.

A well-structured environment requires a culture or climate of support. Teachers convey a general climate of support through expectations of growth and development, ethical excellence, and high achievement. Classroom studies show that these characteristics are particularly beneficial for persons from at-risk situations who must develop support systems as these systems are weak or nonexistent (Benson, Leffert, Scales and Blyth, 1998; Wang, Haertel and Walberg, 1998; Zins, Weissberg, Wang and Walberg, 2004). With increased expertise, students become autonomous within a domain (Zimmerman, 1998). They learn enough skills to be able to monitor their own progress and to change strategies when needed. Teachers must be aware of this development and encourage students in autonomy, self-direction and influence (leadership). The major components of a well-structured environment include teacher warmth, acceptance, support, and modelling; training in social skills; opportunities for helping others; discipline through a sense of citizenship to school; student autonomy, self-direction, and influence; student interaction, collaboration, and participation in open discussion (Solomon et al., 2002). These characteristics foster a climate that engages student ownership and general concern for the wellbeing of the group.

Community Support. Third, students do not flourish alone but require the surrounding community to continually provide the support needed (Bronfenbrenner, 1979). The community is where skills are practiced and honed. Therefore, the educational system must foster strong links to positive elements of the local community. If the purpose of ethical behavior is to live a good life in the community, then together, community members work out basic questions such as: How should we get along in our community? How do we build up our community? How do we help one another flourish? That is, each individual lives within an active ecological context (Bronfenbrenner, 1979) in which, ideally, the entire community builds ethical skills together, for it is in these communities that students express their values, make decisions, and take action. Community members can encourage the desire for nonviolence and develop a sense of empowerment in students to enact internal and social change.

Self-Authorship. Finally, optimal learning environments promote self-regulation in students and community members. The perception of personal agency is formed from our self-regulatory skills and lies at the heart of the sense of self (Zimmerman, 2000). Virtuous individuals must be autonomous enough to monitor their behavior and choices. Where individuals can be coached in domain-specific self-efficacy and self-regulation (Zimmerman, Bonner and Kovach, 2002), once virtues are developed, they must be maintained through the selection of appropriate friends and environments (Aristotle, 1988). That is, individuals have to be active in developing and influencing the systems around them so that the situations they inhabit contribute to their continual prosocial, nonkilling development and do not work against them.

It is vital to start early in shaping the brain to move beyond a Safety Ethic, to shape prosocial emotional systems, to facilitate the ability to deliberate, and to raise capacities for dealing with systems. Adults with children and leaders with group members can actively and consciously work to properly manage the Safety Ethic, both consciously, with self-regulation strategies, and automatically, with group norms and practices. Although the Engagement Ethic is best fostered through early care and caregiver bonding, which facilitate social brain circuitry development, sociality can be fostered by supportive teachers and environments as well (e.g., Watson and Eckert, 2003). Again, social-emotional systems can be rewired to a certain degree with caring relationships. A fully trained Imagination Ethic is key in coordinating instincts, intuitions, goals and actions as well as formulating appropriate judgments, critical skills in ethical development; deliberation skills also require guided practice. Finally, as systems can become dominating, a truly critical education must assist people in assessing systems and the situations systems create. This type of education would also provide skills in civic system development and effective and civil modes of system resistance and deconstruction. Individuals and groups need to learn how to develop moral institutions that facilitate justice among the populace (Trout, 2009). Education then is a major tool in ending killing and reaching those goals set forth by the Center for Global Nonkilling.

What do we teach? Skill development under apprenticeship

The two primary methods of moral education are traditional character education and rational moral education. Traditional character education (Arthur, 2008) understands virtue development as the primary aim of education. It focuses on the educational relationships, habitual action and focus that contribute to the formation of character. Rational moral education (Kohlberg, 1984), in contrast, emphasizes the development of self-directed moral judgment and the proper application of fairness in resolving moral dilemmas as the goal of moral education. Rational moral education focuses on the development of reasoning and autonomy.

Whereas these approaches to moral development are often viewed as opposing one another, they are complementary. Integrative Ethical Education (Narvaez, 2006) integrates the two approaches through moral expertise development. IEE acknowledges the need for character formation, as well as the need to cultivate reflective reasoning and a commitment to justice. Ethical expertise development fosters both conscious rational deliberation, and the habits, skills, and intuitions of moral character, the ethical know-how that can be mentored and self-cultivated to high levels of expertise. But what exactly should be taught?

Table 1. Integrative Ethical Education: Ethical Skills

Ethical Sensitivity – *Notice the need for ethical action, Feel empathy, Put yourself in the other person's shoes, Imagine possibilities, Determine your role.*

- Understand Emotional Expression
- Take the Perspective of Others
- Connecting to Others
- Responding to Diversity
- Controlling Social Bias
- Interpreting Situations
- Communicate Effectively

Ethical Judgment – *Reason about what might be done; Apply your code of ethics, Judge which action is most ethical*

- Understanding Ethical Problems
- Using Codes and Identifying Judgment Criteria
- Reasoning Generally
- Reasoning Ethically
- Understand Consequences
- Reflect on the Process and Outcome
- Coping and Resiliency

Ethical Focus – *Make the ethical action a priority over other needs and goals, Align ethical action with your identity*

- Respecting Others
- Cultivate Conscience

- Act Responsibly
- Help Others
- Finding Meaning in Life
- Valuing Traditions and Institutions
- Developing Ethical Identity and Integrity

Ethical Action – *Implement the ethical action by knowing what steps to take and getting the help you need, Persevere despite hardship*

- Resolving Conflicts and Problems
- Assert Respectfully
- Taking Initiative as a Leader
- Planning to Implement Decisions
- Cultivate Courage
- Persevering
- Work Hard

> The 28 skills [above] were sampled from those considered to be moral exemplars (e.g., Martin Luther King, Jr.), from classic virtues (e.g., prudence, courage) and modern virtues (e.g., assertiveness, resilience), as well as from a review of scholarship in morality, development, citizenship, and positive psychology. Skills include those that promote justice and the flourishing of self and others, individual and community. A minimal level of competence in these skills is required of adult citizens for a pluralistic democracy to flourish.

IEE suggests teaching ethical skills in the four areas of Rest's framework of moral behavior (Rest, 1983; Narvaez and Rest, 1995). The four components—ethical sensitivity, ethical judgment, ethical focus, ethical action—represent the psychological processes that must occur in order to complete an ethical behavior. Table 1 lists the types of skills that can be taught for each process (Narvaez and Bock, 2009; Narvaez and Endicott, 2009; Narvaez and Lies, 2009; Narvaez, 2009). All four processes—sensitivity, judgment, motivation, and action—are highly interdependent. In order for an ethical behavior to occur, all four are required. Otherwise, poor action or no action at all may result.

Ethical Sensitivity. Before an action can be taken, a person must notice the need for ethical action, being perceptive about situational cues. Such *ethical sensitivity* extends to a concern for those involved, including feeling empathy, putting oneself in the other person's shoes, imagining the effects of possible outcomes on others, and the reactions of those involved. Teachers help students with a variety of sensitivity skills such as increasing familiarity with diverse cultures, communicating in appropriate ways for the context, and controlling one's social biases. In application to nonkilling education, this would include teaching sensitivity to situational forces, dehumanizing language and actions (Smith, 2011). Critical from our earlier discussion, it is important for an individual (or group) to stay calm and self-regulated, as sensitivity can be quickly lost when the Safety Ethic is engaged without restraint.

Ethical Reasoning. A second process involved in eventual moral behavior is ethical judgment, an area most related to rational moral education. The skills for ethical judgment include reasoning about possible actions, applying a code of ethics, and judging which possible action is most appropriate. Moral judgments and reasoning structures increase with age and education and are less dependent on differences in culture (Kohlberg, 1984), but are also shaped by habitual thoughtfulness, and by focused training (Narvaez and Gleason, 2007). In application to nonkilling education, students can learn 'attributional charity,' or giving others the benefit of the doubt (Zimbardo, 2007: 212). Students can also conduct ethical analyzes of 'The System' and situational forces, exposing the underlying ethical requirements and assumptions of those systems and situations (see Zimbardo 2007: 245 for consequences of poor analysis). For a formal example of this type of analysis see Walter Schultz's, *The Moral Conditions of Economic Efficiency* (2001).

Ethical Focus. Third, moral behavior does not occur without ethical motivation or focus. For an ethical behavior to take place, a person must prioritize the ethical action identified in the previous step over other needs and goals. This prioritization can either be specific to a situation or more generally prioritized through habituation. This motivation includes focussing on the right thoughts and situational cues. It is important to remember a situation can overwhelm a person without his or her knowledge, destroying ethical motivation (Zimbardo, 2007: 179). For example, intense systems can form a negative present-situation focus only. For example, in Zimbardo's prison experiment, the prisoners' conversation was 90 per cent about the prison issues they were facing. They did not talk about themselves or their lives outside of the prison. Their singular focus on the one system intensified the negativity of the experience and the internalization of the guards' negative attitudes towards them. Zimbardo calls this a 'transformation of character,' where individuals are induced, seduced and initiated into evil behaviors (Zimbardo, 2007: 210). This prevents the initiation of the first stages of the ethical process, ethical sensitivity, and prioritizes immediate relief for some sense of safety. As discussed above, this is precisely the type of context that engages the Safety Ethic and therefore has a strong potential for violence (rage) or unquestioning obedience (fear). Maintaining a sense of multiple systems can facilitate a healthy level of detachment from any particular system (Zimbardo, 2007). The self can maintain a detached resistance. Blasi (Blasi, 1984) and Damon (Damon, 1984) argue that self-concept directly influences ethical motivation in general. For instance, if a person understands the self as compassionate person, then he or she is more likely to prioritize compassionate action no matter the situation. This can be an internal mode of resistance, which is necessary in resisting the forces within 'total situations' (Zimbardo, 2007: xiii).

Ethical Action. The final set of skills required for moral behavior is implementation skills. The person must know how to carry out the desired ethical action and have the perseverance to complete the job. This skill set includes judging feasibility, attaining social support, developing backup plans when things go wrong. Learners must practice the implementation of moral goals multiple times under guided supervision in order to build the skill sets that will work automatically when the need arises. Again, teaching non-violent forms of internal and external resistance, including the use of technology as seen recently in the 2011 Egypt civil uprising, provide both implementation skills and 'ego strength.'

Integrative Ethical Education emphasizes the importance of embedding character education into regular academic instruction. Teachers can slightly shift academic lessons so that they also address an ethical skill. These skills must also be fostered for use in the larger local context—the neighbourhood, town, or city, and are best encouraged by those who live there. The need for practice, guidance by wiser others, and commitment to the community welfare, form the village of support needed for success. The goal of the IEE model is to create effective and committed community members. Engaging the situation, and as discussed above, is key in identifying the right situational forces to engage. Intervention is an ethical and a political action (Zimbardo, 2007). However, not all community traditions and practices are good. Therefore, it is important to facilitate students' ability to have personal checks in place. These include experiences such as participation in multiple communities, skills such as listening to minority voices, empathetic but critical engagement, conscious ethical effort, and modes of nonviolent expression. It should also be pointed out that teachers themselves need to have skills for self-regulation, ethical engagement, and social justice action. The mentors need their mentors too. Again, the IEE model requires the constant practice of skills and this involves the greater public involvement in helping one another achieve and maintain a nonkilling culture.

Conclusion

It is clear there are multiple forces converging on individuals and communities leading to acts of violence and death. There are many reasons that an individual might kill, from poor early nurturing and imagination building to blinding situations that strip away those aspects which allow humans the unique position of ethical compassion, deliberation and behavior. Conditioned and cultivated selves balance internal forces of human evolutionary and cultural development as detailed in Triune Ethics Theory. When a Safety Ethic is activated, it is difficult for anyone to feel or be safe, because its actions can be unpredictable. Fostering ways to keep safety concerns minimal are critical for nonkilling environments.

Individuals and communities are also engaged in systems that create situational forces of their own. These forces can overwhelm the Imagination and Engagement Ethics, leaving the Safety Ethic in charge with its potential for violent self-preservation. Individuals must practice skills that allow them to step away from the power of systems as well as skills in nonkilling resistance when necessary. Extensive, focused practice of critical ethical skills, as detailed in the Integrative Ethical Education model, provides defenses against negative evolutionary, situational and systemic forces. Ethical expertise development, in this way, can help prevent killing. For optimal influence, the instructor should have a caring relationship with the student in a way that is comfortable to the student, but holds high expectations for character and academic success. Moreover, the group relational context, or situational climate, should be positive and supportive to keep the Safety Ethic properly guided and to enhance prosocial emotions. Fostering self authorship under the guidance of community members creates optimal situations for developing effective ethical skills. In this way, moral institutions are cultivated communally, providing *good* systems for proper human development which avoid killing and promote nonkilling and prosociality.

Finally, we emphasize the importance of system regulation. Some factors are vital for creating good situations for system participants such as transparency, policy oversight, and outgroup interaction. Such regulation should extend from small local systems to the many global systems governing the lives of all people on earth. Education in the existence and nature of these systems, system management, and system analysis will foster a culture of system sensitivity and desire for healthy environments, ones absent of killing.

References

Allman, J., Hakeem, A., Erwin, J., Ninchinsky, E., & Hof, P. (2001). The Anterior Cingulate Cortex: The Evolution of an Interface between Emotion and Cognition. *Annals of the New York Academy of Sciences, 935*, 107-117.

Allmand, J., Hakeem, A., Erwin, J. M., Ninchinsky, E., & Hof, P. (2001). The Anterior Cingulate Cortex: The Evolution of an Interface between Emotion and Cognition. *Annals of the New York Academy of Sciences, 935*, 107-117.

Anderson, G., Dombroski, M., & Swinth, J. (2001). Kangaroo care: Not just for stable preemies anymore. *Reflections on Nursing Leadership, 27*, 32-34.

Anderson, S., Bechara, A., Damasio, H., Tranel, D., & Damasio, A. (1999). Impairment of social and moral behavior related to early damage in human preforntal cortex. *Nature Neuroscience, 2*, 1032-1037.

Aristotle. (1988). *Nicomachean ethics.* (W. Ross, Trans.) London: Oxford.

Arpaly, N. (2003). *Unprincipled virtue: An inquiry into moral agency.* New York: Oxford Press.

Arthur, J. (2008). Traditional Approaches to Character Education in Britain and America. In L.P. Nucci, & D. Narvaez (Eds.) *Handbook of Moral and Character Education* (pp. 80-98). New York: Routledge.

Bandura, A. (1999). Moral disengagement in the perpetration of inhumanities. *Personality and Social Psychology Review.*

Bargh, J., & Chartrand, T. (1999). The unbearable automaticity of being. *American Psychologist, 54*, 462-479.

Bargh, J., & Ferguson, M. (2000). Beyond behaviorism: On the automaticity of higher mental processes. *Psychological Bulletin, 126*, 925-945.

Bechara, A. (2005). Decision making, impulse control and loss of willpower to resist drugs: a neurocognitive perspective. *Nature Neuroscience, 8*, 1458-1463.

Benson, P., Leffert, N., Scales, P. C., & Blyth, D. (1998). Beyond the 'village' rhetoric: Creating healthy communities for children and adolescents. *Applied Developmental Science, 2*(3), 138-159.

Blair, R., Jones, L., Clark, F., & Smith, M. (1997). The psychopath: A lack of responsiveness to distress cues? *Psychophysiology, 34*, 192-198.

Blasi, A. (1984). Moral identity: Its role in moral functioning. In W. Kurtines, & J. Gewirtz (Eds.), *Morality, moral behavior, and moral development* (pp. 128-139). New York: Wiley.

Bransford, J. D., Brown, A. L., & Cocking, R. R. (1999). *How People Learn: Brain, Mind, Experience, and School.* Washington D.C.: National Academy Press.

Bronfenbrenner, U. (1979). *The Ecology of Human Development.* Cambridge: Harvard University Press.

Caldji, C., Diorio, J., & Meaney, M. (2003). Variations in maternal care alter GABA(A) receptor subunit expression in brain regions associated with fear. *Neuropsychopharmacology, 28*, 1950-1959.

Cervone, D. (1999). Bottom-up explanation in personality psychology: The case of cross-situational coherence. In D. Cervone, & Y. Shoda (Eds.), *The coherence of personality: Social-cognitive bases of personality consistency, variability, and organization* (pp. 303-341). New York: Guilford Press.

Damasio, A. (1999). *The Feeling of What Happens.* London: Heineman.

Damon, W. (1984). Self-understanding and moral development from childhood to adolescence. In W. Kurintes, & J. Gewirtz (Eds.), *Morality, moral behavior and moral development* (pp. 109-127). New York: Wiley.

Darley, J., & Batson, C. D. (1973). From Jerusalem to Jericho: A study of situational and dispositional variables in helping behavior. *Journal of Personality and Social Psychology, 27,* 100-108.

Darwin, C. (1871/1981). *The Descent of Man.* Princeton: Princeton University Press.

de Quervain, D. J.-F., Fischbacher, U., Treyer, V., Schellhammer, M., Schnyder, U., Buck, A., et al. (2004). The Neural Basis of Altruistic Punishment. *Science, 305,* 1254-1258.

Eisler, R., & Levine, D. (2002). Nurture, nature, and caring: We are not prisoners of our genes. *Brain and Mind, 3,* 9-52.

Ericsson, K. A., & Smith, J. (1991). *Toward a General Theory of Expertise.* New York: Cambridge Univeristy Press.

Frankl, V. E. (1963). *Man's Search for Meaning.* New York: Simon and Schuster.

Giedd, J.N., Blumenthal, J., Jeffries, N.O., & et al. (1999). Brain development during childhood and adolescence: A longitudinal MRI study. *Nature Neuroscience, 10*(2), 861-863.

Gigerenzer, G., & Selten, R. (2001). *Bounded rationality: The adaptive.* Cambridge, MA: MIT Press.

Goldberg, E. (2002). *The Executive Brain: Frontal Lobes and the Civilized Brain.* New York: Oxford University Press.

Harlow, H. (1986). *From Learning to Love.* New York: Praeger.

Hasher, L., & Zacks, R. (1984). Automatic processing of Fundamental Information: The Case of Frequency of Occurrence. *American Psychologist,,* 1372-88.

Hedges, C. (2011). *The World As It Is: Dispatches on the Myth of Human Progress.* New York: Nation Books.

Henry, J., & Wang, S. (1998). Effects of early stress on adult affiliative behavior. *Psychoneuroendocrinology, 23*(8), 863-875.

Hogarth, R. M. (2001). *Educating Intuition.* Chicago: University of Chicago Press.

Hurley, S. (2002). *Consciousness in action.* Cambridge, MA: Harvard University Press.

Jost, J., Glaser, J., Kruglanski, A., & Sulloway, F. (2003). Political Conservatism as Motivated Social Cognition. *Psychological Bulletin, 129*(3), 339-375.

Kahneman, D. (2003). A perspective on judgment and choice: Mapping bounded rationality. *American Psychologist, 58*(9), 697-720.

Keil, F., & Wilson, R. (1999). *Explanation and Cognition.* Cambridge, MA: MIT Press.

Klem, A. M., & Connell, J. P. (2004). Relationships Matter: Linking Teacher Support to Student Engagement and Achievement. *Journal of School Health, 74*(7), 262-273.

Knoch, D., Pascual-Leone, A., Meyer, K., Treyer, V., & Fehr, E. (2006). Diminishing Reciprocal Fairness by Disrupting the Right Prefontal Cortex. *Science, 314*, 829-832.

Kochanska, G. (2002). Mutually Responsive Orientation Between Mothers and Their Young Children: A context for the early development of conscience. *Current Directions in Psychological Science, 11*, 191-195.

Kochanska, G., & Thompson, R. A. (1997). The Emergence and Development of Conscience in Toddlerhood and Early Childhood. In J. Grusec, & L. Kuczynski (Eds.), *Parenting and Children's Internalization of Values* (pp. 53-77). New York: Wiley.

Kodituwakku, P., Kalberg, W., & May, P. (1999). Effects of Prenatal Alcohol Exposure on Executive Functioning. *Alcohol Research and Health: Alcohol-Related Birth Defects: An Update, 25*(3).

Kohlberg, L. (1984). *The psychology of moral development: Essays on moral development, Vol. II.* New York: Harper & Row.

Kruesi, M., Hibbs, E., Zahn, T., Keysor, C., Hamburger, S., Bartko, J., et al. (1992). 2-year prospective follow-up study of children and adolescents with disruptive behavior disorders. Prediction by cerebrospinal fluid 5-hydroxyindoleacetic acid, homovanillic acid, and autonomic measures? *Archives of General Psychiatry, 49*(6), 429-435.

Lapsley, D. K., & Narvaez, D. (2006). Character Education. In W. Damon, & R. Lerner (Eds.), *Vol. 4 (A. Renninger & I. Siegel, volume eds.), Handbook of Child Psychology.* New York: Wiley.

Lapsley, D., & Narvaez, D. (2004). A social-cognitive view of moral character. In D. Lapsley, & D. Narvaez (Eds.), *Moral development: Self and identity* (pp. 189-212). Mahwah, NJ: Erlbaum.

Lapsley, D., & Narvaez, D. (2005). Moral psychology at the crossroads. In D.

Lapsley, & C. Power (Eds.), *Character Psychology and Character Education* (pp. 18-35). University of Notre Dame Press.

Lewis, T., Amini, F., & Lannon, R. (2000). *A General Theory of Love.* New York: Vintage.

Loye, D. (2000). *Darwin's Lost Theory of Love.* New York: Writer's Press.

Loye, D. (2002). The Moral Brain. *Brain and Mind, 3*, 133-150.

Luna, B., Thulborn, K., Munoz, D., Merriam, E., Garver, K., & Minshew, N. (2001). Maturation of widely distibuted brain functions subserves cognitive development. *Neuro Image, 13*(5), 786-793.

MacLean, P. (1990). *The Triune Brain in Evolution: Role in Paleocerebral Functions.* New York: Plenum.

Mathews, V., Kronenberger, W., Wang, Y., Lurito, J., Lowe, M., & Dunn, D. (2005). Media violence exposure and frontal lobe activation measured by functional magnetic resonance imaging in aggressive and nonaggressive adolescents. *Journal of Computer Assisted Tomography, 29*(3), 287-292.

McNeely, C. A., Nonnemaker, J. M., & Blum, R. W. (2002). Promoting School Connectedness: Evidence from the National Longitudinal Study of Adolescent Health. *Journal of School Health, 72*, 138-146.

Meier, B., Robinson, M., & Wilkowski, B. (2006). Turning the other cheek: Agreeableness and the regulation of aggression-related primes. *Psychological Science, 17*(5), 136-142.

Mikulincer, M., & Shaver, P. R. (2005). Attachment security, compassion, and altruism. *Current Directions in Psychological Science, 14*, 34-38.

Mikulincer, M., Shaver, P., Gillath, O., & Nitzberg, R. (2005). Attachment, caregiving, and altruism: boosting attachment security increases compassion and helping. *Journal of Personality and Social Psychology, 89*(5), 817-839.

Milgram, S. (1977). *The individual in a social world: Essays and experiments* (3rd expanded ed.). Pinter & Martin.

Mischel, W. (1973). Towards a Cognitive Social Learning Theory Reconceptualization of Personality. *Psychological Review, 80*, 252-283.

Moll, J., de Oliveira-Souza, R., Eslinger, P., Bramati, I., Mourao-Miranda, J., & Andreiulo, P. (2002). The Neural Correlates of Moral Sensitivity: A Function magnetic Resonance Imaging Investigation of Basic and Moral Emotions. *Journal of Neuroscience, 22*, 2730-2736.

Narvaez, D. (2006). Integrative Ethical Education. In M. Killen, & J. Smetana (Eds.), *Handbook of Moral Development* (pp. 703-733). Mahwah, NJ: Erlbaum.

Narvaez, D. (2007). How Cognitive and Neurobiological Sciences Inform Values Education for Creatures Like Us. In A. D., & J. Chapman (Eds.), *Values Education and Lifelong Learning: Philosophy, Policy, Practices* (pp. 127-159). Springer Press International.

Narvaez, D. (2008). Human Flourishing and Moral Development: Cognitive Science and Neurobiological Perspectives on Virtue Development. In L. Nucci, & D. Narvaez (Eds.), *Handbook of Moral and Character Education* (pp. 310-327). Mahwah, NJ: Erlbaum.

Narvaez, D. (2008). *Integrative Ethical Education: Putting Flourishing back into Character Education.pdf.* Retrieved June 5, 2011, from http://www.nd.edu/~dnarvaez/downloads.html: http://www.nd.edu/~dnarvaez/NarvaezISPP.pdf.

Narvaez, D. (2008). Triune Ethics: The neurobiological roots of our multiple moralities. *New Ideas in Psychology, 26*, 95-119.

Narvaez, D. (2009). *Nurturing character in the classroom, EthEx Series, Book 4: Ethical Action.* Notre Dame, IN: ACE Press.

Narvaez, D. (contracted book in preparation, due 2012). *The Human Canvas: Evolution, Epigenetics and Morality.* New York: W.W. Norton.

Narvaez, D., & Bock, T. (2009). *Nuturing character in the classroom, EthEx Series, Book 2: Ethical Judgment.* Notre Dame, IN: ACE Press.

Narvaez, D., & Endicott, L. (2009). *Nuturing character in the classroom, EthEx Series, Book 1: Ethical Sensitivity.* Notre Dame, IN: ACE Press.

Narvaez, D., & Gleason, T. ((in press)). Developmental Optimization. In D. Narvaez, T. Gleason, D. Narvaez, J. Panksepp, A. Schore, & T. Gleason (Eds.), *Human Nature, Early Experience and the Enviroment of Evolutionary Adaptedness.* New York: Oxford University Press.

Narvaez, D., & Lapsley, D. (Eds.). (2009). *Personality, Identity, and Character: Explorations in Moral Psychology.* New York: Cambridge University Press.

Narvaez, D., & Lies, J. (2009). *Nuturing character in the classroom, EthEx Series, Book 3: Ethical Motivation.* Notre Dame, IN: ACE Press.

Narvaez, D., & Rest, J. (1995). The four components of acting morally. In W. Kurtines, & J. Gewirtz (Eds.), *Moral behavior and moral development: An introduction* (pp. 385-400). New York: McGraw-Hill.

Narvaez, D., Bock, T., Endicott, L., & Leis, J. (2004). Minnesota's Community Voices and Character Education Project. *Journal of Research in Character Education, 2*, 89-112.

Narvaez, D., & Gleason, T. (2007). The Influence of moral judgment development and moral experience on comprehension of moral narratives and expository texts. *The Journal of Genetic Psychology,168*(3), 251–276.

Narvaez, D., Panksepp, J., Schore, A., & Gleason, T. ((in press)). The value of the environment of evolutionary adaptedness for gauging children's well-being. In *Human Nature, Early Experience and the Environment of Evolutionary Adaptedness.* New York: Oxford University Press.

Newman, M., Holden, G., & Delville, Y. (2005). Isolation and the stress of being bullied. *Journal of Adolescence, 28*, 343-357.

Nisbett, R., & Cohen, D. (1996). *Culture of Honor.* New York: Westview Press.

Ochsner, K. N., & Gross, J. (2007). The Neural Architecture of Emotion Regulation. In J. Gross (Ed.), *Handbook of Emotion Regulation* (pp. 87-108). New York: Guilford Press.

Ochsner, K., & Gross, J. (2007). The Neural Architecture of Emotion Regulation. In J. Gross (Ed.), *Handbook of Emotion Regulation* (pp. 87-108). New York: Guilford Press.

Panksepp, J. (1998). *Affective Neuroscience: The foundations of human and animal emotions.* New York: Oxford University Press.

Panksepp, J., & Panksepp, J. (2000). The Seven Sins of Evolutionary Psychology. *Evolution and Cognition, 6*(2), 108-131.

Quirk, G. (2007). Prefrontal-amygdala interactions in the regulation of fear. In J. Gross (Ed.), *Handbook of Emotion Regulation* (pp. 27-46). New York: Guildford Press, pp. 27-46.

Rest, J. (1983). Morality. In P. Mussen (Ed.), *Manual of child* (Vol. 3, pp. 556-629). New York: Wiley.

Roeser, R. M., Midgley, C., & Urdan, T. (1996). Perceptions of the Psychological Environment and Early Adolescents' Psychological and Behavioral Funcationing in School: The Mediating Role of Goals and Belonging. *Journal of Educational Psychology, 88*(3), 408-422.

Rogoff, B. (1990). *Apprenticeship in Thinking: Cognitive Development in Social Context.* New York: Oxford University Press.

Rogoff, B., & Lave, J. (1984). *Everyday Cognition: Its Development in Social Context.* Cambridge, MA: Harvard University Press.

Rosenblatt, A., Greenberg, J., Solomon, S., Pyszczynski, T., & Lyon, D. (1989). Evidence for Terror Management Theory: I. The Effects of Morality Salience on Reactions to Those Who Violate or Uphold Cultural Values. *Journal of Personality and Social Psychology, 57*(4), 681-690.

Schore, A. (1994). *Affect Regulation.* Hillsdale, NJ: Erlbaum.

Schore, A. (2003a). Affect regulation and the repair of the self. New York: Norton

Schore, A. (2003b). Affect dysregulation and disorders of the self. New York: Norton

Schultz, W. (2001). *The Moral Conditions of Economic Efficiency.* Cambridge: Cambridge University Press.

Shaver, P., & Mikulincer, M. (2007). Adult Attachment Strategies and the Regulation of Emotion. In J. Gross (Ed.), *Handbook of Emotion Regulation* (pp. 446-465). New York: Guilford Press.

Smith, D. L. (2011). *Less Than Humans: Why We Demean, Enslave, and Exterminate Others.* New York: St Martin's Press.

Solomon, D., Watson, M., & Battistich, V. (2002). Teaching and schooling effects on moral/prosocial development. In V. Richardson (Ed.), *Handbook of research on teaching* (pp. 566-603). Washington, DC: American Educational Research Association.

Staub, E. (1992). *The Roots of Evil.* Cambridge: Cambridge University Press.

Trout, J.D. (2009). The Empathy gap. New York: Viking Press.

Vogel, C. (Fall 2009). Bearing Witness. *SSA Magazine,* 16-21.

Wang, M. C., Haertel, G. D., & Walberg, H. J. (1998). Building Educational Resilience. *Phi Beta Kappa Fastbacks, 430,* 7-61.

Watson, M., & Eckert, L. (2003). *Learning to trust.* San Francisco: Jossey-Bass.

Watson, M., & Eckert, L. (2003). *Learning to Trust.* San Francisco: Jossey-Bass.

Weaver, I., Szyf, M., & Meaney, M. (2002). From maternal care to gene expression: DNA methylation and the maternal programming of stress responses. *Endocrine Research, 28,* 699.

Wilson, E. (1980). *Sociobiology: The abridged edition.* Cambridge, MA: Belknap Press.

Wilson, T. (2004). *Strangers to Ourselves.* New York: Belknap Press.

Wilson, T.D., Lisle, D.J., Kraft, D., & Wetzel, C.G. (1989). Preferences as expectation-driven inferences: Effects of affective expectations on affective experience. *Journal of Personality and Social Psychology, 56*(4), 519-530.

Zimbardo, P. (2007). *The Lucifer Effect: Understanding How Good People Turn Evil.* New York: Random House.

Zimmerman, B. J. (1998). Academic Studying and the Development of Personal Skill: A Self-Regulatory Perspective. *Education Psychologist, 33,* 73-86.

Zimmerman, B. J. (2000). Attaining self regulation: A social cognitive. In M. Boekaerts, P. Pintrich, & M. Zeidner (Eds.), *Handbook of self-regulation* (pp. 13-39). New York: Academic Press.

Zimmerman, B. J., Bonner, S., & Kovach, R. (2002). *Developing selfregulated.* Washington, DC: American Psychological Association.

Zins, J. E., Weissberg, R. P., Wang, M. C., & Walberg, H. J. (2004). *Building Academic Success on Social and Emotional Learning.* New York: Teachers College Press.

6

Nonkilling Media: A Normative Framework

Philip Lee

World Association for Christian Communication

A concise definition of nonkilling is offered by Joám Evans Pim, based on the work of Glenn D. Paige (2009), in which 'nonkilling refers to the absence of killing, threats to kill, and conditions conducive to killing in human society' (Pim, 2009: 15). Summarising the concepts encompassed by nonkilling, he states that, 'Nonkilling... is the affirmation of the act of not taking the life of another person' (ibid.). In this sense, nonkilling media can be described as those that respect the sacredness of human life and the universality of human dignity.

The theory of communicative action expounded by philosopher and sociologist Jürgen Habermas (1987) explicitly recognizes and affirms the dignity and worth of other human beings. Communicative action depends on the capacity and willingness of everyone to dialogue and to understand or temporarily adopt each other's perspectives and, from that starting point, to develop actions that have just consequences for everyone involved. Mutual understanding, not merely reciprocal influence and certainly not one-sided coercion, are crucial. In this respect, the proactive elements of nonkilling (affirmation and recognition) harmonize with those of communicative action, which asserts that systematic discussion can reveal universal truths and codes of appropriate conduct that enable everyone involved to reach agreements from which they can benefit equally. As Habermas notes,

> The rationality potential in action oriented to mutual understanding can be released and translated into the rationalization of the lifeworld's of social groups to the extent that language fulfils functions of reaching understanding, coordinating actions, and socializing individuals; it thereby becomes a medium through which cultural reproduction, social integration, and socialization take place. (Habermas, 1987: 86)

Among other things, communicative action tries to resolve the problem of universal truths that posit extending morality across all cultures despite differing cultural values and belief systems—a controversial proposition that is the subject of intense debate, for example, in the field of communication ethics (Christians and Traber, 1997; Boltanski, 1999). Communicative action challenges the notion of relativism—that each culture or community has belief systems that cannot conform to universal principles because of cultural practices and experiences. It contests this idea with the foundational assertion that reason is a universal capacity inherent to all human beings. Implementing communicative action would ideally create a globally just society in which all members adhere to a shared principle—the ethic of reciprocity or the 'golden rule'—that:

> Is found and has persisted in many religious and ethical traditions of humankind for thousands of years: 'What you do not wish done to yourself, do not do to others.' Or in positive terms: 'What you wish done to yourself, do to others!' This should be the irrevocable, unconditional norm for all areas of life, for families and communities, for races, nations, and religions. (*Declaration Toward A Global Ethic*, 1993: 7)

Implicit in communicative action is a process of reconciliation with people 'whose freedom has been taken away', based on the core values of genuine communication: 'truth-telling, commitment to justice, freedom in solidarity, and respect for human dignity' (Traber, 1997: 335, 341). That process of reconciliation can only begin in a context of mutual trust in a shared reality: 'Reconciliation requires seeing the world as it is, not as we wish it to be. We cannot make compassion dependent on a transformation to the ideal; we must begin with reality if we want to have any hope of influencing reality' (Sivaraksa, 2001: 41). A clear starting point for genuine communication and compassion is engaged dialogue—a dialogue that involves a desire to hear and understand what other people are saying and how they see the world. It is what Adam Kahane (2004) calls 'deep conversation'.

Kahane models four ways of talking and listening. The first is 'downloading', consisting of polite, socially acceptable, conventional exchanges in which people do not listen carefully and nothing new is explored. The second is 'debating', when people actively search for new information or perspectives and engage in argument. The third is 'reflective dialogue', characterized by placing oneself in the position or circumstances of another person and listening to oneself through his or her eyes and ears. The fourth and most powerful is 'generative dialogue' in which two or more people experience a sense of common purpose and are fully engaged with what is taking place and its potential for change. The premise is simple:

> The way we talk and listen expresses our relationship with the world. When we fall into the trap of telling and of not listening, we close ourselves off from being changed by the world and we limit ourselves to being able to change the world only by force. But when we talk and listen with an open mind and an open heart and an open spirit, we bring forth our better selves and a better world. (Kahane, 2004: 4)

This kind of engaged dialogue is the most democratic, in which everyone is listened to and everyone can take part on an equal footing. It is reminiscent of the talking circle, a traditional instrument for dealing with conflicts, misconceptions, disagreements, or deeper problems that interfere with the everyday concerns of a person or community. Talking circles are where people can search for new directions, abandoning the old, making amends, righting wrongs, and creating new pathways toward conflict resolution and possible reconciliation. They represent a model of 'integrative conversation' that reinforces the skills of listening attentively, making connections, and working cooperatively to address problems and challenges. Individuals place the community in the foreground of their thinking and response and themselves in the background in order to participate in a conversation involving:

> A genuine exchange of ideas, feelings, perspectives, opinions, and so forth, where for each person involved there emerges a sense of self as part of the whole. To participate in integrative conversation, one accepts responsibility not only for actively listening to every perspective, but for creating an integrative story along the way. In doing so, the underlying dynamics of power shift from traditionally myopic, self-centred, and rigid to inclusive, interconnected, and fluid. (Cowan and Adams, 2002: 3)

How might it be possible for mass and community media to adopt the position of communicative action, deep conversation, and engaged dialogue? What models of mass and community media are conducive to the establishment of nonkilling societies and how can they contribute to the paradigm shift identified by Thomas Kuhn (1962) resulting in fundamental alterations to the fabric of society and culture? In attempting to answer these questions, we do well to bear in mind the caveat that:

> A paradigm shift is a long social process that implies significant changes in how disciplines function, slowly modifying views on what is thinkable or unthinkable, altering intellectual strategies for problem-solving and modifying terminology usage and conceptual frameworks in a changing universe of discourse. (Evans Pim, 2009: 19)

In today's information and knowledge sharing societies, such a paradigm shift is unthinkable without the complicity of mass and community media and without reconceptualising the role of public service communication in a globalized context of cultural and religious diversity.

A paradigm shift in media content and practice?

The principles of journalism ethics—including professional journalism's much lauded 'objectivity'—rest on truth-telling, independence and fairness, and a sense of solidarity with humankind. In addition to factual accuracy, truth-telling requires anticipating the possibility of error, rigorous research, and cross-checking based on a sure grasp of the issues in play. Independence and fairness mean striving to avoid bias, giving space to reasonable disagreement, providing alternative points of view and solutions, and avoiding partisan interests. Solidarity with humankind means minimizing harm and standing up for the rights of the 'other'. All these principles implicate those working in the media in an indiscriminate sense of individual and collective moral responsibility. As the MacBride Report underlined 30 years ago:

> Communication, with its immense possibilities for influencing the minds and behavior of people, can be a powerful means of promoting democratization of society and of widening public participation in the decision-making process. This depends on the structures and practices of media and their management and to what extent they facilitate broader access and open the communication process to a free interchange of ideas, information and experience among equals, without dominance or discrimination. (MacBride, 1980: 265)

The concept of journalistic objectivity has been critiqued by many commentators and has decisively influenced the burgeoning field of 'peace journalism' studies. Advocates of peace journalism are attempting to articulate a new set of norms and practices aimed at changing the way the media frame and report war and conflict situations. Critics argue that peace journalism is synonymous with good journalism, but fail to see that journalists' choice of stories, angles, sources, and ways of structuring narratives strongly influence readers' and viewers' attitudes and beliefs. While public consumption of mass media journalism rests firmly on the assumption that stories are fair, balanced, and objective, we do not have to look far for evidence to the contrary.

With a few notable but ultimately ineffectual exceptions, it is now generally accepted that the mass media in the United States colluded in the so-called 'war on terror', aiding and abetting the wars on Iraq and Afghanistan and helping to generate a politics of fear that enabled the Bush Administration and its allies to further their right-wing agendas. Many U.S. broadcasting networks (notably Fox News) and newspapers (such as *The New York Times*) offered a sanitized view of the war, emphasizing patriotism, military technology and heroism, and celebrating 'legitimate' weapons of mass destruction (such as 'smart bombs') as opposed to 'illegitimate' ones such as those used by Saddam Hussein. Apart from notable alternative media sources such as the Indymedia network, the absence of critical judgement or, rather, the presence of government control and the now notorious role played by embedded journalists, led one commentator to observe that:

> Dominant media are complicit in a culture and politics of fear... that fuels the military-industrial complex, the private security industry, the small arms trade, a gated community/fortress mentality, and a foreign policy that, arguably, practices state terrorism, economic exploitation, and cultural domination, fostering hatred amongst subordinate populations. (Hackett, 2007: 4)

A more recent but equally disturbing example can be found in media coverage of the Haiti earthquake of January 2010. Governments and humanitarian agencies around the world responded with immediacy and compassion to the unfolding drama of thousands of people killed and made homeless by the devastation. The mass media descended on Haiti to cover stories of the havoc wrought by the earthquake, the lack of water, food, medicine, and shelter, and the 'miracle' of people pulled alive from the rubble. Within days, however, leading newspapers on all continents were publishing stories criminalizing people desperately searching for a means to keep themselves and their families alive. On its website *The Los Angeles Times* ran a series of photos with captions that included descriptions of 'looting' and 'looters'. The *New York Times* published an op-ed column (January 14, 2010) blaming Haiti's ills on cultural inadequacies and the *Washington Post* published an op-ed column (January 18, 2010) denigrating the Haitian people's ability to determine their own post-earthquake future. It would not have taken an unduly perceptive or sensitive editor to have contextualized what was reported, to have asked 'What would you do in this person's place?', or to have put more faith in the resilience of a people that has struggled for so long against imperialism, corruption, and grinding poverty.

This kind of reporting is an obstacle to distinguishing between what is morally right and what is morally reprehensible. We cannot assume that the mass media represent reality and certainly not the whole truth and nothing but the truth. For this reason, the mass media stand in urgent need of the kind of corrective proposed by peace journalism, since:

> The approach of peace journalism is geared toward the stimulation and maximization of readers' judgement ability and prudence. By challenging routine coverage methods and by providing the broadest possible range of accounts, peace journalism writers entrust the onus of interpretation to their readers. By doing so they do not treat the audience as a passive monolith, but rather supply an elementary and essential commodity for all readers... In summation, peace journalism is about supplying background for questions rather than furnishing answers. (Peleg, 2007: 7)

It is recognized that 'war journalism' is an inadequate term, limited as much by language as it is by a notion of journalistic reporting by aggressors or victors. The *Oxford English Reference Dictionary* (1995) is not alone in defining 'peace' as 'freedom from, or the cessation of, war... a treaty of peace between states etc. at war.' It took the pioneering wisdom of Johan Galtung to shape a broader, more inclusive definition, although the whole notion of 'peace journalism' still has its critics and detractors. Recent research findings seem to imply that there is still a long way to go to validate both its concept and practice, since:

> Neither war journalism nor peace journalism is being consciously practiced on a wide scale, and the prevalence of the former over the latter can be related to news organizations' structures and routines, including journalism's anchorage in the ideologies and power structures of the broader society. (Hackett and Schroeder, 2009: 52)

Yet, it was in 1670 in his *Theological-Political Treatise* that Spinoza wrote, 'Peace is not an absence of war, it is a virtue, a state of mind, a disposition for benevolence, confidence, justice.' If that is true, we need a broader concept of 'peace' as one that takes into account all the sites and forms of human conflict and misunderstanding in society—especially those impacting on the most vulnerable (children, women, and minorities). 'Peace journalism' then becomes 'benevolent journalism' or, since that is rather obscure and what we are really talking about is human dignity and justice, 'just journalism'.

Just journalism can challenge injustices and impunities that lead to killing

Writing in *The New York Times* (March 2, 2009), Archbishop Emeritus Desmond Tutu called on Africa's political leaders to take sides and support the International Criminal Court (IIC) in its attempt to have President Omar Hassan al-Bashir of Sudan indicted for the crime of genocide. Tutu pointedly asks if African leaders are 'on the side of justice or on the side of injustice? Are they on the side of the victim or the oppressor? The choice is clear but the answer so far from many African leaders has been shameful.' Tutu's appeal was in response to the culture of impunity that appears to exist among many of the world's political leaders, few of whom are ever called to account for dubious or downright criminal acts. Bosnia, Rwanda, Chile, and Cambodia may be exceptions (when the political climate is right), although many questions remain unanswered, although we already know that few of the perpetrators of injustice will actually be convicted.

If one takes into consideration the leaders of democracies—who never wage war on each other but only on 'rogue' states—impunity is also the name of the game. France's actions in Algeria, Britain's during the Malvinas/Falklands war, Russia's in Chechnya, the United States' in too many Latin American countries to name as well as in Iraq and Afghanistan—it has to be concluded, as has long been known, that there is one international standard for the power-brokers and another for the rest. Impunity has deep roots. On March 4, 2009, the International Criminal Court finally issued an arrest warrant against Omar Hassan al-Bashir of Sudan on charges relating to the conflict in Darfur, including war crimes. He was accused of running a campaign that killed 35,000 people outright, at least another 100,000 through 'slow death', and forcing 2.5 million people to flee their homes in Darfur. But the IIC stopped short of charging Sudan's leader with genocide because 'it did not find sufficient evidence of a specific intent to destroy ethnic groups in Darfur.' Yet, the UN reported that up to 300,000 people died from the combined effects of war, famine, and disease and more than two million people fled their homes. Al-Bashir stands accused of being criminally responsible for intentionally directing attacks against the civilian population of Darfur that included murdering, exterminating, raping, torturing, forcibly transferring large numbers of civilians, and pillaging their property.

Western media were uncritical in their reporting of the conflict in Sudan and found it difficult to determine what position to take. When the violence and oppression went on relentlessly, news editors turned their attention elsewhere. Similarly, African and Arab-language media have been criticized for ignoring the worsening situation. While it is clear that the mass media cannot prevent war, they can alert, explain, and offer more balanced and insightful opinion. The just journalism option—choosing stories that create opportunities for civil society to consider and value nonkilling responses to conflict—is also an antidote to impunity. The more people know about what is done in their name, about which governments, organizations and groups are doing what to whom, the more likely they are to challenge, contest, and—who knows?—act to prevent.

In his op-ed contribution, Tutu commented that, 'African leaders should be the staunchest supporters of efforts to see perpetrators brought to account. Yet rather than stand by those who have suffered in Darfur, African leaders have so far rallied behind the man responsible for turning that corner of Africa into a graveyard.' The leaders of the world's democratic countries need to take that lesson to heart. They, too, should be the staunchest supporters of international efforts to see the perpetrators of gross injustice brought to account. And those responsible for media enterprises of any kind have a public duty to expose them. When it comes to war, genocide, and human rights violations, there can be no impunity. Only justice.

It is not only the news media that can be scrutinised for its take on moral and political responsibility and accountability. The entertainment media is notorious for a rather cavalier attitude to objectivity, balance, and issues of representation. William Randolph Hearst is credited with instructing artist Frederic Remington not to return from Havana, Cuba, in 1898 without images of war: 'You furnish the pictures and I'll furnish the war.' Indeed, American and Cuban forces soon attacked the Spanish at Guantánamo Bay which led to the eventual defeat of the Spanish and the U.S. military establishing a naval base there. In the James Bond film *Tomorrow Never Dies* (1997), media mogul Elliot Carver is a fictional character modelled on Robert Maxwell, although many viewers saw Carver as a satirical take on Rupert Murdoch. Elliot Carver, head of the Carver Media Group Network, plans to use an encryption device to provoke war between China and the United Kingdom. As the existing Chinese leadership is not receptive to giving Carver Media Group Network exclusive broadcast rights in their country, Carver wants to use a war to eliminate them in favour of politicians more friendly to his plans. Carver quotes newspaper magnate William Randolph Hearst towards the film's climax, updated to 'You furnish the photographs, I'll furnish the war.'

It is to the power of cinema that we turn for a case study of how the mass media can consistently and persistently misportray and misrepresent a whole race of people with lethal consequences.

Case study: Reel Bad Arabs

In a groundbreaking book published in 2001 Jack G. Shaheen provided conclusive evidence that Hollywood films have spent several decades maligning, caricaturing, and misrepresenting Arabs. They portrayed them, deliberately or not, as 'uncivilized religious fanatics and money-mad cultural "others".' *Reel Bad Arabs* reviews feature films with leading Arab characters, the overwhelming majority of which, such as *Prisoner in the Middle East, Wanted Dead or Alive, The Delta Force*, and *Executive Decision* negatively stereotype Arabs. Only a handful of screenplays that surfaced in the 1980s and 1990s featured Arab characters as heroes, such as *The Lion of the Desert* and *The 13th Warrior.*

> In this first comprehensive review of Arab screen images ever published, I document and discuss virtually every feature that Hollywood ever made – more than 900 films, the vast majority of which portray Arabs by distorting at every turn what Arab men, women, and children are really like. In gathering the evidence for this book, I was driven by the need to expose an injustice: cinema's systematic, pervasive, and unapologetic degradation and dehumanization of a people. (Shaheen, 2001: 1)

Shaheen describes a symbiotic relationship between cinema's ability to create fictional narratives and images and its power to create social attitudes, to shape thoughts and beliefs, and to construct prisms through which people view the world and other people. It is an argument that can be extended to mass media generally and especially to the news media.

The first section of *Reel Bad Arabs*, 'The Genesis', discusses the negative stereotyping of Arabs in American pop culture. It is followed by 'Real Arabs' whom Shaheen has known: family, friends, colleagues, and people he has met and worked with. A third section, 'The Stereotype's Entry', articulates how Arab images entered American popular culture as an embellishment of pre-existing caricatures found in European literature, opera, and paintings. One example of this genre is *Oriental Stories* (later retitled *The Magic Carpet Magazine*), a magazine of 1930-34 and an offshoot of Weird Tales, the American fantasy and horror fiction pulp magazine first published in March 1923. *Oriental Stories* specialized in adventure and fantasy stories with Mid-Eastern or North African settings and elements. Its stories were peopled by 'cheating vendors and exotic concubines held hostage in slave markets' and Shaheen concludes that the American public's acceptance of such images tremendously influenced American culture in its relationship with the 'Oriental' Arab.

Reel Bad Arabs describes how Hollywood movies depicted the desert habitat of the Arab: 'The Desert locale consists of an Oasis, oil wells, palm trees, tents, fantastically ornate palaces, sleek limousines, and, of course, camels.' The screen Arab male lives in the desert like Ali Baba with 'curved dagger, scimitars, magic lamps, giant feather fans, and nargelihs' (tobacco water pipes). The Arab female passively accompanies the Arab male in every sort of film imaginable, beginning with two silent, black and white shorts—one censored, the other uncensored—*Fatima* (1897) and *Fatima's Dance* (1907). Both feature the star of the 1896 Chicago World's Fair, as a veiled bosomy belly dancer. To see Arab belly dancers appearing in early films is not surprising. At the turn of the century, dancers were a familiar turn in vaudeville and burlesque. In transferring vaudeville to the silver screen, Hollywood merely emulated them—as did Roscoe 'Fatty' Arbuckle in *The Cook* (1918), in which Buster Keaton consorts with a belly dancer at the Bull Pup Café. The trend continued:

> In Arabian Nights fantasies such as *The Sheik* (1921), *Slave Girl* (1947), and *John Goldfarb, Please Come Home* (1964), Arab women leer out from diaphanous veils, or as unsatisfied, disposable 'knick-knacks' lounging on ornate cushions, scantily-clad harem maidens with bare midriffs, closeted in the palace's women's quarters and/or on display in slave markets. (Shaheen, 2007: 27)

Shaheen puts Walt Disney's *Aladdin* (1992) on trial. The film's opening song immediately turns the Middle East into a dangerous and barbaric place in the minds of young children. The cartoon was unstinting in its depiction of scantily clad belly dancers and moustachioed angry guards with big swords. All good fun, some might argue, until one recalls a reverse scenario. In 1943 Disney produced an animated short film for RKO Radio Pictures called *Education for Death: The Making of the Nazi*. The film featured the story of little Hans, a boy born and raised in Nazi Germany, who is bred to become a merciless soldier. Intended as anti-Nazi propaganda during World War II, a voice track of Adolf Hitler in full demagogic rant is used in a torchlight rally scene and a sequence follows in which Hans becomes a Nazi soldier along with other Hitler Youth. One might struggle to distinguish between the 'propaganda' of *Education for Death* and that of *Aladdin*.

True Lies (1994) with an all-star cast that included Arnold Schwarzenegger and clearly touted as a comedy portrayed Palestinian freedom fighters as bumbling, angry, and fanatical terrorists. Not intended to, it never the less did nothing to acknowledge the grievances of real Palestinians forced from their homes in neo-colonial Israel—in contrast to the non-Hollywood film *Lemon Tree* (2008) directed by Eran Riklis, which sought to offer a Palestinian perspective. Shaheen describes as yet more disturbing the 'inoculation' attempted in *Rules of Engagement* (2000), which begins by making it appear as if Col. Childers was at fault for ordering his men to fire on a crowd of Yemeni citizens. Yet, later in the film the same crowd is portrayed as actually having fired first, even a sweet one-legged girl shown earlier.

Shaheen does not give an entirely negative account of Hollywood productions. He highlights *Three Kings* (1999)—on which he happens to have consulted—which presents a balanced portrayal of Iraqis during the first Gulf War. Some are loyal to Saddam Hussein, but others are depicted as having families and even as victims of State oppression. One scene memorably shows laughing teenage girls: not wrapped from head to toe in black but as human beings. *Reel Bad Arabs* makes a genuine attempt to answer the question: Why the stereotyping? One answer can clearly be found in US foreign policy interests in the Middle East. To further such ends, the Pentagon has collaborated in making movies that portray Arabs as terrorists out to kill Americans and destroy 'the Western way of life.' One example is *Black Hawk Down* (2002), which Shaheen places on his 'worst list'. Backed by the U.S. Department of Defence, it distorts what actually happened in Somalia in 1993 and omits key facts. 'Viewers are never told why so many Somalis are fighting against American soldiers; nor does the film explain that one year earlier, in 1992, the Somalis were very friendly to the Americans' (Shaheen, 2008: 100).

After 9/11, President Bush called a meeting (widely reported) between executives and high-level managers and producers from Hollywood and the White House to discuss how cinema can contribute to 'combating terrorism'. Jack Shaheen's second book (2008) asked if Hollywood's powerful post-9/11 images had smashed stereotypes or reinforced them and, if images had solidified viewers' perceptions of the Arab as the evil 'other', what steps should be taken to resolve the problem. He underlined the essential point that:

> Filmmaking is political. Movies continuously transmit selected representations of reality to world citizens from Baghdad to Boston. Dehumanizing stereotypes emerging from the cinema, TV, and other media help support government policies, enabling producers to more easily advance and solidify stereotypes. (Shaheen, 2008: xviii)

Noting that at the time of publication there were in excess of 1,150 films that defiled Arabs, he analyzed some 100 post-9/11 films in which 22 that otherwise had nothing to do with Arabs or the Middle East contain gratuitous slurs and demeaning scenes, 37 in which Arabs do dastardly things, 12 containing sheikhs caricatured as ugly, evil, or over-sexed, and six in which there were stereotypical portraits of Palestinians.

The survey did, however, commend 29 films that projected worthy Arabs and decent Arab Americans leading Shaheen to comment that, 'thoughtful imagemakers are beginning to rollback slanderous portraits and create fuller, more complicated Arab characters and stories' (Shaheen, 2008: 87). Even so, television has not followed suit. More than 50 post-9/11 TV shows vilify Arab Americans and Muslim Americans, in particular *West Wing, Navy NCIS, Criminal Minds, The Unit*, and *24*. Clearly, much work remains to be done before the entertainment industries begin to construct bridges of understanding and trust, 'illustrating that regardless of colour, creed, or culture, we [humans] are bound together' (Shaheen, 2008: 89).

The 'reel bad Arabs' case articulated by Jack Shaheen serves as a critical point of reference for the discussion of other areas of media content (even though they are becoming increasingly cross-platform and digitally incestuous). How far do today's mass media—

newspapers, television channels, radio stations, magazines, books, blogs—align themselves with the practical implications of Habermas's 'communicative action' explicitly to recognize and affirm the dignity and worth of other human beings? How far do they explicitly or implicitly promote or condone 'conditions conducive to lethality' (Paige, 2009: 77), those in which war, conflict, and violence are not only found to be acceptable but are seen as necessary and inevitable? How far do they negate or denigrate other peoples' cultures, or beliefs? Here, we are not talking about freedom of expression and opinion: the sine qua non of critical reflection and debate, whose purpose is to tease out political, social, and cultural conundrums in order to question, to understand, and to try to reach consensus about ways forward. What is at issue is communication conceived of as a revolutionary political practice leading to social change. As Richard Keeble has pointed out,

> Change will, in fact, only come if based on a radical political analysis of the media and society. This will incorporate an awareness of the possibilities of journalistic activities both within and outside the corporate media and as part of a broader political project to democratise the media and society in general. The strategy will also ultimately involve a radical broadening of the definition of journalism to include intellectuals, campaigners and citizens—all of them articulating their ideas within the dominant and alternative public spheres. (Keeble, 2009)

The questions articulated above apply equally to 'community media' (those genuinely owned and operated by a local community and having the interests of that community at heart) as well as to alternative and citizens' media, Indymedia, and Web 2 networks. Today's world is an exceedingly complex hierarchy of interrelated information and communication networks that exist to a greater or lesser extent in every country. The blogger in Afghanistan is not so far distant from his or her counterpart in Estonia or Chile. Access to technology may be an obstacle, but once in place, access to sources of global information and opinion tends to be a given. The question is how such access can be used to agitate for the reformulation and reconstruction of political, economic, social, and cultural frameworks that are more equitable and more just, and which, in the broadest definition, are 'nonkilling'. Participatory development experts, at least, are forcibly clear that:

> Citizens' media are part of a process of redefining dominant norms and power relations that marginalise and exclude people. Through having the capacities, the ownership, and the control to manage their own media, people can reshape and create the social, cultural, and political spaces in which their voices find expression. This gives meaning and legitimacy to diverse expressions of citizenship, adding depth and value to formal mechanisms of voice and representation (Pettit, et al., 2009: 451).

What would nonkilling media look like and how might they come about?

A necessary condition of nonkilling media is discernment, a willingness to challenge principalities and powers, to serve truth, and to denounce falsehood. In communication terms, discernment includes stimulating critical awareness of the multiple realities constructed in the mass media (and, today, in the virtual worlds of social communications and Web 2.0 technologies) in order to enable people to distinguish reliable information from propaganda, to take into account different positions, and to empathize in the course of reaching decisions. It often means investigating, exposing, and helping rebuild trust as vital steps towards conflict resolution and the long road to reconciliation. The concept of 'just journalism' discussed above is a good example of communication as discernment. Just journalism illuminates structural and cultural inequities as they impact the lives of ordinary people. It equips people to distinguish between self-interested positions and more positive aims and it places the emphasis on conflict prevention or the peaceful resolution of conflict.

A second necessary condition of nonkilling media is an ethical imperative guaranteeing people enough information and knowledge to make critical decisions and providing a framework for acts of indignation that affirm human dignity, sympathize with and take the part of people who are suffering. Michael Traber puts the matter succinctly:

> All affirmation of human dignity takes place through various modes of communication: through intrapersonal reflections and interpersonal and social communications. As the mass media are an important source of meanings for many people, they contribute to our understandings of human dignity and respect for life. When their images and messages rob people of their dignity, we do not remain unaffected. The way they describe and depict acts of violence—from street crime to wars—are of special relevance. They disclose what life is worth and how human dignity is valued or devalued. (Traber, 1997: 341)

The Declaration Towards a Global Ethic endorsed by the Parliament of the World's Religions (1993) identifies such an ethical imperative as 'a fundamental consensus on binding values, irrevocable standards, and personal attitudes.' Leonard Swidler (1994) has pointed out that the Global Ethic was specifically aimed at uniting religious and nonreligious positions and can, therefore, be seen as a humanist endeavour. Swidler went on to propose combining the principles of the Universal Declaration of Human Rights with those of the Global Ethic to create a *Universal Declaration of a Global Ethic* based on the following assumptions: that every human possesses an inalienable and inviolable dignity; that no person or social institution exists outside the scope of moral order; that humans as beings endowed with reason and conscience should act rationally; and that humans are an inextricable part of the universe and as such should act in harmony with nature.

Based on Swidler's claim that the principles of universality, of humanity, and of the autonomy of the human will are found and empirically formulated in all cultures, religious and secular ethical traditions as practical precepts of the ethic of reciprocity, it is possible to formulate at least two characteristics of nonkilling media:

1. *Nonkilling media should treat all human beings as ends, never as means*, respecting their intrinsic worth and dignity. Such respect should be extended to individuals, communities, nations, the world, and the cosmos.

2. *Nonkilling media should observe the right of all humans to hold their own opinions and beliefs*, fostering rational dialogue as the only method of reaching a consensus in which people can live side by side in peace.

As such the content of nonkilling media will be impartial, accurate, honest, gender aware, and contextual.

However, content is by no means the whole problem. There are key issues of corporate ownership and control of the media; government interference and/or censorship; and, crucially, deeply embedded political, social, and cultural ideologies that dictate prejudice, hatred, and injustice. Corporate media giants are silencing diverse voices, abandoning quality journalism, and eliminating local content. In the United States, Free Press (<http://www.freepress.net>)—a national, nonpartisan, non-profit organization working to reform the media—has identified General Electric, Walt Disney, NewsCorp, Time Warner, Viacom, and CBS as the 'Big Six' with revenues in 2009 in excess of US$ 276 billion from television, film, publishing and online holdings (<http://www.freepress.net/ownership/chart/main>). Government interference or censorship in relation to freedom of the press and editorial independence has been a contentious issue since the Vietnam War, notably during the Falklands War (1982), the U.S.-led invasion of Grenada (1983), the First Gulf War (1990-91), the second Gulf War (2003-2011), and the war in Afghanistan (2001-2014). Last but certainly not least, political, social, and cultural ideological differences have led to tension and conflict throughout the world.

Independent media, alternative media, and social media offer better possibilities for communicative action, deep conversation, and generative dialogue. They also challenge the hegemony of traditional mass media enterprises by increasingly providing organized material that is (to a certain as yet ill-defined extent) credible and reliable. Since corporate media are unlikely willingly to diminish their profitability any time soon, and since there will always be a demand for independent public service media, we might imagine a future scenario in which there will be three tiers of media activity that are interwoven and which interact. There will be some kind of integrated public service media at the national level, offering credible in-depth news, information and opinion mainly focused on political, economic, and cultural issues. There will be both independent and commercial media at the community level, offering less structured news, information, and opinion mainly focused on local interests. There will be social media at the ultra local level, offering highly partisan news, information, and opinion mainly focused on small groups of followers. People will dip in and out of all three tiers to varying degrees.

Is it a plausible notion that these three tiers of media activity will take up the principles of nonkilling? The obvious answer is 'no', and yet there is room for optimism. There is increasing awareness and activism around global poverty, ecological and environmental issues, climate change and global warming, gender equality and justice, forced migration, food and water shortages, violence, conflict, and security. These are signs of a growing awareness (acceptance?) of collective responsibility for what are, inevitably, global problems—in short, all the imperatives that challenge the creation of a nonkilling society. More than 20 years ago, Hans Küng wrote:

> For the next millennium a way must be found to a society in which men and women possess equal rights and live in solidarity with one another... a way must be found to a reconciled multiplicity of cultures, traditions and peoples... to a renewed community of men and women... to a society in which peacemaking and the peaceful resolution of conflicts is supported... to a community of human beings with all creatures in which their rights and integrity are also respected. (Küng, 1990: 67-9)

This is the role of nonkilling media. A genuinely democratic world will only accept a communications infrastructure that respects basic notions of justice, equality, and human dignity. Within that framework, nonkilling media would be duty-bound to maintain high standards of probity, accountability, and impartiality, as well as to mediate political, economic, social, and cultural conflicts in constructive and conciliatory ways. Access to public service media would be guaranteed to civil society groups and people's movements, providing openings for ordinary people to dialogue about issues of global, national and local interest. Such a system would be deliberately aimed at actively encouraging a politics of dissent in the interests of greater democracy.

There are many tyrannical institutions and individuals that would object to such a realignment—being content to profit from misery. Nonkilling media would elucidate that reality. Nonkilling media would highlight what Karl Jaspers identified as a form of metaphysical guilt, 'the lack of absolute solidarity with the human being as such—an indelible claim beyond meaningful duty' (Jaspers, 1947: 71). Metaphysical guilt resonates throughout today's globalized world, yet all is not lost:

> Something can be done if we all accept and practice the humanity, the indivisibility in plurality, of one another. Then we might care for human being as such; we might demonstrate a certain solidarity with those whom we feel to be distant otherwise and accord to each person a due measure of the dignity they deserve. That would involve solidarity with the aspiration and need of others to secure the resources of dignity. It would also involve the condemnation of any institutional policies or economic practices which deny access to, or the provision of, the security of those resources of dignity or which allow a surfeit to be allocated to specific groups at the expense of others. (Tester, 1997: 151)

Humanity, indivisibility in plurality, solidarity, and empathy: these are exemplary watchwords and normative principles for nonkilling media.

References

Boltanski, L. (1999). *Distant Suffering: Morality, Media and Politics*. Cambridge University Press.

Christians, C. G. and Traber, M., Eds. (1997). *Communication Ethics and Universal Values*. Thousand Oaks: Sage Publications.

Cowan, D. A. and Adams, K. (2002). 'Talking Circles as a Metaphor and Pedagogy for Learning.'

Declaration Toward A Global Ethic (1993). Section I. Available online at: <http://www.weltethos.org/dat-english/03-declaration.htm>.

Evans Pim, J., Ed. (2009). *Toward a Nonkilling Paradigm*. Honolulu: Center for Global Nonkilling. Available online at: <http://www.nonkilling.org>.

Habermas, J. (1984). *The Theory of Communicative Action. Vol. I: Reason and the Rationalization of Society*. London: Heinemann.

Habermas, J. (1987). *The Theory of Communicative Action, Vol. II: Lifeworld and System: A Critique of Functionalist Reason*. Cambridge: Polity Press.

Hackett, R. A. (2007). 'Media terror?' *Media Development*, 3. Available online at: <http://www.waccglobal.org/en/20073-media-and-terror/469-Media-terror.html>.

Hackett, R. A. and Schroeder, B. (2009). 'Does Anybody Practice Peace Journalism? A Cross-National Comparison of Press Coverage of the Afghanistan and Israeli-Hezbollah Wars,' in Ross, S. D. and Tehranian, M., Eds., *Peace Journalism in Times of War*. New Brunswick: Transaction Publishers.

Jaspers, K. (1947). *The Question of German Guilt*. New York: Dial Press.

Kahane, A. (2004). *Solving Tough Problems: An Open Way of Talking, Listening, and Creating New Realities.* San Francisco: Berrett-Koehler Publishers.

Keeble, R. (2009). 'The Basics of Journalism: Concepts of Ethics, Responsibility and Quality in media and journalism'. Paper given at the Catholic University Eichstaett-Ingolstadt School of Journalism, September 18-20. Available online at: <http://www.ku-eichstaett.de/fileadmin/1303/Downloads/Keeble_Paper.pdf>.

Kuhn, Thomas (1962). *The Scientific Structure of Scientific Revolutions*. Chicago: University of Chicago Press.

Küng, Hans (1990). *Global Responsibility: In Search of a New World Ethic*. London: SCM Press.

MacBride, S. (1980). *Many Voices, One World. Communication and Society Today and Tomorrow*. Paris: UNESCO; London: Kogan Page.

Paige, G. D. (2009 [2002]). *Nonkilling Global Political Science*. Honolulu: Center for Global Nonkilling. Available online at: <http://www.nonkilling.org>.

Paper presented at the Association of Leadership Educators' Conference, Lexington. Available online at: <http://www.leadershipeducators.org/Archives/2002/cowan_and_adams_talking_circle.pdf>.

Peleg, S. (2007). 'In defense of peace journalism: A rejoinder,' *Conflict & communication online*, 6(2). Available online at: <http://www.cco.regener-online.de/2007_2/pdf/peleg.pdf >.

Pettit, J.; Salazar, J. F. and Gumucio Dragón, A. (2009). 'Citizens' media and communication,' *Development in Practice*, 19(4-5).

Shaheen, J. G. (2001). *Reel Bad Arabs*. Northampton: Olive Branch Press.

Shaheen, J.G. (2007). 'Hollywood's reel Arab women,' *Media Development,* 2: 27-29.

Shaheen, J. G. (2008). *Guilty: Hollywood's Verdict on Arabs after 9/11*. Northampton: Olive Branch Press.

Sivaraksa, S., (2001). 'Culture and reconciliation,' *Media Development*, 4: 38-41.

Swidler, L. S. (1994). 'Toward a Universal Declaration of a Global Ethic,' *Dialogue and Humanism, The Universalist Journal*, 4(4): 51-64. Available online at: <http://www.jsri.ro/old/html%20version/index/no_7/leonardswidler-articol.htm>.

Tester, K. (1997). *Moral Culture*. London: Sage Publications.

Traber, M. (1997). 'An Ethics of Communication Worthy of Human Beings,' In Christians, C. and Traber, M., Eds., *Communication Ethics and Universal Values*. Thousand Oaks: Sage.

Nonkilling Campaigns across the Globe

Ir
Hiroshima

Welcome to
Soka University
第170回
家島本島で贈呈式
が晴れの総会
KONARK PUBLISHERS PVT LTD
Launch of
Chief Guest
pan for
ce Award 2016

धर्मो रक्षति रक्षितः

The New Geopolitics
11 - 13 September 2009
Geneva, Switzerland
IISS

CEREMONY

Give
Nonviolence
a Chance

भारतीय विश्वविद्यालय संघ का
92वाँ वार्षिक अधिवेशन
दिनांक १९-२१, मार्च २०१८
of
Age of Disruption.

The 32nd AUAP Annual Conference, Nov. 7~10, Xi'An International University, China

irst Nonkilling
ctorate awarded
Katyayani Singh
On
ioning the Universities of Tomorrow
the Age of Emerging Technologies, Disruption
November 18-21, 2018

EXIT

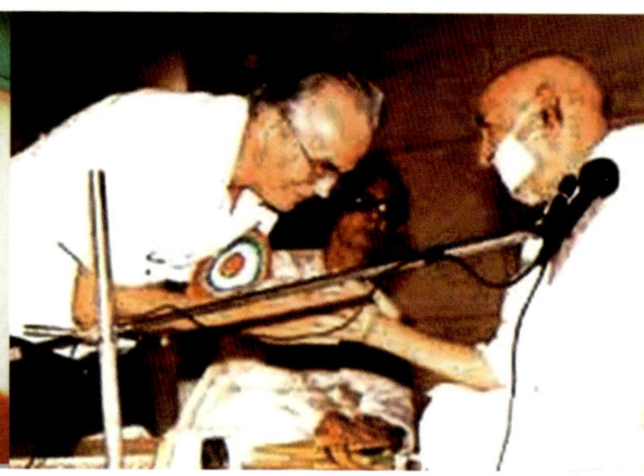

Give Nonviolence a Chance

7

Art – Means for and End of a Nonkilling World

Anis Hamadeh, May 2011

The essay at hand is about art being both a means to reach a nonkilling world and its goal. Definitions first: art is taken to be the part of human life in which inspiration leads to free and meaningful expression, usually in an esthetical, sensual, and communicative way. The concept of art is used here in a rather broad sense, sometimes as broad as meaning 'creativity'. A nonkilling world is a world without killing humans and without threats to kill. The global notion is chosen here, because a nonkilling group or society may still be confronted with killings outside.

We do not live in such a world, but we aspire to. Hardly anybody will not want to live in a world without killing, though many people – probably most people – will not be convinced that such a world is possible. So how can art be instrumental in bringing such a world closer and why should it be that a nonkilling world fosters art in turn?

Art as a Means

In his pioneering essay on the topic 'Nonkilling Arts', Urbain (2009) summarized and augmented the relevant parts of the formative work 'Nonkilling Global Political Science' by Glenn Paige (2009). Paige and Urbain refer to the power of the arts as a motor to 'uplift the human spirit' (Urbain 2009:76) which drives this spirit in the direction of nonkilling. Moreover, Urbain recognizes the elements of 'praising the dignity of life', 'exposing, denouncing, or condemning killing', 'promoting humane causes', and positive 'empowerment' (p 78). All these characteristics can be regarded as potential means for people to bring a nonkilling world closer. The problem with analysis here is that these characteristics are not too tangible, just like art itself, and prone to get lost in abstraction as soon as having entered the discourse, or – if examples are used – may appear random.

At least it can be safely said that art is a means to nonkilling in what is called 'art therapy', including both victim therapy and perpetrator therapy. This is not to say that a crayon in the hand of an offender is the solution, it is merely to show that there is serious work going on, exploring how art can be a systematic or at least a calculable means for peace. Cases of art therapy are legion, a recent one is about a Saudi Arabian (Dr Awad Alyami) experimental rehab center for former jihadists, some from Guantanamo (Durham 2008).

Other art-for-nonkilling factors are the power of art as an eye-opener, the artist as a role model, and the role of art in the self-organization of masses. Before discussing them, let us take a short look at some less complex thoughts on 'art as an end'.

Art as an End

A world without killing and without threats to kill will reduce the general fear index immensely. It is a truism that fear inhibits creativity and thus art. There may be people who claim that situations of suffering are most inducive to art, but there is no proof for that myth. Of course there is the soldier in the trench who writes beautiful poems (cf. Douglas 2000) and of course necessity is the mother of invention. But it is more plausible to assume that strong emotions cause art, rather than strong bad emotions.

For creativity to unfold it needs adequate surroundings, a habitat or climate. A world without killing and without threats to kill is such a climate. Pieces of art here can fill the space of the excitement of killing, together with other elements, like the fulfilling task of peace-keeping, family life, the unfolding of all kinds of talents, exploring the self and the world, exploring inspiration and the power of love.

One of the earliest known examples for art to fill the space of violence is about 5000 years old: the Abydos cemetery in Egypt. Professor Günter Dreyer, who analyzed the site, explains: 'The energy that before was necessary to submit lower Egypt could flow elsewhere. In this case into architecture' (Utzt et al. 2010).

The achievement of a nonkilling world will predictably give rise to pride and entail a constructive, communicative community. There will always be problems and the limitations of life, but it is vital to recall the ideal, because visualization is the first step to bring it closer. It is essential for us to understand why a nonkilling world is most desirable so that working for this cause has a strong motivation.

Art as an Eye-Opener

In some episodes of the famous Simpsons cartoon series, a song is able to solve the most difficult situation. At the end of the song the people around are touched. Suddenly they understand what they did not understand before and change their minds for peace. The scenes make you laugh for their irony (in the real world songs don't work like that), and yet, at the same time, there must be some truth and hope in this scenery (songs should work like that), otherwise we would not laugh. Art can therefore be counted among the means to raise an awareness that leads to change – and change towards nonkilling is a central and not a marginal form of this change.

Investigative journalism may be the most vivid example for the eye-opener phenomenon that can bring about peace and nonkilling. WikiLeaks is an important contemporary token, or take the documentary 'Blood in the Mobile' about the connection of mobile phone production and the civil war in Congo (Poulsen 2011).

A good example for art as an eye-opener is Robert Newman's comedy show 'The History of Oil'. Information Clearing House summarizes: 'Robert Newman gets to grips with the wars and politics of the last hundred years – but rather than adhering to the history we were fed at school, he places oil centre stage as the cause of all commotion'(see Newman 2005).

Picasso's 'Guernica' can be counted into this list and many other works, famous and not famous. Art's special role in awareness raising is rendered by Urbain's list of characteristics mentioned above to which can be added the intrinsic power of some pieces of art like e.g. Guernica or Jimi Hendrix's Woodstock version of the US national anthem which entails a self-explaining authority and the fascination of the affected audience. Also, art can make use of elements like irony and caricature to convey a message, effective means that are not covered in the discourse of investigative journalism or of logical analysis.

It must be stressed, though, that art and creativity do not necessarily work for peace or nonkilling. A striking example of that is Goethe's early novel 'The Sorrows of Young Werther', one of the most successful pieces of world literature. In the wake of its publication in 1774 dozens of 'copycats' committed suicide, a phenomenon known as the 'Werther effect' (Ziegler and Hegerl 2002).

Artists as Role Models

When John Lennon sang 'Come together over me' he was well aware of the fact that artists serve as role models. The consequence he drew from that fact was his deliberate development into a peace—and, if you will: nonkilling—advocate and activist. While in today's zeitgeist such an attitude might be regarded as old-fashioned, naive, or even didactic and pretentious, it cannot be denied that artists by authority of their creativity and freedom have this potential to change the minds of people toward nonviolence and nonkilling.

While Lennon and Ono resorted to staging and orchestrating their pacifist beliefs in order to convey them to others—with events like bed-ins, with songs, huge posters, etc.—there are at least two more levels on which artists and stars can reach the status of role models for peace, and Lennon and Ono have been on these levels, too:

There is the level of own behavior, for one thing. This level is free from didacticism and planned orchestration. Just like children copy the behavior of their parents, fans copy the behavior of their stars. On this level, it is not important whether the role model at hand is an artist or a politician like Gandhi or Petra Kelly or a parent or whatever; yet it can be stated that art has a disposition to go public and thus to reach a wide audience. Take the literary figure of the world-famous inspector Colombo: in none of the episodes Colombo uses a weapon to reach his aims and to arrest the murderer. And in none of the episodes he uses threats of any kind. Even when he is ridiculed, provoked, or under threat himself, he remains calm, sober ... and very efficient. Of course, Inspector Colombo is not a real person, but his case serves the purpose of the argument at hand.

And there is one more level where artists (and other public figures) can bring about peace and nonkilling in a wider sense and this brings us back to the notion of 'come together over me'. For illustration, let us look at one of the biggest icons of the twentieth century: Elvis Presley. Elvis has millions of fans worldwide until today and wherever people, who admire his music, meet, there is an air of community and mutual understanding. This I can say from my own experience in dozens of cases and regarding several countries from all continents. When you are an Elvis fan and meet a stranger who turns out to be another Elvis fan you connect – and this person will no longer be a stranger within an instant of time. You suddenly share a culture and this is enough to overcome distrust and suspicion to an extent that can be recognized as supporting nonviolence. It is not something that Elvis consciously intended, at least it does not have to be. Of course he tried to be a moral man and he is known to have been religious, friendly, and caring, with a sense of social responsibility that certainly distinguishes him from, say, Charles Manson. Elvis is taken as an example here, because he was not a pacifist like Lennon (another Elvis fan) and he did not oppose the war on Vietnam or the military system of the USA. (He also did not explicitly support the war on Vietnam, at least not in public, as did some of his contemporaries, like James Brown). So by mere virtue of his art and personality, Elvis managed to promote peace.

Art and Self-Organization of Masses

The connections and relationships between art and nonkilling accounted for in the essay at hand are not meant to be exhaustive or final.

Rather, they are meant to shed light on some of the major aspects as a brainstorming and a potential inspiration. Certainly, political leadership is an inevitable aspect here. While a discussion of art and creativity in respect to political parties and leaders is worth a monograph of its own, the focus here shall be on the aspect of the self-organization of masses, a topic especially relevant in the grassroot discourse. In how far does art support or even enable successful peaceful calls for change, calls that emerge from a significant and large part of a society?

The case of Woodstock seems relevant here. In 1969, almost half a million people gathered in a farm area in the State of New York to experience a three-day music festival. It was by far the biggest congregation of its kind in history. As can be derived from the German documentary film *Woodstock – How the Myth was Created* the authorities feared an outbreak of violence, simply because of the sheer amount of people who came together without a corresponding controlling power to watch over them. John Morris, the stage manager of the festival, who was also responsible for most of the band bookings, recalled:

> *Nelson Rockefeller, who was the governor of New York, wanted to come in and clear everybody out of the field with the National Guard. I've been on the phone with him and talked to them and was be able to talk to their chief of staff and got them not to do it and got them to send us military medical helicopters instead. And at one point I was on the mike and talking to the audience and it was really hot, just before Cocker, way, way hot. We were trying to get fire-hoses from the fire-engines that were around to spray the crowd 'cause it was so hot. And I could see three or four army helicopters flying from the back of the audience towards the stage. And I thought: oh boy, this is gonna freak people out. So I timed it until they could hear the sound. I mean, this is Vietnam! Everybody knew that sound. I timed it so that I can see them, I can see the audience could hear them and I went: ladies and gentlemen: the US army! And they all went: rrrrhh! … Medical Corps !! And it flipped just like that. And they all cheered and everything else. I talked to one of the guys and he said: That was scary 'cause they booed us and then all of a sudden the roar, positive roar, we also felt we're being bounced with it!* (Morawietz 2009)

As we know today the festival remained peaceful all the way through and the above quote shows that a controlling intervention would even have been counter-productive. Woodstock thus showed that a self-organization of masses is possible. Was art the reason for that in the Woodstock case? Filmmaker and director Stefan Morawietz doubts that:

> *'I think the musical aspect of Woodstock is overrated. After all my conversations with the participants it rather seems to me that the ingroup-feeling was the decisive motif for the behavior of the crowd. For many of them it was the first time to realize that they were not alone. That they were not the only weirdos with long hair like in their hicktowns, but that there were hundreds of thousands of kindred souls. The music mostly only was the trigger and the occasion to meet up and, of course, it was the suitable soundtrack for the event. So in the end I regard Woodstock as a political-sociological phenomenon rather than a musical one.'* (Morawietz 2011, translated from German)

Morawietz's analysis is reasonable and sound, especially when one takes into account other big events where the self-organization of huge gatherings proved successful. To the most prominent ones belong the downfall of the Berlin Wall in 1989 and the Egyptian revolution at Tahrir Square in 2011. It should not be underestimated, though, that the whole so-called 'hippy movement' of the 1960s with its stress on love and peace would have been unthinkable without the artistic expression that went with it: the songs, literature, films, etc. which were part of that new civilization. Joel Rosenman, one of the organizers of the festival, talks about in the mentioned documentary:

> *We tried to organize Woodstock, but this structure basically broke down within the first hours of the festival. And then I saw how half a million of young people created a new civilization without having been pushed to do that from our side. It came from within. And this reminded me of the fact that everybody has got this wonderful spirit in themselves that appears when it is given space. I think that was one of the few true symbols of this kind that can be historically validated. And maybe this is what the myth is about.* (Morawietz 2009, retranslated from German)

It is very hard to assess the role of art in the self-organization of masses, but it undeniably plays a role. The student protests of 1968 had lots of creative and artistic elements, and so has the Egyptian revolution, as, for example, Maysoon Zayid, an Arab-American comedian, witnessed during the first days of the peaceful Cairo uprising. In an Al-Jazeera interview she said:

> *The people in the revolutions themselves use comedy. There were some great posters in Tahrir Square, my favourite being one sign that said: We are looking for a man with black hair, an ego-maniac. If you find him, please send him to the airport. And there was a picture of Hosni Mubarak. They use humour there to get their message across.* (*Al-Jazeera 2011*)

Preconditions of Art and Creativity to Serve Nonkilling Purposes

The essay at hand shall close with the thesis that creativity and art are—like investigative journalism—substantial and valid alternatives to violence and means to overcome violence. Gandhi's salt march was highly creative. The Afro-Americans in the USA of the 1950s used creative methods to overcome segregation. The Gaza flotilla is one of the most creative projects of nonviolent resistance in recent years. Yet, as plausible as this thesis may appear, it faces major structural problems: it is dependent on the sensitization of society through education and values and it needs public response.

To illustrate that, let us take another look at the mentioned Colombo series. William Shatner, known for his role as Captain James T. Kirk in the first Star Trek series, appeared twice as the villain in the Colombo series. The showdown of his second appearance is the following scene: Inspector Colombo and the villain meet on a lonely street outside the city. Colombo, standing next to his car, confronts the villain with the solution of the case, proving his guilt. The villain, who stands some meters apart, listens and then draws a gun, saying something like: 'This knowledge will be of no use for you, as I am going to shoot you'. At this,

Colombo honks the horn of his car and a group of policemen rushes in from around the corner. Happy ending.

Now, what if there were no policemen – or no public, for that matter? Remember the case of the Mavi Marmara. In May 2010, this unarmed boat was forcefully boarded in international waters by the Israeli army who shot nine passengers dead. There was no trial for this murder and no consequences for the perpetrators. Nonviolent, creative resistance especially in Palestine has failed in other places, too, like the village of Bil'in, because the world public does not remotely care enough. Palestine is not the only example, but probably the most striking and obvious one worldwide. A strong public can overcome any injustice; we simply do not have it. We are neither trained nor educated for such issues, as if they were not important.

Similarly, and maybe as a consequence, advocates of nonviolence, be they artists or politicians or others, are rarely promoted by our societies for their advocacy. As mentioned before, someone like John Lennon today would hardly get the chance to really be heard. You can be an activist against land-mines or against famine in the world, but violence and killing as such are so deeply embedded and accepted in our cultures today that most people simply do not understand why nonviolent resistance can be necessary. Even the very strange notion of a military 'war on terror' with the acknowledged inevitability of large numbers of civilian casualties and the many lessons from history that prove that such an idea simply cannot work has not led to the rise of new Lennon and Gandhi – not because there are no candidates, but because the public does not make them big enough.

Here is not the place to discuss the reasons for these phenomena, like the priority of loyalty to groups over loyalty to law and ideas of justice. Or like daily TV brainwash. Or like the current structure of the UN. Also, there surely are exceptions and counter-trends like the Arab Spring. All in all, however, there is not much reason for optimism when we regard the facts. What can be the consequence for those who do understand the significance of nonviolent resistance today? Well, resist.

References

Al-Jazeera English (2011). 'The last laugh', Riz Khan Show, Apr. 28, 2011.

Douglas, Keith (3d edition 2000). The Complete Poems. London.

Durham, Nancy (2008). From Jihad to Rehab, a PBS production, Dec. 17, 2008, see www.pbs.org/wnet/wideangle/episodes/from-jihad-to-rehab/nancy-durham-filmmaker-notes/3839/ and Cathy Malchiodi: Jihad Rehab: Can Art Therapy Cure Terrorism? Dec. 19, 2008, at www.psychologytoday.com/blog/the-healing-arts/200812/jihad-rehab-can-art-therapy-cure-terrorism . Another case at http://sct.temple.edu/blogs/murl/2009/06/25/germantown-art-therapy-for-prison-inmates/.

Morawietz, Stefan (2009). Woodstock – Wie der Mythos entstand (Woodstock – How the Myth was Created). Documentary, Germany, 90 mins.

Morawietz, Stefan (2011). from a personal email, translated from German.

Newman, Robert (2005). The History of Oil. Political Stand-Up Comedy, 45 mins, see www.informationclearinghouse.info/article13416.htm (Google video is embedded).

Paige, Glenn (2009). Nonkilling Global Political Science. 2nd revised edition. Honolulu.

Poulsen, Frank (2011). 'Blood in the Mobile', German/French documentary, arte, Feb. 9, 2011, see www.arte.tv/de/Die-Welt-verstehen/3688366.html.

Urbain, Olivier (2009). Nonkilling Arts. From: Evans Pim, Joám (ed.): Toward a Nonkilling Paradigm, pp 73-91. Honolulu.

Utzt, Suzanne / Remme, Tilman / Feyerabend, Christian (Directors) (2010). Ägypten, Geburt einer Großmacht (Egypt, Birth of a Great Power), Part 1, Documentary, 90 mins, shown on arte on Apr. 2, 2011.

Ziegler, W. / Hegerl, U. (2002). Der Werther-Effekt. Bedeutung, Mechanismen, Konsequenzen. In: Nervenarzt 2002/73, pp 41-49, see www.ipsilon.ch/uploads/media/Werther-Effekt_1__01.pdf (with short English summary).

8

Music in Peacebuilding, the Nonkilling Dimension: A New Prelude to 'Nonkilling Arts'

Olivier Urbain

Director, Min-On Music Research Institute (MOMRI), Tokyo, Aug 6, 2018

It is with deep gratitude that I have accepted the invitation from the editor to republish the chapter entitled 'Nonkilling Arts,' originally published in 2009 in *Towards a Nonkilling Paradigm*, edited by Joám Evans Pim. I've had three types of reactions when reading this piece which was written almost a decade ago: there are passages with which I cannot agree with any more today, others that I feel are even more relevant, and then there is the bulk of the article, which today requires some qualification.

The paragraphs regarding the supposedly 'universal' appeal of Beethoven's Ninth Symphony have been deleted. The comments regarding the effect 'Ode to Joy' has on me personally have been left intact, but my ideas have changed regarding universal vs. culture specific reactions to musicking, mostly thanks to numerous discussions with ethnomusicologists.

There are a few statements in the 2009 version which seem to me even more relevant today, and I will list them here. I believe, more than ever, that…

> 'If we want to move toward a nonkilling society, one of the most crucial elements will be the fostering of positive qualities in ourselves and others' (p. 87).
> 'It is of the utmost urgency for us to learn how to get along and organize our societies on a better basis than killing or the threat to kill' (p. 88).
> "What Glenn Paige has provided to humanity is a way to think about the issue in a systematic way. This set of questions is a pure stroke of genius: 'Is a nonkilling society possible? If no, why not? If yes, why?' For this he deserves our eternal gratitude" (p. 90).

I will now focus on the statements in my 2009 chapter which I believe require some qualification, based on what I learned during the last decade.

In general, I noticed my own (past) refusal to take power balance into account in my (past) prescriptive statements regarding the potential roles of artistic activities in the nonkilling society project. It is true that works of art can inspire us, unite us, and give us hope, but to do what? There are people on this planet who love to kill and to see others killed, and this has to be accepted as an integral part of our reality if we are to make serious progress towards the development of nonkilling societies. Billions of dollars are being made as I write these lines by people who benefit from weapons sales and megadeaths. They may not represent a large percentage of the world population, but they can be found in the highest echelons of power and finance, which is highly problematic for the nonkilling society project to say the least. In addition, we can find power struggles at all levels of human relationships, within ourselves, our families, friendships and community activities. It is quite possible to handle issues of power humanely, creatively and in a way that benefits everyone (see Urbain, 2016), but these issues first need to be acknowledged. Not everyone wants peace and harmony, and as a result, a more robustly realistic approach to the potential of the arts for the nonkilling society project is necessary. To make a long tale short, I had to learn how to include the reality of power struggles into my research endeavours.

During the last ten years, seven major conceptual challenges have emerged in my work regarding music in particular, major ideas that I believe we need to keep in mind when considering the potential application of music in peacebuilding activities, which include activities that promote nonkilling.

1. Ambivalence: music can be used for good or for evil (Kent, 2008), no matter what the music itself is.
2. Musicking: listening, clapping hands, organizing a festival are all 'musicking activities,' and it is necessary to consider music as action (Small, 1998), what we do to ourselves and each other through music, in addition to the qualities of the sounds such as melody, harmony, rhythm, tempo, timbre and the like.
3. Booster: music all by itself would be useless if there was nobody to listen to it. Most human activities, for instance therapy, demonstrations or exposing inequalities, do not require music at all. However, when music is added strategically, the resulting activities are often more effective. In the three examples mentioned, music therapy sessions, chants during demonstrations, and protest songs illustrate the booster effect of music.
4. Non-universality: music is a language that can be found almost universally on planet Earth, but that does not mean that it is the universal language (Cohen, 2008). Different people will have different reactions to the same music based on their social/cultural/economic background, and most of all, based on their individual experiences.
5. Repetition: many wonderful attempts to create reconciliation through music do fail because the positive experiences happen just once during a music camp or a festival. Those experiences need to be repeated for the extraordinary to become the normal (Robertson, 2015). If they remain extraordinary, behavior will not change much.

6. Power balance: all human interactions and relations include a certain amount of desire for power, and so do our musical relations. These have to be taken into account. Case in point: in my 2009 chapter (pp. 82-84), I praise the organization El Sistema that was established in Venezuela in 1975. A few years later, much more information became available, and El Sistema was severely criticized by among others, Geoffrey Baker (2014). The net result is that El Sistema members worldwide have become much more aware of the issues that were plaguing their activities, and have made substantial improvements since then.
7. Industry amplification: the power given to some superstars, who have dozens of millions of fans reading their tweets, is truly frightening, and must be studied in depth.

All of the above being said, I am grateful to be able to present once again some of my ideas regarding nonkilling arts, and I look forward to receiving feedback from the readers, and to continue learning about the most effective ways to apply music in peacebuilding—and nonkilling—activities.

References

Baker, Geoffrey (2014). *El Sistema: Orchestrating Venezuela's Youth*. Oxford: Oxford University Press.

Cohen, Cynthia (2008). 'Music: A Universal Language?' in *Music and Conflict Transformation,* edited by Olivier Urbain.

Kent, George (2008). 'Unpeaceful Music' in *Music and Conflict Transformation,* edited by Olivier Urbain.

Pim, Joám Evans, ed. (2009). *Towards a Nonkilling Paradigm. Honolulu:* Center for Global Nonkilling.

Robertson, Craig (2015). 'Music Sociology: A Focus on Conflict Transformation.'Accessed on Aug. 6, 2018 from http://institute.min-on.org/newsandtopics/item/a-conference-celebrating-the-official-launch-of-the-min-on-music-research-institute-4/Small, Christopher. 1998. *Musicking: The Meanings of Performing and Listening*. Hanover: University Press of New England.

Small, Christopher (1998). Musicking: The Meanings of Performing and Listening. Connecticut: Wesleyan University Press.

Urbain, Olivier, ed. (2015 [2008]). *Music and Conflict Transformation: Harmonies and Dissonances in Geopolitics*. London: I.B. Tauris.

Urbain, Olivier (2009). 'Nonkilling Arts' in *Towards a Nonkilling Paradigm*, edited by Joám Evans Pim.

Urbain, Olivier (2016). 'A statement of values for our research on music in peacebuilding: a synthesis of Galtung and Ikeda's peace theories' in *Journal of Peace Education*, 13:3, 218-237.

9

Nonkilling Arts

Olivier Urbain

Director, Min-On Music Research Institute (MOMRI), Tokyo

> Romain Rolland quotes Tolstoy, '*Art must suppress violence, and only art can do so' (...) Art Young observes, 'Nonviolence is more than a system of political thought; it is the stuff of poetry and of life.' Reminiscent of the importance of martial music for military morale, a maxim in the Kingian tradition maintains, 'If you don't have a song, you don't have a movement.'* (...)
>
> Quotations provided by Glenn Paige, (2009a: 123)

The main question that motivated me to write this chapter is 'What is the role of the arts in making a nonkilling society possible?' As a first attempt to touch upon this vast and complex issue, three answers are provided here. First, Glenn Paige offers several hints in his seminal Nonkilling Global Political Science (2009). Second, I offer the results of some free brainstorming concerning the role of the arts. The third section invites the reader to an exploration of the human qualities enhanced by the arts. Finally in the conclusion, some avenues for further discoveries are suggested.

If we agree to consider the hypothesis that a nonkilling society can be imagined, and that concrete steps toward its realization can be taken, then there is no limit to what can be imagined concerning 'nonkilling arts.' It is to be hoped that a powerful stream of creativity, new ideas, works of arts, and networks will soon irrigate our global human civilization still in the grips of a culture of violence. The ambition of this chapter is to add a few drops to this current toward a society that respects life, and toward governance at all levels that functions effectively with much less, or ideally no more, killing. I wrote this piece from the point of view of an amateur blues pianist, hoping to inspire an endless series of free improvisations around similar themes.

Glenn Paige on the Role of the Arts in the Nonkilling Society Project

> *Synergistic nonkilling creativity among the arts can uplift the human spirit and imagination for the crucial transformational tasks ahead.* (Paige, 2009: 123)

Before starting our explorations of the role of the arts in creating a nonkilling society, we need to go back to Glenn Paige's original set of questions: 'Is a nonkilling society possible? If not, why not? If yes, why?' (Paige, 2009: 21), and especially to the numerous answers provided in his book to the last question: 'If yes, why?' The following passage can serve as a starting point to affirm the crucial role of the arts in endeavours to build a nonkilling society.

> *In December 1987 a Korean professor of philosophy, president of the Korean Association of Social Scientists and political leader in Pyongyang, surprisingly replies without hesitation: 'It's completely possible.' Why? First humans by nature are not compelled to kill. (p. 21)*

Whereas 'equitable distribution' might not be easily enhanced through the arts, everything else on this list—consciousness, reason, creativity, productivity—can be directly inspired by artistic means.

Moreover creativity and the arts have a crucial role to play in 'education' and the 'provision of a proper social atmosphere.' (Ibid) There are many other statements dispersed throughout Paige's book letting us know that he is a strong believer in the power of the arts for the nonkilling society project. Only a few are presented here, and the ambition of this paper is not to offer an exhaustive list. The reader is invited to find many other hints in Nonkilling Global Political Science.

Uplifting, Philosophical and Normative Power of the Arts

Every day we are influenced by the arts, music, dance, films, literature, photography, theatre, painting and sculpture, the use of arts in the media, and more, and the collective power of these artistic energies both expresses and contributes to the overall culture of our human societies. The fact that we need to move toward a 'culture of peace' immediately tells us where we are right now when it comes to the level of humanity with which we treat each other. On 10 November 1998, the United Nations General Assembly (UNGA) proclaimed the period 2001-2010 as the 'International Decade for a Culture of Peace and Nonviolence for the Children of the World' (UNAC, 2009).

What should be the ethical axis of such a 'culture of peace,' and more specifically of a 'culture of nonkilling?' Paige gives an example of the importance of beliefs and values in the shaping of such a culture. He reports findings comparing two Mexican Zapotec villages (emphasis added):

> *With material and structural conditions much the same, the homicide rate in San Andres is 18.1 per 100,000 compared with 3.4 in La Paz. This comparison helps us to understand that pessimism about human nature and community norms condoning violence are correlated with killing; whereas nonkilling beliefs and values predispose to a nonkilling society* (p. 49).

What could be a key concept at the basis of 'nonkilling beliefs and values'? One such normative center, fundamental to a nonkilling culture, is 'Respect for Life.' The phrase appears eight times throughout

Paige's book, as for instance when he affirms that (emphasis added) 'The reality of respect for life in religious and humanist faiths provides a strong spiritual basis for confidence that a nonkilling global society is possible' (Paige, 2009: 41), or that a nonkilling department of political science should try to express the desired traits of a nonkilling society by affirming 'non-sectarian but multi-faith spiritual and humanist respect for life' (p. 132). Paige also uses expressions such as 'uncompromising respect for life' (p. 78) and 'unambiguous respect for life' (p. 121).

Based on the above reaffirmation of the seminal importance of Paige's original explorations, the question at the center of this chapter then becomes: 'How can the arts contribute to the development of a nonkilling society, pervaded by a nonkilling culture, which would be based on an uncompromising respect for life?' First let us take a look at the answers provided by Paige himself throughout his work. Three proposals stand out as part of a coherent plan: using cultural resources, establishing centres, and developing four pillars for nonkilling transformation.

Cultural resources

Paige offers a list of works of art which he includes in the category 'social institutions.' It seems to me that the main point here is to use what we already have to be inspired to do more (emphasis added).

> *Nonkilling cultural resources are creations of art and intellect that uplift the human spirit and inspire advances toward realization of a nonkilling society. These include folk songs ('We Shall Overcome'), opera (Philip Glass, Satyagraha), novels (Bertha von Suttner, Lay Down Your Arms); poetry (Steve Mason, 'Johnny's Song'), art (Käthe Kollwitz, 'Seed for the planting must not be ground'); and films (Richard Attenborough, Gandhi). The Centre for Nonviolence through the Arts, founded in 1995 by Mallika Sarabhai in Ahmedabad, India, seeks to synergize nonkilling creativity for social trans-formation in the visual, performing, and literary arts. (Paige, 2009: 60)*

A systematic exploration of works of art that 'uplift the human spirit' would be fascinating, and we would like to invite the reader to join us in continuing this task.

Centres for creativity and the arts

More concrete than 'cultural resources,' Paige's next proposals advocate the establishment of institutions, promoting a range of positive societal reinforcements from simple celebrations to global recognition of the role of artists (emphasis added).

> *One institutional model—patterned after private centres that sponsor creative communities among the seven arts or among painters, poets, and writers—is to provide opportunities for artists of every inspiration to come together to celebrate transformative nonkilling creativity in response to human lethality… Synergistic nonkilling creativity among the arts can uplift the human spirit and imagination for the crucial transformational tasks ahead. For global recognition, benefactors should establish awards for nonkilling contributions to the arts no less significant than encouragement provided by the various Nobel prizes.* (Paige, 2009: 123)

In the two passages above, Paige mentions the power of the arts to 'uplift the human spirit.' This is very difficult to evaluate, and most of the time the positive impact of the arts cannot be verified empirically. To make this concept more palatable, Paige provides the example of how Thoreau and Tolstoy as literary artists have inspired the major leaders of nonviolent movements, Gandhi and King: 'Nonkilling Americans, such as Adin Ballou and Henry David Thoreau inspire Tolstoy…; Tolstoy inspires Gandhi; Gandhi inspires King; all inspire German Green Party founder Petra Kelly … and many others in a cumulative global diffusion process of emulation and innovation' (Paige, 2009: 70). Along the same lines, the transformative power of the arts can be empirically evaluated in professional fields such as music and arts therapy.

The four elements of nonkilling transformation: the Four S's:

> *The principal elements that need to be combined for nonkilling transformation are clear. Spirit (S1), profound commitments not to kill derived from each and all faiths and philosophies. Science (S2), knowledge from all the arts, sciences, and professions that bear upon the causes of killing and nonkilling transformation. Skills (S3), individual and group methods for expressing spirit and science in transformative action. Song (S4), the inspiration of music and all the arts, making the science and practice of nonkilling politics neither dismal nor deadly but a powerful celebration of life* (Paige, 2009: 130).

The fourth element, Song (S4), clearly represents the power of creativity and the arts in transformational processes. In addition, music and the arts also have major roles to play in the other three S's, namely Spirit, Science and Skill as defined above. My personal conclusion after this brief textual analysis of Nonkilling Global Political Science, is that there is no question that for Glenn Paige, nonkilling arts is an integral and major part of the nonkilling society project. This exercise has only confirmed the content of two long, fascinating and warm personal exchanges between this author and the founder of the Nonkilling movement, in Honolulu on 15 November 2008 and 21 July 2009.

Exploring the Countless Roles of the Arts toward a Nonkilling World

For the possibility of 'nonkilling arts' to make sense, there must be such a thing as 'killing arts.' This might be counter-intuitive, but it is important to recognize that music and the arts have been widely used, and are still used today, to encourage people to kill as many 'enemies' as possible. Hitler, Stalin and other dictators have systematically used the arts to encourage their people to commit mass atrocities through propaganda and other means of indoctrination. Marching songs have given the courage and enthusiasm to soldiers in most historical periods and civilizations to go and kill, and not fear being killed.

In the collective volume entitled *Music and Conflict Transformation* (Urbain, 2008), George Kent dedicates one chapter, 'Unpeaceful Music,' to this issue. He writes:

> *Some music may help to make some kinds of peace some of the time, but, like many other good things, music has a dark side as well. There is music that celebrates war, viciousness, hate, and humiliation. Music does have the power to heal, but we need to see that it also has the power to hurt. Music can bring us together, and it also can divide us.* (Kent in Urbain, 2008: 104)

We invite the reader to continue exploring this topic, which might provide interesting answers to the first part of Paige's original set of questions mentioned above: 'Is a nonkilling society possible? If not, why not? For instance, one possible answer is: 'It is impossible, because even the arts are used for killing!' In this paper, I will continue focussing on the 'If yes, why?' part of the equation.

A personal brainstorming session has yielded the following short list of the positive roles the arts can play in the construction of a nonkilling society:

- To praise the dignity of life, explicitly or not
- To expose, denounce or condemn atrocities and killing
- To promote a cause or an issue conducive to a more humane society
- To empower people in extremely difficult situations, so they can avoid having to kill or being killed
- To enhance positive human qualities that enable people to work toward the development of a less violent society (see next section)

Each of the first four statements will be illustrated by a few examples, and the last one will be more thoroughly explored in the next section. The evaluation of works of art is eminently subjective, and endless debates can be triggered by people's differing tastes and choices. In order to avoid making broad statements that would do not make much sense to anybody else, I will simply state my own likes and dislikes throughout the series of examples examined below. There is no doubt that the reader will easily provide other illustrations, expressing different experiences and a unique appreciation of esthetics and human creativity.

To praise the dignity of life, explicitly or not

Personally, I find Beethoven's Ninth Symphony very moving, and I will focus on the 'Ode to Joy' here. Its power to inspire people to work toward a nonkilling society is implicit and indirect. The voices, sounds, rhythms and timbres do not say 'no more killing,' nor do they say 'violence is bad.' The lyrics, based on a poem by Friedrich von Schiller written in 1785, with additions by Beethoven, do not talk about peace or nonviolence, but about joy and unity, as in this excerpt: 'Joy, bright spark of divinity, Daughter of Elysium, Fire-inspired we tread Thy sanctuary. Thy magic power re-unites all that custom has divided; All men become brothers, Under the sway of thy gentle wings' (classicalmusic.about.com, 2009).

Here I want to use 'Ode to Joy' as an example of a work of art that implicitly provides a message toward the imperative of creating a nonkilling society. The music and the lyrics do not say so directly, but this is the conclusion that some people can draw when enjoying a transformative experience as listeners, spectators, or performers.

I would like to state that art that inspires us to praise the dignity of life, even if the message is not explicit, can contribute to the nonkilling society project. Which work of art inspires whom to feel what is an entirely different question. Other musical pieces that have the same effect on me are most of Beethoven's other symphonies, Vivaldi's 'Spring' from the 'Four seasons,' Mozart's 'Lacrimosa' from the 'Requiem,' and many other Western classical works. Taken at random from other repertoires are Herbie Hancock's 'Chameleon' from Head Hunters, Phil Collins' 'In the Air Tonight,' and Shinji Harada's 'Calling.' None of these songs are about the theme of nonkilling, but do bring out, in at least one listener, an appreciation of life and people that is conducive to the search for ways to realize a nonkilling society.

Sometimes the message can be more explicit, as in Mozart's Magic Flute, in the famous scene when music has the power to avoid bloodshed, or in John Lennon's 'Imagine.' However the problem remains the same. The arts can inspire us to work for the realization of a nonkilling society, but it is hard to define which artwork has what effect on whom. There is also the question of 'bad' art explicitly praising the dignity of life, and spelling out the necessity for a more humane world. Would these have a negative effect on the possibilities of a nonkilling society?

To expose, denounce or condemn atrocities and killing

Pablo Picasso's '*Guernica*' is the best example for me, and the most famous anti-war symbol in Western painting. When I saw the original in Madrid in 2005, I did not feel tremendous 'joy' at being alive, but it did make me think about the dark side of human existence, about the absurdity of war and the omnipresence of killing in our world. The 1937 painting depicts the bombing of Guernica, Spain, by Italian and German warplanes on 26 April of the same year. Innocent civilians and animals are being slaughtered in this navy blue, black and white mural-size composition. On the right, a desperate person has both arms thrown up in supplication. This detail is reminiscent of one of Francisco de Goya's most famous paintings, 'The Third of May,' painted in 1814 to illustrate the events of that took place in 1808 in Madrid, Spain, during the Napoleonic Wars. It shows a man about to be killed by a firing squad, throwing up his arms just like the figure in Picasso's 'Guernica.' Nowhere do these two paintings say: 'stop all wars!' or 'no more killing,' but the viewer is invited to reflect, or avoid thinking, about the issue. There is no guarantee that the sheer number of such works of art describing atrocities and killings will lead to a nonkilling society, but let us imagine their absence for a while. If nobody produces anything describing the dark side any more, that would be a severe impediment toward consciousness raising and education toward a nonkilling society.

Other examples of works of art depicting human suffering, death and killing are Victor Hugo's nineteenth century novels, The *Hunchback of Notre-Dame, Les Misérables* and *Ninety-Three*; Stephen Spielberg's 1993 movie *Schindler's List* based on the 1982 biographic novel by Thomas Keneally; and a series of sculptures by Danish artist Jens Galschiot, each called 'Pillar of Shame'. These 8-metre tall statues represent people suffering from oppression and have been erected in major cities throughout the world since 1997. The 'VII Photo Agency' was established by a group of photographers in 2001 in order to produce a record of the injustices created and experienced by people across the world. Some of their themes are Genocide, 9/11, Afghanistan, Iraq and the Palestinian/ Israeli conflict. The reader is invited to complete the list, starting with Tolstoy's War and Peace, and Oliver Stone's Platoon.

Fulfilling a role quite different from praise for the dignity of life or the uplifting of the human spirit, I believe that art that exposes, denounces or condemns attacks on human dignity has a crucial role to play in the realization of a nonkilling society.

To promote a cause or an issue conducive to a more humane society

Paris-based painter and designer Lida Sherafatmand does not believe that art is only for art's sake. She has published the 'Humanitarian Art Manifesto' in 2004, and has held events to promote its message throughout the world every year, with support and popularity steadily increasing. The 'Introduction' to the Manifesto states:

Now more than ever before, we as people from all disciplines and walks of life, need to pull our forces together to make our dream come true, our dream of peace and humanity.

We will not let discouraging news and threats diminish our hope and we will continue advancing on our road toward humanity and peace with increasing courage and passion.

In previous centuries there have been artworks produced on the themes of peace and humanity, but it is the transnational simultaneousness and the fabulous increase in the number of these works, and the dedication of artists focusing on these themes, that makes this a movement now, at the beginning of the twenty-first century.

We the artists,

- place our creative talents at the service of humanity, and share in the sufferings of those under injustice, with the goal of empowering them with hope and energy
- use the universal language of art to communicate the beauty of humanity and positive peace

- bring to view the need to act with care and compassion instead of inhumanity
- speak for, and on behalf of, our fellow artists who cannot exhibit and share their works because of the suppressive rules under which they live; those artists whose lives are in danger prompt dialogue among different cultures through our art. (Sherafatmand, 2009)

Some of Sherafatmand's paintings have titles explicitly referring to a cause or an issue: 'Children's Hope,' 'Working for Peace,' 'Let's Protect our Children from Wars,' 'Stop Child Labour.' Whereas in Beethoven's 9th and Picasso's 'Guernica' the message in favour of the dignity of life is implicit, the 'Humanitarian Art Manifesto' promotes the creation of art with an explicit message.

A question that comes to mind immediately upon reading the 'Humanitarian Art Manifesto' concerns the necessity of a 'Nonkilling Arts Manifesto.' What would it look like? Would it be radically different from the above manifesto? Or should the nonkilling movement support the Humanitarian Art Manifesto and add a specific component for nonkilling arts?

In our list of examples of the way the arts can help promote a cause or an issue, we must of course add here the theme of nonkilling itself. Paige asks a fascinating question: 'What kind of art will be created when artists are inspired by the belief that a killing-free world is possible and that their art can help to bring it about?' (2009b). Two examples of artists who have already started answering this question are Anis Hamadeh and Francisco Gomes de Matos.

Hamadeh is a German Palestinian musician and writer who wrote the song 'No More Killing' in May 2009 to commemorate Glenn Paige's 80th birthday. The song can be downloaded free from the Internet (Hamadeh, 2009). The first verse goes:

In the land of the free there is no more killing and no threats to kill, and no bets to kill. / Like a bell in the night that is gently ringing, all the kids are singing it now. / We are cheerful and we are proud, that is part of what nonkilling is about. / We vote for nonviolence, all the politicians, senators and presidents.

Gomes de Matos is a prolific Brazilian poet who explicitly states the source of inspiration for his recent volume: Nurturing Nonkilling. A Poetic Plantation (2009). An excerpt from 'A Nonkilling Song' follows:

Nonkilling can be a mission
Does it need everybody's permission? Nonkilling can be a goal
Does it touch every soul? Nonkilling can be a paradigm
Does it make Peace yours and mine? Nonkilling can be a song
Does it make Life 'Number one'? (Gomes de Matos, 2009: 12)

To close this section, I would like to suggest another interesting project along these lines, exploring the activities of famous artists who have made a commitment to a cause. Some of the most well-known include the organizer of the Band Aid and Live Aid projects, Irish rock band Boomtown Rats lead singer Bob Geldof (humanitarian relief for Africa), Colombian rock musician Juanes (victims of anti-personnel mines), US actress Angelina Jolie (refugees), and Irish rock band U2's lead singer Bono (poverty and hunger). They are part of a very long list of accomplished artists who have used their art, their fame, or both, in the service of a cause or an issue.

Note: this section was written and published at a time when basically no critical evaluation of El Sistema was available. This situation has changed, especially with the publication of Geoffrey Baker's *El Sistema: Orchestrating Venezuela's Youth* in 2014.

To empower people in extremely difficult situations, so they can avoid having to kill or being killed

If you were born and raised in the hills surrounding Caracas, your chances of having to kill to survive, or to be killed in the process, would be extremely high. An article dated 16 July 2006 described the barrios (districts, neighbourhoods or more accurately, shantytowns) of Caracas as follows:

> *This is where the poorest of the poor live, millions of people down the side of mountains, without any permanent access to water and electricity, without roads, without a decent sewage system and permanently tormented by the highest levels of crime and violence in the world. Official figures suggest that most of the world's war zones are relatively safer than big Latin American cities like Sao Paulo or Caracas.* (Socialistworld.net, 2006)

How could the arts possibly alleviate the suffering of the millions of people caught in these appalling circumstances? What could music, for instance, offer to people who have to battle every day against destitution, poverty and crime? Actually, music was able to work out nothing less than a miracle:

> *In the violent slums of Venezuela, free classical music lessons have transformed the lives of hundreds of thousands of children and created an unlikely production line of virtuosos … In Venezuela, El Sistema embraces more than 200 orchestras, reaching 250,000 children. It attracts more than £15 million a year of government funding. But it started humbly, with a handful of children playing in a garage.* (Times Online, 2009)

This extraordinary success story is symbolized by the young Venezuelan Gustavo Dudamel, considered today as one of the best conductors in the world, who has risen from the barrios of Caracas thanks to an organization called El Sistema:

> *Inspired and founded in 1975 under the slogan 'Play and fight!' by the extraordinary social crusader Jose Antonio Abreu, El Sistema flourished with a simple dictum: that in the poorest slums of the world, where the pitfalls of drug addiction, crime and despair are many, life can be changed and fulfilled if children can be brought into an orchestra to play the overwhelmingly European classical repertoire.* (Guardian.co.uk, 2009)

The contrast between a life of poverty and crime on the one hand, and the empowerment provided by music on the other, is striking:

> *Across Venezuela, young barrio-dwellers now spend their afternoons practising Beethoven and Brahms. They learn the 'Trauermarsch' from Mahler's fifth symphony while their peers learn to steal and shoot. They are teenagers like Renee Arias, practising Bizet's Carmen Suite at a home for abandoned and abused children, who when asked what he would be doing if he had not taken up the French horn, replies straightforwardly: 'I'd be where I was, only further down the line-either dead or still living on the streets smoking crack, like when I was eight.' Or children like Aluisa Patino, who states plainly that she learns the viola 'to get myself and my mother out of the barrio.'* (Guardian.co.uk, 2009)

Among thousands of testimonies, one more will suffice to make the point:

> *The leader of Los Chorros's orchestra, tipped for a professional future, is Patricia Gujavro. Her face while playing looks as though it knows more than her 17 years should afford, but her lachrymose expression unexpectedly vanishes when she speaks, breezily. Patricia lives in Palo Verde barrio with her two brothers. Her father has 'never been in the family' and her mother disappeared to Ecuador last year. 'I've thought a lot about what my life would have been like if I hadn't started the violin,' she says. 'I suppose I'd be like most 17-year-old girls in Palo Verde—hanging with the gangs and pregnant. One of my friends is 17, with a kid and pregnant again, and no idea how to support them. That... well, that hasn't happened to me yet.' Her ambition, inevitably: 'to join the Simon Bolivar orchestra'—if not, become an engineer, music having 'given me discipline, respect for other people and for myself, unlike the other girls.'* (Guardian.co.uk, 2009)

What is amazing here is not so much that El Sistema has saved thousands of young people in Venezuela, but rather that music has not yet been used in most countries in similar ways to prevent countless precious lives from having to kill to survive or be killed in the process. There are many other examples of the tremendous power of the arts to save lives, and because of lack of space, I will only mention two illustrations of the benefits of music and arts therapy for child soldiers and refugees.

One unique story of musical healing is told by Sudanese hip-hop artist Emmanuel Jal, a former child soldier of the civil war, who is using his music and a documentary called War Child to share his experiences of violence and poverty, and to promote peace and education. At the age of six, Jal was trained as a child soldier by the Sudan People's Liberation Army, to fight and kill his Arab Muslim compatriots. After years in a training camp, followed by rehabilitation, study and hard work in Kenya and Britain, he became a famous artist. He says:

> *Music is the only thing that can speak to your mind, your heart and your soul system, your cells, and influence you without any hard work … I put my fight into music, for two reasons: to cool down my anger, transforming that anger to positivity, and because I want to pass a message to people. At first I was doing it because it's fun [and] it's healthy; now it goes to the people.* (America.gov, 2009)

In 2005, he collaborated with Abdel Gadir Salim for his 'Ceasefire' album, the first to bring together representatives of the opposing sides of the war, a young hip-hop Christian artist and a traditional Muslim Arab singer. Jal has already produced a CD, a book and a documentary, all entitled War Child, and he is making preparations to build a school in his hometown.

Esther Feagan wrote a thesis for her Master of Arts in Arts Therapy at the School of the Arts Institute of Chicago, entitled 'Plotting Transition: Refugees and Survivors of Torture Search for Meaning through Visual and Written Narratives.'

Her research question was: 'Do personal narratives related through visuals, text, and sound enable refugees and survivors of torture who struggle with feelings of futility to recover a sense of meaning in life after migration?' (Feagan, 2009). She worked with adults who had emigrated because of trauma, and helped them to tell their stories through a combination of narrative and art therapies. The conclusion of her research was as follows:

> *Narrative therapy enables the client to find meaning through the process of telling a story. As the client struggles to answer the questions of 'why' and 'for what purpose,' recounting a personal narrative allows the client to map his or her connections between life events and their meaning. The expression of this story through visuals, text, or sound is an outward manifestation of this inward mapping. It brings into existence the elusive pieces of a life once lived, an identity abandoned, and discarded hopes newly restored.* (Feagan, 2009)

The above section is just a small sample of the very different roles the arts can play for the development of a nonkilling society. For those who want to find answers to the question 'If yes, why?' the arts provide a welcome relief from the tough contemplation of death, maiming, killing and destruction affecting humankind, but more importantly, offer pathways toward the transformation of the structural conditions and cultural predispositions of our world.

Human Qualities Promoted by the Arts

In the first section, a Korean professor was quoted as mentioning the qualities of 'consciousness, reason, creativity, productivity' as conducive to a nonkilling society. One of the founders of peace studies, Johan Galtung recommends creativity, nonviolence, and empathy as essential for peaceful conflict transformation. There are many other ways to systematize the importance of human qualities for peace, and another example is the Buddhist leader and peace philosopher Daisaku Ikeda, who recommends courage, wisdom and compassion. The psychologist Martin Seligman has identified six different categories of human qualities leading to happiness and fulfilment. First, Galtung, Ikeda and Seligman's systems are briefly explored, then examples of how the arts do enhance positive human qualities are given.

Why did Galtung choose creativity, nonviolence and empathy? This is linked to his explanation of why conflicts arise. For him it is important to know the attitude, behavior and contradictions (ABC) characterizing the parties to a conflict. Throughout a career that spans decades and has produced more than 1,000 articles and 100 books, and countless workshops and successful conflict transformation sessions, Galtung has affirmed that in order to transform conflicts successfully without violence, the best attitude was empathy, the most appropriate behavior nonviolence, and the most effective way to deal with contradictions creativity (Galtung, 1996).

Galtung often uses the arts in his work for peace. For instance, *A Flying Orange Tells Its Tale* is a children's book about conflict transformation published in several languages, and illustrated by his son Andreas (Galtung, 2007). He often plays the flute to indicate the start and end of his lectures at universities. Galtung has also written a chapter entitled 'Peace, Music and the Arts: In Search of Interconnections' in the volume Music and Conflict Transformation mentioned earlier (Urbain, 2008).

Daisaku Ikeda is the leader of one of the largest lay Buddhist movements in the world, the Soka Gakkai International. He is also a man of dialogue and a philosopher of peace, who has established numerous educational, cultural and research institutions throughout the world, including a fine arts museum and a concert association. The three qualities of courage, wisdom and compassion he recommends as leading toward peace and happiness, are those traditionally characterizing the 'Buddha,' a human being having reached 'enlightenment' (Ikeda, 2002: 10). He is a firm believer in the power of culture and the arts to connect people and enhance peace and nonviolence, and is himself a poet, novelist and photographer. Two online exhibitions of his photographs, entitled 'Dialogue with Nature' and 'This Beautiful Earth' can be found on a website dedicated to his work (Ikeda, 2009).

The qualities of courage, wisdom and compassion emphasized by Ikeda are also found in most other religions and humanist philosophies. Among the six human qualities most conducive to a fulfilling and enjoyable life (and by extension, hopefully, to a life of nonkilling), according to Martin Seligman, the founder of the positive psychology movement, the first three are the same as those recommended by Ikeda: wisdom, courage, love, a sense of justice, temperance, and spirituality or transcendence (Seligman, 2002: 132-133).

There is some overlap between the three lists offered by Galtung, Ikeda and Seligman above, and by adding them up we obtain the following list of qualities: consciousness, reason, creativity, productivity, empathy, nonviolence, courage, wisdom, compassion, love, justice, temperance, spirituality or transcendence. We could easily add hope, kindness, generosity, imagination, and ingenuity.

The point of briefly describing the respective systems of the three thinkers above is to show that human qualities are not floating abstractions, but concrete behavioral structures that are at the basis of entire philosophical and educational endeavours. In this context, the collective level of human qualities displayed by people at a certain point in time determines the quality of the culture of a society. If we want to move toward a nonkilling society, one of the most crucial elements will be the fostering of positive qualities in ourselves and others.

The potential of the arts to promote these qualities is tremendous, more accurately, boundless. In the volume Music and Conflict Transformation mentioned earlier, Felicity Laurence devotes an entire chapter to the power of music to enhance empathy. Most people have tasted the personal satisfaction and sense of accomplishment that accompanies the simplest artistic task.

Creating art collectively has been a way to develop social cohesion for thousands of years. Visual artist Bert Monterona has become an expert at bringing people together through the joint creation of mural paintings, even people caught in opposing sides of violent conflicts.

Music and arts therapy are now recognized for their beneficial power to heal all sorts of physical and mental illnesses, and scientific research has now started into the potential of group music therapy, as in the ground breaking research of Pavlicevic and Ansdell entitled Community Music Therapy (2004).

There are many more examples that show the amazing power of the arts to enhance human qualities conducive to peace, happiness, and collectively, to a nonkilling society.

Conclusion

Before suggesting some avenues for further explorations, I would like to end with a challenging question: if the appreciation of arts depends on the subjectivity of the beholders, and if progress toward a nonkilling society is a question of commitment, where does the process start? Will the arts influence people to make that commitment, or does it all depend on people's commitment from the beginning?

Personally, I think commitments are made as a result of millions of small internal and external events, and are not simply the product of the rational use of our neocortex at some precise point in time. I find it crucial to promote a nonkilling society by any means possible, and especially through the arts. With the impending threats of accelerating global climate change, and resource scarcity including peak oil and water shortages, it is of the utmost urgency for us to learn how to get along and organize our societies on a better basis than killing or the threat to kill.

To end this chapter, I would like to suggest a few avenues for further research or explorations, compiled with the help of some friends[1].

- How do we conduct a systematic exploration of works of art that 'uplift the human spirit' contributing to a nonkilling society?
- What would a 'Nonkilling Arts Manifesto' look like? What would be the best way to optimize the impact of both this new manifesto and the 'Humanitarian Art Manifesto' mentioned earlier?
- Continue the list of artists who have used their art for a cause or an issue; people like Bob Geldof, Juanes, Angelina Jolie and Bono.
- Peter van den Dungen is professor of peace studies at the University of Bradford, UK. He is the founder (1992) and general coordinator of the International Network of Museums for Peace and editor of Peace Museums Worldwide. He believes that peace museums have a major role to play in the development of a culture of peace. He also promotes peace tourism. For instance, he questions the fact that whereas most cities in Europe exhibit on their town squares an equestrian statue of a weapon-wielding man, symbolizing the greatness of local heroes, very few have a sculpture of one person (or more) accomplishing some heroically compassionate actions (Van den Dungen, 2002). What would nonkilling museums and nonkilling tourism look like?

---

1 Many thanks to Itir Toksoz, Terrence E. Paupp and Glenn Paige for providing most of these suggestions.

- How can we evaluate if the use of nonkilling arts makes a difference? Is there any way to collect evidence that people who are exposed to nonkilling arts become more peaceful and less violent? This research can provide new avenues on the links between social psychology and the arts.
- Once people start producing nonkilling arts all over the world, how do we find out which societies create more nonkilling arts (of the explicit type)? Would those be the less violent societies (showing that people express the overall culture of their societies), or the more violent ones (showing that people need the arts to express their most urgent needs)?
- What could be the role of educational institutions such as music conservatories, fine arts institutes, departments of (for instance) peace studies or ethics at universities, in the promotion of nonkilling arts?
- Certain states have funding for the arts. From a policy perspective, how do we encourage states to sponsor public programmes that promote nonkilling arts?
- Explore the use of nonkilling arts at all levels, from elementary to university. What would be the use of integrating such a topic in the regular curricula in different countries? Would there be a difference between the countries considered to be democratic, and those less so? This could contribute to the Democratic Peace Theory if we broaden its scope to include the hypothesis that democracies do not fight each other because their people share a common human heritage of arts and culture, value creativity and the arts, and even focus on nonkilling arts. A related question is: Would countries that introduce nonkilling arts in their regular curricula become more democratic as a result? Or more peaceful without any increase in the democratic level?
- What can international organizations such as UNESCO do to promote nonkilling arts or to do research on nonkilling arts?
- In his speech at Amherst College on 26 October 1963, John F. Kennedy mentioned the links established by Robert Frost between poetry and power. How could decision-makers and people in

positions of power in general become more sensitive to the centrality of the arts and poetry, especially nonkilling arts, for effective and humane governance? The relevant excerpt from Kennedy's speech follows:

> *Our national strength matters, but the spirit which informs and controls our strength matters just as much. This was the special significance of Robert Frost... At bottom, he held a deep faith in the spirit of man, and it is hardly an accident that Robert Frost coupled poetry and power, for he saw poetry as the means of saving power from itself. When power leads men toward arrogance, poetry reminds him of his limitations. When power narrows the areas of man's concern, poetry reminds him of the richness and diversity of his existence. When power corrupts, poetry cleanses. For art establishes the basic human truth which must serve as the touchstone of our judgment.* (Kennedy, 1963)

- The reader is hereby invited to continue the list.

As mentioned at the beginning of this chapter, Glenn Paige did not invent nonkilling. This concept is at least a few tens of thousands of years old, as old as humanity. Moreover, before there were any human beings on the planet to even think about it, we can assume that animals refused to kill every day, based on recent research (see Bekoff; Pierce, 2009). What Glenn Paige has provided to humanity is a way to think about the issue in a systematic way. This set of questions is a pure stroke of genius: 'Is a nonkilling society possible? If no, why not? If yes, why?' For this he deserves our eternal gratitude, which can also be expressed through numerous works of art.

(**Note:** *This chapter was originally published in 2009 in Towards a Nonkilling Paradigm (pp. 73-91), edited by Joám Evans Pim, and is republished here with a few edits by the author.)*

References

America.gov (2009). 'Former Child Soldier Uses Music as Weapon Against Violence,' CrystalOfori, 4 March, retrieved on 18 August 2009: <http://www.america.gov /st/democracyhr-english/2009/March/20090304175753gcirofo0.9383356.html>.

Baker, Geoffrey (2014). El Sistema: Orchestrating Venezuela's Youth. Oxford: Oxford University Press.

Bekoff, Marc; Pierce, Jessica (2009). Wild Justice: The Moral Lives of Animals. Chicago: University of Chicago Press.

Christian, Reginald F., ed. (1978). Tolstoy's Letters: Volume II 1880-1910. New York: Charles Scribner's Sons.

classicalmusic.about.com (2009). 'Beethoven, Translation of "Ode to Joy" by Aaron Green,' retrieved on 16 August 2009: <http://classicalmusic.about.com/od/ romanticperiodsymphonies/qt/Beethovenjoytxt.htm>.

Feagan, Esther (2009). Thesis Abstract on the website of the School of the Arts Institute of Chicago, retrieved on 18 August 2009 from: <http://www.artic.edu/ webspaces/gradthesis/maat05_feagan.htm>.

Galtung, Andreas; Galtung, Johan (2007). A Flying Orange Tells its Tale. Oslo: Kolofon. Galtung, Johan (1996). Peace by Peaceful Means: Peace and Conflict, Development and Civilization. London: Sage.

Gomes de Matos, Francisco (2009). Nurturing Nonkilling. A Poetic Plantation. Honolulu: Center for Global Nonkilling.

Guardian.co.uk (2009). 'Orchestral Manoeuvres,' by Ed Vulliamy, The Observer, Sunday 29 July 2007, retrieved on 16 August 2009: <http://www.guardian.co.uk/music/2007/jul/29/classicalmusicandopera1>.

Hamadeh, Anis (2009). 'No More Killing,' retrieved on 18 August 2009 from: <http://www.nonkilling.org/node/16>.

Ikeda, Daisaku (2002). The Humanism of the Middle Way: Dawn of a Global Civilization. Tokyo: Soka Gakkai.

Ikeda, Daisaku (2009). Online photo exhibitions, retrieved on 18 August 2009: <http://www.daisakuikeda.org/sub/nature/nature.html>.

Kelly, Petra K. (1989). 'Gandhi and the Green Party,' Gandhi Marg, 11:192-202.

Kennedy, John F. (1963). 'Remarks at Amherst College,' retrieved on 18 August 2009: <http://www.jfklibrary.org/>.

Paige, Glenn D. (2009a). *Nonkilling Global Political Science*. Honolulu: Center for Global Nonkilling. (Available at: <http://www.nonkilling.org/>)

Paige, Glenn D. (2009b). Personal correspondence with this author, email dated 18 August 2009.

Pavlicevic, M.; Ansdell, G. (2004). *Community Music Therapy*. London: Jessica Kingsley Publishers.

Rolland, Romain (1911). *Tolstoy.* New York: E.P. Dutton.

Seligman, Martin (2002). *Authentic Happiness: Using the New Positive Psychology to Realize Your Potential for Lasting Fulfillment*. New York, London, Toronto, Sydney: Free Press.

Sherafatmand, Lida (2009). Text of the Humanitarian Art Manifesto, retrieved on 16 August 2009: <http://www.lidasherafatmand.bravehost.com/English.html>.

Socialistworld.net (2006). 'Poverty and destitution in the hills around Caracas,' retrieved on 16 August 2009: <http://socialistworld.net/eng/2006/07/13venezuela.html>.

Times Online (2009). 'Music saved the street children of Venezuela–could it work for Scotland too?' *The Times*, 13 August, retrieved on 16 August 2009: <http://www.timesonline.co.uk/tol/news/uk/article2246441.ece>.

UNAC, United Nations Association in Canada (2009). 'International Decade for the Culture of Peace,' retrieved on 16 August 2009: <http://www.unac.org/peacecp/decade/culture.html>.

Urbain, Olivier, ed. (2008). *Music and Conflict Transformation: Harmonies and Dissonances in Geopolitics.* London: I.B. Tauris.

Van den Dungen, Peter (2002). Personal conversation with this author, University of Bradford, United Kingdom, March 2002.

Young, Andrew (1996). *An Easy Burden: The Civil Rights Movement and the Trans-formation of America.* New York: HarperCollins Publishers.

Young, Art (1975). *Shelley and Nonviolence.* The Hague: Mouton.

10

The Scientific Nature of the Nonkilling Attitude

Antonino Drago
University of Florence and University of Pisa

An Alternative Scientific Tradition inside Western Science

In the twentieth century the people of India, although dominated by a huge colonialist empire, conquered their national independence without weapons. Their leader, Mahatma Gandhi, was inspired by the notion of nonviolence, leading him to reject all offensive means. Surprisingly, Gandhi often reiterated that he experimented with this notion scientifically, so much so that his method should be qualified as science, even as part of the natural sciences.[1]

Western scientists never recognized science in congruence with Gandhi's nonviolent methods. They considered science to be an abstract social product, and deemed it any attempt to correlate it with a personal involvement, as Gandhi claimed, as inappropriate. On the

---

1 It is enough to recall the title of his celebrated book, *An Autobiography, or the Story of my Experiments with Truth* (1909).

other hand, even a follower of the nonviolent way would be perplexed in qualifying his attitude as a scientific one, because science apparently lacks any ethical and religious components.[2] Was Gandhi's claim, an effort to improve mutual understanding with Western people through a naïve appeal to a value of dominant culture?[3] Or, alternatively, does it represent a wise view of science? In the following pages I will support the latter alternative.

Although Gandhi claimed that he was applying a scientific method, he accused Western natural science and technology to be one of the structural violence exported by Western civilization. His claim then probably referred claim to an alternative viewpoint. What was this viewpoint?

Analyzing the history of natural sciences, it can be proven that since the eighteenth century a relevant minoritarian tradition has been present. It can be seen that the foundations of classical chemistry are at variance with the foundations of the theory which dominated science for two centuries, i.e. Newton's mechanics and its improved versions. Let us inspect not only this dominating formulation of mechanics, but also their different formulations, in particular, L. Carnot's mechanics; its foundations are at variance with the foundations of the dominating Newton's mechanics. Other alternative theories include classical chemistry, L. Carnot's calculus, geometry and mechanics, S. Carnot's thermodynamics and Lobachevsky's non-Euclidean geometry (Drago, 2009, 1986, 1991a).[4]

These alternative theories are mostly ignored since some of them are considered as mere variations of the more known formulations of calculus, geometry, mechanics, thermodynamics, non-Euclidean geometries; others (for example classical chemistry, S. Carnot's thermodynamics, etc.) are charged to be 'phenomenological,' 'immature,' Baconian (that is, lacking of advanced mathematics) theories. Yet, in

2 It is his basic criticism of the whole Western civilization. See *Hind Swaraj* (1908).

3 A similar appraisal is given by Sarton (1954).

4 Singh (1996) illustrates a similar philosophical viewpoint, however, lacking formalization.

1905 Einstein triggered an acute crisis in the dominating theoretical physics, as even the foundations of his theory, i.e., special relativity, were at variance with those of Newton's mechanics. This variance is just similar to the previous ones.[5] A comparison of the above-mentioned theories show that they shared common foundations, apparently different from Newtonian ones.

In a previous work (Drago, 2009) I presented a scientific framework for looking at Western science in an entirely new way. As an alternative to the long-held tradition of Western philosophy of knowledge, which conceives a monist representation of science as an application of the unique reason to the real world, this view presents theoretical science as a pluralist enterprise, that provides grounding to nonviolent and nonkilling perspectives.

Taking note of its singularities, the nonkilling imperative, when considered in its full generality, will be equated to the nonviolence principle, which belongs to the millennial Indian tradition and then was renewed by Gandhi; in other words, I will consider the nonkilling imperative as the Western version of the Eastern nonviolence principle as it is intended in modern times.

The Common Foundations of the Alternative Scientific Theories: Nonkilling Scientific Foundations

Each of the above-mentioned theories rather than organized as in Newton's theory—an apodictic system, whose truth flows from few, abstract axioms by means of a purely deductive development—is organized by focussing attention on a universal problem concerning a given field of scientific subjects; for example in the nineteenth century, classical chemistry declared the problem on discovering by which elements matter is constituted; L. Carnot's mechanics dealt with the problem of which quantities stood invariant during an impact of bodies; L. Carnot's calculus dealt with the problem of the reality of the

5 This is the main point missed by previous Sarton's paper; it concludes with the following words: '... there is no freedom of thought concerning that body of scientific evidence.' Notice that Einstein's theoretical revolution occurred at the same time (1905) as the beginnings of Gandhi's revolution (1906).

infinitesimals; L. Carnot's geometry dealt with the problem of calculating all elements of a given figure which is known through some elements only; S. Carnot's thermodynamics dealt with the problem of maximum efficiency when producing work from heat; Lobachevsky's theory dealt with the problem of whether more than one parallel line is possible in geometry; Einstein's theory dealt with the problem of 'conciliating' the principle of relativity in theoretical mechanics with the constant velocity of light in electromagnetism (Drago, 1990, 1991b, 1988, 1991c; Einstein, 1905).

Let us assume that both Freud and Marx did not make appeals to idealized notions from which to draw their theories. The scientific theory of the most intimate conflicts, i.e., Freud's (1925) psychoanalysis, shares the previous feature: it dealt with a problem, i.e. how to cure a deep trauma in a patient. Also, Marx's (1884) theory of social conflicts dealt with a problem, i.e., how to overcome capitalism in mankind's history.

Remarkably, there are some theories which are capable of arguing about many of the factors involved in the most tremendous conflict, i.e., a war. The case of strategic theories is interesting because some strategists did not theorise how to efficiently apply a brute, destructive force; rather they dealt with the universal problem of how to manage a war by linking the best arms' power with given political aims. By reading their books it is apparent that each of those theories does not suggest a technical solution composed of a list of orders imparted to subordinate people. This theoretical attitude in strategic theories characterises at least the three following strategists: Sun Tzu (350 B.C.E.), L. Carnot (1985 [1811]) and Clausewitz (1984 [1838]).

Note also that the theory of nonkilling cannot be drawn from self-evident principles; rather, it deals with a universal problem, i.e. how a conflict in interpersonal relationships can be solved through a final agreement with the opponent.

Each of the above-mentioned theories induce a new method from the commonly shared knowledge, which is capable of solving the previously stated universal problems. Such a feature is apparent in classical chemistry; chemists, although lacking in direct evidence on matter's elements, introduced an excellent method of investigation which combined the analysis and the synthesis of common substances;

by this method alone they obtained an accurate list of all the microscopic elements. Similar notes apply to the other theories. In particular, Einstein started his celebrated paper by introducing a new method for measuring time by means of the usual clocks but by considering the finite value (c) of the signals mutually transmitted by two observers.

Both Freud and Marx referred to common knowledge shared by the wider public in order to discover new methods; respectively, a new curative method consisting of a specific kind of dialogue, and a new method for both forecasting and planning the social revolution.

Also, the above-mentioned strategists started their theories from common knowledge so that their books on strategy addressed laymen. They explained to soldiers too, why each war had to be fought by following a specific method, to be discovered case by case, except for some general guidelines, suggested by those strategists.[6]

Similarly, the theory of nonkilling leads a man involved in a conflict to perform a patient and clever analysis of the commonly shared experiences of human relationships in order to recognize inside the opponent's personality an acceptable aspect, suggesting how to construct a new, specific method, capable of achieving a common agreement which solves the given conflict.

Two centuries ago, the core of the general method to organize a scientific theory in such a way, was qualified in semi-formal terms by L. Carnot in order to improve the old 'synthetic method.' He developed this general method by interpreting infinitesimal analysis, i.e., the most powerful advancement in the history of modern mathematics (Carnot, 1813: 217-253).[7] He remarked that its genius consists of the following sequence of moves. One introduces 'adjunctions' to a given system in order to generalise this system, so that the search for a solution of the problem at issue is made easier. Once the solution is

6 This point is illustrated by the following papers: Angelillo and Drago (1997); Covone and Drago (2000); Drago and Pezzella (2000).

7 He was a scientist, a strategist and one of the leaders of French revolution. In particular, L. Carnot's strategy was aimed at defence only, through the least loss of human lives; he was the first political man favourable to conscientious objectors for political reasons. On his scientific activity see Gillispie (1971). A more recent and complete book is by Charnay (1990).

obtained, the auxiliary variables are suppressed in order to reduce the system to the initial system. For instance, in the ancient infinitesimal analysis one adjoins—to a mathematical system to be solved—some auxiliary variables, called infinitesimals, which, after having obtained the solution, are 'suppressed' through some mathematical trick (for example, by evaluating them as quantities too small to be appreciated; more currently, by a limit process; etc.). In his mechanics, L. Carnot adjoined 'geometrical motions,' which in the simplest case represents changes of the reference frame; since these motions constitute a group of transformations of the mathematical formulas representing the physical system. In fact, Carnot started the first mathematical group theory. By applying the different groups of geometrical-temporal transformations, he obtained the classical invariants of motion.

In Freud's psychoanalysis a patient 'adjoins' his dreams to his personality in order to offer to the analyst a clarification of his psychic 'system.' Marx considered as a trigger eliciting the wanted change in mankind's history, the adjunction of the suitable historical consciousness to the proletariat class, oppressed by the capitalist 'system.'

Among the strategic theories, L. Carnot's defensive one is expressly based upon the notion of 'adjunction.' When a besieged of a stronghold is threatened by a besieger applying a step-by-step strategy for approaching the stronghold with impunity, then the besieged, in order to break the besieger's strategy has to 'adjoin' to his inside defensive activity for some quick outside sorties.

In the theory of nonviolence, Aldo Capitini—the first European nonviolent activist—independently offered a philosophical basis to the method of adjunctions. He considered the whole development of Western philosophy. As it is well-known, Kant recognized that human reason unsuccessfully attempted to know the essence of beings of the external world (*noumenos*); however, Kant (1793) suggested that one can achieve reality through an ethical move, characterized as an 'adjunction.' Hegel's philosophy translated this notion into an idealistic one, the *Aufhebung*, which is an Absolute Spirit's move for transcending the historical reality. Instead, Capitini considered the 'adjunction' at no more than a personal level; it is aimed to raise the level of an even distressing situation of interpersonal relationships, and hence to achieve a higher viewpoint, which makes it easy to envisage a 'choral' solution.[8] According to Capitini, this process constitutes the essence of nonviolence.

Indeed, in Gandhi's conception of nonviolence this notion is substantiated by at least a prayer; or as an intermediate action, a fast; or as his maximum effort, his own sacrifice to death.[9] Therefore, the process of nonkilling solution of a conflict can be modelled by attributing to the notion 'adjunction' the same role it plays in scientific theories (Drago, 2007: section 2.7).[10]

A formal interpretation in logical terms

The common features of these theories now will be qualified in formal terms, first by means of mathematical logic (without, however, involving sophisticated notions). In fact, all these theories follow non-classical logic. In classical logic the law of double negation holds true; it is commonly stated as follows: 'Two negations affirm' (for example the statement: 'It is not true that 2+2 is not 4' is equivalent to the statement: '2+2=4'). But this law may fail; for example, a Court's judgement of 'lack of guilty evidence' is not equivalent to its corresponding positive judgement of 'honesty.' According to recent studies in mathematical logic (Prawitz and Malmnaas, 1968; Dummett, 1977; Dalen and Troelstra, 1988), this failure characterises non-classical logic.

An inspection of the original texts by the authors of these scientific theories shows that they include a lot of double negated sentences (DNSs), whose corresponding positive sentences are not true for lack of scientific evidence. Some instances of DNSs are the following ones: 'It is impossible that matter is divisible in a not finite way' (chemists of nineteenth century); 'The infinitesimals are not chimerical (=not real)

8 Among Capitini's writings on this subject, the most appropriate one is 'L'avvenire della dialettica,' in Cacioppo, Ed. (1973). A short synthesis can be found in Altieri (2008).

9 Also Sarton remarks this point by stressing that Gandhi 'was always ready to be the scapegoat of India' (1954: 97).

10 One may improve this joint theory by considering the theory of impact of bodies as a theory of conflict resolution. See Drago (1996).

beings' (L. Carnot); 'It is impossible a motion without an end' (L. and S. Carnot); 'It is not true that heat is not equal to work' (S. Carnot); 'It is not contradictory the hypothesis of two parallel lines to a given straight line' (Lobachevsky); '... we can attribute no absolute (=not relative) meaning to simultaneity.' Each of the above statements is not equivalent to the corresponding positive statement, since the latter lacks scientific evidence in experimental terms.

Let us say that even the scientific theory of the most intimate conflicts, i.e., Freud's psychoanalysis, share the same features. A Freud celebrated methodological paper illustrates how the analysis of a patient's diseases starts (1925). When a patient, by telling the analyst his dreams, says a negated statement: 'I did not want to kill my mother,' then, the analyst has to add a second negation to this statement: 'It is not true that he did not want to kill his mother.' In such a way he obtains a hint to recognize a patient's trauma.[11]

It is well known that Marx wanted to shape his entire theory by means of a 'new dialectical logic,' where the synthesis between thesis and anti-thesis is obtained by a 'negation of the negation' of the starting thesis.

The original texts about the above-mentioned strategic theories present a great number of DNSs. For example, the main goal of each strategic theory is not to win all wars, but to result in an invincible Army (Sun Szu). L. Carnot's main statement may be considered: 'It is not true that war work is not civil work [to build a stronghold].' Moreover, the most celebrated Clausewitz statement is 'War is nothing else but diplomacy through different means.' (He never wrote the corresponding positive statement which is wrongly attributed to him by almost all scholars.)

Nonkilling thinking is essentially merged in nonclassical logic, since the word nonkilling is not one negation, but two negations—being of course that killing is a negation of life; the same holds true for the word 'nonviolence' (Horn, 1986: 84). In fact, this double negation cannot be

---

11 Actually, Freud was not so explicit. However, his crucial statement 'the negation is a way to get knowledge of the removal,' attributed by him to the patient, also holds true for the analyst. See Drago and Zerbino (1996).

appropriately replaced by a concrete, positive word. According to Gandhi the best candidate for this replacement is the word *satyagraha*; yet, this word sublimates the original meaning of nonviolence into abstract words (in particular, the word 'truth'), overhanging human life. Hence, both words nonkilling and nonviolence are DNSs. As a consequence, any typical slogan which is consistent with the nonkilling attitude is appropriately expressed by two negations; for example 'Do not harm,' 'Never more [nuclear bombing] Hiroshima!' Gandhi also used two more crucial DNSs: *aparigraha* (non-possession) and *advaita* (non-dualism).[12] Christians think that the positive word 'love' is equivalent to—and even more meaningful than—both 'nonkilling' and 'nonviolence'; yet, 'love' is a fuzzy and multi-purpose word, as proved by Christendom's social history which is actually full of wars.[13]

Let us assume that human rights may be viewed as forcing corresponding affirmative versions some DNSs, say the last five commandments (the social ones). In particular, the commandment 'Thou shalt not kill' has been forced into 'Right of survival,' 'Right to develop his own life,' 'Right to have access to life resources,' etc. The examination of this short list tells us that in order to exhaust the meaning of a DNS by translating it into affirmative sentences, one has to produce a lot of them. It is not by chance that the UN Declaration of Human Rights is unsatisfactory to many, who want to add to the list of this declaration the second, third, fourth...generations of rights. Hence, both nonkilling and nonviolence are not equivalent to any finite set of affirmative sentences.[14]

The dichotomy between the two kinds of logic enjoys a noble philosophical origin. Leibniz sketched a 'Science of Science' (Drago,

12 For some instances, see Gandhi (1958, ch. 4, No. 8, 43, 52, 76). However, some more crucial Gandhi words, as *Bramacharya*, are positive words. Hence, Gandhi was not always consistent with the formally inductive way of arguing. In this sense one may remark both 'a confusion' (id., 100) and a 'zigzag' (id., 91), which, however Sarton enlarges to Gandhi's entire thinking.

13 I illustrated this point in the end of Drago (1992).

14 This point is one of the first results on the comparison between classical logic and nonclassical logic. It was obtained by Goedel (1986 [1933]).

1994) whose two basic principles are the principle of noncontradiction and the principle of sufficient reason; the latter one, being in itself a DNS ('Nothing is without a reason') constitutes the best principle for arguing according to nonclassical logic—i.e., in an inductive way—inside an alternative theory (Drago, 2001, 2003). In fact, in each of the above theories, one recognizes the translation of the latter Leibniz' principle in a particular DNS, which in theory plays the role of a specific methodological principle. Respectively: 'No efficient calculus without reason,' that is: 'The infinitesimals are not chimerical (not real) beings' (L. Carnot's calculus). 'Nothing is without parts,' that is: 'As an element we call any substance which is not still decomposed (Lavoisier). 'No parallelism without a proof,' that is: 'We will call parallel line any straight line which by means of a least deviation intersects the base-line' (Lobachevsky's non-Euclidean geometry); 'No motion without a reason,' that is: 'It is impossible a motion without an end' (S. Carnot's thermodynamics).

In Freud's theory: 'No patient's negation without a reason.' In Marx's theory: 'No capitalism's move without a reason'. In strategic theories: 'No move in a war without a reason.' In conflict theory the principle of sufficient reason may be applied almost directly: 'No evil is without a reason.' It leads to directly think which positive reason may be recognized in the opponent.

Some of the above-mentioned theories present one more feature which proves that DNSs play an essential role inside an alternative theory; the mere sequence of DNSs recognized inside an original text faithfully summarises the core of the respective theory. This occurs in S. Carnot's booklet on thermodynamics (Drago and Pisano, 2000), Lobachevsky's new geometry (Drago and Perno, 2004; Drago, 2007), Freud's psychoanalysis (Drago and Zerbino, 1996), and the above strategic theories. This fact gives evidence for the essential role played by the DNS in the development of each of the above theories. Also Gandhi's argument, aimed to positively solve conflicts, includes a great number of DNS. For instance, his celebrated book develops through DNSs (Drago, in press).

A comparative analysis of the above theories show that nonclassical argument by means of double negated sentences achieves results by means of *ad absurdum* theorems. The best instance of them is in thermodynamics—the celebrated S. Carnot's theorem which also presently is taught to the students of Physics and Engineering. [15]

In Marx's theory several *ad absurdum* arguments are included in his works. An example: 'He [the capitalist] is unable to understand that, if really existed one thing as the value of the work and if he really payed this value, [absurd consequence] no capital would exist and his money would not change in capital' (Marx, 1884, Book 1, section XVII).[16]

Also the strategic theories end by *ad absurdum* arguments. In his main strategic writing, L. Carnot presents three *ad absurdum* arguments. The main one is the following one: 'Because, if the enemy is robustly placed on the paths leading to the stronghold, it would be absurd to go to present to him the fight together with a garrison which on the contrary one has to preserve as much as it is possible' (Carnot, 1985 [1811]: 32). Clausewitz presents several *ad absurdum* arguments; for example, the following one: '...in their actual notion, the wars are nothing else than *ad absurdum* manifestations of the politics itself, as we showed in the above. Thus, it would be absurd to subordinate the political views to the military viewpoint, because *the politics generated the war; the former one is the intelligence, whereas the war is nothing else than the instrument*; the opposite would go [*absurdum*] against common sense. It remains nothing else to subordinate the military viewpoint to the political one' (1984 [1838]: book VIII, vi, b.).

---

15 An *ad absurdum* argument concludes by means of a DNS, i.e., *not-not-UT* Classical logic can translate it in the positive sentence *T*, by applying just that law of double negation which fails in nonclassical logic. In a theory arguing through DNSs, the last DNS works as a methodological principle for the next argument; hence, the classical logic is not necessary for advancing lucid and formal arguments according to nonclassical logic.

16 Freud's short paper does not present *ad absurdum* arguments. However, two facts are relevant: an entire page dedicated to the principle of reality, that is non absurdity; the conclusion of the paper is that 'no "not" comes from unconscious,' that is the principle upon which his entire chapter relies, and which could play the role of the principle from which absurd is obtained: 'It is absurd that the unconscious suggests a "no".'

The eventual result of the nonviolent method is obtained by reducing an argument *ad absurdum;* e.g. 'It is absurd that my opponent is not my brother, otherwise God does not exist,' or '...otherwise universal brotherhood is impossible.' Gandhi often argued in such a way; for example, the well-known sentence: 'Eye for eye (meaning the law of the vengeance) makes the world blind'; that is 'Vengeance is absurd; hence it has to be rejected.' He was so rooted in this way of arguing that he claimed 'There is no God but Truth'; in other words: 'In the absurd, no God.'[17]

The final argument of the theory achieves, again by means of an *ad absurdum* theorem, universal evidence concerning all problems at issue, i.e., the universal DNS *not-not-UT*. Owing to its universal nature the author feels justified in changing it in the affirmative predicate *T*, which then is assumed as a new hypothesis from which to draw all possible derivations. This move, changing both logic and the theory organization, is apparent in both S. Carnot's thermodynamics (after this theorem, he changes the resulting DNS ('The efficiency of no reversible heat engine is less than the efficiency of an irreversible heat engine') on the maximum efficiency about all heat transformations in work into a hypothesis ('The efficiency of a reversible heat engine is the maximum one') from which he draws new laws on specific heats and gas) and Lobachevsky's theory (after his main theorem, prop. 22, he changes its result about all straight lines and all triangles in the hyperbolic hypothesis from which he draws all geometrical consequences) (Carnot, 1813: 50; Lobachevsky, 1950 [1840]).

In Freud's paper, the DNSs concerning a patient's trauma is directly stated as an affirmative sentence, 'hence, it is the [relationship of the patient with] his mother [the cause of the trauma],' from which the analyst tries to draw all the consequences of the present patient's personality.

Moreover, *ad absurdum* theorems close both L. Carnot's and Clausewitz' strategic theories. Previous *ad absurdum* argument may be considered Clausewitz's final argument; the final quoted sentence is the universal sentence *UT* concluding the theory.

17 Other instances of this argument in ch. 4, No. 8, 43, 52, 76 (Gandhi, 1958).

It cannot be overemphasized that some of the above scientists, although unaware of nonclassical logic, almost consistently built their theories through both DNSs and ad absurdum theorems so that they followed a common model of organization of a scientific theory.

In the theory of conflict resolution, this last move corresponds to the change from inductive argument may be the key to understanding an opponent's personality, to draw from this key a first initiative, for example, to launch a mutual dialogue for peace. In the case of the above quoted Gandhi's DNS about Truth, after having claimed that 'There is no God but Truth,' he then changed it in his celebrated sentence: 'Truth is God.'

By linking the foundations of conflict resolution with the foundations of some scientific theories, we have characterized in a scientific way both the kind of logic and the alternative organization of a theory of nonkilling. Two more facts support this connection; already in the seventeenth century Leibniz exploited his theory of impact of bodies—where his notion of elastic body interprets a possibly disastrous impact in an exchange of common quantities (i.e., momentum, momentum-of-momentum and energy)[18]—for constructing a theory of interpersonal conflicts where the corresponding notion of a flexible attitude may lead the opponent to recognize common values (Leibniz, 1671; Drago, 1996).[19] Moreover, L. Carnot's celebrated strategy paralleled his general

---

18 His theory was an alternative to Wallis' and Newton's theory of the impact of bodies as based on the idealization of a perfectly hard body, so that it does not bounce. By translating this physical notion in the interpersonal relationships, it is easy to recognize in it a macho attitude.

19 As a further verification, let us remember that recently a similar—since it is a global and conflictual—viewpoint on scientific theories has been reached by seeing all of them from a historical viewpoint. Koyré, Kuhn and some other historians stressed that history of science is essentially conflictual in nature (Koyré, 1957; Kuhn, 1969). By generalizing the categories by both Koyré's and Kuhn's historiographies, I obtained new categories for a new historiography which is capable to faithfully represent the above illustrated conflict inside science (see Drago 1991a, 1994, 2001). Conversely, the conflictual theories of the history of science suggest a general theory of conflict resolution, whose main methodological principle is 'Thou shalt not kill,' and which, moreover, results to include the nonviolent theory (Drago, 1996; 2007a). It results also to generalize Galtung's theory (1976, ch. 1, 2, 1999).

theory of machines (that theory from which originated the modern discipline of technical physics); i.e., he conceived a stronghold as a machine whose laws about the work's balance may suggest how to theorise the principles for stronghold defence (Drago and Sasso (1993).

A Formal Interpretation in Mathematical Terms

Let us assume that not one of the above scientific theories use actual infinity, through infinitesimals or differential equations.[20] In philosophical terms, their infinity is the potential one only; for instance, the numbering of natural numbers, which usually excludes the existence of a maximum number, since it is a manifestly idealistic notion.[21] Yet, scientists introduced actual infinity in mathematics and in theoretical physics too (for example, the extreme points of a straight line, although no one went at these infinite points; or the classical divergences in the central point of a force field, say the gravitational field; or the words: 'All body…' in the statement of Newton's inertia principle, although we will never exhaust the list of all bodies in the world). Whereas the former notion of infinity leads us to see universality as an unlimited addition of ever more units, the notion of actual infinity obtains the universality by a jump to an extreme result, which is detached from any approximation, first of all, in logical terms, by using the word 'all' which is the equivalent of the total quantifier. The former notion leads one to proceed in a step-by-step process of calculation or construction, the latter leads one to proceed by guessing more idealistic notions, provided that their consequences successfully apply to the reality.

In the former one never says 'All…,' but 'No man excluded…'; nor 'There exists…,' but 'One is enabled to construct an instance…' Also the nonkilling attitude can be characterized through its choice for constructing interpersonal relationships involving even more men, rather than possibly mythical ideas or institutions. In particular, it leads one to say: 'No one is an enemy,' not 'All men are brothers.'

---

20 A specific inquiry on Einstein's paper on special relativity shows that the first differential equations can be translated with impunity in mere difference equations.

21 This conflict in the foundations of mathematics, i.e., between the constructive one and the classical one, is illustrated by the 'Manifesto' in Bishop (1967).

By adding this option of the kind of infinity to the above one on the kind of organization, one obtains two dichotomic variables which generalize the two dichotomic variables sketched by Galtung (1976) as generating the notion of four models of development;[22] according to Galtung, these models characterize a nonviolent political theory (Drago, 2007b).

Conclusion

The reader may be surprised that a socio-psychological theory for approaching conflictual relationships, i.e., nonkilling theory, has been linked with scientific natural theories. From a general viewpoint, one can justify this link by remarking that in the above we argued contrary to the common myth, according to which science is a unitarian, monolithic worldview; this myth makes each scientific sentence an abstract and absolutely sure truth of an essentially unitarian scientific thinking.[23] Instead, we recognized inside classical physics an essential conflict between at least two incommensurable traditions. In the twentieth century the new physical theories enhanced this divergence; an incompatibility between relativity and quantum mechanics occurred and even at the present time is unresolved. Moreover, a conflict is even apparent inside the foundations of economy, social sciences, medicine, etc.

On the other hand, the connection of nonkilling theory with scientific theories holds true also in the opposite direction. Indeed, even a scientific experiment is essentially a conflictual process. The outcome may be called a successful scientific result only when an agreement is

---

22 The two dichotomies we have recognized agree with Gita's teaching about human knowledge, as constituted by two irreducible chords, i.e., the Unity and the Infinity [Lanza del Vasto (1993) [1954]: 18-19]. In my view, Unity represents a positive choice on the option on the kind of the organization of the theory at issue, or equivalently on the kind of logic; and Infinity [path to God] represents a positive choice on the option of the kind of infinity, or equivalently on the kind of mathematics of the theory at issue. Let us remark that Lanza del Vasto (1959, ch. 1) was capable of masterly criticising science through two of Christianity's holy texts.

23 So sure to be able to solve any conflict, provided that we are able to formalize it in a scientific way.

reached between the positive answers by the experimental data and the researcher's previous hypothesis. All the above substantiates Gandhi's words on both his experiments with truth and the scientific nature of nonviolence.

When science is conceived as including an essential conflict, its abstract and sure nature collapses in the nature of a merely human initiative, which therefore may be analyzed in connection with interpersonal relationships.

In the past, Western civilization led people to conceive in a unitarian framework all scientific theories on 'reality' and at the same time to consider as an inescapable necessity—at least, in extreme circumstances—the need to judge some conflicts as essentially impossible to solve, so to consider enemies as evil to be suppressed. At present, nonkilling leads us to turn up this attitude; i.e., we have to maintain that the several systems of scientific thinking are mutually incommensurable (like religious beliefs are); and rather, to consider as ethically inescapable to conciliate conflicting persons, by viewing all of them inside the organismic unity of the universal brotherhood, as constituting the only true reality.

This change translates in theoretical terms what in philosophy Capitini had already suggested as the conversion of the human mind to an ethical attitude. Hence the nonkilling attitude is at the same time an ethical attitude and a scientific attitude, provided that for 'scientific' one means the alternative methodology and philosophy of science.

References

Altieri, R. (2008). *The Non-violent Revolution: The Italian who Embraced Gandhi's Satyagraha to Oppose Fascism and War, An Intellectual Biography of Aldo Capitini*. Madurai: Vijayaa Press.

Angelillo, E. and Drago, A. (1997). 'Nuova interpretazione della strategia di Lazare Carnot mediante la logica non classica,' in Drago, A., Ed., *Peacekeeping and Peacebuilding*. Qualevita: Sulmona, pp. 237-250.

Bishop, E. (1967). *Foundations of Constructive Mathematics*. New York: McGraw-Hill.

Capitini, A. (1973). 'L'avvenire della dialettica,' in Cacioppo, G., Ed., *Il Messaggio di Aldo Capitini*. Manduria Lecce : Lacaita, pp. 187-194.

Carnot, L. (1813). 'Note,' in *Réflexions sur la métaphysique du calcul infinitésimal*. Paris: Courcier, pp. 217-253.

Carnot, L. (1985 [1811]). 'De la défense des placefortes,' in Charnay, J.-P., Ed. *Lazare Carnot. Révolution et Mathématique*, Vol. II. Paris: La Herne, pp. 23-97.

Charnay, J.-P., ed. (1990). *Lazare Carnot ou le savant-citoyen*. Paris: Presses de l'Université Paris-Sorbonne.

Clausewitz, Karl von (1984 [1838]). *On War*. Princeton: Princeton University Press.

Covone, G. and Drago, A. (2000). '*L'Arte della guerra* in Sun Tzu,' *Quaderni Asiatici*, 52: 47-62.

Dalen, D. Van and Troelstra, A. S. (1988). *Constructivism in Mathematics. An Introduction*. Amsterdam: North Holland.

Drago, A. (1986). 'What Science for Peace?' *Gandhi Marg*, 7: 733-742.

Drago, A. (1988). 'A Characterization of the Newtonian Paradigm,' in Scheurer, P. B.; Debrock, G., eds., *Newton's Scientific and Philosophical Legacy*. New York: Kluwer Academic Publishers, pp. 239-252.

Drago, A. (1990). 'History of the Relationships Chemistry-Mathematics,' *Fresenius' Journal of Analytic Chemistry*, 337(3): 220-224 [Erratum, ibidem, 340(12): 787].

Drago, A. (1991a). *Le due opzioni. Per una storia popolare della scienza*. Molfetta Bari: La Meridiana.

Drago, A. (1991c). 'The alternative content of Thermodynamics: Constructive mathematics and problematic organization of the theory,' in Martinas, K., Ropolyi, L., Szegedi, P., Eds., *Thermodynamics: History and Philosophy. Facts, Trend, Debates*, Singapore: World Scientific, pp. 329-345.

Drago, A. (1992). 'Teaching History in the Framework of a Problem-based Peace Education,' *Gandhi Marg*, 14: 232-243.

Drago, A. (1994). Interpretazione delle frasi caratteristiche di Koyré e loro estensione alla storia della fisica dell'ottocento. In C. Vinti (Ed.), Alexandre Koyré. L'avventura Intellettuale (pp. 657-691). Napoli: ESI.

Drago, A. (1994). 'The Modern Fulfilment of Leibniz' Program for a *Scientia generalis*,' in Breger, H., ed., *VI International Kongress: Leibniz und Europa*. Hannover: Schlütersche Verlagsanstalt, pp. 185-195.

Drago, A. (1996). 'A paradigm-shift in conflict resolution: War and peace from a history of science viewpoint,' in Koller, P. and Puhl, P. H., Eds., 19TH International Wittgenstein Symposium: *Current Issues in Political Philosophy*. Kirchberg: Austrian Wittgenstein Society, pp. 106-114.

Drago, A. (1996). 'When the History of Physics Teaches Non-Violence: The

Impact of Bodies as a Metaphor of Conflict Resolution,' *Nonviolence and Spirituality*, 3:15-22.

Drago, A. (2001). 'The Birth of an Alternative Mechanics: Leibniz' Principle of Sufficient Reason,' in Poser, H., et al., eds., *Leibniz-Kongreß: Nihil sine ratione*, vol. I. Hannover: G.W. Leibniz Gesellschaft, pp. 322-330.

Drago, A. (2001). 'The several categories suggested for the "new historiography of science:" An interpretative analysis from a foundational viewpoint,' *Epistemologia*, 24: 48-82.

Drago, A. (2003). *La riforma della dinamica di G.W. Leibniz*. Benevento: Hevelius.

Drago, A. (2007). 'There exist two models of organization of a scientific theory,' *Atti della Fond. G. Ronchi*, 62(6): 839-856.

Drago, A. (2007). *Storia e Tecniche della Nonviolenza*. Napoli: Laurenziana.

Drago, A. (2007a). 'Galtung's theory of conflict resolution and beyond,' *Asteriskos*, 3/4: 17-31.

Drago, A. (2007b). 'The Birth of Non-Violence as a Political Theory,' *Gandhi Marg*, 29(3): 275-295.

Drago, A. (2009). 'Nonkilling Science,' in Evans Pim, Joám, ed., *Toward a Nonkilling Paradigm*. Honolulu: Center for Global Nonkilling, pp. 289-323.

Drago, A. (in press). '*Hind Swaraj*: The Birth of a Universal Ethics in Structural Terms,' in Silby, K., ed., *Hind Swaraj. A centennial*.

Drago, A. and Pezzella, A. (2000). 'Logica e strategia. Analisi della teoria di K. von Clausewitz,' *Teoria Politica*, 16: 164-174.

Drago, A. and Pisano, R. (2000). 'Interpretation and recostruction of the *Réflexions* by Sadi Carnot through the nonclassical logic,' *Atti Fond. Ronchi*, 57: 195-215.

Drago, A. and Sasso, A. (1993). 'Entropia e difesa,' in Drago, A. and Stefani, G., eds., *Una Strategia di Pace: La Difesa Popolare Nonviolenta*. Bologna: Fuorithema, pp. 153-162.

Drago, A. and Zerbino, E. (1996). 'Sull'interpretazione metodologica del discorso freudiano,' *Archivio di Psicologia Neurologia e Psichiatra*, 57: 539-566.

Drago, A.; Perno, A. (2004). 'La teoria geometrica delle parallele impostata coerentemente su un problema,' *Periodico di Matematica*, 4:41-52.

Dummett, M. (1977). *Elements of Intuitionism*. Oxford: Oxford University Press.

Einstein, A. (1905). 'Zur Elektrodynamik bewegter Körper,' *Annalen der Physik*, 17: 891-921.

Freud, S. (1925). 'Die Verneinung,' *Imago*, 11(3): 217-221.

Galtung, J. (1976). *Ideology and Methodology*. Copenhaven: Eijlers.

Galtung, J. (1999). *Peace by Peaceful Means*. London: Sage.

Gandhi, M. K. (1927-1929 [1909]). *An Autobiography, or the Story of my Experiments with Truth*. Ahmedabad: Navajivan Publishing House.

Gandhi, M. K. (1958). *All Men are Brothers*. Lausanne: UNESCO.

Gandhi, M. K. (2000 [1909]). *Hind Swaraji, or Indian Home Rule*. Ahmedabad: Navajivan Publishing House.

Gillispie, C. C. (1971). *Lazare Carnot Savant*. Princeton: Princeton University Press.

Goedel, K. (1986 [1932-33]). *Collected Works*. Oxford: Oxford University Press.

Horn, L. R. (1986). *The Natural History of Negation*. Chicago: University of Chicago Press.

Kant, I. (1793). *Über den Gemeinspruch: Das mag in der Theorie richtig sein, taugt aber nicht für die Praxis* [On the Old Saw].

Koyré, A. (1957). *From the Closed World to the Infinite Universe*. Baltimore: University of Maryland.

Kuhn, T. S. (1969). *The Structure of Scientific Revolutions*. Chicago: Chicago University Press.

Leibniz, G. W. (1671). 'Letter to Lambert van Velthuysen,' May 1671.

Lobachevsky, N. I. (1950 [1840]). *Geometrische Untersuchungen ueber der Theorien der Parallelineen*. Appendix to Bonola, R., *Non-Euclidean Geometries*. New York: Dover.

Marx, K. (1884). *Das Kapital*. Hamburg: Verlag von Otto Meissner.

Prawitz, D.; Malmnaas, P. E. (1968). 'A Survey of Some Connections Between Classical Intuitionistic and Minimal Logic,' in Schmidt, H. A.; Schuette, K.; Thiele, H.-J., eds., *Contributions to Mathematical Logic*. Amsterdam: North-Holland, pp. 215-229.

Sarton, G. (1954). 'Experiments with Truth by Faraday, Darwin and Gandhi,' *Osiris*, 11: 87-107.

Singh, N. M. (1996). 'From Descartesian-Newtonian mechanicistic model to Einsteinian-Gandhian holistic consciousness,' *Gandhi Marg*, 17: 478-481.

Sun Tzu (1994 [approx. 350 BCE]). *The Art of War*. Boulder Westview Press.

Vasto, Lanza del (1959). *Les Quatre Fléaux*. Paris: Denoël.

Vasto, Lanza del (1993 [1954]). 'Conversion de la Connaissance, du Coeur et du Corps,' in *Le Grand Retour*. Paris: Rocher, pp. 16-41.

11

Nonkilling, Professional Ethics, and Engineering the Public Good

David Haws
Boise State University

Taking illness to a physician, only a few centuries ago, was likely to result in the unnecessary loss of blood, if not premature death. The source of illness was occult, treatments were dangerous, and so more conservative physicians simply focused on methods that, if ineffective, were at least something less than immediately fatal. Physicians had physical contact with their patients, witnessed their suffering, and felt their loss. The concerned practitioner might draw a little blood, in a variety of ways, and thereby safely demonstrate both erudition and industry—encouraging the patient toward silence, if not health.

But because of the potential for harm, and because of their familial concern for the individual, ancient physicians chose the professional caveat: *Primum Non Nocere*. The potential for harm was, indeed, obvious, as well as morally compelling. And although germ theory gave physicians an important influence on *society*, doctors have retained the Hippocratic Oath in deference to their continued focus on the *individual*.

Engineers, similarly empowered with Baconian methods, address the community need for infrastructure, rather than healthy individuals. As a consequence, engineers primarily consider the potential for harm on a communal scale, and *our* professional constraint is to *hold paramount the public safety, health, and welfare*. Unfortunately, a lot of individuals can and will suffer before the *public* safety, health, and welfare even breaks a sweat. Further, because engineers primarily deal with an abstract social structure, rather than with individuals, engineers do not often see the anguished faces of those they impact. Historically, engineering developed as a branch of the military, and has no *explicit* professional constraint against doing individual harm (killing, being the extreme manifestation).

'Civilian' engineers acknowledge a professional duty to serve the public good, but we, arguably, have an even deeper, personal duty to respect individual life. After all, the public good is not defined by consensus, and even if it were, majority rule is practically, rather than morally compelling. Most governments consist of leaders making decisions (some of which, engineers are expected to carry out) on behalf of the governed. But while even a *tyrant* might choose to define a public good that allows individual, human flourishing, the 'public' is a social construct that does not bleed. When the public good tramples on individual life—even for the greater, actual good of collective individuals—diminished life compels us to respect a remainder obligation toward those suffering a socially imposed burden. While it might be comforting, engineers cannot simply shunt the administration of social justice onto someone else: we are morally obliged by the remainder obligations generated through our work.

The line between killing and letting die is fuzzy at best, and engineers need to re-examine their willingness to let individuals suffer for the greater good generated through engineering projects. Deaths, causally associated with a particular project, might be human or nonhuman; intentional or accidental; foreseeable or unforeseeable; immediate, proximal or distal. But when an individual's death is attributable, at least in part, to an engineering project, that individual bears a kind of ultimate, social burden that cannot be distributed back and relieved by the society in general. Increasing the balance of good *overall* simply is not enough—our engineering projects need to avoid, mitigate, or *at least* respectfully consider the disproportionate burden born by those who suffer and die in the aftermath.

While *ahimsa* (nonkilling) has seldom been the focus of engineering, even with benign projects such as the delivery of clean drinking water, this deficiency is a moral failure resulting from a paternalistic sense of professional duty that 'treats' the beneficiary, and, too often, ignores the collateral individual. This does not make our engineering designs *bad*, it simply makes them incomplete. It would be *wrong* for us to knowingly put forth an incomplete design; or to ignorantly put forth a design that we considered 'complete' as an exercise in wishful thinking. On the other hand, if we *un*knowingly allow an incomplete design to progress through to realization, then we have committed an error of omission. While our motivation remains untainted, we are nevertheless obliged to correct mistakes as they come to our attention, and relieve inappropriately assigned burdens.

For example, the Golden Gate Bridge, completed in 1937, was a stunning engineering achievement, which must have been personally gratifying for the engineers involved. Realizing a greater good for thousands, the bridge was an aesthetic, economic, and moral exemplar. The elegant lines, austere setting, and extreme attenuation (its 4,200 feet was the world's longest clear span at the time of completion) make the bridge a globally identifiable symbol of built beauty. While the bridge was actually constructed *under* budget by $1.3 million, its exquisitely optimized main cables compare tellingly with the grossly over-designed structure of its contemporary, the record-setting Empire State Building (the main cables were so finely tuned as to thwart subsequent attempts to add the second traffic deck, common on less sleekly-spectacular Bay bridges). Finally, as has been frequently noted, Bridge construction pioneered the use of safety nets to protect exposed workers—saving 19 from assumed-fatal falls, and reducing the number of construction deaths to less than a third of what might have been expected by rule of thumb.

Yet, any engineering project interacting with individuals—even drawing nothing but awe and respect from most of us—is liable to entail *some* moral obligations. For this analysis, I would like to examine the bridge, and consider those moral obligations that accrue subject to the potential for loss of life. With regard to *human* life, we need to consider:

- Accidental death during construction, and in traffic (on the bridge itself, but also due to increased regional traffic generation)
- Intentional death through suicide, and from armed attack (on the bridge, as a military or symbolic target of opportunity)
- Increased mortality from economic adjustment (among economic pilgrims, as well as the marginalized and excluded)

Additionally, I think we need to consider the death of animals:

- Directly as roadkill, and indirectly through displaced habitat (attributable to the increased number of vehicles, roads, and communities enabled in the North Bay counties by the bridge's construction)

In each of these instances, Bridge engineers missed an opportunity to lessen the potential for loss of life, failing to commit adequate resources to understand incipient problems and realize effective solutions. If there is a failure here—with the stunning engineering success of the Bridge, and by inference, perhaps, with our more yeoman engineering designs—I feel that it might be justifiably laid at the foot of our professional ethic, which avoids an explicit reference to the individual.

Accidental Loss of Human Life

Compared with the past, we seem less willing to simply accept the untimely death of a distal other. This is equally true of intentional, unintentional, and accidental death. In terms of intentional death, at least some responsible actors in our (US) government believe this, or they would not feel compelled to obscure the level of carnage now taking place in the Middle East (no one similarly placed was concerned enough to conceal our level of troop loss, an order of magnitude greater, 40 years earlier in Vietnam). As for unintentional death, the epidemic of puerperal fever recognized in Vienna by Ignaz Semmelweis, might today generate outrage, rather than a nineteenth century blend of ignorant denial and helpless acceptance. Finally, the expanding scope of current safety features indicates less complacency with *accidental* death, if not an increased willingness to relieve the suffering of victims (still distributing relief primarily on the basis of insurance).

I can remember working on construction projects where safety equipment was minimal to nonexistent by current standards. I also remember a lot of old carpenters with missing digits, and was more-or-less amazed to discover that they had lost fingers, like Civil War saw-bones, through haste and a well-sharpened hand tool rather than the introduction of unfamiliar and obviously dangerous power equipment. The greatest dangers are often concealed—sometimes behind over-reliance on safety devices—but individual accidents derive as much from human attitudes as innately perilous operations. Danger accrues to an industry as a function of process, rather than the ultimate industrial product.

Historically, the risks of a dangerous profession were naively assumed to be inevitable, and the subject of informed consent. Dangerous jobs often entailed higher wages, and the idea was that greater compensation—compensation for risk—was also adequate compensation for the burden of accidental loss. Payment for risk is fine, but the idea that there can be just, monetary compensation for accidental death is ludicrous. No one, in the absence of insanity, terminal illness, unbearable pain, or the duress of an impossible situation, would volunteer to surrender a *limb*, let alone end his or her life, purely for the sake of monetary compensation.

Yet in the recent past, industrial accidents were considered an act of God (or a random act of chance) rather than ultimately preventable occurrences, statistically skewed to particular industries by ignorance, greed, and neglect. Workers were given the economic status of a raw material—to be used up, or replaced by raw material from another source if prices became too dear. (If you believe this practice to occur *strictly* in the past, try hiring your neighbour to raise, slaughter, and clean the chicken you want to cook for dinner.) Injured long-term workers were typically dismissed with some minimal package of benefits, while short-term workers and the families of industry fatalities were left to the spotty care of external charities.

In a similar way, traffic fatalities were accepted as the simple inevitability of hurling people around at 70 miles per hour, surrounded by a ton of glass and metal, and oozing a few gallons of accelerant. The car I have owned for the last 18 years (a 1964 Plymouth Belvedere, which has never had seat belts) was built and originally purchased in 1963, the first year U.S. traffic fatalities topped 40,000. By way of comparison, annual traffic fatalities always exceeded our troop losses in Vietnam (by more than a factor of 3, even during the year of the Tet Offensive). While traffic fatalities reached an apex of nearly 55,000 in 1972, the increasing emphasis on 'safe' vehicles has reduced U.S. traffic fatalities to mid-1960s levels. But historically, so many people died before their time, subject to accidents, infections, treatable or preventable disease, as collateral damage in wars, or subject to the vagaries of food production and famine—we just stoically accepted the fact that our lives would be touched, at various points, by premature death.

We seem more active today, looking for culpability in accidental death and assigning damages. I suppose it is tempting to play a utilitarian analysis with human life. Perhaps we imagine a minimum market value in terms of some abstract utile, like dollars (e.g., how many waking hours might a relatively alert human expect to live, and how much would the reasonably competent require, as compensation, to relinquish one hour). Market force estimations, after all, form the basis of how we value a (nonpet) animal life (so much per mature pork-belly, delivered to the abattoir, depending on timely supply and the instantaneous, global yen for bacon). And, of course, market forces were also used by slave owners, to place a value on 'available' African-Americans before our Civil War.

But the assignment of damages, too often, is a *post hoc* measure of retributive, rather than distributive justice. Since a lost human life is irredeemable, unless, possibly, in exchange for some 'equivalent' human life, justice after the fact is an illusion. Engineers should do their best to design useful projects, which enhance life—not to avoid damages, but because moral behavior is morally compelling. If fatalities occur, we need to correct the immediate and responsible causes, insure that the fatality is not simply accepted as the cost of doing business, and ease the burdens of those who, in Whitman's terms, remain, and suffer. But justice is temporally beyond our grasp. Justice demands our attention *before* dangers become *de facto*.

The Golden Gate Bridge and post-war automobile safety requirements are rightly cited as the beginning of a gentler, more responsible attitude toward the victims of fatal accidents. Innovators like Joseph Strauss and Preston Tucker were obviously unsettled by the existing, callous attitude toward accidental loss of life—and in their own ways, are at least partially responsible for leading our society away from its complacency. But Strauss and Tucker's innovations addressed *familiar* accidents, and made no real attempt to consider safety problems beyond the expected (for example, failing to account for gondolas crashing through safety nets, or lead poisoning from automobile exhaust emissions). Since many engineered works outlive their designers, we need to devote a significant portion of the design effort to considering just how each project might encounter an adjunct failure in unexpected and catastrophic ways (perhaps writing, disseminating, and critiquing imaginative reports). With the collective imagination of the engineering profession, I do not see why we would be unable to anticipate at least some of the new forms of accidents which inevitably follow in the wake of new technologies.

One might argue that the extreme boundaries of killing (intentional) and letting-die (accidental) encompass a well-distributed continuum of possibilities. While no single contribution to an accidental death may be necessary or sufficient, there is perhaps *some* culpability by simple contiguity (this seems to be the direction taken in U.S. civil suits, assigning minimal, potential liability to caterers, for construction deaths at the sites they service). This being the case, there is a fractional aspect of killing associated with accidental death that makes our professional concern morally imperative. Perhaps accidental deaths are simply unintentional killing, as with the ignorant introduction of bacteria during childbirth in nineteenth century Vienna.

Intentional Loss of Human Life

There are probably two types of intentional death one might associate with the Golden Gate Bridge—suicide, which has occurred (often) and should reasonably have been anticipated; and politically-motivated attack—blowing up the Bridge as a military objective, or as a symbol of something else, hateful, yet beyond weapon's range. While both types of deaths are, or would be killing (you cannot really argue Secondary Effect here—that someone might want to blow up the Bridge, without intending to kill the people driving across it in their cars), they otherwise seem to be quite different.

Suicide is certainly a killing, but the *ill* of a suicide's death seems to be a function of motivation; we do not consider willing, self-sacrificial death to be suicide *or* killing—even if the sacrifice achieves nothing concrete. For example, the unsuccessful hero might use his body in a vain attempt to save someone else. Comparatively, a *suicide* might choose to die because he thinks it would be better for his family. Both deaths are untimely, but we hold the suicide particularly culpable because we consider him inadequately informed, and think that he ought to have known better. We are less judgmental of the thwarted hero, and consider the world a better place, because of the occasional human willingness to make the ultimate sacrifice in an attempt—even if unsuccessful—to save the other. But if the suicide cannot know the state of the world in his absence, then neither can we. Further, if the culpability of *accidental* death exists somewhere on a continuum between killing and letting die, then perhaps suicide itself might not be an *absolutely* culpable form of killing (might retain a residual element of the accidental).

If a particular suicide *were* considered morally acceptable—for example, by controlling the manner, rather than the time of death, thereby avoiding a death that could be considered significantly premature—then jumping from the Bridge under the proper circumstances (no witness, no family or musing comrades left behind to wonder, and an out-going tide) might avoid censure. Under the right circumstances, the suicide would mitigate the physical aspects of a messy aftermath; and we know that the 'well-tested' probability of success would be 98 per cent (greater, if the suicide could control the angle of impact).

But if there were a morally acceptable suicide, it would be difficult to differentiate ahead of time. And for the purpose of this analysis, I will assume (along with Kant) that there is a perfect moral imperative against suicide—that suicide is a killing similar to the killing of someone other than yourself. This being the case, the engineers who designed the Golden Gate Bridge should have considered features to deter *all* potential suicide.

Of course, as originally configured with a pedestrian lane, the Bridge might be considered 'suicide friendly.' Does the aesthetic Bay view seen from the walkway (admittedly stunning) offset the 'attractive nuisance' appeal for potential suicides? On the other hand, lazy, or less-ambulatory suicides have certainly been willing to abandon cars on the roadway. More to the point, since suicides were jumping from the Brooklyn Bridge long before the Golden Gate Bridge was envisioned, the bridge's popularity with West Coast suicides should not have really surprised anyone.

As of 2005 (68 years of operation) more than 1,200 Golden Gate Bridge suicides have been documented (currently compiling at about one every two weeks). Importantly, there has been a continuing effort to reduce suicide attempts—through signage, alert officials (many potential suicides being thwarted by the California Highway Patrol) and with the introduction of sensors and strategically placed suicide nets. Perhaps there are additional *post hoc* palliatives (for example handing out anti-depressants at the pedestrian turnstile), but suicide prevention should have been incorporated into the *original* design. Again, as with accidental death, *most* people will eventually recognize a problem and potential solutions, but engineers are particularly well-trained to consider technical problems in the abstract. And a brainstorming of unimagined, destructive applications should be a part of every engineering preliminary design. If this had been accomplished in the 1930s, perhaps the Bridge suicide toll would be less.

In the aftermath of 9/11, I am sure that there must be engineers somewhere considering the possibilities of a hostile impact loading on the Golden Gate Bridge. Because of its exposure to wind and seismic forces, the bridge is probably well designed against the kind of lateral loads that might come from a bomb blast sufficiently small, or at some adequate remove. As a consequence, the problem might become one of keeping potential bombs far enough away from critical structural components (the two towers, the main cables, the two anchorages, the auxiliary cables, and the bridge girders, probably in that order). A military attack might provide enough warning to close the bridge and initiate countermeasures, but a stealth attack by land could use the bridge roadway to access vulnerable features. Further, since the Bridge is an aerial, sight-seeing destination, attack from a private plane might not offer as much warning time as a more standard, military sortie.

Without trying to second-guess terrorists in a morbid way, the Bridge's principal weakness is probably in the material properties of the main cables—steel being particularly susceptible to heat and corrosion. While the ganged cables are statically determinant (enabling catastrophic failure at a single point) the redundant connections to the anchorage would require more points of attack, but correspondingly smaller explosions, and not all of the redundant connections would have to fail simultaneously (this type of failure analysis could be done by any of my upper-division engineering students). If engineers responsible for the bridge are not currently thinking through potential attack scenarios, they obviously should be—in consultation with military engineers, who spend much more of their time trying to figure out how to efficiently blow things up, and how to patch battle damage.

For example, if a private plane loaded with jellied gasoline were to wrap itself around a cable support at the top of one tower, how much warning time would motorists have to vacate the bridge? Should Highway Officials have a mechanism in place (do they?) to more or less instantaneously shut down the approaches (and how far away should vehicles be held)? How could fire retardants be efficiently placed at the site of combustion, or how might the heat of combustion be safely dissipated? If the ends of the bridge were simultaneously blocked, could we safely evacuate motorists by static lines or gondola to the respective shores? Assuming that someone with a grudge will eventually want to attack an American landmark on the west coast, should we 'mis-direct' them by heavily defending the bridge (for example, studding the bridge with anti-aircraft drones), while posting minimal defences, and advertising the 'cultural significance' of some other, attractive target (perhaps San Simeon, from the perspective of historic continuity)?

The point is that a military attack on the Golden Gate Bridge was *not* part of the original design, although it probably should have been (Orson Welles and military planners were certainly considering the possibility of an attack on US soil). Today, there is no excuse for ignoring military/terrorist threats. In fact, since the Oklahoma City bombing, Federal buildings are now being designed to withstand internal blast loading (fairly simple, although perhaps counter-intuitive for someone habituated to thinking in terms of gravity loads).

As a profession, we have made progress in limiting the potential for our designs to further intentional killing. Although such killing is admittedly a bad thing, a determined killing is difficult to prevent. In the end, perhaps the current moral obligation of engineers is to prevent the easy deaths, while playing for time—enlarging the window for a timely response to developing threats. However, not all projects (the Golden Gate Bridge is a notable exception) retain the attention of engineers after their completion, so an exploration of dire contingencies needs to be a significant part of the project's initial conception.

Economic Displacement and the Loss of Human Life

In a finite world, the attraction of resources to one area will preclude their use in another. In the extreme, this polarizes wealth, and leaves behind pockets of marginalized humanity, incapable of realizing the life they desire. Such poverty is often accompanied by the loss of life—killing and otherwise—and the differential of wealth drives migration, taxing the typically minimal services available for new arrivals, and further decreasing the capacity of an abandoned homeland. In addition, indigenous inhabitants or early immigrants, if able to exercise sufficient power, will have an advantage over newcomers, and often use their advantage to exact privilege. In such an environment, the frustration of competing against unwarranted privilege might also motivate conflict resulting in the loss of life.

The history of California is rife with economic struggles between peoples and regions, and the Golden Gate Bridge was rightly seen as an economic stimulus to the North Bay counties (including Sonoma

County, where I grew up). Under Anglo development, the location of San Francisco benefitted from natural port facilities, an existing presidio/mission with support infrastructure, and access along El Camino Real to the lush, surrounding farmlands to the south, and southeast. But originally located as a potential redoubt at the end of a narrow, highly defensible peninsula, San Francisco was separated from the counties to the immediate north by the Golden Gate. As a consequence, commerce to the north was traditionally limited by the availability of ferry traffic within the Bay. North Bay counties were therefore more isolated, agrarian, and economically limited. The Golden Gate Bridge improved access, drew capital as well as wealthier inhabitants, and contributed to the gentrification of the locals (or their exodus farther inland, to less pricey chunks of real estate).

Prosperity in the North Bay counties—augmented by the Bridge—fostered an unwillingness on the part of local inhabitants to do the nasty, or toilsome bits of work. For example, while I was growing up in Santa Rosa (the early 1960s) the public schools did not start until the end of September. Ostensibly, this was to allow school children to aid in the harvest of local prunes and to a lesser extent, English walnuts (both of which involved retrieving product from the ground). Yet, by the time I was there, few locals availed themselves of this opportunity (I certainly did not, although I did work construction jobs during the summer).

Mechanized farm labour is perhaps the most traditionally dangerous, nonbelligerent occupation, and if accompanied by inadequate wages, is understandably rejected by people with other options. However, migrant farm labour (drawn from regions low on options) had been fairly well established by the time of the Great Depression. While the end of the 1960s saw a few locals—otherwise stretching time between meals on communes, such as Lou Gottlieb's Morningstar Ranch—embark on farm labour, the region's less desirable, agricultural jobs (as now, throughout much of the West) were typically taken by 'part-year' transients from Latin America.

This was not a new phenomenon, and the nineteenth century saw waves of Asian emigration—some, such as the Chinese, being met with extreme violence (more than one Chinese was simply killed at the end of the harvest, to avoid the cost of a meagre wage). The point is that from a global perspective, the North Bay counties were already extremely wealthy. The Golden Gate Bridge enhanced this, and so is reasonably seen to contribute—admittedly, in a limited way—to the initial misery of the attracted poor.

Globally, corporations concentrate wealth and exploit the unprotected—particularly where they can operate off the radar of the obliviously empowered. If Malaysian children are working in clandestine, sweat-shop conditions to fabricate sneakers, it is at least partially because some North Bay residents—from a position of relative affluence enhanced in a small way by the bridge—choose to buy cheap footwear. Effort placed in the Third World producing export goods for the First World, gives the rank and file little of value, and detracts from the labour required to produce the food they need to eat, and the other goods that might stay and enhance the local quality of life. I do not know of an Irish Potato Famine in the works anywhere, but the potential mechanism is well understood. The Third World needs fewer 'Hard Rock Café' T-shirts, and a larger percentage of its own resources, to develop local culture and a more satisfying lifestyle. 'Trickle down' failed to work in our own (US) democracy, and it certainly will not work where the receptacles of poverty are so much more ubiquitous and overwhelming.

The problem for engineers is that most of their projects require capital—ready capital being primarily available in the First World. Engineering projects generate economic growth, and so the rich get richer (and, in a zero-sum world, the poor get poorer). If there is a possible solution here, it might be in the kind of *pro bono* engineering work demonstrated by groups like Engineers Without Borders. It would be helpful if such groups received better funding, maybe by levying a surcharge on all engineering projects in the First World. This is not the enormous 'great leap forward' it might first appear to be, since some countries (like Japan) levy a similar engineering surcharge to support things like research and development.

The contributions of the Golden Gate Bridge are admittedly minimal in terms of global economic impact, but we are not justified in assuming they pass unfelt. While the motivation for economic enhancement in the First World is not death in the Third World, the lack of intention, or even ignorance of negative impact, does not absolve us of moral responsibility. Death, attributable to economic disparity is at least *partially* a form of killing, as opposed to letting-die. If the culpability for economic suffering is widely distributed, then the zero-sum impact of regional economic enhancement should be considered as part of the engineering analysis, at least for large, First World projects such as the Golden Gate Bridge. I know of no significant attempt to account for the economic disparity associated with engineering projects, and this certainly was not included in the analysis for the Golden Gate Bridge.

The Accidental Loss of Animal Life

I suppose the intentional killing of animals on the bridge is at least possible (as unimaginable as it is, there are probably individuals who find sport in squishing small animals into the pavement). But the economic growth fostered by the Golden Gate Bridge also meant more space dedicated to human activities, with a correspondingly smaller habitat available for indigenous species. With the encroachment of humans, some species were displaced by others (wild oats and Eucalyptus trees, for example, while alien, have done quite well in northern California). And according to a *replacement* utilitarian theory, 100 happy dogs are equivalent to 100 happy coyotes (although the coyotes might not agree).

Perhaps, from a moral perspective, the most significant problem generated from loss of animal life is the increase in roadkill. For the most part, people who die in traffic accidents make the decision (perhaps ill-informed) to get into a car. While it may go unspoken, it seems reasonable that drivers and passengers, who contribute to the problem of vehicles with a dangerous amount of momentum, implicitly assume a proportionate risk. Do we not always feel worse about a pedestrian or bicyclist hit by a car, as opposed to someone similarly mutilated when two or more cars collide? However, with regard to animals, they seem simply caught in the headlights. Some die instantly and some linger, just as with human traffic casualties—but in the absence of an implicitly accepted risk.

The prevailing attitude with nonfarm animals has always been that those near a road would either develop car-savvy, or would be killed. In the case of feral species, populations would normally diminish (as they might, subject to the sudden introduction of thousands of hungry predators) and the scope of suffering would naturally lessen. On the other hand, sufficiently prolific species like squirrels might simply continue at culled numbers equal to the available food supply. In either case, large, less prolific, non-scavenging populations could easily dwindle and become genetically unviable.

In the case of pets, roadkill was easy enough to replace from the roaming excess of un-neutered animals, and the new pets, if unfamiliar with the perils of traffic, were given a similarly small window to come to grips with the presence of speeding vehicles. While pet roadkill continues, I seem to see fewer mangled pets now than in my youth. Possibly there are fewer free-range specimens among the un-neutered, but (although this evidence is just anecdotal) perhaps we have become better about taking care of our most cherished animals.

While I am currently living in a rural, mountainous part of the Great Basin, I see a lot of feral roadkill, ranging from moose, elk, and mule deer; to the magpies squished *into* the moose, elk, or mule deer they were feeding on. In the 25 years that I have been in this area, I have had two vehicular encounters with mule deer (one became flustered and bolted head-first into the side of my parked car; and the other was head-to-head at 65 miles per hour, totalling my car as well as the deer).

The point is that when I moved to this area in 1985, I was told to watch for deer when their mountain feed became depleted (November through March), and the intent of the warning was to allow me to protect my *vehicle* rather than migrating deer. Hunters might bemoan the occasional roadkill with a nice rack—I have even seen the ignoble taking of coup (like elk eye-teeth) from an otherwise mangled carcass. But even with the massive, post-War addition of rurally-placed 'National Defence' highways, no one was taking measures to limit the time a feral animal might spend in harm's way.

When I first arrived in the area, there still were range cattle and a number of 'cattle-crossing' signs on lightly-used state roads—although one typically saw many more deer on the road than cows. But after I had been living in Utah for a decade or so, a newly completed section of I-40 near Jordanelle Dam was actually engineered for a deer-crossing, using cobbled terrain and fencing to channel the deer migration to a specific, well marked, and highly visible section of roadway. Such a limited application may or may not have saved any *actual* deer (there are still many opportunities to be run down on I-80, a few miles away) but it demonstrates the inkling of an admirable attitude.

The point is that while most humans are less concerned with animal life than human life, we need to recognize that engineering projects, like the Golden Gate Bridge, contribute to the death of a variety of living things, and that to a certain extent, living things—as moral patients—have a claim on us moral agents. As engineers, we should recognize this problem and provide proactive solutions (like engineered deer-crossings). Deer who lose their footing and fall off a cliff may succumb to accidental death; and deer shot by hunters may be killed; but deer that crumple to the side of a road do it from an insufficiently acknowledged engineering neglect.

Conclusions

Death is not the problem; we are all born owing the debt of death. The problem is meaningless death, and the aspect of killing (intentional, unintentional, or partially accidental) implies that someone knowingly or ignorantly dropped the ball—denying the value of life and the meaning of death. Death is supposed to be a *natural* end, at least aesthetically required by our natural beginning, the declining efficiency of our biological containment, as a semi-closed system, and the Second Law of Thermodynamics. But nonkilling is still a significant goal for the engineering profession, and except for the possible, indirect killing related to opportunity cost (born by the Third World for engineering projects designed to economically enhance the First World) engineering as a profession has contributed to a progressive attitude respectful of life. Even with the evils of economic disparity, Engineers Without Borders, as a twenty-first century organization, should certainly be seen as a positive step in the right direction. The problem is that we need to be careful to couch the requirements of nonkilling in an enabling way.

Elizabeth Anscombe (1981) made an interesting comment about pacifism between the two world wars. She held that a typical belief—professed by militant governments—was that pacifism, while noble, was beyond the reasonable expectation of existing regimes. While this categorical denial of a lofty goal is a little self-defeating (like denying hunger because there is no food in your mouth), Anscombe goes on to say that governments, thus self-absolved from nonkilling on practical grounds, took the 'in-for-a-penny, in-for-a-pound' attitude. Since they could not be 'noble' they felt no compunction to be 'decent' (hence, neither side refrained from the indiscriminate bombing of civilian targets).

If engineers claim nonkilling as an absolute, professional goal, and if nonkilling is not within our zone of proximal development (to use Lev Vygotski's term) then the goal of nonkilling might simply be dismissed as unobtainable. 'Ought to imply can'; and if the profession cannot achieve the nobility of nonkilling, at least some might feel absolved from the responsibility of maintaining a decent respect for life. To be absolved at one point, might be construed as a licence to totally ignore one's moral responsibility (certainly, one's moral sensibility might be expected to erode).

Not too many years ago, engineering was simply a branch of the military, and I do not think we are very close to achieving *ahimsa*. Both engineering and the military are currently used to enhance or exact privileged status, and neither pays adequate attention to the holes they tear in our global fabric. Racism, nationalism, religious intolerance, and entrenched privilege are recalcitrant foes—feebly opposed by our efforts in the engineering curriculum, to address the problems of a nonkilling profession. I teach a class in engineering ethics to approximately 300 students a year—and consideration *here* is a miniscule step—but the moral dialogue needs to include active professionals. This is not something you can force with units of continuing professional education, and a serious dialogue may have to wait for the collective will to change. Perhaps volunteer organizations, like Engineers Without Borders will become so overwhelmingly successful that the profession as a whole will desire their institutional subsumption, and be willing to abandon the limited attitudes of centuries past.

A dialogue as to the goals of *ahimsa* might help us to appreciate the negative impact, on isolated individuals, of our otherwise positive projects. With appropriately respectful attitudes, the private good becomes the public good, and recognizing our moral obligation to marginalized victims is an important step. Thus, engineering concern for the individual, comparable to the concern expressed by physicians, seems to be at the core of a viable professional ethic for engineers. As engineers, we must consider the needs of all individuals, along with our first inquiries into the possibilities of engineered solutions in support of the public good.

Reference

Anscombe, G. E. M. (1981). 'War and Murder,' in *Ethics, Religion and Politics: Collected Philosophical Papers Volume III*. Oxford: Basil Blackwell, pp. 51-61.

12

Mathematics for Building a Nonkilling Ethos

Vivek Patkar
Independent Researcher

Mathematics in essence deals with abstract symbols and concepts. But being a human activity, its constructive as well as destructive applications have been witnessed. Of late, mathematics is found providing or guiding instruments used for killing on a mass scale, particularly in warfare. It is high time we pledge to employ only its positive and society binding features to sustain civilization. Mathematical techniques for conflict resolution such as compromise programming, for example, can help to a certain extent in this direction.

Even today killing is frequently resorted to get rid of individuals or groups that may have even marginally differing perspectives of life. Dissimilarities in religion, ideology and culture are often treated as evil and elimination of their adherents is presumed to be a sacred duty in many instances. It is overlooked that such diversity has been and is necessary for human survival and progress. The analogy from geometry namely, the development of non-Euclidean geometries vis-à-vis Euclidean geometry illustrates this point succinctly. There are several other mathematical concepts and methods to assist checking the rise of killing situations.

We need to drive home the message that we should nurture the immense power of mathematics for the furtherance of mankind. Suitable changes in teaching, regular application of mathematical methods to manage the conflicts, and use of information and communication technology to project the positive role of mathematics should be utilized for this purpose.

Introduction

Though mathematics in its rudimentary form started with counting and simple arithmetic, first to facilitate the royal administrative operations like land measure and tax collection and then for common daily transactions, mathematics for the sake of mathematics in large part has been the guiding principle for its development. Only with the Renaissance has its application been systematically undertaken in various fields, and that in turn led to further developments in mathematics. It is amazing to note that in the year 1868 mathematics was divided into 12 branches with 38 sub-branches (Davis and Hersh, 1981), whereas in the year 2000 the number of branches has grown to 63 with more than 4,500 sub-branches. That gives an idea of the rapid expansion and diversification in the field of mathematics. Interestingly, 95 per cent of the existing knowledge of mathematics has developed only since 1900 CE.

Mathematics is primarily a human activity and, therefore, its use for both good and harmful purposes cannot be avoided. On the positive side establishment of computer-based global banking systems, development of metropolitan city-wide water, transport and other utility networks, and launching of satellites for exploring the outer universe have been possible due largely to the assistance of mathematics. Gambling, on the other hand, which irrespective of its form essentially depends on mathematics, has been the cause of ruin of countless individuals and even empires. In other words, mathematics on its own does not dictate the kind of application. Some of its innocuous products, however, are found to be double-edged. That means their beneficial uses in normal times can be found aiding killing forces in war operations. For instance the logarithmic tables that helped Kepler to establish his famous three laws of planetary motion, also proved useful to direct the guns and cannons for increasing firing accuracy in numerous battlefields. It is no wonder that application of mathematical war technology for the purpose of killing on different scales is a fact of life. Sufficient historic evidence is available—particularly from the time of Archimedes (287-212 BCE), to the Second World War, to the latest Iraq and Afghanistan war—to show that mathematics, directly or indirectly, has enhanced our capacity to kill and wipe out the habitat on an unprecedented scale.

The above argument that mathematics, like fire, is basically neutral and pure in its construct and it is man who moulds it to design lethal weapons and other means of destruction or counterattack is true, but only partially. One reason for this skew is that the power of mathematics was recognized early by military establishments, who ensured the adequate flow of funds and other resources for its development to support warfare objectives. Induction of select young mathematicians by the military intelligence agency of Poland in the early 1930s to break the famous 'Enigma' code used for secret communication by German forces is a classic example in this regard (Rakus-Andersson, 2003). Their work was later extended by another mathematician, Alan Turing, who was commissioned by the Defence Ministry of Britain. It is no surprise that next to teaching (formal and private), the department of defence of a nation and its allied agencies all over the world employ the largest number of mathematicians. Their tasks vary from increasing weapon firing efficiency to designing proficient antisubmarine operations in a given section of the ocean. The glamour associated with such work receives more celebrity attention because it leaves a deep impression on the human mind. And, of course, such acts are often glorified by the media, sometimes disproportionately.

It is time to bring the equally important progress and development facilitating power of mathematics to greater prominence. Interplay between abstract constructions of pure mathematics and practical problem-solving capacity of applied mathematics in this respect is to be portrayed. If projected imaginatively, the qualities of mathematics that help deter killing and offer relatively stable solutions for resolving complex conflict by following an all-inclusive approach would be appreciated by people at large. Such promotion is to be done through means such as case study based writing, teaching, public lectures, and demonstration of welfare furthering capabilities of mathematics. Modern communication means of electronic media and the Internet can certainly contribute significantly to these efforts.

The aim of this paper is to show how different concepts from mathematics can help to develop nonkilling attitudes and direct attention to its humanity binding and prospering potential. Support of information and communication technology for this purpose is also highlighted.

Genesis of Killing

Greed for material possession, insecurity due to external and internal threats, and ideological differences due to factors like religion, race, class, language and culture are found to be the leading causes for killing at individual, group and even international levels. Further, human psychology suffers from two sicknesses, namely, promoting vendettas across generations and the tendency to label people as groups responsible for the trouble rather than particular individuals. It is no wonder that more often than not, innocent persons suffer because they simply may fall under such condemned group labels by conditions beyond their control.

A substantial number of killing cases is also found arising out of the following widely-held myopic or fractured adherences; among many:

a) ours is the best worldview (e.g., religion or culture) and, therefore, those holding other views need to be eliminated as they have no right to exist, and
b) Fair distribution of resources is not possible, and therefore, to resort to killing is justified to grab the pie.

Rigid attitudes as reflected by a) above is one of the root causes of conflict which escalates to bloodbath at the slightest provocation. This attitude is counterproductive and is seldom realized and projected. In this context the development from geometry is useful to show that an alternative worldview is perfectly justifiable and co-existence of various systems in fact supplements each other for sustenance. We shall elaborate on this idea in the third section of the paper.

An enormous amount of literature in fields such as mathematical programming, economics, and management offers methods to address the issue of resource distribution raised by b) above. These methods are by and large found effective at a macro level. But at a local level, the technique of compromise programming can be gainfully employed to suggest solutions that can contain the conflicts, at least for some period, during which further options can be developed to settle the issue. That will be the subject matter of our fourth section.

Application of mathematics can amply guide the negotiation process leading to avoidance of human killing. In other words to promote nonkilling conditions, developments from mathematics can certainly help. This also includes cases of killing that occur from accidents due to design failure (e.g., faulty vehicles, poor road geometrics, and signal malfunctioning) and man-made disasters (for example, Bhopal gas leak and meltdown of Chernobyl nuclear reactor). Considerable mathematics-based technological knowledge is available to minimize such tragic incidents. It would be a great folly if we do not understand and exploit the power of this distinct asset of mathematics, which no other living creature on the earth possesses.

Non-Euclidean Geometries

Euclid (325-262 BCE) customarily is given the credit of developing what is now called plane geometry. He systematically drew upon the logical argument framework put forth and fortified successively by Socrates (477-399 BCE), Plato (428-348 BCE), and Aristotle (384-322 BCE) to give a solid foundation to his work. In particular, besides giving 23 definitions (such as point and straight line) and five common notions (such as things equal to the same thing are also equal to each other and the whole is greater than the parts), he assumed the following five axioms to construct the entire edifice of geometry in the form of 465 propositions (theorems) proved in his celebrated 13-part work called *Elements* (specifically, in the papyrus rolls called *Books* I-IV & VI) (Euclid, 1956):

1. A straight line can be drawn from any point to any point.
2. A finite straight line can be extended continuously in a straight line.
3. A circle can be formed with any centre and distance (radius).
4. All right angles are equal to one another.
5. If a straight line falling on two straight lines makes the sum of the interior angles on the same side less than two right angles, then the two straight lines, if extended indefinitely, meet on that side on which the angle sum is less than the two right angles.

Or, equivalently formulated by Playfair as 'Through a point not on line, there is exactly one line parallel to the given line.'

There have been doubts about the self-truth of the above stated fifth axiom, but still for about two thousand years Euclid's geometry was assumed to be perfect, unique and absolutely valid. However, N. Lobachevsky in Russia (1829) and J. Bolayi (1832) in Hungary proved independently that if 'one line' in the above Playfair's formulation of the fifth axiom of Euclid is replaced by 'more than one line' the resulting system contains no contradictions. B. Riemann (1854) found the same if 'no parallel line' is substituted in that place. The basic difference is that geometry developed by Lobachevsky and Bolayi holds well on the hyperbolic surface while that developed by Riemann works on the spherical surface. It is thus implied that Euclid's geometry is valid only for the plane surface and it is one out of many possible geometries that can be constructed. All such other forms are now called non-Euclidean geometries (Gray, 2007; Wolfe, 1945).

Interestingly, Euclidean geometry is still found useful for most daily activities, whereas Riemannian geometry is helpful to study distant galaxies in astronomy, and Lobachevskian and Bolayi's geometry is valuable in sub-atomic physics studies. The study of geometry has expanded ever since this breakthrough and continues to do so fascinatingly (Hartshorne, 2000). All these geometries coexist and none is claimed to be superior to others. Usefulness of each form of geometry depends on the context of application.

There is no doubt that ideas of Lobachevsky, Bolayi and Riemann were quite bold when proposed and they challenged the established mathematical practices of the time. The point to note is that despite the standing of near-perfect Euclidean geometry for more than twenty centuries, efforts to check its soundness and generalization were taken in a professional spirit and results were assimilated in mainstream mathematics smoothly once they were found logically valid. This diversity of geometry has led to beneficial developments in many fields. An outstanding example of this is how Riemannian geometry paved the way for Albert Einstein to develop the 'Theory of Relativity'.

In broader terms the attitude of non-rigidity or acceptance of pluralism in mathematics has helped the subject in its advancement. The same holds true for the survival and progress of human beings. The underlying message is that different beliefs, rituals, life styles and cultural systems are necessary and should not be destroyed unless they cause irreversible damage to the ecosystem. Killing of those who live and conduct themselves differently is not justified on these grounds. It is pertinent to propagate this analogy from mathematics to a wider scale to deter killing for differing viewpoints or faiths as witnessed throughout the history and even currently in many places.

Compromise Programming

Killing to satisfy need or greed also occupies much of our history books. Scarcity of basic resources such as arable land, water sources and domestic animals to support physical survival caused innumerable battles among tribal groups until the establishment of relatively sustainable city states. This, however, was followed by long drawn out battles and wars to satisfy greed—annexing gold and other precious things possessed by others or to subjugate more lands and exploit their people for the advantage by the winner. Some of those campaigns also wore the cloak of settling ideology differences. Unfortunately, it is very difficult to draw a clear line between need and greed. Failure to resolve conflicts over resource distribution, however, has been a principal cause of human suffering at the core. This is now seen more prominently in many local and regional situations in the Indian Sub-Continent and East Africa to name a few.

It may be noted that most of these conflicts over resource distribution build over time. Absence or slow implementation of land reforms to assist landless labourers is one such cause of conflict. The adversarial feeling escalates if not checked before it is too late. Figure 1 shows the phenomenon of increasing intensity of hatred ranging from merely 'not liking' to 'killing' others to meet our perceived needs or goals. In practice, however, the process is not always a gradual five-step one as portrayed in Figure 1. One harsh incidence of considerable intensity can lead to a scene of carnage in no time. Close monitoring of such situations is necessary to initiate controlling actions. Transparency, promotion of reciprocation, and attitude of inclusiveness to avoid the spiralling growth of conflict is another necessity. Keeping the doors open for dialogue and negotiation is the key to avoid the stage of taking lives (Patkar, 2006).

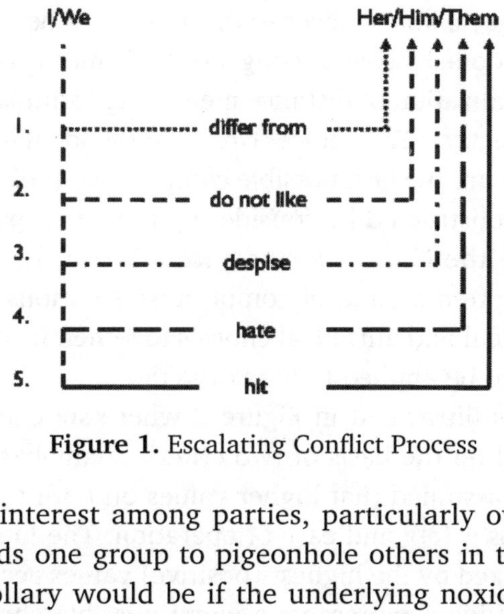

Figure 1. Escalating Conflict Process

Conflict of interest among parties, particularly over resources or ideologies, leads one group to pigeonhole others in the box of foe or rival. The corollary would be if the underlying noxious factor giving rise to conflict could be managed, occasions to deal in killing business would be reduced. A vast amount of serious writing ranging from philosophy to political science deals with this idea. In particular, variety of mathematical models from linear and non-linear programming, game theory and economics are devoted to this theme. Their use in dealing with distribution problems at a gross level is found to be fairly successful in many instances. However, they have limitations in dealing with micro-level conflicts involving actual individuals charged with emotion.

One approach to tackle the issue is based on the principle of discovering a prominent alternative that could be acceptable to all the involved parties (Schelling, 1960). So conflict can be seen as absence of a prominent alternative (Zeleny, 1976; 1982). The theory of compromise programming works on this concept. It represents a family of techniques to address conflicts that may arise either due to several objectives (multi-criterion) or many stakeholders (multi-party). A compromise programming model usually captures viewpoints of the stakeholders for the available choices expressed, for example, in the form of ranking or attributes scores under different criteria. An ideal choice is to be conceived next. If that cannot be done independently, it could be constructed by assigning the best score or ranking on all criteria counts. Obviously it would not likely be realizable in real life. The proximity of available choices to this ideal is to be computed in the next step. This is done by constructing a suitable metric (for example, by employing generalization of distance measuring formula of elementary co-ordinate geometry). The choices *closest* to the ideal according to the distance measure are the best possible compromise choices. Sometimes, an anti-ideal is constructed by considering the worst possible features and in that case the choices *farthest* from it are the recommended solutions. Quite often a band of compromise solutions would emerge by considering ideal and anti-ideal choices together. In such cases some new criterion is to be applied to break the tie.

The process is illustrated in Figure 2 where six choices: C1, C2... C6 are compared on the basis of two criteria, namely Criterion 1 and Criterion 2. It is assumed that higher values on both criteria are to be preferred, such as safety and ease of operation. The ideal represents a choice characterized by the highest (positive) values according to these criteria. The anti-ideal represents a worst possible choice having the lowest (negative) values according to the same two criteria. They are depicted by a 'star' in the second and third quadrant in Figure 2. Distance of each choice from both ideal and anti-ideal choices is determined by using elementary mathematical formula for distance calculation. It is seen that choices C3 and C4 are closer to the ideal than other choices while the choice C1 is farthest from the anti-ideal in comparison to other choices. The tie between C1, C3 and C4 could be broken by employing a criterion other than Criterion 1 and Criterion 2 used originally. In practice, the region bounded by the choices C1, C3, C4 and Ideal could also be explored to generate new choices or prominent solutions. It is clear that the method can be extended to multiple criteria and/or many parties and computer facility can be suitably employed for the involved calculations. The nature of a compromise solution so generated is such that participants would not usually prefer to deviate from it as that would lead to their own disadvantage. This binding capacity of the compromise programming solution is found useful in practice (Patkar, 2009; Zeleny, 1982).

It is clarified that compromise programming basically attempts to *resolve* the conflict. It is therefore not a complete cure, and conflict would surface at the first opportunity. Efforts obviously are needed to *dissolve* the conflict permanently. Generation of additional choices and making the decision process more inclusive and transparent are necessary for this purpose. Compromise programming however provides the vital insight about the situation, and necessary breathing time to work out better solutions and diffuse the tension. To put it differently it increases the threshold of tolerance on the part of the involved parties to a certain degree. We believe that compromise programming provides the methodological revolution envisaged by Paige to adapt methods of analysis and action suitable for bringing about nonkilling transformation (Paige, 2009: 78). To make parties willing to participate in this process still remains a big challenge. Perhaps a few demonstrations of compromise programming application to resolve some relatively less complex community level issues could generate the needed interest.

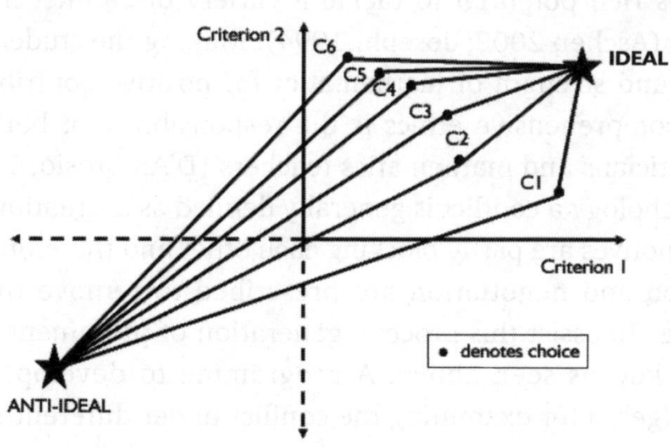

Figure 2. Ideal, Anti-Ideal and Choices

Other Mathematical Leads

Lack of foresight to comprehend the future consequences of actions, capacity to appraise them impartially, and questioning one's own beliefs are identified as, basic causes of discordant behavior and attitude (Bell, 2004). Development of suitable methods under the discipline of Future Studies and prescribing guidelines accordingly for assessing the long term impact of punitive actions and to habituate people to periodically examine their beliefs and perceptions are very much needed. Though the United Nations through its various organs is largely pursuing these very points, the process has produced indifferent results due to various reasons. The outlook of letting go of our own mistakes and letting go of others' mistakes with a resolve not to repeat the same is to be propagated. The post-apartheid regime in South Africa is a shining example in this context. Imparting training to develop necessary skill for this purpose should become an essential part of our education system besides sharpening analytical tools to fathom the underlying complexity of a conflict situation.

Mathematics, as currently taught in schools and colleges all over the world, is projected as an abstract entities manipulation process with the objective of attaining some utilitarian goal, such as increasing efficiency of a product or service. In short, the operational part of mathematics is mainly emphasized. Several other important aspects are in general hardly brought to the notice of students. For instance, study of historical roots of mathematics in different cultures (i.e., ethnomathematics) reveals its rich potential to tackle a variety of conflict management problems (Ascher, 2002; Joseph, 1994). Making the students aware of the profound strength of mathematics for positive contribution along with its comprehensive ethics is the responsibility of both practising mathematicians and mathematics teachers (D'Ambrosio, 1998).

In psychology a conflict is generally defined as a situation where two or more motives are partly blocking each other and therefore discussion, persuasion and negotiation are prescribed to remove the cognitive difference. To assist this process, generation of prominent alternatives hold the key, as seen above. A programme to develop full-fledged conflict algebra for examining the conflict under different perspectives and extending the power of compromise programming is one direction for further mathematical research (Zeleny, 1976).

The theory of a proportioning network provides one more framework to study human interactions mathematically. Various models under this theory examine the responses and counter-responses over time among two or more parties in a real life transaction. Different kinds of end states are predicted by this analysis. Those are determined by the nature and intensity of responses reflecting factors such as commitment to certain viewpoint and availability of information, influencing the situation at a given point in time. These states are: a balanced state of more or less equal reciprocation, or an oscillating state where appropriate reciprocation is extended occasionally, or steady state where such reciprocation occurs as an exception (Zemanian, 1978a, 1978b, 1979). For instance, application of this theory for analyzing the phenomenon of offering a seat to an aged fellow passenger in a crowded city public transport bus over time clearly traces the decline of this normally expected civil courtesy (Modak and Patkar, 1984). The hardening of attitude escalating to killing in human dealings under different circumstances should be studied under this powerful analytical tool of proportioning network and its extensions to guide the design of preventive or diffusing measures.

More often than not a conflict situation is perceived quite differently by the involved parties. Naturally they attempt to find the optimal solution with regard to their own viewpoint. This results in distorted distribution of resources and benefits among different groups causing serious conflicts if not corrected soon. Mathematical models for analyzing such diverse optimality scenarios are available and their application can help to achieve amicable settlement in practice (Patkar, 1993; Zeleny, 1998, 2005).

Studying only some parts of a conflict and resolving them satisfactorily often is not sufficient, because a total situation which is an aggregate of such micro-situations may still lead to failure. A peculiar phenomenon of senescence through a feedforward mechanism may be at work (Patkar, 1993; Rosen, 1978). Ample scope exists to develop a suitable mathematical framework to anticipate and understand this process and suggest methods to track them in real life.

Traditionally game theory has been associated with framing tactics and strategies with regard to armed actions or any competitive situation in general. Its applications for addressing social issues also have received a major thrust (Brams and Taylor, 1999; Brams, Edelman and Fishburn, 2003; Rapoport, 1970). Further advances in game theory in forms such as metagame theory, hypergame theory, drama theory and confrontational analysis provide a rich variety of procedures to assess the degree of hostility under each round of action and reaction and put forward ways and means to avoid the breakdown (Bennett, 1977; Howard, 1971, 1999).

Likewise, methods integrating subjective assessment and analytical techniques such as Analytic Hierarchy Process, Interpretive Structural Modelling and Generic Design Science which have been extensively used for addressing varied conflicts would prove useful to espouse nonkilling mathematics (Patkar, 1988, 2009; Saaty, 1980; Warfield, 1976, 1990). Allowing maximum public participation in the operation of these methods is a significant point of departure. Development of such tools is to be promoted because their use would be imperative for meeting the challenges of serious conflicts that are likely to touch everyone in future. Scarcity of water and food security would be some of the issues.

Support of Information and Communication Technology

Reform in mathematics teaching and education in general is one strategy to spread the message of nonkilling mathematics. However, a large segment of the population, particularly in developing countries, is still excluded from the formal education system. Informing and enlightening such individuals and communities needs urgent attention because they often provide the cadre for carrying out killing missions by different groups. Advances in information and communication technology (ICT) can play a crucial role in the explication process. For instance, globe-covering media, such as television and the Internet, could be employed quite effectively to this end. Mobilizing large-scale public opinion in the framework of compromise programming or any of the above interactive methods could easily be done by such ICT means (for example. SMS system and web-based surveys).

Promotion of altruistic attitudes and behaviors is one theme that needs to be projected, for instance to desist from killing and to counter usual selfish actions. By killing we get into a trap from which it becomes very difficult to escape; cooperation and reciprocity to help everyone should be highlighted (Patkar, 1991). Exploiting the vast reach and rich graphic capabilities of the ICT for a dramatic presentation of this process in terms of stories incorporating simple mathematics can make an immense impact. Suitable scripts and multimedia material are to be prepared for this purpose. Use of cleverly designed videogames can also reinforce this message especially among children and youth. Such productions could be done jointly by mathematicians and media experts.

Similarly, the false notion that by killing so-called offenders our suffering and problems would be reduced is to be expelled from the minds of the masses. One explanation to put forth could be that a phenomenon of conservation of human suffering in societal affairs may be at work (Patkar, 1988). That could again be presented by the imaginative use of mathematics and ICT. Examining different possibilities and pluralities would certainly be strengthened by such broadcasts, or webcasts, or multicasts.

Subject-dedicated web sites, blogs, chat groups and all such evolving ICT-based platforms can inform the mathematics community of its wider responsibility to promote nonkilling mathematics and to share their concerns. For example, discussion of whether a moral commitment like the Hippocratic Oath would help in this direction can generate interesting suggestions.

Concluding Remarks

Conflicts in various geographical sectors are taking a heavy toll on human souls today. Preventing such killings and containing the conflicts should receive top priority. Tremendous scope for mathematics to contribute to building nonkilling society is envisaged in this setting. It can do so primarily in two ways, namely education and practice. One is to impress upon the students the necessity and usefulness of plurality in life by showing various developments in mathematics. Construction of non-Euclidean geometries presented here is one such example. Second, to apply suitable mathematical methods to address the conflicts or at least contain them if they cannot be completely eliminated. Initially addressing a local level problem through this approach is recommended. Based on this experience, higher order conflicts could be considered. Even appropriate mathematical formulation of a conflict situation can supply many new insights which can be pursued in different ways. Models from compromise programming discussed above can certainly serve the cause. Instead of humiliation or annihilation, promoting reconciliation among various groups to arrive at a solution is its basic strength. Only through repeated use of compromise programming and other such interactive techniques discussed in this paper can they be refined to become more effective.

The ICT can be employed to project the role of nonkilling mathematics innovatively on a global scale to benefit everyone. On the other hand, the mathematics community would be made aware of its responsibility and encouraged to resist the harmful use of their subject expertise. Enlightened with such information about peace-supporting application of mathematics, various community groups can put pressure on decision makers to employ mathematical tools only for constructive purposes.

It is not an exaggeration to say that progress of mankind in general depends on the further development of mathematics, both fundamental and applied. And for the advancement of mathematics, prevalence of peaceful societal conditions plays a critical part. The message is loud and clear—our cherished dreams like inter-galactic travel and outer planetary colonization cannot be realized if mathematics is not focused to solve the higher order problems involved in such tasks. Directing mathematics inwardly against humanity for killing and extinction would be the greatest blunder of man. Rich dividends are expected by operations of addition, summation and integration rather than subtraction, elimination and division in human groups for addressing increasingly complex societal problems. Survival with dignity and advance on all fronts will be greatly assisted by nonkilling mathematics.

References

Ascher, M. (2002). *Mathematics Elsewhere: An Exploration of Ideas across Cultures*. Princeton: Princeton University Press.

Bell, W. (2004). 'Who is Really Evil?' *The Futurist*, 38(2): 54-60.

Bennett, P. G. (1977). 'Toward a Theory of Hypergames,' *OMEGA*, 5(6): 749-751.

Brams, S. J. and Taylor, A. D. (1999). *The Win-Win Solution: Guaranteeing Fair Share to Everybody*. New York: W.W. Norton.

Brams, S. J.; Edelman, P. H. and Fishburn, P. C. (2003). 'Fair Division of Indivisible Goods,' *Theory and Decision*, 55(2): 147-180.

D'Ambrosio, U. (1998). 'Mathematics and Peace: Our Responsibilities,' *Zentralblatt für Didaktik der Mathematik (ZDM)*, 30(3): 67-73.

Davis, P. J. and Hersh, R. (1981). *The Mathematical Experience*. Boston: Birkhauser.

Euclid (1956). *The Thirteen Books of Euclid*, edited and translated by Sir T. N. Heath. Cambridge: Cambridge University Press (3 Volumes).

Gray, J. (2007). *Worlds Out of Nothing: A Course in the History of Geometry in the 19TH Century*. London: Springer-Verlag.

Hartshorne, R. (2000). *Geometry: Euclid and Beyond*. New York: Springer.

Howard, N. (1971). *Paradoxes of Rationality: Theory of Metagames and Political Behavior*. Cambridge: MIT Press.

Howard, N. (1999). *Confrontation Analysis: How to Win Operations Other than War*. Washington: CCRP Publications Series.

Joseph, J. C. (1994). *The Crest of Peacock: Non-European Roots of Mathematics*. London: Penguin.

Modak, S. K. and Patkar, V. N. (1984). 'Metamorphosis of Transport Behaviour: The Indian Context,' *Transport Reviews*, 4(3): 277-286.

Paige, G. D. (2009). *Nonkilling Global Political Science*, Honolulu: Center for Global Nonkilling. Available online at: <http://www.nonkilling.org>.

Patkar, V. N. (1988). 'Policy Intent Analysis by Interpretive Structural Modelling,' *Management in Government*, 20(1): 49-54.

Patkar, V. (1991). 'On Promoting Altruistic Behaviour,' *Journal of Social and Biological Structures*, 14(1): 67-72.

Patkar, V. (1993). 'On the Conservation of Human Suffering,' *Journal of Social and Evolutionary Systems*, 16(1): 17.

Patkar, V. N. (1993). 'Challenges of Cognitive Dissonance, Optimality Divergence and Senescence Mechanism in System Management,' *The TMTC Journal of Management*, 3(2): 311.

Patkar, V. (2006). 'Coping with Enmity,' *Manthan* – The Quarterly Magazine of the ICFAI Business School, *Mumbai*, 5(2/3): 15-16.

Patkar, V. (2009). 'Operations Research for Addressing Societal Problems,' *Bharatiya Samajik Chintan*, 7(4): 283-294.

Rakus-Andersson, E. (2003). 'Brains behind the Breaking of Enigma Code before the Second World War,' in Booss-Bavnbek, B. and Hoyrup, J., Eds., *Mathematics and War*. Berlin: Birkhauser, pp. 83-102.

Rapoport, A. (1970). *N-Person Game Theory*. Michigan: Michigan University Press.

Rosen, R. (1978). 'Feedforwards and Global System Failure: A General Mechanism for Senescence,' *Journal of Theoretical Biology*, 74: 579-590.

Saaty, T. L. (1980). *The Analytic Hierarchy Process*. New York: McGraw-Hill.

Schelling, T. C. (1960). *The Strategy of Conflict*. Cambridge: Harvard University Press.

Warfield, J. N. (1976). *Societal Systems: Planning, Policy and Complexity*. New York: John Wiley & Sons.

Warfield, J. N. (1990). *A Science of Generic Design: Managing Complexity through, Systems Design*. Salinas: Intersystems.

Wolfe, H. E. (1945). *Introduction to Non-Euclidean Geometry*. New York: The Dryden Press.

Zeleny, M. (1976). 'Conflict Dissolutions,' *General Systems*, 21: 131-136.

Zeleny, M. (1982). *Multiple Criteria Decision Making*. New York: McGraw-Hill.

Zeleny, M. (1998). 'Multiple Criteria Decision Making: Eight Concepts of Optimality,' *Human Systems Management*, 17(2): 97-107.

Zeleny, M. (2005). *Human Systems Management: Integrated Knowledge Management and Systems*. New Jersey: World Scientific.

Zemanian, A. H. (1978a). 'Balanced State of a Proportioning Network,' *SIAM Journal of Applied Mathematics*, 34(3): 597-610.

Zemanian, A. H. (1978b). 'The Steady and Oscillating States of a Proportioning Network,' *SIAM Journal of Applied Mathematics*, 35(3): 496-507.

Zemanian, A. H. (1979). 'Some Models in the Social and Behavioral Sciences Based on Proportioning Networks,' in Coffman, C. V. and Fix, G. J., eds., *Constructive Approaches to Mathematical Models*. New York: Academic Press, pp. 113-123.

13

Teaching Nonkilling to the States*

Chaiwat Satha-Anand

Thammasat University and Strategic Nonviolence Commission, Thailand Research Fund

There are at least two problems with the topic of this essay besides the problematic natures of both the state and nonkilling. First, based upon the theory of nonviolence from where nonkilling was engendered à la Gandhi and Sharp, nonviolence ordinarily has an oppositional role vis-à-vis the state since it seeks to undermine state power in pursuit of freedom and justice. The question is: does nonkilling locate itself in opposition to the state similar to mainstream nonviolence? Second, due to the nature of the state as the embodiment of violence with the power to kill, can nonkilling be taught to the state? Equally important, perhaps, is the question: even if it can, should the state be taught nonkilling?

This article is an attempt to argue that there is a dire need to 'teach' nonkilling to states in today's world and that it is easier to teach the modern state to accept 'nonkilling' as a policy than 'nonviolence'. I

* This chapter is a reconsideration and modification of my earlier work, Chaiwat (1999), 'Teaching Nonviolence to the States'.

will begin by pointing out the reasons why it is important to teach nonkilling to the states. The strange relationship between killing and the state using Paige's quest for *Nonkilling Global Political Science* (2002, 2007) as an entry point will be discussed in order to argue that it is not impossible to introduce the state to nonkilling policy. Then I will examine my experience in trying to 'teach' nonkilling to the Thai state, especially to its national security agency, focusing primarily on the unique Prime Ministerial Order 187/2546 on 'Coping with conflicts through nonviolence policy' (2003). Arguing that it is easier to teach the state to accept nonkilling policy than to be nonviolent, I will then briefly analyze the dilemmas involved in teaching nonkilling to the states.

Justifications: Why Should States Be Taught Nonkilling?[1]

The most direct and seemingly rhetorical answer to the question of why states should be taught nonkilling is: Because the state kills. But rhetoric aside, there is some truth in this answer. From Beijing to Bangkok, from Rangoon to Jakarta at some points in global history, one can hear stories of state-sponsored violence killing people. The saddest thing about these tales is that they can be told and retold. The plot of these tales is much the same: people without guns demanding freedom or justice in the streets met soldiers with guns in official uniforms authorized by the state to restore order. Sometimes they were ordered not to shoot. But then a shot was heard, a stone thrown, and bloodbath resulted. The day after began with body counts, missing sons and daughters, deep individual wounds, at times mixed with hatred, which later constitute collective traumas that are difficult to heal. Without healing, the cycle of killing could begin anew.

Although it is difficult to ascertain whether in a political confrontation it is the state that starts the acts of killing, it is highly likely that state agents would be the first to use violence.[2] Soldiers and policemen are

1 This part is based on Chaiwat (1999: 186-188).

2 In a comprehensive, though brief, study of American labour violence, Taft and Ross found that trade-unions violence was reactive because strikers would 'virtually always' try to avoid violence and use peaceful means while the employers may not, in which case company guards, the police, or even

trained to perform their tasks with violence. In Asia, they are normally armed, many with guns. In a confrontational situation, fed with frustration and anger, sometimes fuelled with fiery speeches from the other side, those with guns may be more prone to aggression and use what they already possess (Berkowitz and Le Page, 1970: 132-142).[3] It may, therefore, be suggested that there are more factors conducive to killing from the state's side, which would contribute to the possibility of state agents using violence first in a conflict situation. If such is the case, to bring about social transformation toward the possibilities of peace and justice only through educating the people's side with theories, strategies, and practices of nonviolence as well as nonkilling may not decrease the likelihood of a situation of violence, where nonviolent protesters are met with cruel suppression at the hands of the states. The state needs to be educated with nonkilling as well if such a killing situation is to be avoided.

Another reason why the state side needs to be taught nonkilling is its atrocious record. In the latter part of the twentieth century, the late peace researcher William Eckhardt compared his estimate of 10.7 million civilian deaths in civil wars from 1945 to 1990 with Harff and Gurr's account of 12.3 million deaths resulting from 'organized killing by a government or its agents of a people' during the same period. It was stupefying to find that the states, through their agents, kill more of their own civilians during 'peacetime,' occasionally shading into the immediate aftermath of civil wars, than they do in time of civil war (Eckhardt, 1992: 52-53). Using Rummel's figure of 83.4 million deaths by governments, 84 per cent of these killings took place in China and the former USSR, together with Harff and Gurr's estimate, which he suggested may be closer to the facts, Eckhardt arrived at the estimate of fewer than 48 million killed by the states (Eckhardt, 1992: 53). In

---

the National Guard would be brought in (Taft and Ross, 1979: 187-241). They also assert that 'The most virulent form of industrial violence occurred in situations in which efforts were made to destroy a functioning union or to deny a union recognition' (Taft and Ross, 1979: 188).

3 On the anatomy of violence, especially killing, see Grossman (1995: 139-192).

other words, during the last half of this century, the states have killed at least 12 million, if the low estimate is used, or up to 83 million, if the high figure is used. I would contend here that it doesn't matter that much which estimate is more nearly correct because these figures conclusively prove two things. First, states do kill people. Second, these figures of several millions are not mere numbers. They represent millions of human beings, with families and feelings, who have perished at the hands of states. It is therefore extremely important that nonkilling be taught to the state if killing by its 'hands' and in its name is to be avoided. But whereas teaching nonviolence to the state is difficult, is teaching nonkilling to the states equally difficult?

The Strange Case of the State and Nonkilling

In Paige's influential *Nonkilling Global Political Science* (henceforth *NGPS*), there is a change that has taken place in its several incarnations from the 2002 published version to the 2009 electronic book freely available from the Center for Global Nonkilling (<http://www.nonkilling.org>). This strange change, most relevant to the present discussion, is the presence and later absence of the term 'state' in the book that aspires to foster a paradigmatic shift in the discipline of political science.

In the published versions (2002 until 2007), the books' index indicates that the term 'state' appears on pages '3-6, 71, 78 and 79' (Paige, 2002: 237). Using search engine inside the book, it was found that the term 'state' in some forms (for example, including the United States) appear in 93 places throughout the book. But in the 2009 electronic incarnation, the term 'state' is nowhere to be seen in the index! Moreover, it would be interesting to explore that when the term 'state' appears in Paige's *NGPS*, how does it appear?

The term 'state' appears 13 times on pages 3-6, none on pages 71, 78 and 79. According to the index, when the term 'state' appears in the four pages in *NGPS*—in fact only on three pages since it cannot be found on page 3 either, they are in the context of Paige's discussion of the violence-accepting history of political thought and its relationship to 'the state'. As a matter of fact, 'the state' as appeared in *NGPS* takes the following forms:

- as the object of honor and power in Machiavelli's thought.
- as state of nature in the thoughts of social contract philosophers—Hobbes and Locke.
- as the emerging form of political society with the rights to war and conquest from social contract in Rousseau's thought, and then elevated to something akin to the sacred, also in Rousseau's.
- as the 'lethal state' that should be disposed of with violence in Marx's thoughts.
- as the modern state with claims to monopoly of the use of violence in Weber's writing.

Reading Paige's discussion of history of political thoughts in relation to the question of nonkilling and the state, I find that it is easier to imagine a nonkilling state from within the conventional history of political thoughts than from a classic nonviolence theory as advanced, most importantly perhaps, by Gandhi. Given the constraint of space, let me illustrate this point by focusing on Hobbes's *Leviathan* (1651), Kant's *Perpetual Peace* (1795) and Gandhi's thought (1935) as examples. It should be noted that Paige's challenge to the world could be formulated in terms of his global quest. He travelled the globe—Sweden, Russia, Jordan, Japan, Korea, Lithuania, Canada, Colombia, and of course the US, to meet with political scientists and other professionals, including those who were victims of violence and those who had killed others. He met them to ask the question: is a nonkilling society possible? If not, why not? If yes, why? (Paige, 2004: 4). After his long quest, collecting wondrous data, and thoughtful contemplation of more than two decades, he came to a decisive conclusion that a nonkilling society is possible. Therefore there should be 'no more killing'. But I am curious that if Paige could conduct his questioning exercise with these three great proponents of politics and ask them 'Is a nonkilling state possible?', what would be their answers? I suspect that he might have received very strange answers from them. Here is why.

Hobbes' *Leviathan* and the Necessity for a Nonkilling State

Michael Oakshott (1901-1990), an authority on Hobbes' thought, argues that contrary to conventional wisdom, death itself is not significant in Hobbes' argument in his magisterial *Leviathan* since everyone has some expectations about living and untimely death. Most important for Hobbes' advent of the Leviathan—the artificial Man that is the state—is when a human being is killed by another. It is this very type of death-being killed by another human—that is relevant because it signifies failure in the 'race' for precedence which constitutes human life. When killed, people died not in competition with the natural world but in competition with other human beings. Oakshott thinks that this is 'the central point; and this is what is meant by shameful death. To be killed by another man is *eo ipso* shameful or dishonourable because it signified that inferiority vis-à-vis other men which is the centre of all human aversion' (2001: 834). In this sense, being killed by another person is 'the limiting case' in human life (2001: 835). In addition, what a human wishes to avoid is not merely being killed by another, but also *fear of being so killed*. On Oakshott's reading of Hobbes, the *civitas* (state) exists in order to mitigate the effect of this race for precedence that resulted from the act of killing (Oakshott, 2001: 834-836). If the state exists for this very purpose, it would therefore be easier to convince the state of a nonkilling policy since it is in line with both its origin—to get rid of the phenomenon of a human being killing another—and its primary function for existence to prevent such a phenomenon from emerging in the state.

Kant's *Perpetual Peace* and the Possibility of a Nonkilling State

Paige wrote: 'If Kant (1795/1959) can envision "perpetual peace" deriving from steadfast adherence to a no-war categorical imperative, we can now perceive elements needed to transform a nonkilling imperative into global reality' (2007: 91). In fact, I would argue that Kant's proposal for a no-war world began with the question of killing and nonkilling, among other things. In the 3rd preliminary article for perpetual peace among nations on the army, and there are six of these articles, Kant categorically states that 'Standing armies (*miles perpetuus*) shall be gradually abolished.' This article anticipated what has come to transpire in the twentieth century (Kant, 1983: 45)—and made clear in Paige's *NGPS*—that there were 27 countries without armies in the early twenty-first century (Paige, 2007: 45).

But what is most interesting and relevant to the present discussion is Kant's reason for the abolition of standing armies. He argues that they would constantly threaten other nations with war, influence the military race among countries which will in turn incur exuberant costs on the racing countries in maintaining the armies with peoples and killing instruments, among other things. Finally, the cost for maintaining peace this way would 'finally become greater than those of short war, standing armies are thus the cause of wars of aggression that are intended to end burdensome expenditures' (1983: 108).

The next sentence is most important philosophically, however. Kant writes: '...paying men to kill or be killed appears to use them as mere machines and tools in the hands of another (the nation), which is inconsistent with the rights of humanity' (1983: 108). In fact, the standing armies stand in sharp contrast to Kant's ethics since his whole philosophy is based on the notion that no human being should be treated as a means to others in the 'kingdom of ends'. For Kant, killing another human for the country, or I would argue—for some other purpose, is to treat them as means and therefore war cannot be accepted or the ethical foundation that binds people into making decisions and deliberating right from wrong will all but disappear. It should be noted that for Kant, a 'nonkilling state' is possible and in fact preferable since it is conducive to perpetual peace *among nations* when each nation will no longer 'pay men to kill or be killed'. However, Kant believes that a state could continue to have periodic and voluntary military training for citizens to 'secure their homeland against external aggression' (Kant, 1983: 108).

Gandhi's Thought and the Difficulty of Advancing a Nonkilling State

Gandhi wrote in October 1935 that 'The State represents violence in a concentrated and organized form. The individual has a soul, but as the

State is a soulless machine, it can never be weaned from violence to which it owes its very existence' (Cited in Terchek, 2006: 212). Later on March 9, 1940, he wrote that: 'A Government cannot succeed in becoming entirely non-violent, because it represents all the people. I do not today conceive of such a golden age. But I do believe in the possibility of a predominantly non-violent society. And I am working for it' (Gandhi, 1997: 437). It is rather clear that Gandhi is against the state, not only because he seems to think along the Weberian line that the modern state is defined as an organization that is able to kill with its monopoly of legitimate violence, but also with Nietzche, because of the idolatry of elevating the state to be something unchallengeable and sacred (Terchek, 2006: 206-207). In addition, the bureaucratic state proclivity to its expertise also means that it does not have to listen to other voices, reasons, and/or 'truths'. As a result, by claiming neutrality, instrumental reason, and efficiency, the bureaucratic state depoliticizes the world by relegating sites of contested power to margins of political life (Terchek, 2006: 211-212). Perhaps this is why Gandhi's preference is towards less governance. He wrote: 'That state is perfect and non-violent where the people are governed the least. The nearest approach to purest anarchy would be a democracy based on nonviolence' (Gandhi, 1948: 292). Influenced also by Gandhi's thoughts and Thoreau's civil disobedience, among other things, an antistate inclination seems to be prevalent among those in the fields of nonviolence.

Following Gandhi's thought on the state, then it is extremely difficult to invite the state to the path of nonkilling, and it is not easy to argue the contrary, since it is a 'soulless servant' with embodied and concentrated violence in its entity. Though it could be argued that Gandhi had somewhat altered his view on the state from 1930s onwards since he could also see it as a vehicle for social change (Parekh, 1989: 118-121), some scholars warn that Gandhi would not trust the state since: 'To humanize the state and make it the object of love is to put people off guard' (Terchek, 2006: 212). In this sense, it seems that while the creation of a nonviolent and nonkilling *society* is possible for Gandhi, to turn the *state* into a nonkilling machine is much more difficult, if not altogether impossible.

Judging from this reading of Hobbes, Kant and Gandhi, I would argue that it is easiest to introduce the idea of a nonkilling state into the Hobbesian universe whereas it seems most difficult to do the same in a Gandhian political world, while the limited nonkilling state in the Kantian imperative falls somewhere in-between. But why would Gandhi think that it is next to impossible to turn the state to nonviolence/nonkilling? Perhaps it is important to ponder what the state is?

Weber wrote and delivered his speech 'Politics as Vocation' in Munich in 1918. He defines the state as 'a human community that (successfully) claims the monopoly of the legitimate use of physical force within a given territory' (Weber, 2002: 13). Being so defined, the state has become the *only* social institution that can claim legitimacy when engaging in violence and killing. Moreover, he has turned the state into an institution that is *inherently* violent. As a result, a politics that is locked within the state's mental landscape has been deprived of any salvation but to continue with killing and violence. When charged with the task of maintaining existing social orders, it is generally believed that it could do so because it is a monopoly of authoritatively binding rule-making, backed up by a monopoly of the means of physical violence (Mann, 1988: 4). Its occasional use of physical violence induces fear which in turn strengthens obedience to state authority. This is perhaps a most important reason why the Weberian understanding of the state as inherently violent is generally agreed upon by modern state theorists (Giddens, 1987: 18-19; Strange, 1996: 5; Hay, 1996: 3-19).[4] As an institution based upon physical violence, it is natural that state agencies and agents such as the police and the military would find it hard to accept nonviolent actions. But does this mean that the state would not accept nonkilling as well?

Inspired by Benedict Anderson's influential *Imagined Communities*, I have argued elsewhere that the power of the state lies, not only in

4 An interesting aspect of Hay's formulation is in trying to advance an understanding of 'stateness' in two dimensions: moments of stateness, which include the state as nation, the state as territory, and the state as institutions, and levels of stateness from abstract 'category' to concrete 'state structure' (Hay, 1996: 319).

its concrete attributes which includes the monopoly of the means of violence and killing, but also in its abstract quality and artificiality necessary to perform much of its functions (Chaiwat, 1988: 27-41). It is important to emphasize that the state does have other means of enforcement and influence it can deploy, which in fact it normally uses. If I am right in suggesting that the state power lies in its abstraction, perhaps its power lies hidden somewhere while omnipresent in its invisibility. Two decades ago the anthropologist David Kertzer pointed out that because the state power is 'invisible', it must be personified to be seen, symbolized so that it can be loved, and imagined in order to be conceived as a state (Kertzer, 1988: 6). Beyond fear-induced obedience, the technology of power at the modern state's disposal makes it possible for the state to be seen, loved and conceived far more effectively than the use or the threat to use physical violence especially killing. Put another way, if its power lies more in its ability to be seen, loved and imagined, then these attributes can hardly be produced by killing or the threat to kill. In this sense, I would argue that it is easier for the modern state to accept nonkilling as a policy with its concreteness and measurability than the much more problematic nonviolence with its built-in conceptualization that could include a negation of direct, structural and cultural violence. Put another way, because nonkilling is a negation of killing that is at once measurable and concrete, the state with its invisible power is likely to accept it as a policy rather than the more amorphous nonviolence, and therefore much more problematic from its perspective. In becoming a nonkilling state, the state might feel that it could retain much of its power to induce not only obedience, but consent when it is seen, imagined in different forms, and even loved.

Experiences: Teaching Nonkilling to the Thai Security Agency?

Let me begin a discussion of the Thai experience with the case of Zambia's Kenneth David Kaunda. This is a case of a former nonviolent movement leader who gave up nonviolence when he decided to go into politics and later became the president of his country. Kenneth David Kaunda of Zambia is known for his role as a nonviolent leader in fighting against the British imperial power (Levitsky and Way, 2012: 877-878). When he felt the anti-colonial struggle was over, he went to his American friends, Bill Sutherland and Matt Meyer who had helped him along the nonviolent course of action, and said: 'Look, it's quite clear now that we're going to have an election which will provide for majority rule, and the end of British control. I have been with you all this time. I have been nonviolent in principle and I've appreciated and wanted to thank you for all you have done. But I have decided that I am going to be a politician, and to go into government.' He then asked, 'How, as a person who is a believer in nonviolence, am I going to defend the country against the South Africans and the southern Rhodesians and all of these people who are coming in with their spies and attempting to destabilize us from the south?' (Sutherland and Meyer, 2000: 96). Quoting a philosophical principle with a distinctive Weberian ring that 'he who affirms the state affirms violence', Kaunda noted that all but a few 'saints'—who have moved themselves to remote wildernesses—play some role in affirming the state (Sutherland and Meyer, 2000: 98).

Having written about Kaunda and his view on violence and nonviolence in the late 1980s, imagine my surprise when attending a seminar at Chulalongkorn University in Bangkok in 1997, when I heard a deputy secretary general of the Thai National Security Council (NSC) characterized the disturbing conflicts in Thai society at the time as a crisis of trust between the Thai people and the Thai state. In my view, it is quite unusual to find such a diagnosis of the situation from a high-ranking Thai security official. Most important, he believed that a dangerous crisis was imminent, and that the National Security Council, with the Thai prime minister as chairperson, was charged with peacefully courting social change in Thai society.

This experience was the beginning of my attempt to 'teach nonviolence to the states' which I explained in an article more than a decade ago (Chaiwat, 1999). There I discussed my experiences with the Thai state when it began to show interest in nonviolence as seen from a number of workshops the National Security Council organized on nonviolence, trainings offered to government officials around the country, and the establishment of a most unique committee, perhaps the only one in the world, the Strategic Nonviolence Committee

(SNC), within the National Security Council of Thailand, with the Prime Minister as the Council chairman. The SNC, chaired by a former deputy secretary general of the Thai National Security Council, was a group of people comprising academics, senior NGOs, and some security officials. Among other things, its task is to come up with nonviolent alternatives to cope with rising conflicts for the Thai state, through advising the Prime Ministers. Due to changes in governments and the authorities at the NSC, the SNC is no longer within the National Security Council. It has been reconvened outside the security community though continued to be tasked with providing Thai society with nonviolent policy alternatives to problems of oftentimes deadly conflicts and now funded by the independent Thailand Research Fund with me serving as its chairperson.

In 2003, however, the SNC advised the then Thai Prime Minister to mobilize government sectors with nonviolence in preparation for the impending violent conflicts between the Thai state and the people. The result was the historic Prime Ministerial Order 187/2546 on 'Managing Conflict with Nonviolence Policy' which promotes the use of nonviolence from within the security community. In a way, in trying to persuade state security agencies to avoid physical violence, this security policy instrument could be seen as a concrete example of nonkilling policy.

Prime Ministerial Order 187/2546[5]

On August 14, 2001, the then Prime Minister Thaksin Shinawatra approved a proposal: 'Mobilizing Effective Nonviolence in Thai Society', put forward by the Strategic Nonviolence Committee, National Security Council. The proposal consisted of two components: an official declaration of adopting nonviolence as a national strategy and a Prime Ministerial Order aiming to implement the strategy. The Grand Strategy aims at national security construed as attempt to prevent conflict from turning violent and to nonviolently transform conflict (King and

5 This part of the paper is based on my 'Advising Leaders on Nonkilling Politics: Lessons from inside the National Security Community, Thailand'. A paper prepared for the First Global Nonkilling Leadership Forum, Honolulu, October 31-November 4, 2007.

Miller, 2006).[6] Its objective is to enhance trust between the state and the citizens and to reduce prejudices that have adversely affected relationship among peoples of differences in the country.

On September 1, 2003, the now deposed Prime Minister Thaksin Shinawatra signed the Prime Ministerial Order 187/2546 called: Managing Conflict with Nonviolence Policy.[7] Reading the future of the country as ridden with various types of conflict especially between the state and the people, it argues that there is a need to re-evaluate the ways in which conflicts in Thai society have been dealt with since they have not produced a peaceful and just society where everyone is happy. To continue to use violence would bring about hatred and disunity among the people. The use of violence by the state to deal with conflicts, therefore, would engender extremely high social costs, which would in effect, jeopardize national security.

PM Order 187/2546 maintains that it is the way(s) of life of different peoples who are citizens of the Thai state that needs to be protected; and that by protecting and strengthening the ties that bind them together through nonviolence is a national security innovation needed for a new world facing various types of conflict. It categorically states that 'government agencies must give priority to implementing this Managing Conflict with Nonviolence Policy'. But most importantly, perhaps, are its three main principles which serve as the Order's theoretical grounds. They are:

- **Principle 1**: 'In coping with conflicts, "nonviolence" is the *only* way that is just and would engender sustainable peace. It begins with the state and government officials.'
- **Principle 2**: 'The attitude which forms the basis of nonviolence is to reduce prejudices and no hatred to peoples who are different.

6 Though the use of 'nonviolent conflict transformation' seems rare, it has become increasingly visible. See for example, King and Miller (2006).

7 *Prime Ministerial Order 187/2546 on 'Managing Conflicts with Nonviolence Policy'* (Bangkok: Strategic Nonviolence Committee/Institute, National Security Council, n.d.) (A published pamphlet—In Thai). The number 2546 is Buddhist Era or 2003 A.D.

They must not be seen as enemies, but instead as friends in a shared life of suffering. The end of nonviolent means must be just. The state must accept some burdens for the sake of national security and sustainable peace of the people.'

- **Principle 3**: 'The atmosphere and theatre conducive to creativity in order that learning and developing appropriate approaches to conflict in Thai society, informed by pools of local wisdom, must be based on the idea that "cultural diversity and differences of ideas are Thai society's sources of power". This will, in turn, increase nonviolent alternatives in dealing with conflicts.'

These three principles hide three elements extremely important for the constitution of nonviolence policy. They are: inherited nonviolence legacy; local cultural treasures; and political will.

Principle 2 of PM Order 187/2546 has three components: no hatred of anyone; the use of nonviolent actions must be in service of justice; and Thai government officials who follow this Order must be willing to accept self suffering instead of inflicting pain and violence on those who oppose the state. As a matter of fact, this principle is based on a thinly hidden Gandhian legacy of nonviolence. Gandhi once explained that there are four conditions necessary for the success of Satyagraha. They are: no hatred, just cause, acceptance of self suffering, and prayers (Gandhi, 1948: 61). Principle 2 embodies three of these four conditions.

In proposing nonviolent actions and to make global nonviolence work, I have always found it important to look for local elements conducive to the specific context I have to work within. Contrary to mainstream security discourse where differences are often times seen as security threats to a country, principle 3 of the PM Order maintains that cultural diversity is a source of national strength and that there exists sufficient local wisdom conducive to nonviolence policy and practices on Thai cultural soil.

If the Gandhian heritage is the ground on which the PM Order 187/2546 stands, and Thai cultural realities are the local potentials necessary to make this Order work, then principle no. 1 embodies the political will which maintains that nonviolence is *the* direction this country must take for a sustainable national security. I would argue that the uncompromising nature of the statement in principle no.1, that 'In coping with conflicts, "nonviolence" is the *only* way that is just", is at once unprecedented and extremely challenging to both those who are against the use of nonviolence and those who have worked hard to nonviolently transform the world, especially in terms of national policy. The question at this point is how do these principles enunciated in the PM Order 187/2546 relate to nonkilling policy?

Let me turn this question around and ask: can there be any nonkilling policy proposed to the state, imagined or real, that does not include these principles or rely on them? From a general security policy perspective, there is a need for a clear direction grounded in firm political will—in this case a will to move along the course of nonviolence. To make this will work, it has to rely on local realities, power relations informed and legitimized by cultures. In implementing such a policy, there will be some costs that the state needs to undertake. In this case, the state declares its intention to allow its security forces and other officials to accept suffering as a result of adopting nonkilling policy rather than to inflict sufferings (read – including killing or threat to kill) on ordinary people. These three principles, I would argue, contain clear grounds to call the PM Order 187/2546 a nonkilling security policy.

Lessons Learned

One of the first questions often raised about this unusual episode of nonkilling security policy of a country is: why did the Prime Minister who is known for his acceptance of the use of violence accept the proposal by the SNC in the first place and, more importantly, to sign this historic PM Order? (Puangthong, 2010). One way to deal with this question is to be brutally candid and point out that nonkilling security policy in Thailand has come this far not because the leaders understand and accept it, but because they either do not understand it or do not believe that it could pose a threat to traditional security, both in terms of its theoretical grounds and effectiveness. In addition, based on the theoretical understanding of the modern state discussed above, some visionary government leaders such as the former Prime Minister

Thaksin might have thought that taking away the force of killing from the state in matters related to imminent conflicts does not mean that the state has lost other means of control which the state could continue to exercise with a better legitimizing principle – that it is doing all it could to maintain peace, law and order without trying to harm, do violence or to kill its own citizens.

Apart from political leaders' perspectives on nonkilling, in recent years I have found that nonviolence security policy that seems to be acceptable to the state has been primarily based on nonkilling, perhaps with the exception of the state's responses to the problems of drugs and southern violence. This could be a result of the dynamics of a contemporary working state, understood as the embodiment of physical violence—epitomized by its monopolization of the use of killing, in the context of increasing democratization and the globalized gaze. By arguing that killing its own people will compromise the legitimacy of the state in a situation where conflicts are on the rise, the space for accepting the proposal on nonviolence security policy understood more and more by the state as nonkilling within the security community has been critically expanded.

More importantly, in my experiences, the work for nonviolence policy from within the security sector is both difficult and challenging for two reasons, among others. First, the degree of resistance to nonviolence policy options depends on changing political contexts. In a democratic setting, if the politicians believe that violent options will be more acceptable to the majority, they will not be hesitant in toeing the voters' line. Second, while the idea of nonviolence security policy is radically different from conventional security discourse, I found that officials working on security issues would either try to relegate it to marginal importance within the security community or to accommodate nonviolence as a form of their more familiar discourse such as psychological warfare or public relations efforts. In the latter case, it is not difficult to work with them into accepting this new security policy as a nonkilling policy. Again, this is another reason why proposing nonkilling policy to the state might be easier than to teach nonviolence to it.

Dilemma: Is it Right to Teach Nonkilling to the State?

I have earlier discussed the dilemma of teaching nonviolence to the state (Chaiwat, 1999: 193-194). But teaching nonkilling to the state has different problems. First, as indicated in the PM Order, the word nonkilling was nowhere to be found in the policy document. Given its absence, can this be considered a nonkilling policy? Second, if this policy is indeed a nonkilling policy, what does it do to nonviolence? This is a curious issue since it belies the complex conceptual relationship between nonkilling and nonviolence. I believe that these two challenges are profoundly connected and need to be addressed, though the second problem will require a much more careful and critical discussion which is beyond the scope of the present essay.

As discussed above, the principles that govern the PM Order are clearly based on principled nonviolence as advanced by Gandhi. The question is when one transports Gandhi's notion of nonviolence, born from the womb of a nonviolence theory that is deeply suspicious of the state, to inform the national security policy of the state, what would be the result?

The state, especially its policy makers could come to a conclusion that their tasks of ensuring national security could be performed without killing. This possibility is a result of both a realization of its own diverse power bases short of the use of killing as well as a recognition of nonviolent actions carried out by ordinary people as they engage in conflicts in pursuit of justice, among other things. Once the state recognizes nonviolent actions, it is likely that its responses would be less violent despite the state's violent nature. If they could identify people's peaceful collective actions as nonviolent, they may be able to use nonviolent language to characterize or describe them. In a way, this is a process of questioning the normality of violence where nonviolent discourse could enter into a discursive battle with violent discourse (Chaiwat, 1991). An understanding of the communicative quality of nonviolent actions would help the state see that these actions are indeed attempts to communicate in the public sphere, that there are structural problems such as the lack of freedom resulting from uneven distribution of power or poverty resulting from uneven distribution of wealth.

In addition, the realization of its own power other than killing should strengthen a newfound confidence in the state and its nonkilling power while the recognition of the people's resistance to the state comes with an understanding stipulated in the PM Order that they are not the enemies of the state but those whose lives and well-being are for the state security officials to protect, and to fulfil such a task even if it means to accept suffering on their behalf. The fact that it is possible at all to have a state accepting such a policy could be seen as an innovation both in the field of security policy and an experiment in advancing a nonkilling approach. The fact that it has not been successful attests to the challenges facing anyone who chooses to work on such a project with the state and its security apparatus. But the fact that it has been attempted at the national level also suggests that it is a critical experiment awaiting the genuine test of a state that one day will choose to secure national security by nonkilling.

References

Berkowitz, Leonard and Le Page, Anthony (1970). 'Weapons as Aggression Eliciting Stimuli,' in Mcgargee, Edwin L. and Hokanson, Jack E., eds., *The Dynamics of Aggression*. New York: Harper & Row, pp. 132-142.

Chaiwat Satha-Anand (1988). 'Of Imagination and the State,' in Silva, K. M.de, et al., eds., *Ethnic Conflict in Buddhist Societies: Sri Lanka, Thailand and Burma*. London: Francis Pinter; Boulder: Westview, pp. 27-41.

Chaiwat Satha-Anand (1991). 'From Violent to Nonviolent Discourse,' in Boulding, Elise, et al., eds., *Peace Culture and Society: Transnational Research and Dialogue*. Boulder: Westview Press, pp. 24-32.

Chaiwat Satha-Anand (1999). 'Teaching Nonviolence to the States,' in Tehranian, Majid, ed., *Asian Peace: Security and Governance in the Asia Pacific Region*. London and New York: I.B. Tauris, pp. 186-193.

Chaiwat Satha-Anand (2008). 'Advising Leaders on Nonviolent Politics,' in Paige, Glenn D. and Evans Pim, Joám, Eds., *Global Nonkilling Leadership: First Forum Proceedings*. Honolulu: Center for Global Nonviolence, pp. 265-268. Available online at: <http://www.nonkilling.org>.

Eckhardt, William (1992). 'Death by Courtesy of Governments, 1945-1990,' *Peace Research*, 24(2): 51-56.

Gandhi, M. K. (1948). *Non-Violence in Peace & War, Vol. I*. Ahmedabad: Navajivan Publishing House.

Gandhi, M. K. (1997). *The Selected Works of Mahatma Gandhi, Vol. VI: The Voice of Truth*. Ahmedabad: Navajivan Publishing.

Giddens, Anthony (1987). *The Nation-State and Violence: Volume Two of A Contemporary Critique of Historical Materialism*. Berkeley: University of California Press.

Grossman, David (1995). *On Killing: The Psychological Cost of Learning to Kill in War and Society*. Boston: Little, Brown.

Hay, Colin (1996). *Re-stating Social and Political Change*. Buckingham: Open University Press.

Kant, Immanuel (1983). *Perpetual Peace and Other Essays*. Indianapolis: Hackett Publishing Company.

Kertzer, David (1988). *Ritual, Politics and Power*. New Haven: Yale University Press.

King, Mary E. and Miller, Christopher A. (2006). *Teaching Model: Nonviolent Transformation of Conflict*. Addis Ababa: University for Peace.

Levitsky, S. R. and Way, L. A. (2012). 'Beyond Patronage: Violent Struggle, Ruling Party Cohesion, and Authoritarian Durability,' *Perspectives on Politics*, 10(4): 869-889.

Mann, Michael (1988). *States, War and Capitalism*. Oxford: Blackwell.

Oakshott, Michael (2001). 'Letter on Hobbes,' *Political Theory*, 29(6): 834-836.

Paige, Glenn D. (2002, 2007). *Nonkilling Global Political Science*. Honolulu: Center for Global Nonkilling. Available online at: <http://www.nonkilling.org>.

Paige, Glenn D. (2004). 'Is a Nonkilling Society possible? If no, why not? If yes, why?' in Abueva, Jose V., Ed., *Towards a Nonkilling Filipino Society: Developing an Agenda for Research, Policy and Action*. Marikina City: The Aurora Aragon Quezon Peace Foundation and Kalayaan College at Riverbanks.

Parekh, Bhikhu (1989). *Gandhi's Political Philosophy*. Notre Dame: University of Notre Dame Press.

Puangthong Pawakarapan (2010). 'Militarizing Drug War Campaign in Thailand,' in Satha-Anand, ed., *Violence hides/seeks Thai Society*. Bangkok: Matichon (In Thai).

Strange, Susan (1996). *The Retreat of the State: The Diffusion of Power in the World Economy*. Cambridge: Cambridge University Press.

Sutherland, Bill and Meyer, Matt (2000). *Guns and Gandhi in Africa: Pan African Insights on Nonviolence and Armed Struggle and Liberation in Africa*. Trenton: Africa World Press.

Taft, Philip and Ross, Philip (1979). 'American Labour Violence: Its Causes, Character and Outcome,' in Graham, Hugh Davis and Gurr, Ted Robert, eds., *Violence in America: Historical and Comparative Perspectives*. Beverly Hills: Sage, pp. 187-241.

Terchek, Ronald J. (2006). 'Gandhi's Politics,' in Johnson, Richard L., ed., *Gandhi's Experiments with Truth: Essential Writings by and about Mahatma Gandhi*. Lanham: Lexington Books, 198-227.

Weber, Max (2002). 'Politics as a Vocation,' in Besteman, Catherine, ed., *Violence: A Reader*. New York: Palgrave Macmillan, pp. 13-18.

14

The Image of a Nonkilling Future

Dennis Morgan
Hankuk University of Foreign Studies

Throughout history, all civilizations have faced timely challenges to their existence. These challenges are so critical that the capacity of a civilization to recognize and respond to the challenges within a fixed window of time, determines whether that civilization will rise and flourish or decay and collapse, due to intrinsic or extrinsic forces or, in most cases, a combination of both. Such was the challenge-and-response thesis of the twentieth century historian, Arnold Toynbee. Furthermore, when a civilization fails to respond to the crisis and thus collapses, Toynbee (1947) faults the leadership of the 'creative minority' for its poverty of 'creative power' to recognize and respond to the challenges; hence, the 'creative minority' thereafter simply becomes the 'dominant minority,' presiding over the masses in a desperate bid to cling to power during the time of the collapse.

During the 1950s, a Dutch sociologist, Fred Polak, obviously influenced by Toynbee's challenge-and-response theory of the rise and fall of civilizations, linked a civilization's challenge and response and rise and fall to the image of the future that the civilization held. For Polak (1971), the 'challenge' is the challenge of the future, and the key to a civilization's survival depends on whether it can recognize this challenge and respond to it through a creative image of its own future, which acts as a positive force to help overcome challenges posed; in other words, the vigor of a civilization depends upon a positive and hopeful vision of itself in the future, which enables it with the capacity to meet these challenges and overcome them as part of the process of realizing itself in time. Thus, if a society loses its vision of the future, it will fail to recognize and thus respond to critical challenges and will then fall into decay and eventually collapse; however, if it possesses a positive image of the future, it will recognize, respond to, and overcome the challenges, and thus flourish and progress.[1]

Glenn Paige (2009), in his manifesto for a nonkilling world, considers the challenge to civilization that a killing world represents and the needed response to shift toward a nonkilling world. Such response revolves around the crucial role of the creative minority to recognize the self-destructive nature of the killing crisis and then create a basis to shift toward a productive, nonkilling world in the future. Hence, I see Paige's efforts, in addition to the contributions of others in the nonkilling world project, playing the positive role of Toynbee's creative minority. Yes, Paige acknowledges the predicament and challenge of a killing world, which rationalizes and justifies killing daily as an 'unfortunate' but 'necessary' price to pay for territorial expansion, 'progress,' social control, 'civilization,' and a future world. However, Paige rejects the ends-justifies-the-means rationalizations in these legitimizing efforts; instead, he questions the embedded assumptions (exposing the pseudo-logic) and counters them by elaborating on the evolving prospects for realizing a nonkilling world.

As a way of also contributing to those 'evolving prospects,' I investigate the historical basis as a reality starting point for imaging a nonkilling future and discover, from archeological sources, that a mostly nonkilling world did indeed exist from approximately 5000 to 3000 B.C.E. and quite likely throughout much of prehistory before then. Nevertheless, the age of 'Empire' emerged and brought about the rise and fall of civilizations, which, almost without exception,

---

1 See Morgan (2002) for more on Polak's view of the image of the future.

embraced killing and war as perceived necessities for growth, expansion, occupation, domination, and social control. The same pattern has continued throughout the ages and has only intensified through technological developments of the weapons of war—the instruments of killing and destruction in the modern era—which have become so lethal on such a large scale that they threaten the future of humanity, thus representing the self-destructive, civilizational challenge and crisis that Paige and others are responding to.

In the context of such lethality, as well as the autonomous nature of technical civilization, which continually desensitizes the masses concerning the rationalizations and justifications for killing and perpetual war, I question whether the modern image of the future is capable of embracing the image of a nonkilling future and conclude by identifying this image from a postmodern rather than modern origin and perspective, which requires a major shift of consciousness in order to realize a nonkilling world. Finally, I examine the leadership role of the postmodern, creative minority to realize a nonkilling future and conclude that a nonkilling world and future can only come about through the evolution and transformation of consciousness in a paradigm shift from Global Empire to Earth Community.

The Thesis for a Nonkilling World

Glenn Paige's seminal study (2009) begins with a question: 'Is a Nonkilling world possible?' Then, Paige explores the various reasons given for answering the question in the negative. Representing the prevailing rationalizations of current political thought, he cites three main reasons given by 20 American political scientists: (1) humans are natural killers, (2) scarce resources dictate the need to kill for them, and (3) the possibility of rape justifies the need to kill in defence of females. Thus, the primal arguments 'of human nature, economic scarcity, and sexual assault served sufficient to make unthinkable the practice and science of nonkilling politics' (p. 22). Furthermore, Paige (2009) refers to classic political philosophy, which offers thorough support to discount the notion of a nonkilling world. Many of the world's great philosophers (Plato, Aristotle, Machiavelli, Hobbes, Locke, Rousseau, Marx, and Weber) all give various justifications for killing. Moreover, as Paige (2009) recounts, American blood-filled political history, 'violence-accepting' religious tradition, and popular culture resonates with killing, mandating it as if it were fundamental to the American identity. The history of killing began with the very foundation of the American republic and then extended throughout its expansion for two centuries, not only continentally but globally, until it founded a global empire, whose lethality is unquestionable, upheld by weapons of mass destruction—historically unparalleled.

However, according to Paige (2009), political philosophy and national political tradition are not necessary to convince Americans that a nonkilling society is impossible since 'killing in everyday life confirms it' (p. 27). Paige (2009) then cites how much Americans kill each other on a daily basis—'news' that they are continually reminded of by mass media such that violence in the US is 'socially learned and culturally reinforced' (p. 29). Finally, as if this were not enough, Americans can look beyond their own borders and their own history for ample evidence of a world drenched in blood—the twentieth century having the notable distinction for being 'mankind's most murderous era' (p. 32). Paige (2009) cites the following research by Rudolf J. Rummel (1994), who gives a rough yet conservative calculation of the overall magnitude of human killing. In his study, Rummel distinguishes between 'democide' (state killing of its own people) and 'war' to conclude that almost 400 million people have been killed.

When you consider that these conservative totals do not figure in homicides, deaths as an indirect consequence of war, and is only until 1987, then the total must surely now be 400 million killings or more. It should be no surprise then, as Paige concludes, that most Americans consider the prospects for a nonkilling society as utterly inconceivable.

However, when interviewing people from other countries, Paige (2009) finds that the responses are remarkably different. These responses range from: (1) 'I've never thought about the question before ...' (2) 'It's thinkable, but ...' (3) 'We know that human beings are non violent by nature, but ...' (4) 'It's not possible, but ...' and (5) 'It's completely possible ...' (p. 34-5). The remarkable difference is that where the question itself is considered absurd or preposterous by most

Americans, people from other cultures and historical traditions seem to be more open-minded about the possibility, and some even affirm it. One has to consider then the role that cultural bias plays when confronted with this question.

Also, from the American denial of even considering the possibility of a nonkilling world, one can glean from some responses a common characteristic of American culture: exceptionalism—and the use of exceptions to undermine and distract from the rule. For example, two common objections to the possibility of a nonkilling world are: (1) 'What about Hitler? Nonviolence is completely ineffective when confronted with a tyrant like Hitler,' and (2) 'One must reserve the right to kill in self-defence.' Yet, both of these responses are indicative of begging the question and using the exception to distract from and undermine the rule. In the case of the Hitlerite retort, the historical example is abstracted from its social and cultural context as if the phenomenon of Hitler arose out of thin air. What is not considered is that a Hitler rising to power could only occur in a social, cultural, and global context of a violent world that rationalizes and legitimizes killing. World War II, not World War I, was the 'war to end all wars.' It was a watershed moment in history in which the world finally realized the horror of war and, through the U.N. Charter, took steps to prevent and eliminate wars of aggression. Of course, that doesn't mean that all wars have been eliminated since then, but it does mean that there has been a shift in consciousness toward realizing a world without war so that the phenomenon of another Hitler rising to power will not be repeated.

Likewise, the response about reserving the right to kill in self-defence also begs the question and uses the exception to undermine the rule. The overall thrust of proposing a nonkilling society and world is to change the mindset such that killing would be considered as an example of the pathological condition of a culture that rationalizes and legitimizes killing in the first place. If this condition is recognized as pathological and treated as such, then killing will be minimized to such an extent that one would almost never be confronted with having to defend oneself from killing by killing in the first place; this scenario would be more of a hypothetical nature than a reflection of the real world, which by its very nature has thoroughly rejected killing, especially the rationalizations that serve to legitimize it socially and culturally. In other words, when such rationalizations exist in the form of state-sanctioned killing, as a form of social control and power maintenance through the threat of lethality, then the underlying, subtle message to the members of that society is that the way to power is through killing—that it's okay to kill as long one can rationalize the exception—much like Raskolnikov did in Dostoyevski's classic (2004), *Crime and Punishment*. As long as the state continues to rationalize killing and reserves for itself the 'license to kill,' as a means of control, power, and global expansion, then the people also pick up on this message and reflect its pathology through individual acts of killing. In a killing culture, one can surely maintain the right to defend oneself from killing by killing, but in a nonkilling culture, this becomes a mere hypothetical question since the act of killing itself is unacceptable under any circumstances and is truly considered a pathological condition. In other words, the situation would only very rarely occur (if at all) rather than be a commonplace, everyday 'fact of life' continuously reaffirmed by the news media and celebrated by a Hollywood culture. Instead, it would truly be the exception rather than the rule; however, when killing is accepted as the rule by a culture, albeit reserved for those in power as a matter of social control, with the pretence that it's the exception, and celebrated in the popular culture, then a twisted message is transmitted to the members of that culture, who begin to view killing as an exceptionalist means to power—the social pathology of our times reflected in daily killings in which one has to defend oneself by also killing—in a vicious cycle. The fact that one responds as such by defending the right to kill in self-defence merely reflects that one is unable to step outside of this killing cycle—that one refuses to get the bigger picture of killing.

In Chapter 2, 'Capabilities for a Nonkilling Society,' Dr Paige (2009) delivers the 'bigger picture' by giving a historical overview as the grounds for considering why a nonkilling society is indeed possible. Despite the hundreds of millions of historical instances of killing, humans are not 'natural born killers' but are nonkilling by nature. Statistically speaking, only a very small percentage of people kill, and even the vast majority of these, through military training, have to overcome their 'deep resistance to killing' (Paige 2009, p. 39).[2] Throughout Chapter 2, Paige (2009) masterfully brings to light the historical and present resources and capacities to realize a nonkilling society and world. Drawing upon spiritual and humanistic traditions as well as scientific, anthropological, and sociological studies, he exposes the undercurrent of consciousness and social change movements that have been gradually building up through the ages and are now ripe for the transformation of values that instead advocate a new, peaceful social contract, which does not use violence and killing (or the threat of the same) to maintain control. Moreover, as Paige (2009) points out, 'salient manifestations of nonkilling capabilities' are appearing in a number of ways throughout various societies. Remarkable examples of political decisions 'tending towards the realization of nonkilling societies are found in countries that have abolished the death penalty, countries that have no armies, and countries that recognize the right of conscientious objection to killing in the military' (p. 51). Regarding the abolition of the death penalty, Paige (2009) inquires why and how so many countries came to this nonkilling decision, and what the historical processes are that can account for this global shift. Furthermore, Paige (2009) gives specific instances of how social, spiritual, educational, economic, training, security, research, and problem-solving institutions have adopted nonkilling principles, and how nonkilling-based cultural resources and communications media have emerged, along with nonkilling political struggles, to bring about social transformation. Surely, Dr Paige provides persuasive and convincing evidence to consider the possibilities of the emergence of a nonkilling world, which is the basis for the image of a nonkilling future.

However, at the same time, the historical record of killing cannot be ignored or denied and so must also be taken into account and fully

2 As Paige (2009) explains, the process of overcoming this 'deep resistance to killing' can drive one insane, and then the very conditions of war can drive one further down the path of insanity—where killing becomes 'second-nature,' while other 'aggressive psychopaths' are insane to begin with, so they 'naturally' adapt to military training and then lustfully thrive on the conditions of war, unable to ever adapt to a life of peace in civil society. (p. 39)

understood in order to realize the transition to a nonkilling world and future. Understanding the justifications and rationalizations that legitimate killing is an important component for deconstructing the prevailing modern image of the future, based on violence and killing (or the threat thereof) as a tool for social control and global dominance. Besides, we should also investigate the past in order to determine whether or not a prototype nonkilling civilization has previously existed. If so, though social evolution will not allow us to 'go back' to this civilization, nevertheless, the argument for a nonkilling world and the image of a nonkilling future will be further clarified and thus strengthened by such a discovery, for the 'can do' spirit will then be provided a solid historical foundation, which will make it even less 'theoretical' and thus more probable.

A Prototype for the Image of a Nonkilling Future

Recent archeological discoveries have confirmed that a mostly nonkilling world did indeed exist from at least 5000 to 7000 years ago (and perhaps much further back) chiefly through the advent of horticulture.[3] According to Leonard Shlain (1998), before the advent of horticulture, humans lived in predominately gatherer/nurturer-hunter/killer tribes, which were essentially unchanged for almost three million years; then, somewhere, sometime, someone noticed that where seeds had fallen around the kitchen midden, grain consistently appeared the following season. This observation led inevitably to the insight that if seeds were *intentionally* planted and tended, they could ensure a reliable food supply' (p. 32). Also, around the same time, people discovered that some animals could be domesticated and bred; thus, for the women, who had primarily been gatherers/nurturers, the transition to horticulture and husbandry did not require a drastic psychological adaptation as it did for the men, who until then had been primarily hunters/killers. Farming was not very '... exciting compared to the chase. Suddenly, the male was required to fend off *other* predators who were determined to eat *his* ripening harvests and cull *his* flocks' (Shlain 1998: 33).

3 Whereas agriculture is large-scale farming, horticulture is small-scale gardening.

This cultural shift from gatherer/nurturer-hunter/killer to farming / husbandry was so dramatic, relates Shlain, it rapidly replaced the way of life of wandering nomadic tribes, who began to adopt the revolutionary new lifestyle whenever the two cultures brushed up against one another. Comparatively speaking, since the nomadic way of life had been predominate for almost three million years, this shift occurred in the blink of an eye. Beginning around seven thousand years ago, 'farming societies began to sprout all across the Mediterranean and southern Europe.' (Shlain 1998: 33)

Moreover, since the advance seemed to have sprang from the gather/nurturer, a powerful female deity, Earth Mother, emerged, whom men worshipped as well as women. However, psychologically speaking, this sudden shift was traumatic for men, whose psyche had been honed for hunting and killing throughout much of his evolution. Though agricultural advances increased, according to Shlain (1998), these bloodless activities could hardly replace the thrill of the kill, so the male's '... pent up aggression began its toxic accumulation. Sport hunting, contests of courage, ritual killings, and human sacrifices came into being because of men's need to replace the excitement of the hunt. Eventually, war-to-the-death superseded the hunt as the principal means of periodically lancing the boil of the men's innate combativeness.' (p. 34)

Shlain (1998) writes that, due to farming, man's 'predatory impulses' had been reined in by 'yoking his killer instincts to the plow,' and then held in check and suppressed for at least 2,000 years until its 'toxic accumulation' built up and then re-emerged through sports hunting, contests of courage, ritual killings, human sacrifices, and war-to-the-death, which brought about a new era marked by killing through conquest, domination, social control, and empire building. However, Shlain (1998) does not offer much evidence to support his 'toxic accumulation' theory and later seems to contradict this theory by offering alternate possibilities to explain why nonkilling societies disappeared. Moreover, his theory of a 'killer instinct' is problematic for a number of anthropologists. For example, as Schoenherr (2006) reports, Sussman and Hart (2005) argue that primates, including early humans, 'evolved not as hunters but as prey of many predators, including wild dogs and cats, hyenas, eagles and crocodiles.' The idea of 'man the hunter,' asserts Sussman, is mostly derived from 'a basic Judeo-Christian ideology of man being inherently evil, aggressive and a natural killer'; yet, as Sussman explains, when you '... really examine the fossil and living nonhuman primate evidence, that is just not the case' (Schoenherr, 2006). What they discovered through an analysis of the evidence is that *Australopithecus afarensis*s were not 'dentally pre-adapted to eat meat'; so, asks Sussman, if they 'couldn't eat meat, why did they hunt?' (Schoenherr, 2006). Furthermore, we can see the simple evidence in the teeth of humans today; they are not sharp, predator teeth designed by evolution for eating meat. As Sussman relates, it was not 'possible for early humans to consume a large amount of meat until fire was controlled and cooking was possible' (Schoenherr, 2006). Finally, as Barbara Ehrenreich writes, quoting anthropologists Clifton B. Kroeber and Bernard L. Fontana, 'It is a large step from what may be biologically innate leanings toward individual aggression to ritualized, socially sanctioned, institutionalized group warfare.' Or as a 1989 conference on the anthropology of war concluded, 'The hypothesis of a killer instinct is . . . not so much irrelevant as wrong.'

Nevertheless, regardless of whether or not one can posit a 'killer instinct,' which was temporarily reined in by the shift to farming during a prehistoric era of two to three thousand years, as Shlain (1998: 34-35) maintains, still, archeologists have uncovered evidence from the period between 7000 and 4000 B.C., suggesting a muting of violence in many early farming communities. Settlers frequently located their villages in the rich bottomlands of valleys, and many of these communities lacked fortifications, suggesting that these people were not concerned about attackers (Baring and Cashford, 1991). Sifting through the artifacts of such settlements, archaeologists do not find the preponderance of war weapons over domestic utensils characteristic of later civilizations. Their deities are not depicted carrying spears or hurling thunderbolts, and their gravesites do not include elaborate tombs of warrior kings buried with their retinues and great material wealth (Eisler, 1988). Women are often buried in more favorable locations than men. There is little evidence confirming the domination of the many by the few. While archeologists cannot know with certainty what transpired in the day-today lives of these prehistoric peoples, these clues suggest an existence relatively free from the strife that seems to have characterized most of recorded history. And everywhere in the ruins of these cultures there are statue fragments of a female deity (Baring and Cashford, 1991).

In fact, archeologists have unearthed a number of societies who share these characteristics during this same time period; thus, regardless of whether a 'killer instinct' can be argued to have been in effect throughout prehistory prior to that time, it does seem that for at least 2,000-3,000 years, the world was, indeed, for the most part, a peaceful place to live in, remarkably absent of the phenomenon of war and killing,

However, this era came to an end roughly 5,000 years ago. Though scholars have speculated and proposed various theories explaining why it ended, no one is quite sure, but some notable changes are consistent: (1) agricultural techniques became more sophisticated and large-scale, (2) warrior sky gods displaced the Earth Mother and other goddesses, (3) the advent of writing (cuneiforms-phonograms), an abstract, left-brain activity exhibiting mostly masculine features, replaced oral authority through the formulation of 'laws' and (4) war, conquests, and domination schemes founded empires in which the use of violence and killing was standardized as a means of power and control.

Another anthropological interpretation of this shift from largely nonkilling farming and nomadic tribes to successive killing civilizations for 5,000 years up to the present era is that of Les Sponsel (2009), who points to the rise of horticulture and then agriculture that spawned violence over property, which erupted into the killing cycles of civilization. Thus, Sponsel (2009) offers the following narrative (as summarized by Dator[4]) to explain the shift to the era of successive civilizations characterized by war and killing:

> It seems to me that humans lived for tens of thousands of years in small, nomadic, egalitarian, peaceful societies of abundance (what is often called by anthropologists 'subsistence affluence'). It was only with the rise of horticulture and then agriculture (probably caused by rapid human population growth facilitated by the evolution of

4 Private email correspondence.

> speech, and our overall propensity to exploit our environment to extinction and move on until we could no longer move anywhere) that humans were forced to become sedentary; property and killing in defence of property (including women and children) became important; hierarchies and eventually hereditary leaders maintaining power by killing force emerged; tribal squabbles became wars with professional warriors; free-floating matriarchal spirituality became organized patriarchal religion with orthodox texts and priests; peasants and slaves (of war) were ruled by urban elites; cities grew into empires and all the rest—all enabled by the invention of writing.

So it appears that all of prehistory can be mostly characterized by the absence of war and killing and that the 'killer instinct' is mostly a myth used to justify killing throughout the 5,000 years that followed the prehistorical era of mostly nonkilling tribes and societies. In fact, John Zerzan (2005-6), in 'The Origins of War,' claims that, based on the archeological evidence, 'it is now a tenet of mainstream scholarship that pre-civilization humans lived in the absence of violence—more specifically, of organized violence.' Zerzan (2005-6) then goes on to reference a number of anthropologists whose interpretation of the evidence challenges and overturns previous anthropological scholarship, blinded by the Hobbesian framework for interpretation, to instead propose a new, mostly nonkilling perspective on prehistoric man. This new perspective is promising, for it bolsters the claim that it is indeed possible to conceive of and realize a nonkilling world, and through the evolution of consciousness during the past 5,000 years, especially considering more recent nonkilling historical sources (as recounted by Paige, 2009), perhaps a transformation toward a new, stable, nonkilling era is now possible.

Such is the thesis of David C. Korten in *The Great Turning: from Empire to Earth Community*. Like Shlain, Korten (2006) also believes that the relatively peaceful and nonkilling era of prehistoric tribes and societies holds clues that can help form the image of and blueprint for a new, nonkilling era in the transition from 'Empire' to 'Earth Community.' As Korten (2006) relates, 'One of the best kept historical secrets is that practically all of the material and social technologies fundamental to civilization were developed before the imposition of a dominator society' (p. 94). The foundations of complex social organization had been laid through the development of the institutions of law, government, and religion; also, the arts of dance, pottery, '... basket making, textile weaving, leather crafting, metallurgy, ritual drama, architecture, town planning, boat building, highway construction, and oral literature' had been cultivated (Korten, 2006: 94).

However, according to Korten (2006), what is also remarkable about these early societies is the relatively 'egalitarian nature of their social structures,' a critical dimension that gender-biased anthropologists and historians had often neglected. As Korten (2006) writes, recognizing the distinctive role '... of women in the initial humanization of the species, we can more easily understand the enormous cost to our humanity of 5,000 years of imperial repression of women, the importance of gender balance, and the essential role of women leaders in birthing Earth Community' (p. 94). Moreover, 'as best we can determine,' continues Korten (2006), early humans were '... relatively undifferentiated by occupation, status, or power.... Burial practices and the generally uniform size and design of houses further suggested generally egalitarian societies with little of the differentiation by class, race, and gender that is characteristic of the societies that followed. The varied artworks of these Neolithic civilizations support a similar conclusion. There are no scenes of battles, images of noble warriors and wrathful gods, nor depictions of conquerors dragging captives in chains' (p. 97-8).

Korten (2006) writes that this nonkilling era prior to the emergence of the 5,000 years of Empire may have been much longer than 2,000-3,000 years—that its origin can be traced to the end of the Ice Age 11,000 years ago, which makes it comparable to the 5,000 year era of Empire. The contrast is stark; during this comparable era, the emphasis in the 'Goddess societies was on the development and application of technologies that nurture life. Humans were expected to enter into partnership with the productive processes of nature, an activity for which women—the life givers of the human species—were presumed to have special affinity' (Korten, 2006: 98). Of course, one should guard against sweeping generalizations that tend to idealize the past, and Eisler's research has received considerable criticism; nevertheless, as Korten (2006: 99) points out, our concern here is '... not whether women-led societies are always more peaceful and egalitarian than male-led societies, but merely to note the evidence of the rich variety of the early human experience, which included peaceful, egalitarian, highly accomplished societies in which women had strong leadership roles'.

According to Korten (2006), the transition from a largely peaceful, settled, egalitarian, nonkilling world, based on generative partnership power relations associated with the feminine, to the era of Empire, associated with violent male sky gods, warrior cultures, social institutions based on the pursuit of power, domination, and technologies of destruction, came about through the division between settled agriculturalists and nomadic pastoralist tribes who sought to improve themselves through the development of more effective technologies of destruction rather than technologies of production (p. 100). The nomadic pastoralists' focus on developing better and better weapons eventually gave them 'an advantage in subsequent combat with the more prosperous agriculturalists, whose lands and labour they eventually appropriated through conquest' (id.). Thus began what

> Eisler calls 'a bloody five-thousand-year domination detour.' As the pre-Empire societies honoured the power to give life, so later societies honoured the power to take life. Kings and emperors bolstered their demands for obedience with claims of personal divinity or divine appointment. Angry male gods representing dominator power displaced the female and male gods representing generative power. Priestesses were gradually stripped of power and replaced by priests. Wives became the chattel of their husbands. The poor became the servants of the rich. The regenerative power of the Spirit gave way to the dominator power of the sword. Humans came to mistake dominance for potency, domination displaced partnership as the organizing principle of society, and the era of Empire was born (Korten, 2006 100-101).

Moreover, Korten (2006) notes a 'striking change in the pattern of distribution' as conquered societies entered into this new era. Whereas in previous times pre-Empire societies focused primarily on improving the overall standard of living, one chief characteristic of Empire societies is that they are hierarchical, with 'men at the top' appropriating the 'bulk of the wealth and power,' while their subjects are forced to make-do with the trickle-down crumbs falling from their tables. Those who achieved '... their positions of power by destroying and appropriating the wealth of conquered peoples continued their established pattern of appropriation, distributing the spoils among those who faithfully served them—a pattern that remains familiar to this day' (p. 101).

Sifting through the archeological evidence, Shlain and Korten piece together a convincing picture of a largely nonkilling world during the era prior to that of Empire. Though some may question the interpretation of this evidence or whether it is conclusive; nevertheless, one should recognize that such objections often come from narratives that are also ideologically-based, focusing on exceptions to the rule rather than challenging the consistent pieces of the puzzle, which fit together to form the overall, compelling image of a mostly nonkilling world—in stark contrast to the image of 5,000 years of blood-filled history that mainstream anthropological and historical narratives in the past supported and justified. More importantly, this image of a nonkilling prehistorical past bolsters support for the image of a nonkilling future by providing a prototype of an era comparable to that of Empire; this new narrative also tells the story of what went wrong—the 'detour' into Empire. This 'detour' has only accelerated in the modern, technological era, as killing and war have became an accepted 'reality of life' and the 'price that has to be paid' in the name of 'progress' and the 'March of Civilization.'

The Modern Image of the Future as the 'Technological Society'

In the modern era, we discover the culmination of 5,000 years of successive empires that have legitimized violence and killing as a means of territorial expansion, domination, and social control. So, the modern consciousness is one that has evolved from this foundation by accepted killing as the price of the 'good life' that modernity brings through the advances of science and technology. In fact, one could very well say that the modern image of the future is that of the technological society. If this is indeed the guiding vision of the modern future, then the question of the position of the technological society toward killing is critical. In other words, is the technological society 'neutral' when it comes to killing, as some contend, or is killing fundamental to its modus operandi?

According to Jacques Ellul (1964), in his classic study on the technological society, the notion that 'technique' is neutral is 'naïve' and 'useless' because it doesn't really understand the dynamic, autonomous, self-augmented, monistic, universal nature of technique in the modern era. The pursuit of technique has come to define the modern image of the future, subsuming everything else in its path. Hence, throughout modern history, as wars of conquest spread all over the world, vanquished peoples were filled with such a mixture of admiration and fear that they adopted the conquerors' machines, which 'came to replace their gods' (Ellul, 1964: 118). The machine became the supreme symbol of power since, at the same time, it posed 'the possible means for liberation from these conquerors' (p. 118). It's not as if the vanquished peoples had a choice in the matter; they could either embrace the machine as the means of liberation or face extinction. In other words, they had to embrace the killing power of the machine or else be exterminated by it if they refused.[5] This led to the birth of the arms race, and all 'the instruments of power began to flourish as a means of provoking insurrection'; moreover, to the degree that '... these peoples became better organized and technicized, rebellion became a national affair....War provokes the sudden and stupefying adaptation of the 'savage' to machinery and discipline' (Ellul, 1964: 118).

This process of assimilation through advances in the techniques of war is the ritual of initiation into the vicious killing cycle of modern

5 As the American writer and environmentalist Derrick Jensen (2006) puts it, 'So, given the choice between Christianity or death, slavery or death, civilization or death, is it any wonder that at least some do not choose to die?'

civilization, which cultivates a machine-like consciousness that seems to transcend the moral concepts of 'good' and 'evil' in favour of that which is most efficient instead—as the 'means' become an 'end' in itself, and the war industry increasingly attains a permanent status and feature of technical civilization. Ellul (1964: 142) presents a convincing argument that humankind does not master technique for either 'good' or 'evil'; rather, technique is the master, whose modern image of the future is the image of the machine, impervious to moral judgment. Technique does not accept the '... existence of rules outside itself, or of any norm. Still less will it accept any judgment upon it. As a consequence, no matter where it penetrates, what it does is permitted, lawful, justified.'

Some may object and contend that technique can be transformed and wielded for only good purposes, as if the 'end' of technique is human good. However, as he elaborates on the autonomous nature of technique, Ellul (1964) argues that this view is wrongheaded, for technique is totally 'irrelevant' to the notion of human good; instead, it evolves in '... a purely causal way: the combination of preceding elements furnishes the new technical elements. There is no purpose or plan that is progressively realized. There is not even a tendency toward human ends. We are dealing with a phenomenon blind to the future, in a domain of integral causality' (p. 97-8).[6]

---

6 Ellul (1964: 97-98) elaborates on the nature of technique by reasoning thus: Hence, to pose arbitrarily some goal or other, to propose a direction of technique, is to deny technique and divest it of its character and its strength....To say of such a technical means that a bad use has been made of it is to say that no technical use has been made of it, that it has not been made to yield what it could have yielded and ought to have yielded. The driver who uses his automobile carelessly makes a bad use of it. Such use, incidentally, has nothing to do with the use which moralists wish to ascribe to technique. Technique *is* a use. Moralists wish to apply another use, with other criteria. What they wish, to be precise, is that technique no longer be technique....There is no difference at all between technique and its use. The individual is faced with an exclusive choice, either to use the technique as it should be used according to the technical rules, or not to use it at all. It is impossible to use it otherwise than according to the technical rules.

For example, let's take a look at the technical process involved in the invention of the atom bomb. As Ellul (1964: 99) explains, the fact that the atom bomb was created

> before the atomic engine was not essentially the result of the perversity of technical men. Nor was it solely the attitude of the state which determined this order. The action of the state was certainly the deciding factor in atomic research.…Research was greatly accelerated by the necessities of war and consequently directed toward a bomb. If the state had not been oriented toward the ends of war, it would not have devoted so much money to atomic research. All this caused an undeniable factor of orientation to intervene.

As Ellul (1964) concludes, if the state had not supported this effort, no atomic research would have been conducted in the first place, so no question of the peaceful use of nuclear energy would have been posed. Therefore, continues Ellul (1964: 99), the atomic bomb is a

> transitory, but unfortunately necessary, stage in the general evolution of this technique. In the interim period represented by the bomb, the possessor, finding himself with so powerful an instrument, is led to use it. Why? Because everything which is technique is necessarily used as soon as it is available, without distinction of good or evil. This is the principal law of our age. We may quote here Jacques Soustelle's well-known remark of May, 1960, in reference to the atomic bomb.… 'Since it was possible, it was necessary.'

This 'principal law of our age,' which defines our civilization through its image of the future, as being a *technical civilization*, is what is of concern here regarding the image of a nonkilling future. In Ellul's words, *technical civilization* means that 'our civilization is constructed *by* technique (makes a part of civilization only what belongs to technique), *for* technique (in that everything in this civilization must serve a technical end), and *is* exclusively technique (in that it excludes whatever is not technique or reduces it to technical form)' (1964: 128).

This involves an 'inversion' that distinctively marks the modern era. As Ellul notes, without exception, in the course of history,

> *technique belonged to a civilization* and was merely a single element among a host of nontechnical activities. Today *technique has taken over the whole of civilization*. Certainly, technique is no longer the simple machine substitute for humanlabour. It has come to be the 'intervention into the very substance not only of the inorganic but also of the organic'. (1964: 128)

That's why today we find that nuclear weapons, the supreme symbol of the power to kill, have increasingly attained an autonomous nature. In other words, nuclear weapons systems have evolved out of human hands as they have become more computerized with automated alerts in place in the event of a nuclear attack. Once an attack begins, whether by accident, 'glitch,' or intentional, the system responds automatically, while the possibilities for human intervention have become increasingly less and less.[7] In this 'decisive evolution,' we should be warned of the grave, fatal consequences; consider Ellul's (1964: 93) insight on the autonomous nature of the evolution of technical systems, in which humans do not play a part.

> Technical elements combine among themselves, and they do so more and more spontaneously. In the future, man will apparently be confined to the role of a recording device; he will note the effects of techniques upon one another, and register the results.

The problem with this scenario, of course, is when, for one reason or another, a 'glitch' in the complex, automated, nuclear weapons system causes its responses to spin out of control—erupting into global nuclear holocaust.

Under such conditions, the prospects for a nonkilling world are no longer a matter for humans to even consider; it is out of the question since no longer do humans have a say about killing or nonkilling. This is

---

7 For more on scenarios of nuclear war, see Morgan (2009).

the very nature of the technological society within technical civilization; increasingly, in the interests of technical efficiency, the decision-making process has been taken out of human hands and placed under the jurisdiction of the machine, which does not conform to the norms of human morality or judgment, whose only interest is the interest of efficiency, transforming everything, including human life, into means. Ellul (1964: 146-7) asks a rhetorical question, which still reverberates almost 50 years later:

> The tool enables man to conquer. But, man, dost thou not know there is no more victory which is thy victory? The victory of our days belongs to the tool. The tool alone has the power and carries off the victory....The individual obeys and no longer has victory which is his own. He cannot have access to his apparent triumphs except by becoming himself the object of technique and the offspring of the mating of man and machine.

The Image of a Nonkilling Future as a Reflection of Postmodern Consciousness

Since modern civilization is defined by its image of the future as the technological society, it cannot conceive of a nonkilling future, for the killing machine of technical efficiency stands outside of human morality and judgment and thus has no regard for human life if such life attempts to resist assimilation into the technological society. Its logic is the logic of social-Darwinism, which rationalizes and justifies killing as ever-so-natural in the course of evolution. Furthermore, the distinction between 'peaceful industry and military industry is no longer possible,' for every industry, every 'technique, however humane its intentions, has military value' (Ellul, 1964: 110-1). Even nature itself is under attack by the artificial environment, which destroys, '... eliminates, or subordinates the natural world, and does not allow this world to restore itself or even to enter into a symbiotic relation with it. The two worlds obey different imperatives, different directives, and different laws which have nothing in common....When we succeed in producing artificial *aurorae boreales*, night will disappear and perpetual day will reign over the planet' (Ellul, 1964: 79).

Once we understand this driving force and modus operandi of the modern image of the future, we realize that it is impossible to consider a nonkilling image of the future from within the modern consciousness and paradigm. That is the precise reason why the 20 American political scientists interviewed by Dr. Paige *could not even conceive* of a nonkilling world. It simply did not conform to their worldview, which is but a product of the technical civilization—a machine-like consciousness that has been fully technicized.

So, if a nonkilling image of the future cannot appear from within the modern consciousness, from whence does it originate? I propose that this image of the future springs from a *postmodern* rather than modern consciousness, for it is only within the postmodern consciousness that critiques of and alternatives to the modern paradigm can be considered. Yet, at the same time, one should understand that the postmodern consciousness has its historic origins within modernism, even as it is a reaction to modernism. Though its literal meaning is 'after' or 'beyond' modernism, its sources are often from the Romantics, anarchists, existentialists, humanists, and spiritual philosophers who have resisted and critiqued the modern paradigm, especially its image of the future as the technological society.

Every stage of consciousness contains its own pathologies as well as the seeds for its own transcendence, often in the form of critique; hence, the modern consciousness provided the basis for its own critique and transcendence in the form of postmodernism – the emergence of a new stage of consciousness *out of* modernism, which transcends the technical civilization paradigm to provide the basis for alternative images of the future to emerge, such as the image of a nonkilling future. It is an alternative future for a civilization that has become alienated and desensitized by the modern image of the future as the technological society.

However, the postmodern image of a nonkilling future is in a minority position since perhaps only five per cent (if that) of the population has evolved into postmodern consciousness[8], which is characterized

8 In this description of the postmodern consciousness, I am mostly referring to the 'affirmative postmodernists' rather than the 'skeptical postmodernists,' a useful distinction made by P. Rosenau (1992).

by universal pluralism/ multiculturalism / holism; the dignity of the individual; subjective truth; New Age spirituality; alternative medicine and therapy; sensitivity to the repressed, marginalized, and exploited; support of authentic, direct democracy; progressive politics; social activism; planetary awareness and global consciousness; environmental/ecological conservation/sustainability/restoration; rejection of scientism, materialism, reductionism, utilitarianism, and technical rationality; recognition of the pathologies of modernism; sensitivity to feminine, intuitive, and 'right brain' ways of knowing; opposition to militarism, imperialism, corporatism, and capitalism; anti-globalization/pro-localism; anti-war; civil disobedience; peace studies and the principles of nonviolent conflict resolution and social interaction; and a refusal to accept the metaphor of the machine as the dominant metaphor in its vision of the future.[9]

As was stated, the postmodern consciousness sprang from within the soil of the modern consciousness. That's why many aspects of postmodern consciousness can be also located within the Enlightenment ideals of modernity; nevertheless, postmodern consciousness also recognizes the pathologies of modernity, which betrays itself through its inherent contradictions. For example, even though the ideal of democracy is an expression of modern consciousness, at the same time, modernity embraces the capitalist economic system and industrial civilization, which is essentially antithetical to democracy. As a matter of fact, capitalism works quite well with slavery, which can be found throughout the modern era, principally in the form of wage slavery. In this case, the value and dignity of the individual is compromised in favour of the 'freedom' of capitalism to expand, monopolize, and dominate with machine-like efficiency. The individual is given an ultimatum to accept this compromise and become a cog in the machine or else die; resistance is futile. The slow-killing global economic machine grinding away at the billions who live on less than $2 a day represents one of the pathologies of modern consciousness that postmodernism rejects.

---

9 See McIntosh (2007) for more on the description of postmodern consciousness.

Postmodern consciousness also rejects outright killing and violence (or the threat thereof) of militarism, which upholds, maintains, and advances the ruling interests of the hierarchal, authoritarian power elite of Empire, who use democratic ideology and rhetoric through its lapdog and mouth organ, the corporate media, to manufacture consent of the masses and thus legitimize its rule. Of course, this corporatocracy would rather use soft power ('smiley-faced fascism') than outright violence to maintain its rule, but the threat of violence is always present in case soft power doesn't work. For the corporatocracy, democracy is just a sophisticated shell game by which it can manage the masses more effectively than outright violence, but if one were to call its bluff, putting it to test by opening the curtains to expose the corporate wizard pulling all the strings, then the violent nature of its rule would surely reveal itself for what it is. Hence, disillusioned postmodernists are reluctant to participate in mainstream elections. If they do, they vote for marginalized third party candidates who do not have a chance of being elected; otherwise, they don't vote at all.

The realization of a nonkilling future is at once a local and global effort within postmodern consciousness. Both efforts are interlinked so that success in one level automatically impacts success in the other. Local activism represents pockets of resistance to 'politics as usual' and to dependency on Global Empire and its rule by the power elite of the corporatocracy; on the other hand, postmodern global activism networks these pockets of resistance to form a movement of the rising multitude[10] toward authentic global democracy, with its image of the future being that of Earth Community, for it is only when Global Empire has been transformed into Earth Community, can the image of a nonkilling future be realized.

These pockets of resistance began in the 1960s through the advent of localized organic farming communities, who were founded on the principles of nonviolence and who strove to be completely nondependent on the global economy. For example, one such self-sustainable organic farming community is that of 'permaculture,' which is the art and science 'of designing human beings' place in the environment. Moreover,

10 See Hardt and Negri (2005).

permaculture teaches how 'to understand and mirror the patterns found in healthy natural environments' so that one can then 'build profitable, productive, sustainable, cultivated ecosystems' that can include people, and 'have the diversity, stability, and resilience of natural ecosystems.'[11]

Such movements like permaculture represent the nucleus of the postmodern image of a nonkilling future, for it is only when humans learn to live in harmony with their environment and each other can the principles of nonviolence be activated in a very real way. In such an environment, killing becomes unthinkable. However, these independent 'pockets of resistance' need to link up with others globally to form Earth Community. In this case, it is not necessary to completely abandon technology, since technology has always been an aspect of human societies and evolution. It's just that, as it was in pre-modern times, technology will be only one feature among many in Earth Community, and under the strict scrutiny of sustainability, made to benefit the whole of humankind—as a servant rather than an organizing, autonomous principle and ends in itself.

Now, let's examine what the image of a nonkilling future would look like within the context of Earth Community. As Korten (2006: 295) writes, the turning from Empire to Earth Community has two primary elements. First is a turning from money to life as our defining value. Second is a turning from relations of domination to relations of partnership based on organizing principles discerned from the study of healthy living systems.

Immediately one recognizes that when *life* itself becomes our defining value, and relations of domination are replaced by relations of partnership, based on principles of healthy *living* systems, then the underlying paradigm in which killing emerges has been transformed into a paradigm in which killing is unthinkable.

Then, if we apply this supreme value of life paradigm based on healthy living principles to daily interactions within postmodern society,

11 See Morgan (2010) for more on the role of the efforts of localized organic farming communities like permaculture to realize a new culture and alternative paradigm that is not dependent on and in opposition to Global Empire.

what image of life can we envision? Here are some features, as described by Korten (2006: 295-6):

- Locally rooted, self-organized, compact communities
    - Work, shopping, and recreation nearer to residences
        - Saves energy and commuting time
        - Frees up more time for family and community

          (Less fragmented and thus more coherent living; Community bonds denser, stronger, and more trusting; Youth more engaged in community life)
    - Less dependency on automobiles
        - Reduces CO_2 emissions and dependence on oil
        - Land devoted to roads and parking converted to bike lanes, trails, and parks
    - Local governance more authentically democratic
- More food grown on family farms
    - No toxic chemicals
    - Processed nearby, saving transportation costs
    - Compost organic wastes recycled back into the soil
- Environmentally efficient buildings
    - Designed for specific micro-environments
    - Constructed by local materials, thus saving transportation costs
- Energy mostly produced through wind and solar sources
- Education philosophy and school curriculum redesigned to include vital life skills: developmental psychology; responsible citizenship; parenting skills; application of life skills through community service and mentoring of younger children.
- Elders upheld as caretakers, educators, mentors, and wise advisors
    - Restoration of respect and honor of elders
    - Elders more unlikely to suffer from longing for or fear of death
    - Elders serve as models to guide potential of the youth
    - Elders act as guides to individual and community futures

Korten's image of Earth Community is just a preliminary sketch that can certainly be fleshed out more to include how localism interacts within a larger framework, which includes the state, the nation, and the world. For example, while Korten does advocate the break-up of large corporations, he doesn't seem to be as ready to advocate the break-up of the nation-state or at least large nations, yet authentic, functional democracy dwindles in proportion to the expansion of the nation-state and Global Empire. In other words, how do all the pieces fit together to form the global picture of functional democracy at each level to transition from Empire to Earth Community? Moreover, while direct democracy is achievable at a local level, is it possible to initiate direct democracy at the state, national, and global levels? If so, should representational democracy be scrapped, or can it still play a positive role if separated from financial influences?

While it is beyond the scope of this paper to attempt to answer these questions, which would help to flesh out the image of Earth Community as the new paradigm in a postmodern world, it is important to note that since the image of a nonkilling future can only be realized on the foundation of postmodern consciousness, as manifested through the paradigm of Earth Community, then questions concerning the functionality of democracy in larger contexts are also quite relevant. In other words, the image of a nonkilling future cannot be separated and treated as if it were a thing-in-itself, disconnected from social change in general, especially when you consider that the solution to the problem of killing cannot be resolved within the same framework that produced it; thus, it's a matter of changing the framework from which killing emerges. From this perspective, the frustrations that people feel as a result of disenfranchisement, of alienation and disempowerment, because the system itself is merely a democratic farce to legitimize authoritarianism by corporate soft power, as a form of smiley-faced fascism, then these frustrations can easily boil over and erupt into violence and killing in reaction. Furthermore, such reactions are viewed as pathological by those at the top of the hierarchy only because they are perceived as threats to the social order, while the violence and killing perpetrated by the power elite are justified as necessary to maintain the social order; thus, violence that preserves the social and global order is permitted and rationalized while individual violence out of frustration, repression, or defiance by those who are lower in the pecking order is considered as a 'pathological' threat to the hierarchy of power. This hypocrisy itself only leads to further frustration that perpetrates the cycle of violence and killing. Therefore, once the problem of functional democracy is addressed in a way that people are enabled and empowered to make meaningful contributions to society, then this will also help to alleviate the problem of violence and killing.

Conclusion

As Toynbee (1947) pointed out, the 'creative minority' has the historic responsibility to recognize and lead the responses to meet the challenges that face a civilization; otherwise, that civilization will perish. The modern image of the future as the technological civilization has fatal, structural flaws that cannot be fixed within the same framework that produced these flaws; instead, a new, wiser conceptual framework must be realized by the creative minority during the time of crisis, or better yet, through the exercise of clear foresight, in anticipation of the crisis. The time of crisis has already appeared on the horizon. As Immanuel Wallerstein (2004: 76) puts it, this is not just a 'difficult period,' since if the difficulty can be resolved in some way, it does not constitute a real crisis: 'True crises are those difficulties that cannot be resolved within the framework of the system, but instead can only be overcome by going outside of and beyond the historical system of which the difficulties are a part'.

More than 5,000 years ago, for a time period of at least 2,000 years, and perhaps thousands of years more—from the end of the Ice Age until the age of Empire—much of the world was composed of mostly peaceful, nonkilling, horticultural societies. However, while the horticultural societies had turned their swords into plowshares, some nomadic tribes perfected their weapons (their 'instruments of mass destruction') until they were able to successfully wipe out the communities of peace. Thus even the very beginning of the era of Empire was initiated through the advent of new techniques of war and weapons designed for the express purpose of killing in order to conquer, destroy, dominate, and enslave others, and such has been the story of empire after empire throughout the past 5,000 years. But now, as Korten relates, it's time to change the story, for the world faces a critical juncture, a very real 'crisis,' of weapons of mass destruction that possess the lethality to kill millions, in which it must ask itself whether or not the age of Empire *must* come to an end—to usher in instead the age of a peaceful, nonkilling Earth Community.

The image of a nonkilling future has a strong case to make based on anthropological and historical precedents, as well as current sociological research. Paige and others who have contributed to the conceptualizations of a nonkilling world can surely be said to be doing the good work of Toynbee's 'creative minority' to help lead the way to realize a future in which the dominant metaphor is the sanctity of human life rather than the power of the killing machine. The question now is whether the creative minority will have enough influence to play a timely leadership role in the shift of consciousness toward the realization of this new image of a nonkilling future.

References

Baring, A. and Cashford, J. (1991). *The Myth of the Goddess: Evolution of an Image*. New York: Viking.

Dostoevsky, F. (2004). *Crime and Punishment*. New York: Barnes and Noble.

Ehrenreich, B. and Pollitt, K., et al. (1999). 'Fukuyama's Follies: So What If Women Ruled the World?' *Foreign Affairs*, 78(1): 118.

Eisler, R. (1988). *The Chalice and the Blade*. New York: Harper.

Ellul, J. (1964). *The Technological Society*. New York: Vintage Books.

Hardt, M. and Negri, A. (2005). *Multitude: War and Democracy in the Age of Empire*. London: Penguin Books.

Jensen, D. (2006). *Endgame: the Problem of Civilization*. New York: Seven Stories Press.

Korten, D. C. (2006). *The Great Turning: From Empire to Earth Community*. Bloomfield: Kumarian Press; San Francisco: Berrett-Koehler Publishers.

McIntosh, S. (2007). *Integral Consciousness and the Future of Evolution*. St. Paul: Paragon House.

Morgan, D. R. (2002). 'Images of the future: a historical perspective.' *Futures* 34(9/10): 883-893.

Morgan, D. R. (2009). 'World on Fire: two scenarios of the destruction of human civilization and possible extinction of the human race.' *Futures* 41(10): 683-693.

Morgan, D. R. (2010). 'Civilizational futures within the integral futures framework: the plural quadrants.' *Foresight* 12(6): 69-90.

Noble, T. (2000). *Social Theory and Social Change*. New York: Palgrave.

Paige, G. D. (2009). *Nonkilling Global Political Science*. Honolulu: Center for Global Nonkilling. Available online at: <http://www.nonkilling.org/node/18>.

Polak, F. (1971). *The Image of the Future*. Amsterdam: Elsevier Publishing.

Rosenau, P. M. (1992). *Post-modernism and the Social Sciences: Insights, Inroads, and Intrusions*. Princeton: University Press.

Rummel, R. J. (1994). *Death by Governments*. New Brunswick: Transaction.

Shlain, L. (1998). *The Alphabet Versus the Goddesse*. New York: Penguin.

Schoenherr, N. (2006). 'Man the Hunter' theory is debunked in new book.' Washington University in St.Louis 'Newsroom.' Available online at: <http://news.wustl.edu/news/Pages/4582.aspx>.

Sponsel, L. (2009). 'Reflections on the Possibilities of a Nonkilling Society and a Nonkilling Anthropology.' in Evans Pim, Joám, Ed., *Toward a Nonkilling Paradigm*. Honolulu: Center for Global Nonkilling, pp. 17-54.

Sussman, R. W. and Hart, D. (2005). *Man the Hunted: Primates, Predators, and Human Evolution*. Cambridge: Westview Press.

Swimme, B. and Berry, T. (1992). *The Universe Story*. San Francisco: Harper.

Toynbee, A. J. (1947). *A Study of History: Abridgement of Vols. I-VI*. London and New York: Oxford University Press.

Wallerstein, I. (2004). *World-Systems Analysis: an Introduction*. Durham and London: Duke University Press.

Zerzan, J. (2005). 'On the Origins of War.' *Green Anarchy*, 21: 12-13, 15.

15

Leadership, Followership and the Nonkilling Paradigm

Katyayani Singh and Anoop Swarup

Political leadership and statesmanship play an important role not only in maintaining state sovereignty and integrity but also the maintenance of stability and peace and the affirmation of the nonkilling paradigm so much critical for the spiritual advancement of the society and the country. Ancient history reveals the importance of leaders in protecting these attributes both by means of peace and war. The role of two immensely successful leaders one in the west and the other in the east respectively, Alexander[1] (356-323 B.C.) and Ashoka[2] (304-232 B.C.), though contemporaneous but in different cultural contexts for instance decided the destiny and fate of their kingdoms for the better. It was their remarkable leadership and followership, foresight and vision and the strategic wisdom that was unmatched for its times that

1 Walbank, F. W., 2018. *Alexander the Great.* [Online] Available at: https://www.britannica.com/biography/Alexander-the-Great[Accessed 15 May 2018].

2 Adolf, Antony, (2009). Peace: A World History, Cambridge, Polity Press.

led to humankind's incremental advancement through a period of great political turmoil and anarchy. In fact, these leaders in a short period of time brought about a distinct civilizational change that fostered stability, peace and even spiritual awakening that catches one's imagination even by today's standards. Also, interestingly enough, the adjective 'great' has been used for both of them though in complete contrast, Alexander is called 'great' because of his remarkable military conquests that brought stability and peace while Ashoka is called 'great' because of the way he transformed himself from a violent path of military conquests to settle for a nonviolent and peaceful one. Rather he earned the title only when he transformed not just himself but his state through the spread of *Buddhism*[3]far and wide. As a result, it is the hypothesis being set here that such contrasting but charismatic personalities may predicate the rise of future 'great' leaders who may in their own way, dictate the future course of human consciousness that would lead to a nonkilling paradigm and peace in the time to come

Leadership Studies: East versus West

The idea of leadership in Indian philosophy was initially explored by Kautilya in *Arthashastra and* later in western philosophy by Machiavelli in *The Prince.*[4] The similarity was that both these philosophers represented strong, charismatic and authoritative personalities with the difference that while Kautilya checked the acts of the king by binding him to *Dharma*[5] *(*a holistic word that implies religion, duty and righteousness*)* the rule of the righteousness, whereas Machiavelli made no such effort to restrain the king. However, no subsequent studies on leadership were made that probed into the qualities of leaders and its impact on the society. It has been pointed out by Glenn D. Paige in '*Scientific Study of Political Leadership*'[6] that leadership studies in

3 Ibid, Chapter 3: Peace in the Ancient East: India, China and Japan.

4 Machiavelli, N., 1532. The Prince. In: T. Parks, ed. London: Penguin Groups.

5 Kautilya, 2012. *Kautilya's Arthashastra.* 6th ed. Mumbai: Jaico Publishing House.

6 Paige, G. D. (1977). Scientific Study of Political Leadership. California: The Free Press.

the discipline of political science have found lesser recognition then it should have been the case. He points out that though the discipline has made significant studies on the concept of: power, decision making, value allocation, cybernetics, political economy and even structural functionalism but no direct studies on political leadership have been made (Paige, 1977). Paige points out that though some of these concepts like cybernetics and value allocation have given an indirect insight into the importance of leaders but even these did not make any significant contribution with respect to leadership studies. It was only in the period of 1970's says Paige, that some political scientists like: Merriam, Shannon & Seligman and those belonging to the behavioral schools stressed on the study of political leadership for creating and maintaining a democratic society. Further leadership studies were developed by sociologists like Max Weber[7] wherein he characterized authority into 3 types on the basis of political obligations: *Traditional, Charismatic and Legal Rational.* However, a study on leaders and their premise of peace not to speak of nonkilling is something that still hasn't found a firm ground in most academic works on political leadership, thought and process.

Conceptualizing the Theory of Nonkilling Leadership

George Simon seeks to create a link between humanism, nonkilling and leadership. Without the presence of humanist traits in leaders they would never be able to practice nonkilling[8] (Simson, 2008). In other words nonkilling leaders refer to those leader who in their endeavour to protect the power paradigm or the sovereignty of the state did not put human lives at stake rather tried to find an alternative way to give protection to their state or achieve their ends. Though it can be argued that leaders alone do not make policies for the state the organizations and institutions are largely responsible for making decisions but Paige offers an explanation to this dilemma, he says, '*World politics*

7 Gauba, O.P., 2003. An Introduction to Political Theory, New Delhi, Macmillan.

8 Simson, G., 2008. Humanism, Nonkilling and Leadership. In: J. E. Pim, & G. D. Paige, eds. Global Nonkilling Leadership. Honolulu: Center for Global Nonviolence, pp. 35-37.

is the politics of world individuals. A nonkilling global society depends upon individuals who do not kill'[9] (Paige, 2009). Indeed, the political organizations work at the behest of leaders; their responsibility cannot be diluted in the camouflage of organizations and their processes.

According to Glenn D. Paige, 'a nonkilling paradigm shift requires perfection of principles to assist individuals and social decisions from daily lives to global politics'[10] (Paige, 2009). These principles include respecting our own life as well as of other, creative and constructive ways to solve conflicts, drawing strength from life respecting sources, seeking reconciliation in conflict rather than humiliation, degradation or annihilation and to be creatively courageous in withdrawing support from violence in any form. The presupposition, that nationhood, national integrity, national pride, ideological dogmas take precedence over 'human life' as such is a fallacious one. Rather it is argued by the authors that reverence to life takes precedence over all other factors and undeniably the entire argument and logic for human rights, humanism and human dignity would fall in place vis-a-vis these secondary considerations. The biographical and philosophical works of some prominent charismatic leaders helps us to understand in depth as to how much reverence they had paid to human lives. It may not be out of place to mention that leaders such as Mao, Hitler, Lenin and other such leaders with self-centric approach to power often provoke violence and killing in the name of nationalism, freedom or equality.

Why Affirmative Nonkilling?

If the national integrity of a nation is at stake, can the dignity of the individuals be at ransom and should it be withheld by denying them the fundamental rights of liberty, expression, opportunity, equality or justice? Should injustice and exploitation be tolerated for the purpose of peace? The answer is No! Where there exists no dignity in human relations between individuals and society, between individuals and state and between the individuals themselves, peace of mind or even of the

---

9 Paige, G. D., 2009. *Nonkilling Global Political Science*. Honolulu, pp. 90: Center for Global Nonkilling.

10 Ibid, pp. 76.

society at large is indeed in a disturbed state. The disturbance may or may not have manifested itself in the external world but it does not mean that where there is no such manifestation in a society or a state as representation of peace. Subjugation and oppression needs to be fought but with the principle of affirmative nonkilling in its backdrop as human life is non-negotiable. Thus it leads us to the next rational course, as to why should affirmative nonkilling i.e. *creating the nonkilling processes and products or the conditions that lead to reverence to life in the civilizational discourse* be actively practiced against such oppressors and the oppression? To understand the importance of affirmative nonkilling there are certain other concepts that need to be comprehended well: *consciousness for life, principles in action, and civilizational progress.*

Consciousness for Life

Rabindranath Tagore explains that life was found in a cell initially but then with the power of growth and adaptation it could gain enormous and various forms. Life in universe has evolved through complex interrelationship amongst such cells maintaining a perfect co-ordination of function. This is called the 'creative principle of unity;[11] a process of voluntary association where each unit is given adequate freedom of expression and autonomy at the same time. The principle of life is that it evolves through expansions however; all expansions become a burden if they try to break the rhythm of life. Hitler became a burden when he tried to expand his control in the neighbouring countries; those capitalists are a burden who tries to expand their profit by exploiting the resources of nature and marginalizing the needs of other men. Although, they undertook these actions to get power which was thought to give them joy and satisfaction, it never could fulfil their desire. This is because happiness is not the ultimate quest; the ultimate quest is uniting our soul with that of the universe.[12] Though happiness is a legitimate goal for human beings yet it has to be seen within the larger quest for

11 Tagore, R. (1931). The Religion of Man. New York: The Macmillan Company.

12 Tagore, Rabindranath, (1915). *Sadhana* – The Realization of Life, New York, The Macmillan Company.

moral excellence.[13] Therefore morality cannot be sacrificed for either personal or collective happiness and morality rests in recognizing and acknowledging each soul in this universe as our own. Harming others doesn't just affect the others but us too.

Principles in Action

Action is better known as *Karma* in Hindi language; all action is *Karma*.[14] Every small action of ours: breathing, listening, talking, thinking and the aggregate of these actions defines the effect on us. Hence, the act of killing on our part even for a just cause is bound to have certain effect not only on our character as a society but also the civilizational ethos for all time to come. Logically putting it, Newton's third law of motion states 'every action has an equal and opposite reaction', hence, to stop exploitation and injustice if killing is resorted to; it will not end by killing the oppressors but would rather initiate a vicious cycle of killing. Actions are the means while its effects constitute the end; an action cannot be separated or differentiated with its ends. Implicitly a wrong action cannot be undertaken to produce the right end; if indeed it is taken then that the end is bound to get corrupted. An action affects us, the conscious environment and also the purported end for which it is undertaken. Lenin in his early days thought, talked and wrote on violence. Through his writings he glorified violence and leaders with terrorist fervour and finally was able to seize power through the October Revolution.[15] But the violence did not die after the revolution and neither was the dignity restored to the people. Rather it resulted in an environment where there was protracted carnage. All this was done to bring equality in society and unity in state. But social or political cohesion achieved through authority and coercive measures does not bring stability and does not last long for any nonkilling peace being deceptive by its very nature. Rather when such extreme measures are

---

13 Bowdown, T. B., 2017. *'Immanuel Kant Critique of Pure Reason'* 50 Philosophy Classics. London: Nicholas Brealey Publishing.

14 Vivekananda, Swami, 1896. Karma Yoga, Available from: https://www.thoughtco.com/top-free-ebooks-by-swami-vivekananda-1770693.

15 Service, R., 2011. Lenin: A Biography, London: Pan Macmillan Limited.

followed, it may result in its own destruction, as can be observed in the case of the dissolution of many a state such as the downfall of the Union of Soviet Socialist Republic (USSR).

Civilizational Progress

History has witnessed the emergence and decay of various civilizations. Though the progress of the civilization depends upon the power it has acquired yet its sustenance cannot be guaranteed by such power. In the progress report of the 16TH Sustainable Development Goal in 2017 it has been reported that violent conflicts have increased in recent years, while homicides have declined slowly, however, few high intensity armed conflicts have caused large number of civilian casualties.[16] Thus, it is our case that over the years there have been warning signals and mankind has to be aware of the dangers in the future ahead of us. Civilizations have decayed and died owing to causes which produced

> 'callousness of heart and led to the cheapening of man's worth; when either the state or some powerful group of men began to look upon the people as a mere instrument of their power; when, by compelling weaker races to slavery and trying to keep them down by every means, man struck at the foundation of his greatness, his own love of freedom and fair-play.'[17] (Tagore, 1915)

Tagore described the perils associated with power: '*The people who grow accustomed to wield absolute power over others are apt to forget that by so doing they generate an unseen force which someday rends that power into pieces*[18](Tagore, 1931)'. To measure the progress of civilization, one should not depend upon its economic development rather on its

16 Sustainable Development Knowledge Platform, 2017 Progress of Goal 16 in 2017. Available from: https://sustainabledevelopment.un.org/sdg16. (1 August 2018).

17 Tagore, Rabindranath, 1915. *Sadhana* – The Realization of Life, New York, The Macmillan Company, p. 62.

18 Tagore, Rabindranath, 1931, 'The Religion of Man', p. 127, The Macmillan Company, New York.

expression for the love of humanity through its laws and institutions.[19] The prominent civilizations of the ancient period: Egyptians, Greeks and Romans fell after turning ruthless on its own people and other nations around them to expand their power.

Fighting a Just Cause

Human killings hamper the soul of the individuals as well as that of the society. They bring misery and destruction all around even if they were committed for a noble cause. But that does not imply that one should not undertake any struggle to attain a better standard of life or to come out from oppression. The twentieth century has seen various leaders such as: Mao Tse Tung, Lenin, Hitler, Fidel Castro, Mohandas Karamchand Gandhi, Nelson Mandela, Martin Luther King (Jr.) and Rabindranath Tagore who strived hard to fight oppression and achieve certain ends, however, their struggles differ by the manner in which they are fought. While some leaders showed reverence to human lives in their struggle others showed reverence to certain ideologies such as freedom, equality or justice.

Mao and Lenin were fighting against the imperial rule which had plunged their country into poverty and exploitation. In Cuba and Germany though the governments were democratic in nature but they were highly corrupt. The governments wielded great powers and to overthrow them greater power was needed. The power of mass revolt had been dealt extensively with by Karl Marx and Friedrich Engels and each of these leaders except Hitler (who despised communism) sought to modify communism to suit their situation. The philosophy of communism carried certain traits of violence and it was this feature of the philosophy that by and large attracted the leaders towards it rather than its ultimate objective. It has been noted by Jung Chang that Mao was inspired by communism mainly because of its violent trait and he

19 Pettinger, Tejvan, 2009, 'Rabindranath Tagore', Oxford, UK. www.biographyonline.net. Available from: http://www.biographyonline.net/poets/tagore-rabindranath.html.

seemed to have enjoyed it.[20] Chang in her interview states all books in China were being burnt when she was growing.[21] Similar such views have been found in the biography on Mao by his private physician Dr. Li Zhisui. While referring to Mao he states: '*He may have been a communist but he held greatest admiration for the most ruthless emperors of China and tried to identify with them*'[22] (Zhisui, 1996). Zhisui describes the period of Cultural Revolution in which not only leaders were purged but also died by committing suicide. Moreover, if a member of the communist party committed suicide he/she was treated as a traitor and their family was subjected to despicable lives[23] (Zhisui, 1996). Likewise Lenin too was inspired by leaders with terrorist fervour. While developing his idea of revolution, Lenin focused solely on violence and terror and this was well reflected in his writings and his idols. The piece of work which made Vladimir recognized as Lenin was '*What is to be Done*'? He wrote it under the pseudonym of N. Lenin and it was recognized not because of producing some outstanding theory but for causing controversy on the subject amongst the Marxist intellectuals (Service, 2011).[24] On one hand he wanted a revolution to overthrow the monarchy but on the other hand he did not mingle with the workers rather 'He saw the factories and commercial offices of St Petersburg only from the outside. He lived as a middle-class rentier[25] (Service, 2011).' There were streaks of violence and terrorism in all his writings. Other Marxist intellectuals felt 'his Marxism retained an excess of the more violent aspects of Russian agrarian-socialist terrorism[26] (Service,

---

20 Chang, J., 2005. Dispelling the myth of Mao: Jung Chang sheds new light on the Communist leader, The World Today. Available from: http://www.abc.net.au/worldtoday/content/2005/s1419468.htm. (30 April, 2018).

21 Ibid.

22 Zhisui, L., 1996. The Private Life of Chairman Mao, Toronto: Random House of Canada Limited, p. 122.

23 Ibid, IV: 1965-76, p. 465.

24 Service, R., 2011. Lenin: A Biography, Chapter IV: 1965-76, London: Pan Macmillan Limited, Chapter 8 An Organisation of Revolutionaries: 1900–1902.

25 Ibid, Chapter 6. St Petersburg: 1893-95.

26 Ibid.

2011).' Lenin did not care for the lives of the lower class. He had been unmoved by the Volga famine of 1891–2. He had cared little when the number of casualties had soared in the Russo-Japanese War in 1904–5 and the experience of the soldiers of the First World War did not move him[27] (Service, 2011). Fidel Castro held that violence was not bad in itself it depended upon the motive.[28] Though Castro was never in favour of direct assassination but he felt that change could only be brought through revolution and not election. Adolf Hitler may differ from Mao, Lenin and Castro in his political orientation but he shares with them the similarity of considering themselves as a messiah. His statement '*In standing guard against the Jew I am defending the handiwork of the Lord*'[29] (Hitler, 1925) corroborates this notion all the more. It was owing to this feature in their personalities that these leaders either killed people directly or let them die as a result of their failed policies. The art of propaganda and communication was mastered by them in such a way so as to make the people believe that true salvation lay under their leadership.

Where on one hand violent means attracted some leaders to fight against oppression there were also leaders on the other hand who were attracted by nonviolent means in their struggle. Gandhi fought for the cause of Indians in South Africa and in India, Nelson Mandela and Martin Luther King (Jr.) fought for the rights of the blacks in South Africa and USA respectively and Rabindranath Tagore tried to fight for the oppressed sections in the Indian society. Though Gandhi and Tagore were more of social leaders than political in strict sense yet they had political influence. But rather than wielding power they wanted to educate the society about the true meaning of power. Tagore in particular devoted himself to literary works that spoke against the social traditions in the society that made human life bleak.[30] He himself

27 Ibid, Chapter 13: Fighting for Defeat- 1914-15.

28 Coltman, Leycester (2013). The Real Fidel Castro, London, Thistle Publishing, p. 32.

29 Hitler, Adolf, (1925). *Mein Kampf*, Mumbai, Jaico Publishing House, p. 69.

30 Tagore, R., 1983, Three Plays: *Mukta Dhara, Natir Puja, Chandalika*, translated by Marjorie Sykes. Oxford University Press.

taught in a school where he endeavoured to inculcate the feeling of love towards nature and sensitivity in human relations with the help of literature, festive ceremonials and by religious teachings. He sought to create spiritual power in the people and not political power for the purpose of liberation from the oppression in the society. In similar way Gandhi sought to create power within the individuals[31] rather than over others. King and Mandela were political leaders in true sense but while King was an ardent follower of nonviolence principle Mandela used nonviolence only as a tool and not principle in his early struggle period.[32] He even organized a military wing of the ANC known as Umkhonto we Sizwe (The Spear of the Nation) or MK for short. As a result of his acts he got imprisoned for 27 years. In his period of imprisonment, he learned that there was a human side to the opposition as well and they could be won over by love. Martin Luther King had stressed on the element of reconciliation from the very start in his nonviolent movements. He wanted to reconcile with the oppositions and not create them as enemies. This was explicitly mentioned in the speech on April 15, 1960, in Raleigh, North Carolina[33] (King, 1998). He did not want to instil in the people the element of hatred as he regarded it as a virus that grows and spreads indiscriminately thereby making the atmosphere inclement for everyone.

Philosophy, Principle and Propaganda

Philosophy without principle but with great propaganda has great ramifications on the society in future. It seeks to gradually justify and legalize immoral acts on the part of those in power. Power that is usually sought for enhancement of interest, be that of self, community or nation hampers the rights of the 'other person', community or nation.

---

31 Summy, R. 2013. 'Changing the Power Paradigm' In Pim, Joám Evans (ed.) *Nonkilling, Security and the State,* Honolulu, Center for Global Nonkilling, pp. 48-50.

32 Mandela, N., 1995. *The Long Walk to Freedom.*Boston. Little Brown & Company, Chapter 41.

33 King (Jr.), Martin Luther, 1998. The Autobiography of Martin Luther King (Jr.), ed.Carson, Clayborne, New York, Warner Books. Chapter 14: The Sit in Movement.

There is always a purpose behind those who seek power. According to Robert Dahl, leaders seek power for collective interest, self-interest and unconscious motives[34] (Paige, 1977). In the cases mentioned here the purpose to seek power was mostly self-interest combined with community (national) interest. Hitler sought power not just for himself but also for his race and nation; he identified his humiliation with that of his people and the nation, and wanted to make both so powerful that no questions could be raised with regard to their capabilities. Psychologists Evelin Lindner describes Hitler as a man seeking recognition and acknowledgement[35] (Lindner, 2000) thereby, he felt committed to make bold decisions even if it involved killing. Mao, Fidel and Lenin were no different they too were seeking mass adulation and in this endeavour only they went on a killing spree. Through themselves they wanted to make their nation or community also great and knowing that they lack in principles they needed something to conceal their shortcomings.

The art of propaganda was thus developed which not only hid the despotic attitude of the ruler but was also able to justify it where it couldn't be hidden. The revolutionary leaders are mostly held in reverence for their attachment to the locals, to their roots and to the working class that is exploited the most. But in reality, these leaders never identified themselves with the lower class or even if they did such feelings were soon vanished after they usurped power. Service says that although Lenin was inspired by ideas of Russian agrarian socialism, he never felt pity for the peasants. Lenin did not care for the lives of the lower class. He had been unmoved by the Volga famine of 1891–2. He had cared little when the number of casualties had soared in the Russo-Japanese War in 1904–5 and the experience of the soldiers of the First World War did not move him[36] (Service, 2011). Castro had used draconian methods to discipline his army; treachery and desertion

34 Paige, G. D., 1977. *Scientific Study of Political Leadership*. California: The Free Press, p. 17.

35 Lindner, E., 2000. The Psychology of Humiliation: Somalia, Rwanda / Burundi, and Hitler's Germany, p. 29, PhD Thesis, University of Oslo, Available from: http://www.humiliationstudies.org/documents/evelin/DissertationPsychology.pdf.

36 Ibid, Chapter 13: Fighting for Defeat – 1914-15.

were punished by deaths. As a result of his oppression, there have been reports of mass killings[37] (Goldman, 2016) as well as mass exodus in Cuba which occurred in four phases: 1959-62; 1965-74; 1980; and 1985-84.[38] Hitler openly accepted that he loathes the Jews but this doesn't imply that he had love for others; he considers the poor class as a victim of the poisonous surroundings and he felt that they need to be corrected so he does not identify himself with them either. In contrast, Mao was ready to sacrifice 10 or 20 million of his people as he believed China had lots of people, he expressed these thoughts first to Jawaharlal Nehru in 1954 which disturbed him and later in 1957 at Moscow he said in his speech that 'he was willing to lose 300 million people—half of China's population'.[39] The inhumane thoughts and actions thus, were justified and the situation today is that in the name of power, freedom, justice and other fundamental rights people feel killings can be justified. This is being stated from an online survey in which more than 500 people took part and in which 50 per cent of the respondents were peace practitioners:

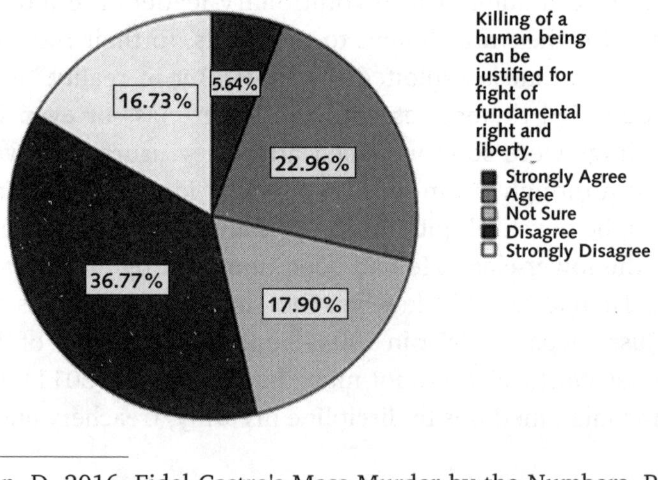

37 Goldman, D. 2016. Fidel Castro's Mass Murder by the Numbers, Pjmedia, Available from: https://pjmedia.com/spengler/2016/11/28/fidel-castros-mass-murder-by-the-numbers/. (29 April 2017).

38 Pedraza, S. 1998. Cuba's Revolution and Exodus, The Journal of the *International Institute*, Vol. 5, Issue-2, Available from: http://hdl.handle.net/2027/spo.4750978.0005.204. (29 April 2017).

39 Zhisui, L., 1996. *The Private Life of Chairman Mao*, Toronto: Random House of Canada Limited, II: 1949-57, p. 125.

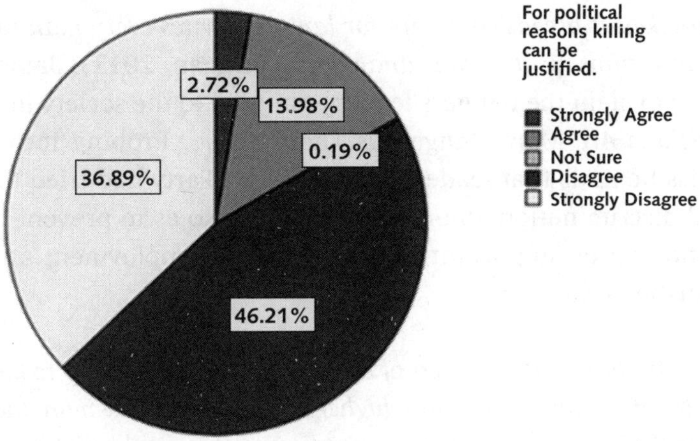

Some of these people hold the view that killing is inevitable in the course of establishment of peace and having a dignified life that guarantees freedom, liberty, equality and justice so much so they even consider killing as an inherent nature of human beings. The violent history, philosophy and leaders are accountable for such wrong notions and hence, philosophies without principles but with propaganda can be fatal for all humanity.

Affirmative Nonkilling Society, Leaders and Followers

The prevalence of nonkilling and nonviolence in ancient societies has been observed by anthropologists and historians. Violent behavior and war have only appeared in some last thousand years and are considered to be product of cultural conditioning, hence the literature and mythology that persists on brutal violence seems to have been sustained by some vested interest[40] (Giorgi, 2010). Few elites in every society try to maintain division not for specificity in functions but for privilege, subsequently to maintain that privilege oppressive laws and customs were introduced in the society. States and leaders assumed themselves to be omnipotent and made decisions that endangered human lives. Louis Brandeis states that, '*Crime is contagious. If the government becomes a*

40 Giorgi, P. P., 2010. Not Killing Other People. In: J. E. Pim, ed. *Nonkilling Societies.* Honolulu: Center for Global Nonkilling, pp. 83-100.

lawbreaker, it breeds contempt for laws; it invites every man to become a law unto himself; it invites anarchy'[41] (Gilligan, 2011). James Gilligan tries to explain the dangers leaders can pose to the society in *Why Some Politicians Are More Dangerous Than Others.* Probing into American politics he finds that leaders of Republican Party had tried to maintain racial discrimination amongst their people so as to prevent them from questioning on important issues such as unemployment and poverty. He further says:

> '*It is in the political interest of the very rich for the country to have high rates of violent crimes, since higher the crime rate, the more the voting population is able to be divided and conquered, as the high crime rates alienates the middle class from the poor, and the poor from each other – the nonviolent majority from the violent minority by whom they feel most directly and immediately endangered.*'[42] (Gilligan, 2011)

Leaders themselves are product of the environment in which they had been brought up in, but they always have in their possession choices by which they may just not change their own destiny but also of their society and the country. Benevolent and nonkilling leadership allows for criticism and suggestion while leaders with absolute approach to power do not leave place for any such criticism. Such a society lives under fear and ignorance; their political obligation is not just based upon the fear of their leader but also on the ignorance of the true nature and principles of their political leader. They hold their political leader in high esteem for bringing about the revolution in their society but they fail to understand that neither one factor alone nor a leader alone can bring such revolutions. It is the unity of events and actions that is responsible for bringing any change in society. Out of sheer political obligation such societies start undermining human lives and dignity and there always persist some kind of threat if the leaders have turned absolutists. The goal of Paige therefore, 'that calls for absence of

41 Gilligan, James, 2011. Why Some Politicians Are More Dangerous Than Others, Polity Press, p. 131.

42 Ibid, p. 80.

threats to kill' for a nonkilling society cannot be achieved with absolute power in the hands of the leaders that may dictate the followers but only conducive societal conditioning that promote and facilitate an affirmative nonkilling paradigm.

Conclusion: an Affirmative Nonkilling Paradigm for Civilizational Progress

Since ancient time political leaders of multifarious cultural and religious fervour have in the name of freedom, justice, rights and equality waged wars. These wars can be classified under two dimensions—violent wars and nonviolent wars. The violent wars guaranteed faster restoration of the desired goal but not the guarantee for perpetual peace and nonviolent and nonkilling existence while nonviolent wars did ensure the desired end but only after a prolonged struggle and persistent fight. The course of civilization change and human existence therefore largely depends on the role of political-social leaders, statesmen and followers. Whenever leaders with authoritarian and totalitarian values have risen they have been observed to commit protracted carnage. However, such leaders attract the people who may be great followers, especially in times of crisis such as economic depression leading to inequality and poverty, societal conflicts and cultural rifts that disturb the life and dignity of individuals. Such leaders may overcome prevailing crisis but they have also been instrumental in giving birth to a new kind of crisis wherein human lives have come under great peril and have jeopardized the very course of future human existence. The problem becomes all the more complex when leaders are only analyzed by the end result and not the process and means by which they ruled. It was due to this reason that Hitler was vilified while leaders with similar mind-set and activities that led to genocide have been revered as father of nations or even freedom fighters. The future destiny of humankind is thus largely a function of the affirmative nonkilling paradigm of our society and our own consciousness as we determine and construct where the end not only has to be justified by the means but also by the right choice of leaders, followers and the processes that lead to those right choices.

References

Adolf, Antony, (2009). *Peace: A World History.* Cambridge: Polity Press.

Almagor, R., 1991. Foundations of Violence, Terror and War in the Writings of Marx, Engels, and Lenin. *Terrorism and Political Violence,* 3(2), pp. 1-24.

Bowdown, T. B., (2017). 'Immanuel Kant Critique of Pure Reason' 50 Philosophy Classics. London: Nicholas Brealey Publishing.

Chang, J., (2005). *Dispelling the myth of Mao: Jung Chang sheds new light on the Communist leader.* [Interview] (21 July 2005).

Coltman, L. (2013). *The Real Fidel Castro.* London: Thistle Publishing. [Accessed 7 May 2018].

Gandhi, M. (1925). *An Autobiography or. The Story of My Experiments With Truth.* Ahmedabad: Navjeevan Publishing House.

Gauba, O.P. (2003). An Introduction to Political Theory. New Delhi: Macmillan.

Gilligan, James, (2011), Why Some Politicians Are More Dangerous Than Others. Polity Press.

Giorgi, P. P., (2010). Not Killing Other People. In: J. E. Pim, ed. *Nonkilling Societies.* Honolulu: Center for Global Nonkilling.

Goldman, D. (2016). *Fidel Castro's Mass Murder by the Numbers.* [Online] Available at: https://pjmedia.com/spengler/2016/11/28/fidel-castros-mass-murder-by-the-numbers/.[Accessed 29 April 2017].

Hitler, A. (1925). *Mein Kampf.* Mumbai: Jaico Publishing House.

Kautilya, (2012). Kautilya's *Arthashastra.* 6th ed. Mumbai: Jaico Publishing House.

King, M. L. J. (1998). An Autobiography of Martin Luther King (Jr.). In: C. Carson, ed. New York: Warner Books.

Lindner, E. (2000). *The Psychology of Humiliation: Somalia, Rwanda / Burundi, and Hitler's Germany.* Oslo: University of Oslo.

Machiavelli, N. (1532). The Prince. In: T. Parks, ed. London: Penguin Groups.

Mandela, N. (1995). *The Long Walk to Freedom.* Boston: Little Brown & Company.

Paige, G. D. (1977). *Scientific Study of Political Leadership.* California: The Free Press.

Paige, G. D. (2009). *Nonkilling Global Political Science.* Honolulu: Center for Global Nonkilling.

Pedraza, S. (1998). Cuba's Revolution and Exodus, *The Journal of the International Institute,* 5(2).

Pettinger, T. (2009). *Rabindranath Tagore.* [Online] Available at: http://www.biographyonline.net/poets/tagore-rabindranath.html. [Accessed 7 May 2018].

Service, R. (2011). *Lenin: A Biography.* London: Pan Macmillan Limited.

Simson, G. (2008). Humanism, Nonkilling and Leadership. In: J. E. Pim, & G. D. Paige, eds. *Global Nonkilling Leadership.* Honolulu: Center for Global Nonviolence.

Summy, Ralph (2013). 'Changing the Power Paradigm' In Pim, Joám Evans (ed.) *Nonkilling, Security and the State.* Honolulu, Center for Global Nonkilling.

Tagore, Rabindranath, (1915). *Sadhana – The Realization of Life.* New York: The Macmillan Company

Tagore, R. (1931). *The Religion of Man.* New York: The Macmillan Company.

Tagore, R. (1983), Three Plays: *Mukta Dhara, Natir Puja, Chandalika,* translated by Marjorie Sykes. Oxford University Press.

Vivekananda, Swami (1896). Karma Yoga, Available from: https://www.thoughtco.com/top-free-ebooks-by-swami-vivekananda-1770693.

Walbank, F. W. (2018). Alexander the Great. [Online] Available at: https://www.britannica.com/biography/Alexander-the-Great [Accessed 15 May 2018].

Zhisui, L. (1996). *The Private Life of Chairman Mao.* Toronto: Random House of Canada Limited.

16

Spirituality and Nonkilling: Theoretical Basis and Practical Evidence

Piero P. Giorgi
National Centre for Peace and Conflict Studies, University of Otago, Dunedin (New Zealand)

Nonkilling is a relatively new concept (Paige, 2009 [2002]) but it has been explored in relation to many social aspects and from the point of view of several academic disciplines.[1] The topic of spirituality is perhaps the most difficult one. In this work we will analyze first the theoretical aspects of spirituality and nonkilling. Then we will review some practical examples of the relationship between these two practices.

In the literature about religion(s) the terms spirituality and religion are generally used as synonymous. In a number of occasions (see, for example, Giorgi, 2008, chapter 5) we have, on the contrary, emphasized the different origins of these two phenomena and their diversity. Establishing such a difference is very important in the present discussion.

---

1 See <www.nonkilling.org>.

Definitions always carry personal biases, but they are necessary for the reader to know what the author means when using a certain word. Regardless of whether one agrees or not with his/her definition, it will help understanding the author's reasoning. I define *spirituality* as the human potentiality of asking metaphysical questions[2] and attempting some answers. I define *religion* as the original human spirituality framed inside later acquired concepts of divinity, priesthood, moral rules and rituals. Let us explore this difference.

Spirituality is a natural potentiality of human beings

Human beings emerged as a species (*Homo sapiens*) about 150,000 years ago in Eastern Africa and about 70,000 years later began moving gradually into all five continents. About 40,000 years ago human beings started producing art (Palaeolithic rock art) in the form of painted cave walls and mobile art (carved bones and stone figurines) (Anati, 2000). Several millions of rock art images from five continents have already been described and classified by palaeo-anthropologists. The interpretation of these images strongly suggests two aspects that are central in our discussion: Palaeolithic humans did not use violence against each other (Giorgi, 2001, Giorgi and Anati, 2004, Giorgi, 2008, chapter 3)[3] and had a relevant level of spirituality. Importantly,

2 In this case metaphysical questions concern aspects of life other than physical sustenance, avoiding physical pain and seeking physical pleasure. They concern, for example, thinking and discussing about the meaning of life and death, our origins, the origin of nature, how we should relate to nature, and how we should relate to other human beings. This is a restricted view of spirituality, but it can suit the context of our discussion.

3 The present work is not meant to discuss the evidence of nonviolence in Palaeolithic humans, as already presented in Giorgi (2001, 2008). Here it is enough to remind that human beings emerged through a process of biocultural (not just biological) evolution; that violence and nonviolence are complex social behaviors; and that social behavior cannot be defined by genes. As a consequence we are neither violent nor nonviolent by nature (or genes). A nonviolent culture would offer children nonviolent social models (hunter-gatherers); a violent culture would offer children violent social models (last 7,000 years in food-producing culture). A nonviolent

these two human traits have also been found in the last century in contemporary hunter-gathering cultures, which were the best available models of a possible prehistoric life style. They have been studied by cultural anthropologists, but now they have practically been eliminated through forced re-location and cultural genocide.

In rock art we can find several pictorial symbols that meant infinity and movement, or represented mythological beings associated with the origin of natural structures and human beings (Anati, 2000). Interestingly, these metaphysical symbols seem to have had a general use in different continents, when comparing cultures that could not have had any form of contact (Von Petzinger, Nowell, 2010).

Contemporary hunter-gatherers verbally reported similar metaphysical concepts to enquiring anthropologists (Evans Pim, 2010). They proved to have an interest in the origins of human beings and nature, in particular rivers, the sea, mountains, plants and animals. Of course, they were concerned with the type of behavior they should adopt towards other human beings, not in terms of moral rules (religion) but as a practical application of their nonviolent culture.

A very different type of evidence supporting the congenital nature of human spirituality is the presence in our brain of a functional region that specifically mediates metaphysical and spiritual thoughts. This was tested with functional magnetic resonance imaging (Aletti, 2006). But, as for most human cognitive functions, a well-developed spirituality must be acquired (not learned; for terminology, see Giorgi 2008, section 2.3.3) after birth through specific experience, just as we must develop after birth the functional potentialities of bipedal gate, speech and hand dexterity, which are not congenital functions (instincts). If children do not experience enough spirituality in their cultural environment, they cannot express their own spiritual potentialities and remain prisoners in a material world without being able to fly higher as human beings should. The spiritual poverty of modern life in part explains the general acceptance of daily human killing in both the civilian (assassinations and death penalty) and military world (war).

---

transformation of our culture is therefore, possible as the emergence of violence in the late Neolithic was a purely cultural change. Here we concentrate on the evidence of spirituality among hunter-gatherers.

Religion is a 'recent' cultural acquisition

As indicated above, we consider religion as the world of spirituality framed inside new practices introduced in the Neolithic by the cultures that produced food. The chain of events that inevitably followed food production (as opposed to hunter-gathering) has already been discussed elsewhere (see Giorgi, 2001: 152-161 and Giorgi, 2008, section 4.3). Among these events, we must consider the importance of the process of social stratification and the position of power of astronomers, who introduced the concept of the divine associated with moving stars and the commanding role of the chief priest, as the intermediate between human beings and gods. The chief priests also introduced a moral code of behavior and the rituals to be performed to appease the gods. The addition to spirituality of these new ideas and practices (priesthood, gods, moral codes and rituals) corresponded to the birth of polytheistic religions, which became a necessary system of power in communities that had become too large to self manage themselves and also suffered of the social malaise introduced by a new relation of fear with nature.

The anthropological and archaeological literature generally does not make a clear distinction between spirituality and religion, and often attributes to pre-historical human beings religious concepts, such as the veneration of gods and the practice of rituals. A 'religious spirit' in prehistory has been mentioned by Facchini and Magnani (2000), a term that does not contribute to clarify issues. We hold, instead, that religion, as described here, did not exist before the Neolithic (Giorgi, 2007, 2008). The distinction between spirituality and religion is important for the analysis of the relationships between spirituality and killing (see below).

Power systems and religion

The egalitarian cultures of hunter-gatherers did not know those post-agricultural institutions we refer to as power systems. These institutions did not emerge from an innate human desire for power; they became gradually necessary when the size of human settlements became too large for collective decision-making. We suggest that the evolution of religions followed the same cultural trend and religious authorities joined civil powers in the new effort of controlling a large, stratified population. The different forms of power enjoyed by religious authorities changed according to different cultures, from the coincidence of kings and great priests in antiquity, to the assignment of the same land benefits of counts to bishops and abbots in the Middle Ages, and to the title of prince of the Church later assigned to cardinals. In the past, religious authorities acted as ministers of the king and prelates were part of His Majesty's court.

In the occasion of wars, religious authorities have blessed troops and weapons assuring everybody that God was on their side, while the clergy of the enemy were stating the opposite. This ambiguous situation nurtured the idea that religion could be the cause of many wars. In reality religion was only part of a convincing propaganda: the enemy wants to take our land, rape our women and destroy our gods. That was enough to convince poor peasants to kill other poor peasants, while they would have preferred to stay home and continue working the land. Wars are decided and wanted by high authorities for a variety of reasons other than religion.

Gandhi, nonviolence and spirituality

Although Mohandas Karamchand Gandhi (1869-1948) is considered the father of nonviolence, this behavioral trait was the normal result of human biocultural evolution (see above) and, as a strategy to resolve conflicts of interest, was also practiced in antique and modern times before him (Sibley, 1963). Moreover, Gandhi lacked current anthropological and neurobiological information and believed that we are violent by nature (Pontara, 2006; Manara, 2006). His philosophy of *ahimsa* (nonkilling, nonviolence) was, therefore, based on moral principles (without a scientific support) and on the belief that a person can be converted to the idea of not causing pain to others. Interestingly, this position is the one that now motivates most people engaged in the peace movement and in peace studies. It is a worthy position from the ethical point of view, but very ineffective for the purpose of a nonviolent transformation of society: it would be much better *stopping the current violent education of small children and adolescents*, rather than trying to convert people to nonviolence after having educated them to violence.

Regardless the intellectual source of Gandhi's nonviolent teaching, he has been very clear in stating that *one cannot be really nonviolent without having a good level of spirituality* (Pontara, 2006; Manara, 2006). He insisted on the spiritual, not religious, qualities of a person practicing nonviolence. In fact Gandhi, although of Hinduism upbringing, avoided being associated with one particular religious faith and probably paid with his life the determination of maintaining good relationships with the Muslims of the Indian subcontinent.

Unavoidable violence, still a very popular belief

We have become aware only recently of the rich humanity that characterized the Paleolithic cultures (see above) and of the need to include that period as part of our human adventure, in order to understand who we are. As long as we limited our interest to the so called 'history', that is, the shorter period beginning when we started producing written records (about 6,000-7,000 years ago), we obviously believed in congenital violence: direct violence and war also started at the beginning of that 'history'. Two additional factors contribute to uphold this wrong but popular belief. The first one is a psychological trap. The hypothetical unavoidable occurrence of violence produces a soothing feeling in both citizens and authorities: we don't need to do anything to prevent and eliminate violence, a process that would involve radical and unpopular changes in people's life style and political programmes.

The second factor maintaining the *status quo* is the vested interest of several businesses that a strongly competitive life style and overt violent social interactions continue in society. An oppressive commercial-media system effectively promotes egoism and individualism among people, thus discouraging grass-roots initiatives aiming at social promotion. Just a few examples of what works against the prevention of violence: the weapon industry, powerful movements promoting intolerance and nationalism, associations exploiting the ambiguity of legal rights such as the National Rifle Association, the industry of passive entertainment (violent films and sport events), the industry of unhealthy food, the industry of competitive physical appearance, etc.

While we have grown accustomed to think that an increasing rate of chronic depression, drug dependence, diseased people, corruption and poverty are unavoidable aspects of modern life, we also have the emergent proposals and experimentation of a nonviolent economy, a nonviolent civilian defence, a nonviolent education, etc. The future non-competitive, nonkilling, nonviolent society with true democracy—an unavoidable transformation in order to avoid extinction—would be composed of happy, healthy and spiritual people with enough material resources.

The unhappy, sick and poor soldiers

The postmodern war machine has removed all the attractive aspects of being a soldier. The glorious service of noble ancient worriers, the honourable obligation of medieval citizens and the professionalism of modern armies have gone. Now a young man joins the army to learn a job, to obtain a degree, or to pay the house loan during a dangerous assignment abroad. But the price to pay is often too high. In Russia one can see return soldiers begging in the street; in the Unites States a proportion of Vietnam veterans and other former 'heroes' are guests of psychiatric clinics or members of outlaw gangs.

A strong evidence denying congenital violence in humans is the many cases of mentally disturbed soldiers, especially those returning from 'dirty' wars, where armies of industrialized countries fight against irregular troops in Third World countries, operations often called 'peace missions'. Chronic depression, violent behavior, drug addiction and other syndromes are becoming a serious health problem among war veterans. If it was true, as most people believe, that violence is a natural human characteristic (see above), soldiers returning home should be happy, satisfied, well balanced people, while quiet post office clerks should be mentally disturbed. This obviously nonsensical suggestion is based on the conclusions reached by Sigmund Freud when he discussed this very topic in a very reputed book at the age of 74, 10 years before his death (Freud, 1961; Giorgi 2009: 103-107).

Religious training

Most readers must have attended, to a certain extent, Sunday school or a similar programme within a certain religious creed. The aim of most types of religious training is to inspire (or inculcate, depending on the teacher's style) the love of God, the foundations of specific beliefs, formal rituals, and moral rules. These rules are very important, but they should be demonstrated since birth by the parents with their lifestyle, not instructed verbally and too late by a religious authority. For our discussion it is interesting comparing the religious training of a child with the training of a soldier.

Military training involves, besides specific strategies to kill, the numbing of critical thinking, of unfettered human empathy (*agape*), and of a general spiritual view of life (see above). The training of a soldier involve, therefore, the suppression of the main functions that make us human, let alone the concept of uncritical obedience, the biggest insult to that freedom of deciding for ourselves that was granted to us by our Creator. But these terrible features of military training are necessary for the profession of war; so it is the idea of war that is wrong, not the preparation of a diligent soldier for the killing. There is a rich literature on the theory and practice of the nonviolent defence of a country (Sharp, 2005), but the public is accurately prevented from knowing about it. Military personnel are encouraged, indeed, to embrace a given religious faith, but with the added attitude of intolerance toward other forms of belief. This does not justify, however, the idea that religions are the cause of war.

The spirituality of nonkilling animals

The ancient nutritional choice of vegetarianism is becoming increasingly popular and is inspired by various motivations. The purely nutritional approach holds that plants can provide the whole requirement of proteins we need and that eating meat causes a number of health problems. The environmental approach holds that feeding animals to feed humans is inefficient and damages natural resources. The ethical approach is inspired by the discomfort of causing pain to animals.

Interestingly, the last two approaches belong to the domain of spirituality. Being concerned about the environment involves asking metaphysical questions on our relationship with nature and about the future of humanity. Being concerned with animal suffering involves metaphysical questions about our relationship with other living beings on earth. One could object to this interpretation by noting that the choice of answers to those metaphysical questions depends on ethical principles, not so much on spirituality. Two comments. One should not automatically assume that the only source of ethical principles is religion; we have a rich history of secular ethics. In fact spirituality is a natural faculty of human beings (see above) long before the emergence of religion and it has always inspired the collective mind as part of a healthy social culture, especially in small communities. Furthermore, the teaching (formal catechism) of most Christian denominations contains little or nothing about protecting nature and animals.

The relationship between spirituality and nonkilling

Cultural anthropologists have reported that surviving hunter-gathering cultures did not have a moral code as such, one like the Ten Commandments for example. Children acquired an ethical behavior growing up in a community where people displayed solidarity and did not lie, steal and kill, apart from occasional extra-marital breaches (Evans Pim, 2010). Adolescents also received information about mysteries and taboos from the elders during initiation. The whole community had sophisticated methods to prevent the rare possibilities of violence and injustice.

Hunter-gathering cultures had essentially a high level of spirituality. This means that they were asking questions about the origins of natural features and of human beings, and about their relationship with nature; these were answered with mythological explanations. They were interested in how one should relate to other human beings: this had been culturally selected to be nonviolent relationships.[4] Interestingly, contemporary hunter-gatherers did not engage in war, they were unlikely to use man-to-man violence (Fry, 2013) and were wounding in a leg somebody guilty of a bad crime, while capital punishment was

4 Like other social species, *Homo sapiens* emerged after a bio-cultural (not just biological) evolutionary process, with social behavior not being defined by genes. This means that we are neither violent nor nonviolent by nature, and nonviolence was selected and maintained by cultural transfer from one generation to the next because it was the most suitable behavior for the advantage of the community (adaptive).

unknown. This view of hunter-gathering cultures has nothing to do with the idea of the 'noble savage' of Jean-Jacques Rousseau, who had no notion of anthropology and imagined that 'savage' as a lone idiot not doing any harm because too stupid for doing so (see Giorgi, 2001, note 7).

If we compare the above model with the opposite social situation, a large city of an industrialized country, we find essentially a severe lack of spirituality. The origins of the physical world and the wonders of living creatures are unwillingly learned at school and soon forgotten. The origins of human beings are badly described at school and soon forgotten or misunderstood or substituted with the catechism of creationism. How we should behave toward each other—cooperation, solidarity and nonviolence—is not taught at school, is hopelessly advocated at religious classes, is denied in history classes, and negatively displayed in the family and the general public—individualism, competition and egoism, if not worst.

Moreover, people are not told about the emergence of inhuman behavior, violence and killing in the periods of the Late Neolithic and the Bronze Age, which are still recorded only for the achievements of food production and technological advances. Who has a vested interest in perpetuating this ignorance?

Specific case studies

One may ask the question of whether there is a relationship between the practice of killing and the level of spirituality of a nation.

There are three cases when the State authorizes killing human beings: death penalty sentenced by the judiciary, striking in self-defence carried out by police officers and citizens, killing people who are considered a danger to the country (enemies) carried out by soldiers or special services. Death penalty is the most interesting one.

All countries of the European Union, Canada, Russia, Australia, New Zealand and 10 others have abolished death penalty for all crimes. The United States, Indonesia and many countries of East Africa and Southern Asia retain death penalty. The rest have intermediate or unclear situations. The case of USA is particularly interesting because this country is so much represented by media and fiction to become internalized by the public, like in the advertising strategy, as the social model to imitate. Well, of the 50 States comprising the USA, only 18 have no death penalty statute, while most of the remaining 32 have performed executions since 1976 (after a suspension by the Supreme Court between 1972 and 1976). While in Europe one is currently discussing about the illegality of life imprisonment because the main aim of imprisonment should be attempting the redemption of the inmate, the USA is still allowing death penalty as it was in Europe 100 years ago. Moreover, the unique percentage of US citizens owing a gun is well known, as well as the unique frequency of shooting in schools and public places.

Interestingly, the US has a level of religiosity (people attending church) much higher than Europe (41 per cent vs. 15 per cent in France or 10 per cent in the UK, according to Gallup International). It is difficult to determine the level of spirituality of a person and, worse, of a country, but this human trait surely requires the ability of deep thinking, abstract reasoning and metaphysical interests. After having lived long periods in several different countries, it is the impression of this author that, apart a culturally privileged minority, US citizens are generally more materialistic and superficial than European citizens. I present this personal impression with due caution, because it should be supported by proper evidence-based data, but I would doubt that the US is on the way of becoming the spiritual leader of the world. On the contrary, the US is currently the country fighting more official wars than any other one, besides being involved in many covert operations without Congressional oversight. A programme of research should be undertaken on the relationship between high levels of killing and low levels of spirituality.

The causes of our low level of spirituality

In this work the idea has been defended that spirituality and religion are different human traits, one being innate and the other recently added by purely cultural evolution. As mentioned above, it is relatively easy to assess the level of religiosity of a society, but that of spirituality seems to escape quantitative methods. From the psychological and behavioral traits mentioned above, one could, however, select the quality of interpersonal relations and perhaps direct violence as a measurable parameter, although the concept of spirituality is a much more complex than that. In this case it would be easy to assess the displays of individualism, egoism, greed and wild competition to determine, by default, the level of spirituality. Unfortunately, these attitudes and behavioral traits are those considered as winning strategies by the current neo-liberal trends, which would explain the difficulties we face in expressing our spiritual potentialities. If this reasoning is correct, we could follow the same line of thinking to elucidate the cause(s) of the current low level of spirituality in industrialized countries.

One cannot blame certain philosophical ideas, such as positivism or Marxism or existentialism, because they are intellectually dead or survive in a small minority of learned people. In any case, these outmoded ideas were associated with anti-religion positions and do not concern spirituality. In fact, one can meet self-declared 'atheists' or 'agnostics' who display high levels of spirituality.

In the majority of people, human and spiritual poverty is cunningly promoted by *economic power systems that need both vulnerable workers and uncritical consumers*. Workers have won many battles in the past to have their rights recognized by employers, but they are gradually losing their achievements through the strategy of guided 'economic crises' (during which very rich people are doing even better) that force them to lower down their demands. Added to this is a new, and so far unknown, form of oppression of citizens as consumers perpetrated by the commerce-media system (a form of structural violence). Its overt selling mantra is freedom and liberty ... to buy much more than what one need.

Greed, corruption, habituation to killing, need of violent entertainment, and psychiatric conditions are the intended outcome of the above mentioned hidden power system that aims at obedient and gullible citizens, who become even more vulnerable if somehow depressed and not fully healthy. One can well imagine how these new weapons of behavioral control may impede the expression of people's natural potentiality for spirituality. Conversely, one can imagine how a population with a good level of spirituality would be protected from such effective attempt of oppressing them.

Within the commercial-media oppression system, the military industry needs citizens that are drugged with violent entertainment and habituated with both home and international violence as a normal human affair. Here the selling mantra is 'security', aiming at having all police and army interventions justified, while hiding the fact that violent military solutions enjoy a very low rate of success when compared with the excellent record of nonviolent movements (Zunes et al., 2007; Drago, 2010).

Conclusion

It is clear that the culture of violence we are experiencing today gradually emerged 6,000-7,000 years ago and was perpetrated from generation to generation by cultural transfer through unconscious repetition. The expression of the innate human spiritual potentiality was at the same time inhibited for thousands of years by the new social context of large food producing cultures and, perhaps, also by the dry, ritualistic practice of religion. In recent times, especially after World War II, new economic strategies have consciously been put into place to enhance the alienation of people and to oppress them both as workers and consumers. Now we are surrounded by violence, corruption, and killing in fictional entertainments and in our real daily life; this makes us worried, unsecure and poor enough to be easily manipulated.

The recovery of human dignity and peace will need a spiritual and a Political transformation—the capital letter distinguishes the future service Politics from the current power politics. In our opinion, this will occur with what we (see <www.neotopia.it>) call a *nonviolent, slow, legal and local revolution* (in a sense of radical change). 'Nonviolent' refers to the theory and practice of Gandhi, Galtung, and Sharp; 'slow" means a probable duration of two or three generations, because the final targets will be children; 'legal' means that the methods adopted will be in line with local laws; 'local' means that spiritual and Political actions will come from the bottom (active citizenship) in small towns and will be adapted to local resources. A good strategy for the type of 'revolution' mentioned above is to distinguish short-term projects from medium-term projects and long-term projects, which should all be started at the same time. The first type would deal with simple remedial actions that do not resolve the basic problem (as they do not deal with its cause) but make people (especially adult) aware of the situation of oppression (structural violence) in which we find ourselves. The second would be destined mainly to adolescents by appealing to their residual capacity of idealism and rebellion and proposing nonviolent methods, such as simply saying 'no' to the many chimeras of the commercial-media oppression, to start with. The third one would be destined to small children and their parents, who would provide a very different social environment for them, one offering the same advantages of babies born in a hunter-gathering band.

The aim of this ambitious, but inevitable, project is to begin a nonviolent transformation of local communities first and wider social entities later. This model of a nonviolent, slow transformation of society is meeting with a powerful opposition from the commerce-media interests that favour religious sermons to active spiritual and nonviolent solutions.

References

Aletti, M. (2006). 'Tra dati neurobiologici, contesti culturali e attribuzioni personali – La specificità dell'approccio psicologico alla religione,' in Aletti, M. et al., Eds., *Religione – Cultura mente e cervello*. Torino: Centro Scientifico Editore, 138-197.

Anati, E., ed. (2000). *40,000 ans d'art contemporain* (40,000 years of contemporary art). Capo di Ponte: Edizioni del Centro.

Drago, A. (2010). *Le rivoluzione nonviolente dell'ultimo secolo – I fatti e le interpretazioni*. Milano: Edizioni Nuova Cultura.

Evans Pim, J., Ed. (2010). *Nonkilling Societies*. Honolulu: Center for Global Nonkilling. Available online at <www.nonkilling.org>.

Facchini, F. and Magnani, P., eds. (2000). *MIti e riti della preistoria* (Myths and Rites of Prehistory). Milano: Jaca Book.

Freud, S. (1961). *Civilization and Its Discontents*. New York: W.W. Norton.

Fry, D. P., ed. (2013). *War, Peace and Human Nature – The Convergence of Evolutionary and Cultural Views*. Oxford: Oxford University Press.

Giorgi, P. P. (2001). The Origins of Violence by Cultural Evolution. Brisbane: Minerva Education & Science. Available online at <www.pierogiorgi.org>.

Giorgi, P. P. (2007). 'A new interpretation of female symbols and figurines produced in prehistoric Europe – The hypothesis of the centrality of women' in Bloom, M.; Giorgi P. P. and Pietroboni, G., Eds. *Rock art in the framework of the cultural heritage of humankind*. Capo di Ponte (Italy): Edizioni del Centro, 185-191.

Giorgi, P. P. (2008). La violenza inevitabile – Una menzogna moderna. Milano: Jaca.

Giorgi, P. P. (2009). 'Nonkilling human biology', in Evans Pim, J. Ed., *Toward a nonkilling paradigm*. Honolulu: Center for Global Nonkilling, 95-122. Available online at <www.nonkilling.org>.

Giorgi P. P. and Anati, E. (2004). 'Violence and Its Evidence in Prehistoric art – A comparison of ideas'. In Anati, E., Ed. *Prehistoric and Tribal Art. New Discoveries, Interpretations and Methods*. Capo di Ponte (Italy): Edizioni del Centro, 263-269.

Manara, F. C. (2006). *Una forza che dà vita – Ricominciare con Gandhi in un'età di terrorismi*. Milano: Edizioni Unicopli.

Paige, G. (2009). *Nonkilling Global Political Sciences*. Honolulu: Center for Global Nonkilling. Available online at <www.nonkilling.org>.

Pontara, G. (2006). *L'antibarbarie – La concezione etico-politica di Gandhi e il XXI secolo*. Torino: Ega Editore.

Sharp, G. (2005). *Waging Nonviolent Struggle – 20th century practice and 21st century potential*. Manchester: Porter Sargent.

Sibley, M. Q. (1963). *The quiet battle – Writings on the theory and practice of nonviolence resistence*. Boston: Beacon Press.

Von Petzinger, G. and Nowell, A. (2010). Article published by *New Scientist*, 21 February 2010, 31-34.

Zunes, S.; Kurtz, L. R. and Asher, S. B., eds. (2007). *Nonviolent social movements*. New York: Backwell Publishing.

Epilogue
The Scientific Nature of Nonkilling Movement

Balwant Bhaneja

Posing the right question is critical in science. Once you have found the question, search for the answer(s) begins. Prof. Glenn D. Paige was primarily a scientist. 'Is Nonkilling Global Society possible?' was his Eureka moment. This question was to become the central thesis of his seminal work, 'Nonkilling Global Political Science' (2002, 2009), to be followed by the establishment of a Center for Global Nonkilling in 2008 which was awarded Special Consultative Status with the UN Economic and Social Council in 2014.

CGNK has a unique mission that is aimed at both individuals and societies for inspirational and transformative purposes to prevent violence: *'To promote change toward the measurable goal of a killing-free world by means open to infinite human creativity in reverence for life.' (CGNK website: www.nonkilling.org)* The paradigm is beyond traditional dichotomy between rich-poor, urban-rural, and weak-powerful.

Concentrating on 'evidence based approach' to the problems of violence, it draws upon, advancing and combining, the Spiritual, Scientific, Skill, and Arts capabilities of humankind for change.

Science and Civilization advance by questioning the seemingly impossible. For Paige, Nonkilling was not only about political science or politics but primarily 'finding some scientific grounds for confidence in nonkilling human capabilities'. (Paige, 2002:30) As he states: 'By science is meant broadly all forms of knowledge gained by questioning and experimentation—facts, theories, and methods for determining validity and reliability. A harbinger of scientific revolution is when some philosophers begin to question accepted thinking' (p. 30). This covered both production and application of knowledge across the whole gamut of social and natural sciences seeking solution to local, regional and global issues.

On killing and nonkilling, Paige was influenced by the work of A. Richard Konrad who had challenged in 1974 the conventional assumption that readiness to kill was the only effective way to cope with violence from rape to holocaust. (Paige, 2002: 31) Konrad argues that the thesis of the single violent problem-solving alternative rests upon three assumptions: that all nonviolent alternatives have been identified; that all have been tried; and that all have failed. But these assumptions are untenable as nonviolent problem solving alternatives are hypothetically infinite. (Paige, 2002:31)

Nonkilling is a holistic term. It is beyond using nonviolence as a tactic for bringing political change through strategic or principled nonviolence, it is a means for creating an open ended global transformation requiring research and problem solving processes and institutions in place to deal with societal issues having zero killing as its ultimate goal. Nonkilling paradigm defines politics in a complete new form different from traditional Hobbesian focus of politics on violence assuming power and its transfer and control to a body politic of state (and non-state actors). As Paige writes: 'Where killing is assumed to be inevitable and acceptable for personal and collective pursuit, there is less urgency to understand and to remove causes of lethality.' (Paige, 2002:72)

Concept of Causation and Nonkilling Analysis

In Nonkilling analysis, Paige asserts, 'the concept of causation is central, every case of killing demands causal explanation: wherever killing occurs—from homicide to genocide to atomic annihilation—we need to understand processes of cause and effect, however complex and interdependent.' (2002:72) His four-part logic of nonkilling political analysis underscores the causes of killing, the causes of nonkilling, the causes of transition between killing and nonkilling; and the characteristics of completely killing free societies. (2002:72) A main impediment to studying the possibility of Nonkilling paradigm has been on grounds that other values such as freedom, equality, or security are more important than nonkilling. Paige maintains: 'Nonkilling is at least of equal importance because humanity has arrived at a condition where all of these values are threatened without a powerful commitment to nonkilling ethic in political science and political life. Materialism and morality have arrived at the same conclusion. If tradition has taught us that we must kill to be free, equal, and secure—the present teaches that unless we stop killing not only freedom and equality are in jeopardy but our very survival—individual, social, and ecological—is periled. We have reached a point where the science and practice of politics must be aligned with the life-supporting forces of society and nature.' (Paige, 2002.154)

The Nonkilling 'Big Science' Project

The multi-disciplinary essays in this volume confirm thrusts identified in Paige's Nonkilling Global Political Science about existing Nonkilling capabilities in a variety of scientific disciplines e.g. anthropology (Paige, 2002: 32-3, 37-40), bio-neuroscience (2002:34), ecology (2002: 116, 120-21), economic (2002:113-17), ethology (2002: 31-33), medicine (2002:146-47), philosophy (2002: 30-31), physics (2002: 32), psychiatry (2002:36-37), psychology (2002: 31-32) etc. New institutions with life enhancing mandates and new ways to problem solving are imperative for realizing nonkilling societies. This may appear to be daunting but elements of Nonkilling capabilities and capacities are already in place as shown above, and since 2007 on the nonkilling research done as shown under the publications tab on CGNK website (www.nonkilling.org). The findings therein need nurturing and support for next level of research, advocacy and institution building. A Big Science Nonkilling Society project for example with zero killing as its goal can be a step in right direction, with a research agenda identifying and facilitating responsiveness to nonkilling needs of all, in a way similar to the effort that was garnered for launching many international projects of the last century e.g. Manhattan, Apollo Moon-landing, International Space Station, Human Genome, etc. A multinational concentrated effort of changing our ways and beliefs from lethality to non-lethality, global in discovery, creativity, diversity and effectiveness could have significant impact in development of violence preventing peacebuilding policies and programmes in the twenty-first century.

At one of the Center for Global Nonkilling (CGNK) international youth leadership workshops in Honolulu in 2009, a female student from Haiti enquired—'Why Nonkilling?' Prof Chaiwat Sath-Anand, one of the course facilitators responded: 'Nonkilling is the Alpha and Omega of life. It is a prerequisite, *a priori* condition, an ethical imperative, and a guide to action for individual and societal transformation to achieve the highest human potential.' Nonkilling is indeed 'the measure of human progress'. Killing stops that progress; but when killing is stopped the human progress resumes. Reverence for life is fundamental to survival and continuity of humanity. Without nonkilling everything else is meaningless whether we are talking about environment, security, or poverty.

One of the strengths of nonkilling paradigm has been its open-endedness grounded in philosophy of reason and tolerance with an emphasis on the use of evidence in human affairs that we as people and societies can improve our lot. It takes the view of the modern secularists that existence precede essence rather than that of religionists which was based on the notion that essence precede existence. Three centuries of humanist revolution through scientific and philosophical advancements among other fields in evolutionary biology, psychology, sociology and cosmology has shown that life on this planet is unique and worth living unlike ephemeral other worldly visions of religionists. In such thought, culture has come first and religion later. Nonkilling as a focal point has clarity and a baseline that defines its purpose without any ambivalence or ambiguity despite its conclusions, may be transient in nature.

Peace, Nonviolence and Nonkilling

Paige liked precise formulations that could be examined, analyzed and tested. For example, on Peace, Nonviolence, and Nonkilling, he was adamant that these three concepts were non interchangeable. Though all of these were part of the same family, each had specific meaning. He had the following intellectual argument about nonkilling's non interchangeability. Note his following formulation on the subject: 'Nonkilling will certainly contribute to Nonviolence and Peace. But Peace and Nonviolence do not necessarily lead to nonkilling.' He then went on to explain the rationale behind his above statement. He would remark: 'Examples, Gandhian leaders in recent past professing nonviolence have supported India's nuclear weapons programmes, death penalty, wars, etc. US policymakers are talking of nonviolence as complement to military actions in Afghanistan, Iraq, etc. As you may know, 'Peace is our Mission' is the motto of the US nuclear Strategic Air Command. Wars are fought for peace and veterans who kill are lauded in the US for bringing peace.

'Thus unqualified nonviolence and peace do not necessarily require nonkilling. But nonkilling by nature must contribute to conditions of nonviolence and peace. However, nonkilling, nonkilling nonviolence, and nonkilling peace can become a powerful linguistic transformational troika to carry humanity to a killing-free world—free of the psychological, economic, and environmental consequences of killing. Nonviolence and Nonkilling are mutually compatible and interdependent. The goal of nonkilling is to enable attainment of *Ahimsa* within, it elevates from presence of a sense of nonkilling peace.'

Humans in all cultures may have violent tendencies but by their own definition—they are not necessarily killers or wish to describe themselves that way. Most often their reluctance to kill can be only overcome in their training as in the case of soldiers through demonizing their adversary as barbarians and murderers.

Paige in his 2016 commendation for a honorary doctorate from Jagran Lakecity University in Bhopal, India, states: 'Kill, killing is a concern to the world. It dates from the dawn of humanity and is universal. History has been marked by killings, conflicts and wars occurring in all seasons and areas. Murders, killings in wars or massive exterminations are countless. From ancient conquests, independence wars, world wars, and regional wars of liberation to jihadist terror, killing remains a big challenge. Humanity must find an effective solution to killing. Indeed it is urgent at global, international and local levels, that initiatives be taken to bring about a nonkilling society where people live in harmony with each other.'

WHO Report on Violence and Health (WHO, 2002) concluded, 'violence is a preventable disease'. Like the 'Nonkilling Global Political Science' book, it concentrated on 'evidence based approach' to the problems of individual, interpersonal and collective forms of violence. Systemic trees of remedial actions can be developed for each of the above three kinds with a serious anatomy of violence/killing and cures, that is, focusing upon something measurable in how much collective, inter-personal, and personal violence was/can be reduced/alleviated/eliminated? How many suicides, homicides, wars/conflicts etc., were or can be prevented or reduced?

The nonkilling paradigm has demonstrated: One, we humans are not inherently killers, humans are essentially non-killers. We may be aggressive by nature, but not killers. Nonkilling societies are possible. Two, there is an empirical problem to be solved. Because vast resources for human security are skewed to military interventions and warfare, a shift in support and resources is badly needed to create alternate structures to enable new policies, mandates, programmes and institutions aimed at prevention of lethality. It was only when such national legislation and processes are in place, that an effective global monitoring system and support could be nurtured for prevention of violence nationally and globally.

Research Agenda

The book, *Nonkilling Global Political Science* is strewn with questions which Paige called 'a constructive invitation to creative thinking'. In the chapter, *Implications for Political Science*, he seems to be setting a research agenda demanding that 'we need to know who kills whom, how, where, when and why and with antecedents, contextual conditions, individual and social meanings and consequences. And, of course we need to discover cross-case patterns of lethal casualty for intensive, parsimonious, typological explanation... Similarly we need to understand the causes of nonkilling. Why do humans not kill? Why has the idea of nonkilling arisen in human life? Why have humans committed themselves in nonkilling principles? Why have some people throughout history—in the face of ridicule, ostracism, exile, deprivation, imprisonment, torture, mutilation, and threats of deaths up to assassination, execution, and collective extermination—held fast to the principle of life over lethality?' (Paige, 2002: 72-73) The chapter is full of such curiosity, pointing to the need for research for a measurable evidence based nonkilling paradigm. (2002: 75-77)

Nonkilling Possibilities

In conclusion, I share below insightful notes excerpted from Paige's emails sent over in recent years on cutting edge themes, revealing his inquisitive mind, both advising and grappling with challenging themes transcending boundaries of faith and ideals yet with 'nonkilling possibilities'. Below are some of his perceptive thoughts on Nonviolence Limits of Jains of India; Abortion; Death of Self, Cures for Killing/ Lethality disease; and Policy and Politics connection.

On Nonviolence Limits of Jains of India: 'I have been very close to the Jains of India, the most comprehensively nonkilling religion-philosophy perhaps ever seen in the world. Animals, insects, plants microbes, atmosphere, you name it. One exercise in a 10-day Jain meditation camp I attended some years ago to raise consciousness is to walk barefoot in sandy ground and watch out not to step on ants. Monks cannot ride horses, cars, boats, or planes because they kill life. They walk barefoot all over India. Laypersons cannot become farmers or fishermen. Strict vegetarians. Women in cutting fruit must not cut seeds. Use water sparingly (water is life). Do not clap hands since sound and force do violence to life in air. Recommend search Google for Jain religion. But even they are weak on not killing human beings. Some are military officers. Don't protest against patriotic wars or nuclear weapons. Not visible in campaigns against death penalty in India.

So I prefer to concentrate at least on the deliberate killing of humans by humans. If others want to extend nonkilling to everything that exists in the universe that is perfectly fine and admirable–but not as a prerequisite to squarely facing up to ending killing of humans by humans from homicide, crime, terrorism, to war. Totalitarian nonkilling need not be a prerequisite to not killing humans with all its antecedents and consequences for the psychological, social, and material consequences for humanity and life on the planet.'

On Abortion: 'Somewhat the same argument holds for abortion. Yes we must progress to such respect for creating human life (including ending rape, unwanted pregnancies, advancing science to prevent and treat abnormalities, and creating economic and social conditions that sustain life) that there is no need/justification for abortion. But advocacy of the practice of abortion need not become a prerequisite to focusing on not killing humans after birth. In the US the most anti-abortion, 'pro-life' advocates, especially fundamentalist evangelical Christians, are some of the most militaristic in favour of armed forces, guns, and advocates of the death penalty. The appeal to them can be: Can you extend your respect for the God-given sanctity of life before birth to not killing humans after birth? While working to respect life before birth.

'In short, while working toward the goal of a human killing-free world we can walk humbly with the knowledge that we are all killers of many other things in life and nature on this scientific and spiritual miracle of Planet Earth on which we have been born. And can extend our work for not killing each other to not killing other things that sustain life.

'How this initiation is to be accomplished in a widespread manner now remains for us to devise.'

On Death of the Self: Paige had an interesting exchange of emails with neuroscientist and philosopher Professor Bruce Eldine Morton on the possibilities for subduing an ego-driven killing ideology. It had started with an open-ended conversation on fasting and nonkilling to which Morton replied: 'Fortunately, there is a SOLUTION to this problem of killing. It is brought about by a rite of passage where in one experience we are transformed from a killing primate into a nonkilling human being. The core element of this rite of passage to humanhood has always been the production of a near-death experience where the grip of the ego is temporarily lost and one is confronted with the existence of one's Higher Intelligence, awaiting hidden within. One is forever transformed by this contact. ...The extremely valuable concept of the rite of passage by death of the self to the entrance to the larger whole has been lost by modern man. We are now deathly afraid of self-death and in our alarm have proscribed any procedure that threaten the domination of the Ego. This makes use of psychedelics to find their nonkilling God within illegal. As I mentioned, the Ayahuasca churches originating from the Amazon offer some hope in this regard. Ideally, at the age of 18, everyone would be inoculated against the killing disease by an injection of short acting DMT, causing a temporary collapse of one's Ego and a five-minute introduction to one's Higher Power. This would have a lasting transforming impact and recognition that life above all is the ultimate value...'

Paige replies: 'Mahalo for precise explanation... I have a question about psychedelics and homicide, suicide, and intra/intergroup killing among communities/cultures that use them. Like Ayahuasca in Amazon. Suggests need for interdisciplinary research with colleagues of the Nonkilling Anthropology Research Committee?

'The question comes from reading about military killers (maybe suicide bombers too?). Invariably using alcohol and drugs in conquering fear in killing and in reactions to killing. Like Vietnam vets. Or Ukrainians slaughtering Jews for the Nazis. Or Japanese kamikaze pilots—seems ancient practice—and can't conceive of war without it. What is the difference in the two processes and outcomes? One suppresses killing, the other enables it.

'Idea for another book in your creative exploration seems very promising. Would be a best seller for societies seeking how to end killing. Like psychological self-help books now. But would likely be suppressed by societies that need military killers, etc....'

On Cures for Killing/Lethality disease: 'It has to be more than repetition of mere lamentation and being horrified.' Paige points to CGNK publications, in particular, a collection of essays by theorists and practitioners in the volume entitled, *Nonkilling Security and the State*.

On Policy and Politics connections: 'I have just discovered and strongly recommend James Gilligan, *Why Some Politicians Are More Dangerous Than Others* (2011). You and students can freely read its thesis online. Go to Amazon for the book, look inside, and read Introduction for explanation of the thesis and empirical grounds for it.' From 1900-2007 suicide-homicide rates have gone up during Republican administrations and down in Democratic ones! I'm amazed that media has not picked this up to my knowledge since 2011. Every political science student and citizen-voter in US should know about the thesis and the method by which it is substantiated. Political science ignorance is perhaps the result of disciplinary compartmentalization: Gilligan is a professor of psychiatry at Yale Medical School and has been working on suicide and homicide for years. Good example for why NKGPS (Nonkilling Global Political Science) needs to be multidisciplinary as well global.

Would the thesis hold that political leadership correlates with variations in suicide-homicide rates if comparable data and comparable political rules could be matched in other countries?

Another groundbreaking book by James Gilligan to note: *Violence – Reflections on a National Epidemic* (1996): The attached pages are from Chapter 2 'Dead Souls' in James A. Gilligan, M.D, *Violence: Reflections on a National Epidemic* (New York: Vintage Books, 1996). They remind us of the worst case killings by individuals as a challenge to CGNK work. On the other end, of course, are mass killings by political leaders and others (supported by many) who have had 'normal' parental care. Gilligan's work, emerging from 25 years of experience as a prison psychiatrist seeking to understand and help the most violent prisoners, needs to be paired in CGNK understanding with the brain scan work of Nonkilling Neuroscience Research Committee colleague Adrian Raine, *The Anatomy of Violence: The Biological Roots of Crime* (New York: Vintage Books, 2014). {'Look Inside' at Amazon}.

Gilligan in 1996, anticipating CGNK and WHO, called for the interdisciplinary scientific study of violence as a 'disease'. He was among those who founded the WHO Violence Prevention Alliance and is a longtime colleague of Dr Bandy X. Lee, Yale Medical School, with whom CGNK Director Joam Evans serves as coordinator of its academic collaborations initiative. Winie Wang CGNK UN representative in New York is a student of Bandy Lee and knows Gilligan's work well.

While killing has many forms and causes, I hope this reminder of the bioneurological challenge to CGNK nonkilling work will interest you amidst your busy lives.

* * *

Dawn of Nonkilling Era

With emergence of interlinked problems of the world poverty, security and environment in the new millennium, a shift from nation-state to a global society is gradually emerging with a new consciousness of ourselves as a human, our humanity, and of a humane world. Ultimately impact of epoch-changing scientific discoveries is going to be down on the earth and its solar system than in the galaxies and black holes; it will be how we view ourselves and our planet? That will be unraveled by next generations.

For Paige to be a scholar of a nation state and its citizen was too narrow and a quaint description – his vision transcended such definition of a scholar. For his Honorary Doctorate from Jagaran Lakecity University when the university wanted to put Political Scientist beside his name, he insisted that this be corrected to 'Global' Political Scientist. It was not for status. But to emphasize that social scientists have to rise above the confines of a national citizenship, religion or ideology in their research, he wanted his work to be judged on the grounds of empirical evidence in defence of why and how Nonkilling paradigm should prevail.

The dawn of a Nonkiling Era continues to unfold; it is already there as Paige's work pointed out a decade ago. It will be rapidly accelerating because killing or its consequence is unsustainable at micro level in resolution of a localized land or ethnic dispute or catastrophic destruction of the planet through a nuclear war. Eventually, there is no independent play – the consequence of an action small or larger will increasingly be felt globally be it related to war, poverty or degradation of the planet or beyond. In the first two decades of 21st Century, such statement is no longer a theoretical assumption, but in reality already being witnessed globally – the truth becomes transparent today in myriad ways despite efforts of the vested interests to hide or manipulate it. The impact of new technology, new knowledge and its rapid diffusion has unleashed alternatives that cannot be put aside and ignored. They have to be mediated through a process of consensus building in a long-term process of education, confidence-building and just institutions grounded in global nonkilling ethos.

There is a need for raising nonkilling consciousness in relation to concepts, vocations and our everyday living at primary, tertiary and secondary levels. Time has come to put concerted effort on Nonkilling as a fundamental imperative in the twenty-first century. Ignoring Nonkilling paradigm, it is likely that any other approach for peacebuilding is likely to end up with a limited comprehension and a stop-gap resolution of the problem. Once Nonkilling becomes the basis of our raison d'être, chance of sustainable peace will be more imminent.

References

Gilligan, James D. (1997). *Violence – Reflections on a National Epidemic*. New York: Vintage Books.

Gilligan, James D. (2011). *Why Some Politicians Are More Dangerous Than Others*. Malden, MA: Polity Press.

Konrad, A. Richard. *'Violence and the Philosopher'*. Journal of Value Inquiry, 8: 37-45.

Morton, Bruce Eldine (2011). *Neuroreality: A Scientific Religion to Restore Meaning, or How 7 Brain Elements Create 7 Minds and 7 Realities*. Megalith Books.

Paige, Glenn D. (2002, 2009). *Nonkilling Global Political Science*. Philadelphia: X-libris Corporation, Honolulu, HI: Center for Global Nonkilling.

Raine, Adrian. (2014). *'The Anatomy of Violence:The Biological Roots of Crime'*, New York: Vintage Books.

Sponsel, Leslie E. (2015). *'The Anthropology of Peace and Nonviolence.'* Diogenes 2:107-134.

WHO (World Health Organization). (2002). *World Report on Health and Violence*. Geneva, Switzerland.

Contributors

Anis Hamadeh has Master of Arts in Islamic Studies, English and linguistics. He is a writer, musician, painter, journalist, editor of Anis Online, author of *Understanding Islam: A Practical Handbook* (2013, in German) and translator of *Nonkilling Global Political Science* into German (2009).

Anoop Swarup is the recipient of Hiroshima Peace Award, Tokyo, Amrita Devi Environment Award and Presidential Award of Republic of India and a Fellow of Royal Society of Arts, London and Fulbright Visitor to United States. He is the Founding Vice Chancellor of Jagran Lakecity University at Bhopal (2012 to date), Chairman of Center for Global Nonkilling (UN Affiliate) at Hawaii and Founder Chairman of Global Knowledge Alliance at Melbourne. He has been the Vice Chancellor of Shobhit University, Commissioner at Government of India, Executive Director of Nehru Yuva Kendra Sangathan (largest Youth Organization in the world), UNSC Representative at United Nations and a Global Environmental Outlook Reviewer (UNEP 2007). Notable amongst his books are *Aloha* and *Arcadia* (Books of Poems), *Give Nonviolence a Chance*, *Indian Civilization through the Millennium*, *Regional Economics Engagement and the Free Trade Agreements – Analytical Insights and Policy Options* and *The World of Money Laundering, Commercial Frauds and Financial Crimes.*

Antonino Drago graduated in Physics and taught History of Physics at Naples University as well as subjects of nonviolence at Florence and Pisa University. He participated in the struggles of Neapolitan favelas, student movements, Pisa and Peace Transcend movements of conscientious objectors, and movements of the objectors to the military taxes. He was also the first President of the Ministry Committee for the civil non-armed and nonviolent defence.

Antony Adolf is the author of *Peace: A World History* (Polity Press), and is a teacher, public speaker and independent scholar. He is the publisher of *One World, Many Peaces*—a provocative commentary on current events worldwide aimed at creating a better future. He regularly speaks at popular and academic events related to peace studies, peace history, and peace activism around the US and globally.

Balwant Bhaneja, born in Lahore and living in Canada since 1965, is the author of five books. He has written widely on politics, science and arts. His recent works include collaboration with Indian playwright Vijay Tendulkar, entitled *Two Plays: The Cyclist* and *His Fifth Woman* (2006) published by Oxford University Press (India), and *Quest for Gandhi: A Nonkilling Journey* (2011) published by the Center for Global Nonkilling, Honolulu, Hawaii. Bhaneja's short fiction has appeared in South Asian periodicals and his plays have been produced by the BBC World Service and Toronto's Maya Theatre at Harbourfront.

Chaiwat Satha-Anand is a prominent peace activist and Associate Professor of Political Science at Thammasat University, Thailand. He was previously a Senior Research Scholar with the Thailand Research Fund. He also served as Vice-President of the Strategic Nonviolence Committee, National Research Council of Thailand; Vice-President of the Foundation for Children Development; and Director of the Peace Information Center. He served as Action-Policy Team Leader of the CGNK between 2008 and 2011. At present he is the Vice Chairman of CGNK.

Darcia Narvaez, PhD, is a Professor in the Department of Psychology at the University of Notre Dame. Her research explores questions of species-typical and species-atypical development in terms of wellbeing, morality, and sustainable wisdom. She examines how early life experience (the evolved nest) influences moral functioning and wellbeing in children and adults. Her 2014 book, *Neurobiology and the Development of Human Morality: Evolution, Culture and Wisdom,* won the 2015 William James Book Award from the American Psychological Association and the 2017 Expanded Reason Award for research. She also writes a popular blog for *Psychology Today* called 'Moral Landscapes'.

David Haws is a Professor in the Civil Engineering department at Boise State University.

Dennis Morgan is professor at Hankuk University of Foreign Studies (HUFS), South Korea. Morgan has an MA in Applied Linguistics for TESOL (2004) and an MS in Futures Studies (1992). He has published many papers in the field of futures studies. At HUFS, besides teaching four-skills language courses, he also teaches courses on Globalization, American Studies, Intercultural Communication, and Introduction to Global Futures Studies.

Francisco Cardoso Gomes de Matos is Emeritus Professor of Linguistics, Federal University of Pernambuco, Recife, Brazil. He teaches Linguistic Rights at that University's Specialization Course in Human Rights and Applied Linguistics. Prof Gomes de Matos has presented more than 80 papers in national, regional, and international conferences. A world pioneer in Peace Linguistics since 1993, he has published four books there on, two of which are in Portuguese and two in English. Gomes de Matos is internationally known for his work in Linguistic Rights: he is the author of the pioneering (1984) *Plea for a Language Rights Declaration* and has chaired the UNESCO-sponsored International Seminar in Human Rights and Cultural Rights at the Law School, Federal University of Pernambuco (1987), the outcome of which is the Declaration of Recife (on Linguistic Rights). Active in Human Rights,

Dr Gomes de Matos is a co-founder of the Dom Helder Camara Human Rights Commission, Federal University of Pernambuco. He is also co-founder of ABA Global Education, an organization established in Recife, Brazil, 25 years ago, and co-founder of the World Dignity University initiative. His most recent book is Dignity – A Multidimensional View, published 2013. Another sustained commitment of his is centered on applications of the Nonkilling Approach, as can be seen in his book *Nurturing Nonkilling*. He likes to characterize his current mission as that of helping contribute to the global education of DIGNIFIERS.

James Tyner's research centers on the intersection of political and population geography. His most recent work has addressed war, violence, and genocide. Jim has a regional interest in Southeast Asia; recent travels have taken him to Cambodia, the Philippines, Vietnam, Laos, Thailand, Burma, Malaysia, Singapore, and to Japan, and China. He is the author of 13 books, including *War, Violence, and Population: Making the Body Count,* which received the AAG Meridian Book Award for Outstanding Scholarly Contribution to Geography.

Joám Evans Pim is Director of the Center for Global Nonkilling and also teaches seasonally at Åbo Akademi University and Universitat Jaume I. Edited volumes include *Global Nonkilling Leadership* (2008, with Glenn Paige), *Toward a Nonkilling Paradigm* (2009), *Nonkilling Societies* (2010), *Engineering Nonkilling* (2011), *Nonkilling Psychology* (2012, with Dan Christie), *Nonkilling Futures* (2012, with Jim Dator), *Nonkilling Security and the State* (2013), *Nonkilling Balkans* (2015, with Rifet Bahtijaragić), *Nonkilling Spiritual Traditions* (2015, with Pradeep Dhakal) and *Nonkilling Education* (2017, with Sofía Herrero). He also authored the entry on nonkilling in *The Oxford International Encyclopedia of Peace* (2010). Before working for CGNK, he lectured at the University of Santiago de Compostela and directed the Galizan Institute for International Security and Peace Studies, having followed graduate and undergraduate studies in Journalism, Anthropology and Politics (Peace Studies).

Joshua F.J. Inwood has a PhD from the Department of Geography at the University of Georgia. Inwood is an Associate Professor in the Department of Geography and a Research Associate in the Rock Ethics Institute. He is committed to understanding the material conditions of peace and justice and is engaged with these concerns through a variety of research and teaching projects. At its heart, his research seeks to understand the social, political and economic structures that make human lives vulnerable to all manner of exploitations, as well as how oppressed populations use social justice movements to change their material conditions. Most recently, he has worked on the movement to address human wrongs through truth and reconciliation commissions, specifically the burgeoning truth movement within the United States. Other research projects that he has been involved in connect Civil Rights and labour struggles in the US South following the end of segregation, and the way legacies of racism, violence and social activism continue to frame contemporary anti-racist struggles. Inwood contributes to literatures on urban spaces, political geographies, justice and historical and cultural geographies as well as others. In 2015, Inwood received the Glenda Laws Award for outstanding contributions to geographic research on social justice issues. He has also received the Stanley Brunn Young Scholar Award in 2016.

Leslie E. Sponsel has a BA in Geology (geomorphology), Indiana University, 1965, MA in Anthropology (biological and cultural), Cornell University, 1973, PhD in Anthropology (biological and cultural), Cornell University, 1981. Previously visiting instructor or professor at Indiana University, University of Saskatchewan (Saskatoon), Mount Royal College (Calgary), Cornell University, University of Massachusetts (Amherst), Venezuelan Institute of Scientific Investigations (Caracas) as Fulbright Fellow, and Prince of Songkla University (Pattani, Thailand) as Fulbright Fellow. Joined the faculty at the University of Hawai'i in 1981. Hired to develop and direct the Ecological Anthropology Programme from 1981-2010 attracting national and international recognition.

Neelakanta Radhakrishnan is Gandhian scholar and activist. He has organized many university and village *shanti sena*, and trained more than 5,000 young volunteers over 20 years. He took up assignment under the Government of India as Director of Gandhi Smriti and Darshan Samiti, also establishing the Indian Council of Gandhian Studies; Gandhi Media Centre; G. Ramachandran Institute of Nonviolence and Shanti Sena; and Missionaries of Nonviolence Foundation India. He has authored over 50 books.

Olivier Urbain is Director of The Min-On Music Research Institute, Founder and Director of the Transcend: Art and Peace Network, an online organization promoting research on the links between peacebuilding and the arts, and Former Director of the Toda Peace Institute (Tokyo and Honolulu). He is also Member of the Board of Directors of the International Peace Research Association Foundation. He has a PhD in Literature (University of Southern California, USA) and a PhD in Peace Studies (University of Bradford, UK). Publications include *Music and Conflict Transformation: Harmonies and Dissonances in Geopolitics* (2008), *Music and Solidarity: Questions of Universality, Consciousness and Connection* (2011) and *Music, Power and Liberty: Sound, Song and Melody as Instruments of Change* (2015).

Patricia Friedrich is an Associate Director & Associate Professor in the School of Humanities, Arts and Cultural Studies (SHArCS). Dr Friedrich is a sociolinguist whose scholarly interests include Critical Applied Linguistics, Critical Theory, Cross-cultural Communication, and language and peace.

Philip Lee, a British national, joined the World Association for Christian Communication (WACC) in 1975 and is currently Deputy General Secretary and editor of the international journal *Media Development*. Publications include *Requiem: Here's Another Fine Mass You've Gotten Me Into* (2001); *Many Voices, One Vision: The Right to Communicate in Practice* (ed.) (2004); *Communicating Peace: Entertaining Angels Unawares* (ed.) (2008), and *Public Memory, Public Media and the Politics of Justice* (co-ed.) (2012). In 2013, he was conferred Doctor of Divinity (honoris causa) by the Academy of Ecumenical Indian Theology and Church Administration in Chennai, India.

Piero P. Giorgi feels strongly about avoiding specialization in academia and creating bridges between science and humanities. Since 1967 he has worked in developmental biology and specialized in the development of brain and behavior in vertebrates since 1970 and humans since 1990. This last aspect was related to the application of modern neuroscience to sociology and peace studies, which is now (since 2004) his major research interest. From 1988 to 2002 Piero has done research on the history and philosophy of medicine. This has now developed into a keen interest in the philosophy of biology. In 1991 Piero, with other colleagues at the University of Queensland, established the first degree programme in Australia of Peace and Conflicts Studies (still offered in 2017). From that date to 2003 he has been teaching at the Faculty of Social Sciences for that programme. From 1995 to 2002 Piero had an active involvement in multiculturalism and in the promotion of the Italian culture in Australia, particularly as the founder and editor of *Convivio*, a bilingual journal of ideas in Italian studies.

Todd Junkins is a Clinical Social Worker Specialist in Chicago, Illinois. He graduated with honours in 2014 from the University of Chicago. He specializes in social work and clinical social work.

Vivek Patkar holds BSc (Hons.) in Mathematics and MSc and PhD in Operational Research, all from the University of Delhi. He was a Faculty of Quantitative Methods and Operations Management at the ICFAI Business School, Mumbai. Prior to that, he worked for 25 years as an Operations Research Specialist in the Planning Division of Mumbai Metropolitan Region Development Authority (MMRDA). He was involved in numerous schemes and projects pertaining to land-use planning, infrastructure financing, and area and transport development. A comprehensive Regional Information System employing geo-referencing tools of Remote Sensing (RS) and Geographic Information System (GIS) for urban planning and management was established in MMRDA by the unit guided by him. He is now an independent researcher and engaged in research on different aspects of the research. He has conducted several workshops on research methodology for both the natural and social sciences. Patkar is regularly invited as a resource person to the courses and seminars organized by the ICSSR—Western Regional Centre, and Departments of Geography, Mathematics, Statistics, Economics, Law, Computer Science and Civics and Politics of Mumbai University and its affiliated colleges, and many universities and institutions in the country. Besides the 11 books to his credit, he has written over 300 research papers and articles.

Index